Personality and intelligence

Personality and intelligence

Edited by

ROBERT J. STERNBERG

PATRICIA RUZGIS

Yale University

CAMBRIDGE
UNIVERSITY PRESS

Published by the Press Syndicate of the University of Cambridge
The Pitt Building, Trumpington Street, Cambridge CB2 1RP
40 West 20th Street, New York, NY 10011-4211, USA
10 Stamford Road, Oakleigh, Melbourne 3166, Australia

First published 1994

Printed in the United States of America

Library of Congress Cataloging-in-Publication Data

Personality and intelligence / edited by Robert J. Sternberg, Patricia Ruzgis.
    p.   cm.
    Includes bibliographical references and index.
    ISBN 0-521-41790-2. – ISBN 0-521-42835-1 (pbk.)
    1. Personality and intelligence. 2. Personality and intelligence –
Testing. I. Sternberg, Robert J. II. Ruzgis, Patricia.
BF698.9.I6P47   1994
153.9′3–dc20
                            93-21757
                              CIP

A catalog record for this book is available from the British Library

ISBN 0-521-41790-2 hardback
ISBN 0-521-42835-1 paperback

Contents

Part IV   Personality, intelligence, and culture

Part V   Integration

    Peter Salovey and John D. Mayer

    Name index   319

    Subject index   329

Contributors

Paul Baltes
Max-Planck Institute für Bildungforschung
D-1000 Berlin 33, Germany

Jonathan Baron
Department of Psychology
University of Pennsylvania
Philadelphia, PA 19174

Nancy Cantor
Department of Psychology
Princeton University
Princeton, NJ 98544

Chi-yue Chiu
Department of Psychology
Columbia University
New York, NY 10027

Carol Dweck
Department of Psychology
Columbia University
New York, NY 10027

Hans Eysenck
Institute of Psychiatry
University of London
London SE5 8AF
United Kingdom

Martin Ford
Graduate School of Education
George Mason University
Fairfax, VA 22030-4444

Elena Grigorenko
Department of Psychology
Yale University
New Haven, Connecticut 06520

Robert Harlow
Department of Psychology
Princeton University
Princeton, New Jersey 98544

Nick Haslam
Department of Psychology
University of Pennsylvania
Philadelphia, Pennsylvania 19174

Jutta Heckhausen
Max-Planck Institute für
  Bildungforschung
D-1000 Berlin 33, Germany

Ying-yi Hong
Department of Psychology
Columbia University
New York, NY 10027

Anna G. Maciel
Max-Planck Institute für
  Bildungforschung
D-1000 Berlin 33, Germany

John D. Mayer
Department of Psychology
University of New Hampshire
Durham, New Hampshire 03824

Patricia Ruzgis
Department of Psychology
Yale University
New Haven, Connecticut 06520

Peter Salovey
Department of Psychology
Yale University
New Haven, Connecticut 06520

Sergei Dmitrievich Smirnov
Department of Psychology
Moscow State University
Moscow 103009, Russia

Robert J. Sternberg
Department of Psychology
Yale University
New Haven, Connecticut 06520

Elliot Turiel
School of Education
University of California
Berkeley, California 94720

Preface

This book was motivated by our belief that much of the most interesting work on intelligence is now being done at the interface of intelligence and other constructs such as creativity, wisdom, and, perhaps most generally, personality.

The fields of intelligence and personality have, in some respects, curiously parallel histories. Both went through periods of "grand theories," in which theorists tried to formulate overarching theories of the constructs as a whole. Some theorists, such as Raymond Cattell and Hans Eysenck, contributed to both literatures, and suggested possible interfaces between the two constructs. For example, intelligence is a factor in Cattell's theory of personality, and intelligence is closely related to personality in Eysenck's theory.

Both fields have also been primary targets for the method of factor analysis. In factor analysis, a correlation or covariation matrix is decomposed in order to reveal the latent traits alleged to underlie the observable measures that are being correlated. This psychometric approach has played a prominent role in the development of both fields, although today it is only one of a number of approaches that are being used.

Finally, both fields have developed beyond factor-analytic approaches in similar ways. Both have gone through stages in which people have argued that the construct is situational (as it is sometimes called in the personality literature) or domain-specific (as it is sometimes called in the intelligence literature). Today, some theorists have gone beyond saying that personality or intelligence resides wholly in the individual or wholly in the situation and are looking at person–situation interactions.

All of the approaches to personality and intelligence mentioned above are described in this book, the goal of which is to present the current state of the literature with respect to the interface between the constructs of personality and intelligence. The chapters in the book have been written in a way that should be comprehensible to students and professionals alike, whether or not they happen to specialize in the topics covered.

The book is divided into five main parts. The first four parts deal with different aspects of the relations between personality and intelligence, whereas the fifth part serves to integrate the first four.

Part I deals with personality traits and intelligence. This part contains two chapters. Chapter 1, by Eysenck, represents the most "traditional" of the approaches in the book. Much of the work described looks at correlations between personality traits and various measures of intelligence. But Eysenck also considers newer, experimental approaches to the interface. Chapter 2, by Haslam and Baron, focuses on the relation between intelligence and a particular personality trait: prudence. Haslam and Baron suggest that intelligence, broadly conceived, involves "intellectual personality traits," which together constitute prudence.

Part II deals with personality development and intelligence. This parts contains two chapters.

In Chapter 3, Maciel, Heckhausen, and Baltes present a life-span perspective on the interface between personality and intelligence. These authors view multidirectionality and multidimensionality as two key aspects of intellectual development in general. Multidirectionality refers to the observation that the development of intelligence does not proceed in just one direction, but rather in many directions. Thus, it is more like a branching road than a single path. Multidimensionality refers to the notion that intelligence is not a single thing, but rather is multifaceted. From their perspective, the development of intelligence involves selective optimization with compensation: we try to optimize our performance in a subset of areas in which we find we can excel, and try to compensate for things we do not do as well, especially as we grow older and find that certain fluid abilities start to wane.

In Chapter 4, Chiu, Hong, and Dweck propose an integrative model of personality and intelligence. They propose that both intelligence and personality can be understood at three basic levels: the level of basic processes, the level of the knowledge base, and the level of actualized behavior. At the basic-process level, intelligence involves basic mental operations, whereas personality at this level involves basic motivational and affective processes. At the knowledge-base level, intelligence involves factual knowledge and skill (procedural knowledge), whereas personality involves values, beliefs, and standards. Finally, at the actualized-behavior level, intelligence involves academic problem solving, whereas personality involves moral–ethical problem solving. At the interface of intelligence and personality one finds interpersonal problem solving, which involves elements of both constructs.

Part II considers the relation of personality to particular manifestations of intelligence. This part contains three chapters.

In Chapter 5, Cantor and Harlow look at the relation of one manifestation of intelligence—social intelligence—to personality. According to these authors, social intelligence represents the efforts of individuals to solve the problems of daily life and to work toward desired goals. These authors suggest that people develop a repertoire of problem-solving strategies and schemas that they use to solve problems of these kinds. The socially intelligent person is able to use these strategies and schemas flexibly in the pursuit of solutions to the problems they face in their lives.

In Chapter 6, Sternberg suggests that the interface between personality and intelligence can be found in a construct he refers to as the "thinking style." The basic notion is that such a style is not intelligence itself, but a way of utilizing one's intelligence. In other words, people can choose to exploit the abilities they have in multiple ways—for example, as lawyers, doctors, or scientists—and their effectiveness and choices in life will be influenced at least as much by styles as they will be by abilities and personality.

In Chapter 7, Martin Ford looks at yet another manifestation of intelligence, namely, "personal intelligence." He does so through what he refers to as a "living-systems approach" to the integration of personality and intelligence. The basic notion underlying this approach is that the processes of human functioning are intimately interconnected in complexly organized ways to form a whole person who is continually interacting with the environment in goal-directed sequences of activity. Ford suggests that personality is most directed at the content of a person's thoughts, feelings, and perceptions, whereas intelligence is most directed at the effectiveness of these same things. Thus, personal intelligence deals with both content and effectiveness in people's interactions with the environment.

Part IV deals with personality and intelligence and their relation to culture. This part has three chapters.

In Chapter 8, Smirnov considers the roles of intelligence and personality in the theory of activity. According to the theory, activity is a nonadditive unit of life, not just a combination of various physical actions mediated by cognitive processes. Activity forms the basis of a bidirectional connection between the individual and the world. Smirnov introduces the concept of "image of the world" and states that it is both a product and organizer of the individual's cognitive activity. The concept of image of the world provides an original approach to understanding the relation of the individual to his environment. In this view, the individual's image of the world generates cognitive hypotheses that are modified by the environment; in turn, the environment modifies the image of the world. By placing the origin of cognitive activity in the individual's image of the world, Smirnov provides a new approach for studying the personality–intelligence dichotomy.

In Chapter 9, Ruzgis and Grigorenko investigate cultural meaning systems, intelligence, and personality. Drawing heavily on psychological anthropology and the work of culture theorists, they argue that culture consists of a system of meanings that, to a large extent, shape reality. In other words, the reality we perceive and the way we think about things are always filtered through a cultural lens. What we see as "objective" is conditionalized upon culture, so the beliefs and practices that seem "natural" in one culture may seem quite unnatural in another. Ruzgis and Grigorenko examine implicit theories or folk conceptions of intelligence from a range of cultures and the relation of these folk conceptions to cultural meaning systems. They support the currently popular definition of intelligence as adaptation to the environment. However, they argue that our view of the environment and the process of adaptation must be expanded to include cultural meaning systems if we are to understand cross-cultural variations in notions of intelligence and their relation to personality. Simply put, intelligence and personality must be viewed within the context of cultural meaning systems.

In Chapter 10, Turiel considers relations among morality, authoritarianism, and personal agency in cultural contexts. Turiel considers the large extent to which culture shapes the way we perceive the world. People within a culture often form stereotypes of outgroups, which then become the bases for the way these groups are treated. As an example, Turiel draws on the classic but sometimes forgotten work on the authoritarian personality done by Adorno and colleagues. This work showed the extent to which people showing a high level of a particular personality trait, authoritarianism, stereotyped outgroups such as Jews, and then proceeded to act as though their stereotypes were reality.

Part V, which attempts to integrate the other contributions to the book, contains just a single chapter, Chapter 11, by Salovey and Mayer. In this chapter, the authors present some final thoughts about personality and intelligence. They review the various chapters in the book, and also suggest that the topic of emotion may have received less attention in the book than it deserves. To this end, they introduce their concept of emotional intelligence, or the ability to monitor one's own and others' feelings and emotions, to discriminate among them, and to use this information to guide one's thinking and actions. Salovey and Mayer elaborate on the notion of emotional intelligence, present a case study, and also discuss empirical data relevant to the construct.

To conclude, we believe that *Personality and Intelligence* covers many of the multifaceted relations between two of the most important constructs in psychology: personality and intelligence. The book highlights where the interface between these two constructs is today, and where it may be in the research of tomorrow.

RJS
PR

Part I

Personality traits and intelligence

1   Personality and intelligence: psychometric and experimental approaches

H. J. Eysenck

Introduction

A discussion of the relationship between two concepts requires some definition, however preliminary, of these concepts. Intelligence, as I have argued (Eysenck, 1988), has three major meanings in contemporary writings: biological intelligence, psychometric intelligence, and social intelligence. Figure 1.1 illustrates these 3 meanings. Biological intelligence is concerned with the physiological, neurological, and anatomical bases of intelligence; the existence of such bases is mandatory given the strong genetic determination of individual differences in this field (Eysenck, 1979, 1985).

Psychometric intelligence is defined in terms of the IQ; it constitutes Spearman's (1927) *g* factor (general intelligence), plus the various primary factors isolated since (Eysenck, 1979). It is determined largely by biological intelligence, but is also affected by environmental and social factors, in the ratio of 7:3, roughly speaking. Finally, social or practical intelligence (Sternberg, 1985; Sternberg & Wagner, 1986) is essentially concerned with the application of IQ to success in life; this depends largely on IQ but also on a variety of other factors as shown in Figure 1.1 (Sarton, 1969).

In this chapter I have concentrated on the definition of intelligence in terms of IQ, although scientifically I would argue that biological intelligence is more securely based (Eysenck, 1982). However, too little work has been done on the relation between biological intelligence and personality to make such an endeavor feasible. Practical intelligence is by definition almost bound together intrinsically with personality, insofar as personality determines very largely the use a person makes of his intellectual gifts (Eysenck, 1988). Psychiatric disorders, alcoholism, impulsivity, addiction, and promiscuity can fatally impair a person's ability to use his IQ to the best advantage, and will hence lead to impairment of "practical intelligence." This use of the term "intelligence" is too broad to be scientifically useful, and will hence not be used in this chapter. For readers interested in this concept, a recent paper by Miller, Omens, and Delwadia (1991) contains ample material.

Personality will here be used in terms of a hierarchical trait model, that is, a model based on primary, first-order factors, correlating to make up higher order concepts

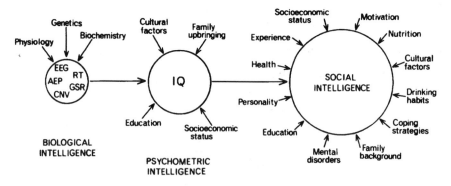

Figure 1.1.   Different meanings of "intelligence." (From Eysenck, 1988.)

like extraversion (E), neuroticism (N) or anxiety, and psychoticism (P), as opposed to super-ego functioning (Eysenck & Eysenck, 1985). As regards the *relations* between these two concepts, I will emphasize the contrast between purely psychometric relations, a theoretical and purely heuristic, and a theoretical–experimental one, that is, based on experiments conducted to test a specific theory. I hope to show that little of importance has been found by authors using the first approach (unfortunately much the more numerous group), while potentially important findings have been made by authors using the second approach. The reasons why the theoretically and practically less promising approach has been so much favored is difficult to discern, unless it be that it is much easier, demands only routine collection of data, and can be done *ambulando.*

Intelligence and psychopathology

It is usually assumed, with good reason, that intelligence, as defined by Spearman's *g*, is not correlated with personality. A good deal of work has been done, for instance, on the possible relation between the WAIS, as a good measure of intellectual ability, and the MMPI, as a measure of personality. Gaines and Morris (1978) found that " . . . there are no lawful relationships between WAIS subtests and MMPI clinical scales" (p. 400). Similarly, Bloom and Entin (1975) concluded that "apparently no lawful relationships exist between WAIS and MMPI scales, and further investigation seems unwarranted" (p. 698). Again, Lacks and Keefe (1970) report lack of relationship, and conclude that "further pursuit of WAIS–MMPI relationships is apt to be fruitless" (p. 430).

On the other hand, Holland and Watson (1980), Turner and Horn (1976), and Watson, Davis, and McDermott (1976) do claim to have found relations between the two tests, as do Berg, Ingersoll, and Terry (1985). The last-named may serve to illustrate the possible degree of relationship that may be found. Using 197 psychiatric inpatients, they administered MMPI and WAIS tests, and subjected valid raw subscale scores to bivariate, multivariate, and canonical correlational analyses. Twenty-four percent of the bivariate correlations and 50% of the multiple correlations were significant, and a canonical R of .609 was found between the WAIS subtests and the MMPI clinical scales, and a canonical R of .394 between the WAIS subtests and the MMPI validity scales. Tables given by the authors show the bivariate and multivariate correlations between MMPI and WAIS subtest scores.

How can we interpret the observed relations? The authors suggest that their canonical analysis has characteristics of a cognitive factor, for example, memory, for the clinical scales; for the validity scales, they suggest an intellectual factor. Holland and Watson (1980) had suggested an intellective factor to account for the clinical scales and their relation with the WAIS also, but of course all these interpretations are speculative. Perhaps all that these studies show is that when there are large differences in psychopathology, the degree (and possibly the kind) of pathology may depress WAIS scores selectively. For normal samples there should be little correlation, and that is what is usually found. Making avoidable errors seems correlated with high 428 and 987 MMPI profiles and may be the mediating factor between pathology and IQ (Fracchia, Fiorentiur, Sheppard, and Merlis, 1970).

Is there a relation between kind of psychopathology and intelligence? The MMPI is hardly an instrument to use when looking at differential pathology, due to its psychometric deficits, but Wechsler has from the beginning emphasized, on the basis of his clinical intuition, that certain patterns of WAIS profiles are in fact diagnostic of different pathologies (1940). Matarazzo (1972) has surveyed the literature; so have Rabin (1965) and Franks (1970). What did they find?

Matarazzo (1970) says, "Hundreds upon hundreds of studies on the use of profile, pattern, or scatter analysis with the Wechsler scales . . . fail to produce reliable evidence that such research would be fruitful." (p. 430). There would be little point in giving long lists of all these researchers with their negative or controversial findings, but it may be useful to consider why this obviously promising idea failed. The first reason, of course, is a psychometric one that should have been apparent from the beginning. The variables considered, whether they be profiles, patterns, or scatter analyses, are essentially measures of differences between subtests, and as such are subject to the damaging fact that differences between tests have much lower reliabilities than do the tests themselves. These lower reliabilities would make any meaningful findings very unlikely, and Meehl and Rosen (1955) and Cronbach and Gleser (1965) have presented the relevant statistical arguments in some detail; it is unfortunate that researchers in this area have neglected such considerations that, for all practical purposes, foredoom these empirical approaches to failure.

The second and equally important factor is the unreliability of the criterion, that is, the type of psychopathology involved. Psychiatric diagnoses are notoriously unreliable, and hence prediction of such unreliable diagnoses, even with a perfect test, would still show only very low correlations. Given this unreliability, Matarazzo points out that "a correlated index such as the Wechsler profile, no matter how promising, cannot produce anything but . . . confusing, or otherwise frustrating findings."

There is a third reason why one would not expect such studies trying to use patterns or profiles on the Wechsler subtest as a diagnostic aid to succeed. Most of the studies were based on a simple blunderbuss approach; in the hope of finding correlations you administer a large number of tests and randomly correlate them with whatever takes your fancy, in anticipation of finding correlations (and judiciously forgetting to correct the observed probability values for the number of comparisons made!). This is the major fault of the WAIS-MMPI correlations; with so many correlations and no *a priori* hypothesis, the data are simply not worth calculating.

Clinicians often object to such criticisms by saying that their research is based on clinical "insights" which serve the purpose of a hypothesis. It is difficult to give credence to such arguments because the term "insight" is ill-defined. Usually it means little more than a guess on the part of the clinician, based on a certain amount of experience perhaps, but certainly not suggesting that his "insights" are anything but guesses. There is no theoretical rationale, based on sound laboratory evidence, and in the absence of such evidence the claim to possess some deep "insights" must be taken with a grain of salt. Matarazzo discusses in great detail the relationship between the Wechsler subtests and the Gittinger Personality Assessment System, which he regards as a theoretical model based on clinical insights. I know of no evidence to suggest that these "insights" have any relation to reality, or lead to any replicable relationships with Wechsler subtests.

It is fair, in retrospect, to deplore the time and energy spent by so many (mainly clinical) psychologists in trying to achieve something that in the nature of things was impossible. Rather than use unreliable and probably invalid clinical criteria (diagnoses or MMPI scores), they might have been better advised to try to improve the methods of diagnosis, particularly, replacing the categorical system with a dimensional one that seems to fit the facts much better (Eysenck, 1970). Furthermore, they might with advantage have improved their acquaintance with statistical methods and conclusions, thus avoiding the collection and analysis of data foredoomed to be inconclusive. Finally, they might have tried to elaborate more general theories that might predict relationships between intelligence and personality. This chapter is now pretty well closed, although some courageous souls are still searching for the Holy Grail in this unlikely area.

A slightly more hopeful relationship is that, originally suggested by Wechsler, between psychopathic personality and having a higher PIQ than VIQ. As Wechsler (1958, p. 176) put it, "the most outstanding single feature of the sociopath's test profile is his systematic high score on the Performance as compared with the Verbal part of the Scale." Matarazzo (1972) listed about 30 studies that generally support this view, although he urges caution in individual diagnosis. Moffit and Silva (1987) are less optimistic about the usefulness of this index. Kandell et al. (1988) find that high IQ acts as a protective factor for subjects at high risk for antisocial behaviour, but VIQ is equally protective as high PIQ. This agrees with the more general finding that IQ correlates negatively with criminality (Eysenck & Gudjonsson, 1989). What is clearly needed is more systematic, focussed research of an experimental rather than a purely psychometric kind.

Personality and the structure of intelligence

It is usually taken for granted that the structure of intelligence is defined in terms of factorial investigation of correlations between tests. Thus, many studies have been done of the Wechsler scales (Maxwell, 1960; Canavan, Dunn, and McMillan, 1986), extending to abnormal groups, such as patients with unilateral cerebral lesions (Warrington, James, and Maciejewlski, 1986), and in many different countries (e.g., Drago, Daum, and Canavan, 1991) with similar results. Based on this assumption, we now have in addition to *g* some two dozen "primary factors" of intelligence, derived from many different tests (Eysenck, 1979). Similarly, the analysis of matrices of correlations between items of personality questionnaires, or of personality scales themselves, has given rise to numerous factors (Eysenck, 1970). Are these procedures justified?

The problem that arises may perhaps be put as follows: when a factor analysis of personality inventory scales is carried out, a number of factors, such as extraversion, neuroticism, etc., usually result. Similarly, when a factor analysis of intelligence test scales is carried out, a number of factors, such as verbal ability, perceptual ability etc., usually result. These factors are independent, in the first case of intelligence, in the second case of neuroticism or extraversion, as long as we preserve the rule that we are only concerned with linear relations. But we may enquire whether similar factors and relations would emerge if we extracted personality factors from populations differing in intelligence level, or intelligence factors from populations differing in degree of neuroticism.

A study by Shure and Rogers (1963) has attempted to answer the first question. They administered the eighteen scales of the California Psychological Inventory (CPI) to three student groups differing without overlap in IQ level, and then intercorrelated and factor analyzed the resulting scores for the three groups separately. They found that while there was considerable overall similarity in the solution, the total factor variance associated with their neuroticism factor dropped by over 30% in going from the high-ability group to the low-ability group. (The sum of squared loadings is, respectively, 5.18, 4.64, and 3.48 for the three groups.) No such change was observed in their extraversion factor, the sum of squared loadings being 3.46, 3.76, and 3.17, respectively, for the three groups. While confirmation is, of course, essential before too much credence can be given to this finding, it would appear that factorial studies of personality may not give invariant results under change of ability level.

The other problem raised is perhaps even more important from the educational point of view: would factorial studies of abilities be invariant under change of personality composition of the groups under analysis? The only paper concerned specifically with this problem is one published by Lienert (1963). His work is based on 1,003 school children with a mean age of between 15 and 16; three-fifths of the children were male. These children were administered thirteen intelligence tests of the Thurstone type, constituting the so-called Leistungspruefsystem of Horn (1962a). Also administered was a personality questionnaire, modeled after Eysenck's Maudsley Medical Questionnaire by Horn (1962b) that gives a measure of neuroticism and also contains a lie scale. Seventy-seven subjects were excluded from the analysis because they had not completed all the tests or because of unusual lie scale scores. Of the remaining subjects, 259 labile and 262 stable children were selected as constituting the 25% highest-scoring and lowest-scoring subjects, respectively, on the neuroticism scale. There were no differences between the groups in age but there were more girls in the labile group. However, Lienert was able to show in a preliminary factor analysis that sex had no effect on the factorial structure of the tests. A product–moment correlation of the summed standard scores on the thirteen tests with neuroticism gave a value of −0.16. While statistically significant because of the large numbers, this is for practical purposes equivalent to a finding of orthogonality between the two variables.

Separate matrices of intercorrelations were calculated for the labile and stable subjects, respectively, and split-half reliabilities were calculated for all the tests for the two groups. Reliabilities did not differ, but the average intercorrelation of the tests was slightly and significantly higher for the stable group (.33 as opposed to .27).

Next, Lienert carried out a multiple factor analysis following Thurstone's procedure. It was found that eight factors could be extracted from the stable group and only four from the labile group. Communalities were lower for the labile than for the stable group and specific factors were more important for the labile than for the stable group. After rotation, it was found that three factors could be interpreted for the labile and six for the stable group; the latter were said to be closer to Thurstone's primary factors, whereas the former were much more mixed. These figures suggest strongly that children high and low on neuroticism differ very significantly in the way their mental abilities are structured. This conclusion is so important that a thorough critical analysis of the study seems in order.

Such a study was undertaken by Eysenck and White (1964), whose analyses in essence supported Lienert. Cohen and Wittemann (1967) attempted to replicate Lienert's study, and administered 14 standardized intelligence tests to 2,000 eighth-graders. They used a different neuroticism test from that used by Lienert, and their sample was more homogeneous with respect to age. They failed to support Lienert's results, the factor structure of high-, medium-, and low-neuroticism groups corresponding to a high degree. There the matter rests at the moment. It is sad that so important and fundamental a question is left in such an unsatisfactory state. It is perhaps typical of psychology that a theoretically important question like this only attracts a few students, while utterly meaningless clinical studies such as those considered in our second section are repeated time and time again.

Intelligence and introversion–extraversion

In this section I shall try to show how theory can suggest relationships between intelligence and personality, in contrast to the blunderbuss approach criticized in the first and second sections. Before discussing specific hypotheses, let us consider a distinction that is very important but seldom made in this field. Students of learning and conditioning will be familiar with the distinction between learning and performance; we may have learned a specific response, but whether that response will actually be made (performance) depends on many additional variables. Low problem solving in an IQ test is a measure of performance; personality may influence performance rather than abstract intellect, with measurable effects on the IQ. An IQ test lasts for up to 1 hour or more, and considerations of fatigue, vigilance, arousal, etc., may very well play a part.

Speed of working is another important variable that is closely connected with extraversion (Eysenck, 1967). Jensen (1964) has reported a study on 50 university undergraduates demonstrating the relevance of this factor. The Raven Progressive Matrices were administered to subjects individually, without time limit; however, the total time taken by the subject in doing the test was recorded by the tester without the subject knowing it. Correlations of E (extraversion) and N (neuroticism) with total score (−.13 and +.15) were insignificant, but E correlated −.46 ($p < .01$) with total time spent on doing the test. Raven scores were completely uncorrelated with time spent on the test. These findings suggest that had the test been given under timed conditions, the more extraverted subjects would have had a distinct advantage. It is this type of deduction that seems well worth testing, derived as it is from well-established theories. (N showed a completely insignificant correlation with speed of working.)

I have suggested that introverts are characterized by higher cortical arousal than extraverts, and hence show greater vigilance and less inhibition in extended performance tasks (Eysenck, 1967; Eysenck & Eysenck, 1985). This suggests a crucial test: extraverts should show a decline in performance on IQ tests during a lengthy administration. The first attempt to test this hypothesis was carried out by D. Furneaux, in an unpublished study (Eysenck, 1957).

The test used consisted of sixteen easy letter-series problems, preceded by two problems that were not scored, and followed by an insoluble problem, also not scored. The problems are so easy that in the population of university students tested errors do not occur; consequently, the score used is the time taken over each problem. The problems are roughly equal in difficulty, as determined by prior research. Under these conditions we would expect inhibition to affect the speed of work, and we would expect it to do so differentially for extraverts and introverts. No more precise prediction can be made, as the test which is being analysed was preceded by other tests of intelligence, thus making the situation too complex to allow precise prediction.

Subjects were given the Guilford personality scales, and 12 markedly extraverted and 15 markedly introverted subjects chosen for a comparison of their scores. The most reliable type of score was found to be the rate of work for a given item, divided by the average rate of work for the whole test. The difference between the groups was found to be statistically significant, thus lending support to both our points—inhibition affects the rate of work, and it does so differentially for extraverts and introverts. Furneaux took one further step. Using a new sample of 130 students, he plotted each subject's scores and gave him a new score (pattern score) according to the degree to which his pattern of scores approached the extraverted or the introverted pattern. These pattern scores would be expected to correlate with extraversion–introversion scores on the questionnaire, and indeed a very significant correlation of .35 is reported by Furneaux, thus cross-validating the differential patterns found (Eysenck, 1957, pp. 132–133).

In a replication of the Furneaux experiment, Eysenck (1959) predicted that in the process of solving the 60 problems of the Morrisby Compound Series Test (Morrisby, 1955), a nonverbal intelligence test, extraverts would show greater reactive inhibition, and consequently a falling off in performance during the last quarter of the test as compared with the first three quarters. From 137 adult male and female neurotics, who were given the Maudsley Personality Inventory, were then chosen an introverted group (E score of 16 or below) and an extraverted group (E score of 30 or above). Nineteen extraverts and 28 introverts were available for testing. They were administered the test individually, without time limit, and each item was separately timed.

There were no differences in the total number of items correctly solved, or in the speed with which all items were finished. There was, however, a significant difference in the speed with which correct solutions were produced. On the first 45 problems, introverts were insignificantly slower than extraverts; on the last 15 problems, extraverts were significantly slower than introverts. When we turn to the speed with which items were abandoned unsolved, we find that there were no significant differences on the first 45 problems, but that on the last 15 problems extraverts gave up significantly more quickly. (A one-tail test was used for this comparison because the outcome had been predicted.) It is concluded that extraverts show greater work decrement on an intelligence test by taking longer to obtain correct solutions toward the end of the test, as compared with introverts, and by giving up more easily toward the end.

These studies show that general laws, such as those linking vigilance with introversion, extend to performance on IQ tests; problem solving behaves just like other types of performance, cognitive and noncognitive (Eysenck, 1967). It is interesting that in such attempts to apply general psychological principles to the specific problems of intelligence, personality interactions have been so rare; this would seem to be an interesting and rewarding field.

A rather different theory-driven approach has been pioneered by Robinson (1985). As he says, "Previously reported findings indicate that variation of EEG evoked-potential parameters is strongly related to both personality and intelligence differences" (Robinson, 1982a). These data and the associated theory imply that personality should relate to intelligence-test performance. Results are described in this report indicating that subtest profiles obtained with the Wechsler Adult Intelligence Scale (WAIS) differ significantly for subjects scoring highest and lowest on the Extraversion (*E*) scale of the Eysenck Personality Questionnaire (EPQ); introverts tend to do better on the "Verbal" subtests while extraverts tend to do better on the "Performance" measures (Robinson, 1982b).

Using a complex system of weights, Robinson did find the expected relationship, as shown in his Figure 2. In view of the small number of subjects used by Robinson, a replication was carried out by Barrett and Eysenck (1992). We used two separate scales, namely the WAIS-R (individual) test and the Jackson Multidimensional Aptitude Battery (MAB) group test, which purports to measure similar abilities to the WAIS. There is no Digit Span subtest in the MAB, and this scale also assesses Spatial Ability, a subtest not included directly by name in the WAIS. The subject data are taken from a total sample of 268 subjects (for the MAB) and 149 subjects (WAIS), matching introverts and extraverts by age, and using subjects one SD or more above or below the mean of the Eysenck and Eysenck (1975) EPQ extraversion scale.

Results lend little support to Robinson's theory. Overall the two sets of data (extraverts and introverts) do not differ significantly on either test. The data suggest that extraverts and introverts do not differ in IQ on a representative set of scales, whether tested individually or in groups. Saklofske and Kostura (1990) arrived at a similar conclusion. It should not be assumed that these data completely disprove Robinson's theory, particularly as he has reported a replication of his earlier work which gave very positive results (Robinson, 1986). The situation is probably much more complicated than originally assumed, as shown by a study introducing time stress (Rawlings and Carnie, 1989). In their study

The EPQ and four tests derived from WAIS subtests (Arithmetic, Information, Digit Span, Picture Arrangement) were given to 40 subjects under both timed and untimed conditions. On the basis of Eysenck's arousal theory of extraversion, it was predicted that introverts should be more adversely influenced by time–pressure than extraverts. The prediction was supported by a highly significant extraversion by time–pressure interaction. A highly significant extraversion by subtest interaction was also established: extraverts showed superior performance on the Information subtest and introverts showed superior performance on the Digit Span subtest, but only under untimed conditions. A two-way interaction between sex and psychoticism, and a three-way interaction between sex, psychoticism, and time–pressure were also revealed. The results provide support for earlier studies, showing interactions between personality and time–pressure and suggest an alternative explanation for Robinson's model relating personality to intelligence.

A recent study by Kirkcaldy and Siefen (in press) lends modified support to Robertson. Using the German version of the WAIS on 84 psychiatric patients, they found that "Introverts did exhibit higher intelligence scores across *all* Wechsler subtests compared to extraverts, the difference being most pronounced for those scales, information and similarities constituting the factor, verbal intelligence." In addition, the Picture Completion task, which assesses the ability to differentiate essential from nonessential details and is supposedly loaded on the performance intelligence factor, was done better by introverted individuals, consistent with Robinson's (1985) findings that this subtest, unlike the other nonverbal tasks, does not require any obvious overt motor manipulation and is passive. To that extent, it resembles verbal subtests involving an active search for an appropriate associate. The superiority of introverts on sensory associative tasks has been considered due to their generating excitation from stimulus analysis in contrast to extraverts who outperform on motor tasks, since they generate excitation from response organization and inhibition from stimulus analysis (Brebner, 1985).

Differences between extraverts and introverts may be more apparent in performance parameters than in total scores. Thus Eysenck (1947) found that extraverts tended to be faster but less accurate than introverts; these features may be mutually compensating to produce equal total scores, or, depending on type of test, scoring methods etc., that may favor one group or the other. Howard and McKillen (1990) put this hypothesis to the test. They used the Perceptual Maze Test (PMT: Elithorn, Jones, & Kerr, 1963), in which the testee has to connect points in a maze such as to make a path that connects as many points as possible; no backward moves are allowed. Figure 1.2 shows a schematic example.

This test, particularly in its computer-automated form (Jones & Weinman, 1973),

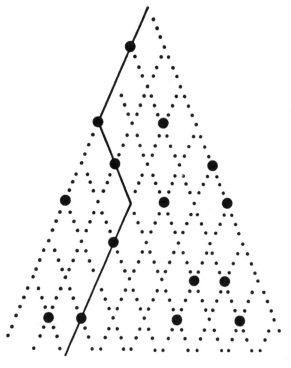

Figure 1.2.   Schematic examples of a maze from the Perceptual Maze Test, showing a solution path. (From Howard and McMillan, 1990.)

is a powerful tool for examining different aspects of task performance; it is easy to administer and score, and it is possible to vary task complexity according to the S's level of performance, and to present each item with or without information regarding the optimal solution available, or with and without time limits of various kinds. In an earlier study, Weinman, Elithorn, and Cooper (1985) had found that extraversion was related inversely to the proportional search or inspection time, i.e., extraverts spent a lower proportion of total time inspecting the maze prior to entering it, indicative of a lack of "reflectivity." (Neuroticism was associated with slower performance.) These differences in performance related to personality were more apparent in the "without information" condition, which can be construed as containing more ambiguity. In a replication study by Howard (unpublished, quoted in Howard and McKillen, 1990), fast responders in the "no information" conditions were significantly more extraverted than slow responders.

In the Howard and McKillen (1990) study, results were in agreement with the hypotheses stated. As they say, "We can summarise our results by saying that extraverts, in comparison with introverts, displayed a cognitive style characterised by faster, less accurate, and less reflective performance in the perceptual maze. This difference in cognitive style emerged most clearly in the more ambiguous condition, where no information was given regarding the optimal solution. As the situation became more ambiguous (i.e., changed from the "with information" to the "without information" condition), extraverts speeded up and tended to become less reflective. Introverts, in contrast, slowed down and tended to become more reflective. This cannot be accounted for by a practice or time-on-task effect, since extraverts showed essentially the same phenomenon in the "without information" condition in the pilot study, where condition (with versus without information) was varied between different groups of Ss. The difference in cognitive style was also reflected in the type of strategy used to solve the maze. Extraverts opted for a nonreflective strategy, aiming their responses towards the area of the maze with the highest density of dots. This strategy might be considered as analogous to the confrontational coping strategy which extraverts appear to use in stressful interpersonal situations (Howard, 1988). Introverts, by contrast, opted for a more planful, reflective strategy, mapping out a pathway through the maze before entering it. Our findings are in agreement with Eysenck's (1947) original suggestion that the speed/accuracy ratio is high in extraverts and low in introverts.

We may conclude this section by saying that in contrast to the blunderbuss, atheoretical approach of the authors in the first section of this chapter, these workers have (1) articulated specific hypotheses to test, (2) used appropriate measures to test their hypotheses (usually not simple total score or IQ measures), and (3) concentrated on style of solution rather than undifferentiated outcomes. While unfortunately this approach has usually been followed only by a small proportion of researchers, it would seem to hold out much more promise than the simple-minded, undifferentiated approach criticized earlier on.

Intelligence and neuroticism–anxiety

Having failed to find any connections between Wechsler subtest patterns or profiles and psychiatric classification, psychologists turned to the more clearly defined and (in principle) measurable concept of anxiety, using for the most part the Taylor Manifest Anxiety Scale (Taylor, 1953). Here, too, however, findings were mostly negative or at best contradictory; Matarazzo (1972) has summarized the earlier evidence, and nothing since has changed the situation. As he puts it, "the overwhelming weight of evidence suggested little or no correlations between a person's TAS anxiety level and his measured intelligence. The few significant correlations which were reported by the earliest investigators were beginning to appear, in retrospect, to be the result of sampling or a similar methodological artifact." (p. 442.) He cites the Spielberger (1958) study as fairly conclusive. Spielberger (1958) carried out an extensive study in which he showed that although the correlation between ACE intelligence and TAS score was an insignificant −0.02 for a total sample of 1142 Duke University students, comprising six consecutive semesters (samples) of classes of students taking introductory psychology, the r for any one semester (sample) of such students ranged from one value of −0.01 to another of −0.34 (p of 0.01) for male students, and an r of +0.62 (p of 0.05) to an r of −0.19 for female students. Spielberger very convincingly argued from such a large sample of individuals, and subsamples of them, that there was *no* correlation between TAS and ACE and, also, that the subsamples in which the level of intelligence (ACE scores) *was low* were more likely than others to produce a significant negative correlation between anxiety and intelligence. (The ACE is a timed IQ test which earlier research had suggested might impose stress on the subject leading to higher correlations with anxiety.) The results are unlikely to be in dispute.

It seems more than likely that the divergent results reported in the literature are due to different conditions of motivation, stress, and felt anxiety; as Cicero (see Eysenck, 1983) pointed out before Christ was born, feelings of anxiety may arise in people not having an anxious disposition, and fail to arise in people who do have that disposition. Situations, and individual reactions to specific situations, determine state anxiety, which is correlated with trait anxiety, but not identical with it. More recent research has been concerned with state anxiety and its influence on intelligence measurement. Note that again we are concerned not with intelligence as a dispositional cognitive trait, but with performance variables; state anxiety has a purely temporary influence on an individual's performance on an IQ test, but need not be (and probably is not) correlated with *true* IQ.

A few studies may be looked at in some detail to illustrate the methodologies used. State anxiety may be inferred (1) on the basis of the subject's own self-report, or (2) experimentally induced stress. This may involve threat of electric shock or other techniques of transient fear arousal in the individual being tested; instructions or other statements that the individual being tested is less intelligent than his peers, or otherwise is inferior in his performance; use of a warm and encouraging intelligence examiner versus a more cold, bland one; the examiner's open use of a stopwatch in order to put temporary "time pressure" on the tested individual versus absence of such situational pressure; gazing directly into the eyes of the individual while he is verbally reciting digits forward and backward versus not gazing in this manner, etc.; (3) any combinations involving two or more of these types of state anxiety measures, or combination of one of them with a measure of trait anxiety such as the TAS.

One of the earlier studies is by Mandler and Sarason (1952), who used the Kohs Block Design Test and Digit Symbol Test with undergraduate subjects divided into High Anxiety and Low Anxiety subsamples on the basis of their own self-report on how much anxiety they felt during their examination. They found that the examiner's use of a success or failure instructional set for the student had a different effect on the high-anxious individual relative to the low-anxious individual when both samples were administered these two intelligence subtests. Mandler and Sarason concluded that in examining the anxious individual, the optimal condition is one in which no reference is made to the individual's performance, while for low-anxious individuals, telling them that they were failing would improve their performance, presumably by increasing their motivation.

In another study, Siegman (1956a) used the TAS to separate Ss into high and low trait anxiety groups. He then compared the WAIS performance of these two groups on those subtests which were timed versus those which were not timed. He found that the low anxious group did as well on the timed as on the untimed tests, but the high anxious group subjects performed poorer on the timed tests than on the untimed ones, presumably because of the imposed stress of the timing. In a later study Siegman (1956b) confirmed this finding on a larger group of clinical and psychiatric patients.

One further set of studies must suffice to illustrate the procedures used. All were carried out by Walker and his colleagues, the first being one by Walker and Spence (1964), where no relationship was found between a student's TAS score and his performance on the WAIS Digit Span Subtest. In addition to this control group Walker and Spence also used an experimental group for which they modified the standard administration procedure with the Digit Span Test by having the examiner first tell each of the subjects that he was selected for this individual intelligence examination by the instructor because he had performed poorly on two personality questionnaires that had been administered to the whole class. This procedure was intended to produce state anxiety, and the success of the procedure was tested by asking each individual in the experimental group how he felt when he was told that his previous test scores had been different. Over half of the students in the experimental group said they were disturbed, and they showed a significant decrement in the IQ test relative to the controls; students who had not felt disturbed failed to show such a decrement.

In a later test, Walker, Neilsen, and Nicolay (1965) imposed another type of situational stress by imposing unavoidable failure on the subjects attempting to complete the WAIS Object Assembly Subtest. The control group did not have this failure experience. Of those who experienced the failure, three subgroups were formed and given the standard form of the test. The groups differed in terms of the instructions given, which could be bland, somewhat encouraging, or definitely suggesting that the next item would be easier. For the control group there was no correlation with TAS score, or any of three other measures of anxiety administered. For the first experimental subgroup, i.e., those presumably under greater situational stress, performance correlated −0.45 with their score on the TAS; correlations for the two remaining experimental groups were all insignificant. The authors concluded that "the personality variable of anxiety is negatively related to intelligence-test performance under stress conditions provided that such conditions are directly associated with a testing instrument" (p. 402).

In a final study Walker, Sannito, and Firetto (1970) repeated the Walker and Spence study but utilized all five verbal subtests of the WAIS rather than the Digit Span test alone. The results confirmed and extended the earlier finding in that the subjects who were told that they were given the WAIS because the instructor had said that their earlier responses to a personality questionnaire were questionable, did significantly poorer than on the information, similarities, arithmetic, and digit-span tests, and marginally so on the test of comprehension. Matarazzo (1972) pointed out the importance of this contribution by saying that "in all three studies Walker et al. have found evidence that situations producing state anxiety or other immediate, task-related situational stress can reduce performance on measures of intellectual functioning. Conversely, a subject's score on a measure which tests an individual's more chronic TAS-anxiety does not correlate with such decrements; or, if it does, does so only in the presence of superimposed situational stress (state anxiety)" (p. 446).

Matarazzo (1972) lists some studies using threats of electric shock as anxiety-inducing variables, without finding any effect of this type of state anxiety. Saltz (1970) has shown that the type of neurotic anxiety involved in these studies is concerned with social, not physical threats; this is an important finding to be born in mind when designing or evaluating research in this area.

Again, in reviewing this area, we find that blunderbuss atheoretical approaches have completely failed to produce positive results of any kind. As Matarazzo (1972) points out, "three decades of examination of various samples of psychiatric patients, those diagnosed anxiety neurotic and others, failed to find a differential Wechsler profile, pattern, or scatter. Additionally, when the criterion of anxiety was shifted to an objective measure like the TAS, this, too, failed to show any relationship to Digit Span or other subtest performances." (p. 447). Nothing could better indicate the bankruptcy of traditional approaches to the topic. There are well-established theories of anxiety that mediate many interesting predictions for learning, intelligence, and stress (Eysenck, 1973). It seems sad that these theories have for the most part not been used to guide research.

One of the most interesting consequences, for instance, of looking at the theoretical and experimental literature on anxiety is the argument that anxiety, regarded as a drive, may be linked in a curvilinear fashion (inverted-U shape) to intelligence; in other words, obeying the Yerkes-Dodson Law we would expect both high and low anxiety to be sub-optimal for performing well on IQ tests. Lynn and Gordon (1961) have furnished some evidence in favour of this hypothesis, but of course much more needs to be done to establish the truth or otherwise of this view. In particular, the degree of threat presented by the testing situation would have to be borne in mind in order to mediate specific predictions. Nevertheless, this example may serve to give an idea of how the results of experimental research and proper theorizing may be used to give testable deductions in this field.

Divergent intelligence, creativity, and psychoticism

Divergent thinking, as opposed to convergent thinking, has for a long time been suggested as the model for originality and creativity, as opposed to rigidity and formalism (Hudson, 1966). The concept (though not the name) originated with the Spearman school in the form of "fluency" tests (Hargreaves, 1927); Spearman was one of the first to use multiple factor analysis (long before Thurstone), and found that fluency was a primary factor which remained after *g* had been extracted from the table. Later developments have been detailed in Glover, Ronning, and Reynolds (1989); it seemed that convergent and divergent tests of intelligence correlate at low IQ levels (up to about 120), while at typical student levels they become independent. This suggests that at such levels of IQ, the traits of creativity and originality, as measured by divergent ability tests, may have an origin in personality, rather than in cognition (Eysenck, 1983).

The personality dimension, which in the past has been most closely related to genius and creativity, is, of course, psychiatric illness (Prentky, 1980); it is unlikely that actual illness (i.e., schizophrenia and manic–depressive illness) would be helpful, but *spectrum* disorders, i.e., schizoid, psychopathic, and other similar rather milder disorders, frequently occurring in close relatives of psychotic probands, do appear to show above-normal creativity and originality, as Bleuler already suggested when he originally introduced the concept of "schizophrenia" at the beginning of the century [Bleuler, 1978 (translation)].

I have suggested the concept of "psychoticism" as the third major dimension of personality (Eysenck and Eysenck, 1976), and also formulated the hypothesis that creativity was closely related to this continuum. The demonstration of such a relation demands some clear, measurable definition of "creativity"; actually there are two such: creativity as a trait, measurable by means of divergent tests of intelligence, and creativity as *achievement,* measurable in terms of worthwhile and original works (poetry, music, science, etc.). These two types of measures are not closely correlated because trait creativity is only one of several conditions needed for achievement creativity, others being high IQ, persistence, special abilities (verbal, numerical, visuospatial, socioeconomic status, etc.). These are conceived of as interacting synergistically, thus producing a J-shaped distribution, although divergent thinking tests produce a normal distribution. Support for the theory would thus necessitate (a) a strong correlation between divergent thinking and psychoticism, and (b) higher P scores for creative persons, as shown in actual creative achievement. Both types of support have been forthcoming (Eysenck, 1993).

Some of the early studies linking psychoticism and creativity have been discussed elsewhere (Eysenck and Eysenck, 1976). Thus, Farmer (1974) found two factors (fluency and originality) in a factor analysis of correlations between divergent-thinking tests. P had a small loading of .24 on fluency, but a very high one on originality ($r = .74$). Kidner (see in Eysenck and Eysenck, 1976, pp. 186–187) used IQ and divergent-thinking tests, creating an "index of creativity" by subtracting the standardized sum of the IQ tests from that of the creativity tests; this correlated .31 with P, and –.23 with L. The correlation with E was .21. In another experiment he replicated the correlation of P with creativity, and also found that P correlated with overinclusiveness and slowness in categorization, aspects of schizophrenic thinking often found.

Here, I will concentrate on two studies, one concerned with trait creativity, the other with achievement creativity. These two studies have been selected for detailed discussion because they bring out particularly well certain points of theoretical interest. The first of these two studies is by Woody and Claridge (1977), and was designed especially to test the hypothesis of a strong relationship between creativity and psychoticism. The tests used were the Eysenck Personality Questionnaire (Eysenck and Eysenck, 1975), the Wallach-Kogan (1965) creativity tests, and the Nufferno Speed Test as a measure of intelligence (Furneaux, 1950). Subjects were 100 Oxford University students, sampling widely from the various fields of specialization; mean age of the group was 20 years, S.D., two years.

Consider first the correlation of P with the 5 tasks constituting the creativity test – instances, pattern meanings, uses, similarities, and line meanings. For each of these divergent tests, there are two scores, one for numbers of suggestions (fluency) and the other for consequences (originality); correlations with P were .32, .37, .45, .36, and .38 for number score, and .61, .64, .66, .68, and .65 for uniqueness. Overall the correlations with Extraversion and Neuroticism were quite insignificant, but those for L (Lie Scale) were significant and in the –.20 region. (For groups such as this, L probably measures social conformity rather than lying, and correlates negatively with P.) It is worth noting that the ten indices of creativity were all highly intercorrelated, with correlations ranging from .37 to .83; thus it appeared that the tests were tapping a unitary factor. Correlations between the creativity and personality variables, on the one hand, and intelligence, on the other, were insignificant.

Using all ten tests of creativity predicted P at a high level (multiple R = .84). While replications would no doubt give a lower value for R, using the same prediction formula, the fact that the R is higher than the reliability of P does suggest an astonishingly close relationship between the two variables, and thus supports the original theory. Of course, these results refer only to creativity as a trait; they say nothing about creativity in terms of achievement.

This problem has been tackled by Gotz and Gotz (1979a,b), two internationally known German painters who were successful, because of their inside position, in getting 147 male and 110 female artists of renown to return completed forms of the EPQ. Painters and sculptors were included in this sample. Mean age was 47 years, with a range of 29 to 78 years. Three hundred male and 300 female controls were also tested, with a similar age range (mean 41 years, range 21 to 79 years). Testing was done individually or in small groups.

Male but not female artists were more introverted than respective controls; perhaps women need more dominance and urgency to compete! Male but not female artists were more neurotic than respective controls. Most important from our point of view, male artists had higher P scores than male controls (6.53 vs. 5.79), and female artists had higher P scores than female controls (6.18 vs. 4.32). The SDs were around 3.00. Both differences were highly significant, and are in the predicted direction. Note the exceptionally high P score of the female artists; this is expected on the basis of the dual threshold hypothesis (Eysenck and Gudjonsson, 1988), and is similar to findings concerning P scores for male and female criminals. For L, there is no difference for males, but a large one for females ($p < .001$). It should be noted that comparisons between artists and controls may, as stated, appear less significant than they really are because P declines with age (Eysenck, 1987), and the artists were significantly older by 6 years.

In a recent study (Gotz and Gotz, 1979b), 60 well-known artists were divided by experts into 37 more and 23 less successful ones. The more successful ones had significantly higher P scores. Some artists who were successful had low P scores, but these tended to be in the high age group, where P scores tend to drop. Altogether, being a successful artist correlated well with P, and distinguishes artists from non-artists. This is very much in line with our theory. These two studies are thus complementary in linking P with both definitions of creativity.

Would we expect psychotics to show high creativity? Hasenfus and Magaro (1976) have found significantly depressed performance of schizophrenics on tests of creative thinking. As we shall argue, creativity demands a combination of high P and high ego strength; there is considerable evidence for the necessity of combining these two apparently antithetical properties.

It may be more illuminating to consider persons within the psychotic Erbkreis, but who are not themselves psychotic. This can be done by looking at relatives of psychotics, to see if they show unusual amounts of creativity (Eysenck, 1983). Thus Heston (1966) studied offspring of schizophrenic mothers raised by foster parents and found that although about half showed psychosocial disability, the remaining half were certainly successful adults, pursuing artistic talents and demonstrating imaginative adaptations to life to a degree not found in the control group. Karlsson (1968, 1970) found in Iceland that among relatives of schizophrenics there was a high incidence of individuals of great creative achievement. McNeil (1971) studied the occurrence of mental illness in highly creative adopted children and their biological parents, discovering that the mental illness rates in the adoptees and in their biological parents were positively and significantly related to the creativity level of the adoptees.

Such findings give powerful support to a link between psychoticism and creativity. More experimental is another approach.

It has often been suggested that schizophrenic thinking is characterized by a cognitive style that has been variously called overinclusive, allusive, loose, or characterized by the term "mental slippage." Such overinclusiveness would seem to be similar in nature to the gentler slope of the associative gradient, or the broader associative horizon often suggested to be crucial in accounting for creativity.

Our theory would demand that some good and appropriate measure of "over-inclusion" should (a) be commonly found in schizophrenics and/or in other psychotic patients; (b) should correlate with measures of psychoticism in normal people; and (c) should correlate with creativity. The obvious choice for such a test must be one of word association, because it has been known for a long time that unusual associations are highly characteristic of schizophrenic patients; I have reviewed the literature elsewhere (Eysenck, 1993). Does the giving of unusual word associations correlate with creative performance? An excellent test of this hypothesis comes from the work of IPAR (Institute of Personality Assessment and Research, Berkeley). MacKinnon (1962, 1965) has described the study in detail; it is concerned with groups of creative, somewhat creative, and noncreative architects ($n = 124$) who made up the sample.

MacKinnon (1962) starts his account with a reference to a study by Bingham (1953), who tested Amy Lowell, the poetess, with (among other tests) the word association test and found that "she gave a higher proportion of unique responses than those of anyone outside a mental institution" (p. 11). With his architects, MacKinnon found the same; the unusualness of responses correlated .50 with the rated creativity of the architects. Thus Architects I (the most creative) scored 204; Architects II scored 128; and Architects III, the least creative, scored 114.

Gough (1976) has reported on a similar study done with 60 engineering students and 45 industrial-reward scientists. The subjects were rated for creativity, and given two word-association tests, one a general one, and one using a scientific-word list. Both correlated with creativity, but the scientific-word list gave rather higher correlations. This is an intriguing finding that ought to be followed up in future research.

Similar results have also been reported by Miller and Chapman (1983), using the Chapman and Chapman (1980) scales as measures of schizotypal behavior. Using a continuum word-association test they found that subjects with high scores in Perceptual Aberration/Magical Ideation gave a larger number of idiosyncratic responses. It is also relevant that Griffiths, Mednick, Schulsinger, and Diderichsen (1980) reported more deviant associations in the children of schizophrenic parents.

Finally, we come to the predicted association between unusual word associations and psychoticism. The most relevant study is one by Upmanyu and Kaur (1986) in which 140 university students were tested on the Kent–Rosanoff Word Association test and the Eysenck Personality Questionnaire (Eysenck and Eysenck, 1975). Unique responses correlated .32 with P; E, N, and the Lie scale failed to show any correlation, as did intelligence. The reliability of the WAT was .72, that of the P scale was .68; correcting for attenuation gives us a correlation between P and unique responses of

.46. Ward, McConaghy, and Catts (1991) reported similar results. The third requirement of the theory seems to be fulfilled.

There seems little doubt that there is a fairly close relationship between some aspects of personality (psychoticism) and some aspects of intellect (divergent thinking). In the past such cross-discipline associations have been rather disregarded; yet some of the most interesting areas of psychology seem to lie here. Perhaps the next few years will see a rapid development of this promising field.

Intelligence and personality in children

In children, intelligence and school achievement are closely related, and seem to be related with personality in a manner which changes with age. Thus Eysenck and Cookson (1969) studied some 4,000 11-year-old boys and girls who had been given IQ tests, personality tests, and scholastic-achievement tests. Intelligence was tested on two Moray Home verbal-reasoning tests, with a mean of 100 and a S.D. of 15. On both tests extraverted children significantly surpassed introverted ones, both sexes giving similar results. Table 1.1 shows the main outcome of the study.

It is apparent that extraverted boys and girls do significantly better than introverted ones; that ambiverts are intermediate; and that girls do better than boys. The differences in IQ between extraverts and introverts are not inconsiderable, amounting to between 4 and 9 points of IQ. Similar differences between extraverts and introverts were observed in respect of achievement (Mathematics, English, and Reading); a proportion of grammar-school entrants also showed the same difference.

Entwistle & Cunningham (1968), working with 13-year-olds, failed to find an overall correlation between extraversion and school achievement; extraverted girls and introverted boys tended to be more successful in school work than children with the opposite personality characteristics. There seems to be a vital change in the direction of correlations between extraversion, on the one hand, and ability and achievement, on the other, coinciding roughly with the passing from primary to secondary education. S. B. G. Eysenck (1965) clearly demonstrated this inversion in her study. Correlating Junior Eysenck Personality Inventory scores with intelligence test scores, she found that this turned from positive at age 11 (.22 for girls, .27 for boys) to negative at age 14 (−.25 for girls, −.10 for boys). Other authors finding

Table 1.1

	Introverts		Ambiverts		Extraverts	
	M	F	M	F	M	F
Test 1	92.20	93.52	94.41	96.48	96.57	100.35
Test 2	95.11	97.11	99.32	100.09	99.65	104.39

positive correlations between ability/achievement and extraversion in young children are Elliot (1976), Entwistle (1972), Jones (1960), Morrison, MacIntyre, and Sutherland (1965), Ridding (1967), Rushton (1966), Savage (1966), and Wilson (1972); the first author to have documented the switch from positive to negative correlation seems to have been MacNitt (1930), although in his case it came several years later than in the British studies.

A recent study of 2,185 children aged 7–15 years, carried out in Hungary, supports Entwistle and Cunningham (1968) in their finding that sex plays a role in the change-over of the direction of correlation between extraversion and ability/achievement, with girls continuing to show a positive correlation (Kalmanchey and Kozcki, 1983). At age 14 and 15, they found *positive* correlations for girls (.311 and .28), but none or a negative one for boys (.00 and –.03). Yet a change-over point must come even for girls, because at higher age levels correlations with ability become negligible, and with achievement negative (Wankowsky, 1973).

Why this turnover? The cause of this reversal from primary to secondary school is not precisely known, but it seems possible that it is related in part to the change from the free-and-easy atmosphere at primary school, which accords well with the extraverted, and possibly the anxious, temperament, to the more formal atmosphere at secondary school and university, which agrees better with the introverted temperament (Banks & Finlayson, 1973). In partial support of this suggestion may be cited a study in which children were tested at a school that combined primary and secondary classes under the same roof, and in which both were equally formal; here correlations with personality were similar for both the younger and the older children (Whitlock, 1969), favoring introverts.

An interesting alternative theory for the reversal of the extraversion–attainment correlation has been suggested by Anthony (1973). There is good evidence that the time course of the development of extraversion shows an increase up to the age of 13 or 14 years, followed by a decrease into middle age and beyond. Ability, on the other hand (as shown by conventional IQ scores) apparently continues to increase until the twenties (Bayley, 1970). These two different developmental courses would, according to Anthony, produce the observed cross-over relationships. Speaking of personality development, he says that

A child who is consistently *early* in this development would at first be more extraverted than his age-mates, but he would reach his peak sooner than they, and in later years would be *less* extraverted (more introverted) than his age-mates. Similarly, a consistently late developer would in early years be more introverted than his age-mates, but in descending late from the peak, he would in these later years be more extraverted than his age-mates. . . . The occurrence of early and late peaks in the development of a measured characteristic tends to invert the rank order of individuals in the characteristic, i.e., it tends to reduce the retest reliability over the period where the peaks are occurring. This would account for the low retest (stability) correlations in Eysenckian extraversion mentioned by Entwistle (1972, p. 146).

Anthony then invites us to suppose that, at any given time, a person who is ahead of his age-mates in the development of extraversion is also likely to be ahead in the development of ability, and that, similarly, a person who is behind in the development of extraversion is also likely to be behind in the development of ability. This is purely a supposition, though a natural one, which will enable us to make sense of the correlations between extraversion and ability. It follows, then, that in early childhood the child who is ahead in these developments will be high in ability *and* high in extraversion, whereas the child who is behind will be low on both, and therefore there will be a positive correlation between extraversion and ability. But as a group of children approach the age of thirteen, some among them who are ahead reach their peak extraversion early and start "downhill" towards introversion, while they are still increasing in ability, for the peak of ability is still many years ahead. Since those ahead are still the most able but *not* now the most extraverted, the correlation is weakened. As the average children pass over their extraversion peaks, the correlation becomes zero; and when, after fourteen, most of the group is decreasing in extraversion, the children who are ahead are the least extraverted but the most able, while the children behind are the most extraverted but the least able; that is to say, the correlation between extraversion and ability in these (hypothetical) children is now negative.

Anthony goes on to review the literature in order to support the hypothesis just outlined; he shows that there is indeed considerable empirical support, but we shall not discuss the details of this support here. Of more interest is a later analysis carried out by Anthony (1977) in an attempt to come to even closer grips with the factors determining the interaction between personality and achievement/ability as a function of age. He used data from a longitudinal study of 266 children tested at 10–11 and again at 15–16 years of age.

The crude idea that the more able children become introverted while less able children become extraverted, may be reformulated as the idea that ability is correlated with decrease in extraversion. A second alternative . . . may similarly be reformulated in terms of extraversion being correlated with decrease in ability, . . . Is it . . . that the more able children become introverted while the less able children become extraverted . . . or, alternatively, is it that the extraverts fall behind in the development of ability while the introverts make faster progress?

These alternative hypotheses become testable, using an ingenious formula devised by Anthony, and this he applies to the data, separating out scores in intelligence and on school-attainment tests. Two conclusions emerge from his analyses.

(1) The more intelligent children, and those able in English, tended to become relatively more introverted than the less intelligent and the less able in English. (2) The more extraverted children tended to become less able in English and mathematics than the introverted children. Previously the change in extraversion–ability correlations could be hypothetically attributable to *either* of the two kinds of transformation envisaged, whereas it is concluded here that *both* kinds of transformation are significantly involved.

The results suggest that the prevalence of one or other kind of transformation depends on the kind of ability tested. The correlation between introversion and the increasing relative success in academic examinations is plausible, since such success is presumably facilitated by private study which is an introverted type of behavior (Banks & Finlayson, 1973). The correlation between intelligence and decreasing extraversion, on the one hand, may be attributed to the earliness versus lateness of development in the 10–16 year age group.

When we turn to neuroticism, the picture is much less clear. Thus Child (1964) failed to find any relationship between IQ and N; Callard and Goodfellow (1962) obtained a low but significant negative correlation, while Lynn and Gordon (1960) found a curvilinear relationship. Eysenck and Cookson (1969) found a slight positive effect for stability as opposed to neuroticism, while Entwistle and Cunningham (1968) found a slightly stronger positive effect. Kalmanchey and Kozeki (1983) also found such an effect, which did not seem to vary much with age, certainly not in any systematic fashion; some of the correlations were quite respectable. The only real exception to the pattern of negative N–IQ correlations occurred among the youngest girls, 8 years old, ($r = 0.29$), which may be compared with 13-year-old girls ($r = -0.34$). Psychoticism had a uniformly negative correlation with IQ, as it also has in adults (Eysenck and Eysenck, 1976). In adults N is also more likely to correlate with achievement, but hardly with IQ; in a large-scale comparison of neurotic and non-neurotic subjects, Eysenck (1943) found little evidence for any intellectual differences between the groups. The reasons for the divergences of findings have already been discussed in the last section.

What may we conclude from all these studies? With the very large samples we seem to find some low correlations between personality and intelligence, but results are often contradictory and difficult to replicate. Saklofske (1985) has reported a study in which he measured intelligence with the Kaufman Assessment Battery for Children (Kaufman and Kaufman, 1983), which yields scores for simultaneous and sequential processing as well as the Woodcock–Tolman Brief Scale (Woodcock, 1977). As he summarizes his results, he finds that

In all, results support Eysenck's hypothesis that personality and intelligence are uncorrelated and essentially independent psychological constructs. These findings are also meaningful because the main intelligence measures employed in this study distinguish between how information is processed (sequentially or simultaneously) and problem-solving ability on the one hand, and "fact-oriented or skill-based tasks" comprising the Ach scale on the other. (p. 432)

He does find low negative correlations with P, but on the whole it clearly requires an $n > 500$ to obtain significant results; such correlations are statistically significant but scientifically and socially not very important.

The interrelation between personality, intelligence, and achievement are in fact too complex to be disentangled by univariate studies of the usual kind. McKenzie (1989) has indicated the way these factors may be interwoven in an interesting study.

The investigation examined the relationship between neuroticism and academic achievement in a sample of 204 Independent Study students by following up a previous finding by McKenzie (1988a) that although neuroticism correlated negatively with success on the Diploma of Higher Education (Dip.H.E.) programme it correlated positively with success on the third year B.A./B.Sc. (Hons) Degree by Independent Study. These results supported Eysenck and Eysenck's contention that neuroticism only correlates positively with achievement in groups that have been highly selected. In testing for possible interactions, the investigation discarded Spielberger's (1962) contention that neuroticism aids achievement only in highly intelligent students. An alternative hypothesis advanced by Furneaux (1980) that neuroticism correlates positively with achievement only in students who have been selected on some coping factor associated with traits such as Cattell's superego strength or independence (Saville, 1978) was supported, positive correlations being found between neuroticism and degree result for students in the high superego group. The presence of the neuroticism–superego interaction or Furneaux Factor was much more marked when allowance for the effects of dissimulation was made, the correlations between neuroticism and degree result being significant at the 0.05 level and beyond. The results were replicated across sexes. An internal validation showed that the Furneaux Factor was present in each of the 1981, 1982, and 1983 intakes, positive correlations between neuroticism and degree result being reported for the high superego group in all intakes. An external validation supported the hypothesis that the Furneaux Factor would be less apparent in students following a less academically demanding course. It was suggested that the Furneaux Factor has significant implications for learning theory in general and for student selection and counselling in particular. In addition it may be able to provide an objective assessment of the academic rigour of programmes of higher education.

Summary and conclusions

Any study of the relationship between intelligence and personality and intelligence is likely to find that (1) IQ is not related in any meaningful way to personality, (2) nor are patterns or profiles on IQ tests. However, (3) actual *performance* on IQ tests is meaningfully related to personality variables. This finding serves to underline my conclusion that simple attempts to correlate any old IQ test that comes to hand with any old personality test that happens to be available, or any diagnostic psychiatric groups that happen to be around, are doomed to failure, and are a waste of time and energy. Such studies attempt to make use of material that happens to be readily available, such as WAIS and MMPI scores on psychiatric patients, disregard obvious statistical warnings, such as the high standard errors of difference data, and come to conclusions having no scientific meaning or social usefulness. This way of doing research can only undermine the credibility of work in the fields of personality and intelligence.

The approach suggested is to look at well-established theories concerning performance data, arrange experimental conditions to test deductions from these theories, and interpret results cautiously in the light of the theories in question. Several examples of this experimental approach have been given, and it is suggested that a good deal of information has been gained along those lines. We now know that (trait) anxiety does influence performance in IQ tests when conditions are so arranged as to make subjects differentially anxious (state); it should have been obvious from the beginning that a dispositional trait, such as anxiety, can only affect performance when the situation involves stress, danger, or threat.

The experimental approach should extend well beyond the psychometric isolation of different factors in the fields of intelligence and personality. We might consider the experimental separation of global IQ into separate factors of mental speed, persistence and error checking, and the separate correlations of these with different aspects of personality (Frearson, Eysenck, & Barrett, 1990). This approach has already shown some evidence of fruitfulness, but has not often been tried.

Altogether, it seems that we are still plagued by the separation of Cronbach's (1957) "Two disciplines of scientific psychology," that is, the psychometric and the experimental. Until and unless we manage to unite these into one seamless garment, new attempts to understand better the nature of personality and intelligence and their interaction will be severely compromised.

One line of research which is perhaps particularly important has not been discussed because so little work has been done along the lines of improving performance when inhibited by factors related to personality. Thus, hyperactivity in children is characterized by highly extraverted behavior that interferes with performance on IQ tests; such behavior is modifiable by behavior therapy (Redd, Porterfield, & Anderson, 1979). Similarly, work on transcendental meditation has suggested that performance on IQ tests over the years employing this technique can be improved, as compared with a control group. It seems likely that transcendental meditation increases introversion and reduces neuroticism, although the links with personality is not firmly made in the original publication (Cranson et al., 1991).

In a discipline noted for its atheoretical and sometimes antitheoretical outlook (the MMPI is the most widely used clinical instrument in the world, yet it completely lacks any theoretical basis), the stress on experimental testing of theories grounded on laboratory investigations may not be welcomed, but it is difficult to see how else advances are likely to be made. Simple-minded correlational studies have not yielded any worthwhile conclusions over the last 50 years or more; surely the time has come to adopt a more promising approach!

References

Anthony, W. S. (1973). The development of extraversion, of ability, and of the relation between them. *British Journal of Educational Psychology, 43*, 223–227.

Anthony, W. S. (1977). The development of extraversion and ability: an analysis of Rushton's longitudinal data. *British Journal of Educational Psychology, 47*, 193–196.

Banks, O., & Finlayson, D. (1973). *Success and Failure in the Secondary School.* London: Methuen.

Barrett, P. T., & Eysenck, H. J. (1992). Brain electrical potentials and intelligence. In: A. Gale and M. W. Eysenck, *Handbook of Individual Differences: Biological Perspectives,* pp. 255–285. London: Wiley.

Bayley, N. (1970). Development of mental abilities. In: P. H. Mussen (Ed.), *Carmichael's Manual of Child Psychology,* Vol. 1. New York: Wiley.

Berg, A. J., Ingersoll, G. M., & Terry, R. L. (1985). Canonical analysis of the MMPI and WAIS in a psychiatric sample. *Psychological Reports, 50*, 115–122.

Bingham, M. T. (1953). Beyond psychology. In: *Homo sapiens auduboniensis: A tribute to Walter Van Dyke Bingham,* pp. 5–29. New York: National Audubon Society.

Bleuler, M. (1978). *The Schizophrenic Disorders.* New Haven: Yale University Press.

Bloom, R. B., & Entin, A. D. (1975). Intellectual functioning and psychopathology: a canonical analysis of the WAIS and MMPI relationships. *Journal of Clinical Psychology, 31*, 697–698.

Brebner, J. (1985). Personality theory and movement. In: B Kirkcaldy (Ed.), *Individual differences in movement.* Lancaster and Boston: MIT Press.

Callard, M. P., & Chapman, J. P. (1980). Scales for rating psychotic and psychotic-like experiences as continua. *Schizophrenic Bulletin, 6*, 476–489.

Callard, M. P., & Goodfellow, L. L. (1962). Three experiments using the Junior Maudsley Personality Inventory. Neuroticism and Extraversion in schoolboys as uncovered by the JEPI. *British Journal of Educational Psychology, 32,* 241–251.

Canavan, A. G. M., Dunn, G., & McMillan, T. (1986). Principal components of the WAIS-R. *British Journal of Clinical Psychology, 25,* 81–85.

Chapman, L. J., & Chapman, J. P. (1980). Scales for rating psychotic and psychotic-like experiences as continua. *Schizophrenia Bulletin, 6,* 476–489.

Child, D. (1964). The relationship between introversion and extraversion, neuroticism and performance in school examinations. *British Journal of Educational Psychology, 34,* 187–196.

Cohen, R., & Wittemann, K. (1967). Eine Untersuchung zur Abhaengigkeit der Intelligenz Struktur vom Neurotizismus. *Zeitschrift fuer experimentalle und angewandte Psychologie, 14,* 71–88.

Cranson, R. W., Orme-Johnson, D. W., Gackenbach, J., Dillbeck, M. C., Jones, C. N., & Alexander, C. N. (1991). Transcendental meditation and improved performance on intelligence-related measures: a longitudinal study. *Personality and Individual Differences, 12,* 1105–1116.

Cronbach, L. J. (1957). The two disciplines of scientific psychology. *American Psychologist, 12,* 671–689.

Cronbach, L. J., & Gleser, G. C. (1965). *Psychological Tests and Personnel Decisions.* Montana: University of Montana Press.

Drago, M. C. G., Daum, I., & Canavan, A. G. M. (1991). A factor-analytic study of the Wechsler Intelligence Scales as administered to a clinical sample in Chile. *Personality and Individual Differences, 12,* 993–998.

Elithorn, A., Jones, D., & Kerr, M. O. (1963). A binary perceptual maze. *American Journal of Psychology, 76,* 506–508.

Elliot, C. D. (1976). Personality factors and scholastic attainment. *British Journal of Educational Psychology, 42,* 23–32.

Entwistle, N. J. (1972). Personality and academic attainment. *British Journal of Educational Psychology, 42,* 137–151.

Entwistle, N. J., & Cunningham, S. (1968). Neuroticism and school attainment – a linear relationship? *British Journal of Educational Psychology, 38,* 123–132.

Eysenck, H. J. (1943). Neurosis and intelligence. *The Lancet,* Sept. 18, 362.

Eysenck, H. J. (1947). *Dimensions of Personality.* London: Routledge and Kegan Paul.

Eysenck, H. J. (1957). *The Dynamics of Anxiety and Hysteria.* London: Routledge and Kegan Paul.

Eysenck, H. J. (1959). Personality and problem-solving. *Psychological Reports, 5,* 592.

Eysenck, H. J. (1967). *The Biological Basis of Personality.* Springfield: C.C. Thomas.

Eysenck, H. J. (1970). A dimensional system of psychodiagnosis. In: A. R. Mahrer (Ed.), *New Approaches to Personality Classification,* 169–208. New York: Columbia University Press.

Eysenck, H. J. (1970). *The Structure of Human Personality.* 3rd Edition. London: Methuen.

Eysenck, H. J. (1973). Personality, learning and "anxiety." In: H. J. Eysenck (Ed.), *Handbook of Abnormal Psychology,* 390–419. London: Pitman.

Eysenck, H. J. (1979). *The Structure and Measurement of Intelligence.* New York: Springer.

Eysenck, H. J. (Ed.), (1982). *A Model for Intelligence.* New York: Springer.

Eysenck, H. J. (1983). Cicero and the state–trait theory of anxiety: another case of delayed recognition. *American Psychologist, 38,* 114–115.

Eysenck, H. J. (1983). The roots of creativity: cognitive ability or personality trait? *Roeper Review, 5,* 10–12.

Eysenck, H. J. (1985). The theory of intelligence and the psychophysiology of cognition. In: R. J. Sternberg (Ed.), *Advances in Research in Intelligence,* Vol. 3. Hillsdale, Erlbaum.

Eysenck, H. J. (1987). Personality and aging: An exploratory analysis. *Journal of Social Behaviour and Personality, 3,* 11–12.

Eysenck, H. J. (1988). The concept of "intelligence": Useful or useless? *Intelligence, 12,* 1–16.

Eysenck, H. J. (1993). Creativity and Personality. *Psychological Inquiry, 4,* 147–178.

Eysenck, H. J., & Cookson, D. (1969). Personality and achievement in primary school children. I. Ability of achievement. *British Journal of Educational Psychology, 39,* 109–122.

Eysenck, H. J., & Eysenck, M. W. (1985). *Personality and Individual Differences: A Natural Science Approach.* New York: Plenum.

Eysenck, H. J., & Eysenck, S. B. G. (1975). *Manual of the Eysenck Personality Questionnaire*. London: Hodder & Stoughton.

Eysenck, H. J., & Eysenck, S. B. G. (1976). *Psychoticism as a Dimension of Personality*. London: Hodder and Stoughton.

Eysenck, H. J., & Gudjonsson, G. H. (1989). *The Causes and Cures of Criminality*. New York: Plenum.

Eysenck, H. J., & White, O. (1964). Personality and the measurement of intelligence. *British Journal of Educational Psychology, 24,* 197–202.

Eysenck, S. B. G. (1965). *Manual of the Junior Eysenck Personality Inventory*. London: University of London Press.

Franks, G. H. (1970). The measurement of personality from the Wechsler tests. In: B. A. Maher (Ed.), *Progress in experimental personality research, 5,* 108–184. New York: Academic Press.

Fraschia, J., Fiorantino, D., Sheppard, C., and Merlis, S. (1970). Raven Progressive Matrices avoidable errors as a measure of psychopathological ideational influence upon reasoning ability. *Psychological Reports, 26,* 359–362.

Frearson, W., Eysenck, H. J., & Barrett, P. (1990). The Furneaux model of human problem-solving: its relationship to reaction time and intelligence. *Personality and Individual Differences, 11,* 235–357.

Furneaux, W. D. (1950). *Manual of Nufferno Speed Tests*. London: National Foundation for Educational Research.

Furneaux, D. (1980). Historical Considerations. In: R. Holder and J. Wankowski, (Eds.), *Personality and Academic Performance*. Guildford: SRHE.

Gaines, T., & Morris, R. (1978). Relationships between MMPI increases of psychopathy and WAIS subtest scores and intelligence quotients. *Perceptual and Motor Skills, 47,* 399–402.

Glover, J. A., Ronning, R. Q., & Reynolds, C. R. (Eds.). (1989). *Handbook of Creativity*. New York: Plenum.

Gotz, K. O., & Gotz, K. (1979a). Personality characteristics of professional artists. *Perceptual and Motor Skills, 49,* 327–334.

Gotz, K. O., & Gotz, K. (1979b). Personality characteristics of successful artists. *Perceptual and Motor Skills, 49,* 919–924.

Gough, H. G. (1976). Studying creativity by means of the Word Association tests. *Journal of Applied Psychology, 61,* 348–353.

Griffiths, J. J., Mednick, S., Schulsinger, F., & Diderichsen, B. (1980). Verbal associative disturbances in children with high risk of schizophrenia. *Journal of Abnormal Psychology, 89,* 125–131.

Hargreaves, H. L. (1927). The "faculty" of imagination. *British Journal of Psychology,* Monograph Supplement, 10.

Hasenfus, N., & Magaro, P. (1976). Creativity of schizophrenia: An equality of empirical constructs. *British Journal of Psychiatry, 129,* 346–349.

Heston, L. C. (1966). Psychiatric disorders in foster-home reared children of schizophrenic mothers. *British Journal of Psychiatry, 112,* 819–825.

Holland, T. R., & Watson, C. G. (1980). Multivariate analysis of WAIS-MMPI relationship among brain-damaged schizophrenic, neurotic and alcoholic patients. *Journal of Clinical Psychology, 36,* 352–359.

Horn, W. (1962a). *L-P-S Leistungspruefungsystem*. Gottingen: Hogrefe.

Horn, W. (1962b). *S-O-F Stabilitats una Offenheitsfragebogen*. Gottingen: Hogrefe.

Howard, R. C. (1988). Telic dominance and coping. In: M. J. Apter, J. H. Kerr, and M. P. Cowles (Eds.), *Progress in Reversal Theory,* pp. 83–93. Amsterdam: Elsevier.

Howard, R., and McKillen, M. (1990). Extraversion and performance in the perceptual maze test. *Personality and Individual Differences, 11,* 391–396.

Hudson, L. (1966). *Contrary Imagination*. London: Methuen.

Jensen, A. R. (1964). *Individual differences in learning: Interference factor*. Washington, D.C.: Office of Education, U.S. Department of Health, Education and Welfare.

Jones, D., & Weinman, J. (1973). Computer based psychological testing. In: H. Elithorn, and D. Jones (Eds.), *Artificial and Human Thinking,* 83–93. Amsterdam: Elsevier.

Jones, H. G. (1960). Relationship between personality and scholastic attainment. *Bulletin of the British Psychological Society, 40,* 42.

Kalmanchey, G. M., & Kozeki, B. (1983). Relationship of personality dimensions to social and intellectual factors in children. *Personality and Individual Differences, 4,* 237–243.

Kandell, E., Mednik, S. A., Kirkegaard-Sorensen, L., Hutchings, B., Knop, J., Rosenberg, R., & Schulsinger, F. (1988). IQ as a protective factor for subjects at high risk for antisocial behavior. *Journal of Consulting and Clinical Psychology, 56,* 224–226.

Karlsson, J. L. (1968). Genealogic studies of schizophrenia. In: D. Rosenthal & S. S. Kety (Eds.), *The Transmission of Schizophrenia.* Oxford: Pergamon Press.

Karlsson, J. L. (1970). Genetic association of giftedness and creativity with schizophrenia. *Hereditas, 66,* 177–182.

Kaufman, A. S., & Kaufman, N. L. (1983). *Kaufman Assessment Battery for Children.* Circle Pina, Minnesota: American Guidance Circle.

Kirkcaldy, B., & Siefen, G. (in press). Personality correlates of intelligence in a clinical group. *Personality and Individual Differences.*

Lacks, P. B., & Keefe, K. (1970). Relationship among education, the MMPI and WAIS measures of psychopathology. *Journal of Clinical Psychology, 26,* 468–470.

Lienert, G. A. (1963). Die Faktoren struktur der Intelligenz als Funktion des Neurotizismus. *Zeitschrift fuer experimentalle und angerwandte Psychologie, 10,* 140–159.

Lynn, R., & Gordon, I. E. (1960). The relation of neuroticism and extraversion to intelligence and educational attainment. *British Journal of Educational Psychology, 31,* 194–203.

McKenzie, J. (1988). Three superfactors in the 16 PF and their relation to Eysenck's P, E and N. *Personality and Individual Differences, 9,* 843–850.

McKenzie, J. (1989). Neuroticism and academic achievement: The Furneaux factor. *Personality and Individual Differences, 10,* 509–515.

McNeil, T. F. (1971). Rebirth and postbirth influence on the relationship between creative ability and recorded mental illness. *Journal of Personality, 39,* 391–406.

McNitt, R. D. (1930). *Introversion and Extraversion in the High School.* Boston: R. G. Badger, The Gorham Press.

MacKinnon, D. W. (1962). The nature and nurture of creative talent. *American Psychologist, 17,* 484–495.

MacKinnon, D. W. (1965). Personality and the realization of creative potential. *American Psychologist, 20,* 273–281.

Mandler, G., & Sarason, S. (1952). A study of anxiety and learning. *Journal of Abnormal and Social Psychology, 47,* 166–173.

Matarazzo, J. (1972). *Wechsler's Measurement and Appraisal of Adult Intelligence.* 5th Edition. Baltimore: Williams and Wilkins.

Maxwell, A. E. (1960). Obtaining factor scores on the Wechsler Adult Intelligence Scale. *Journal of Mental Science, 106,* 1060–1062.

Meehl, P. E., & Rosen, A. (1955). Antecedent probability of the efficiency of psychometric signs, patterns, or culling scores. *Psychological Bulletin, 52,* 194–216.

Miller, E. N., & Chapman, L. J. (1983). Continued word association in hypothetically psychosis-prone college students. *Journal of Abnormal Psychology, 92,* 468–478.

Miller, M. L., Omens, R. S., & Delwadia, R. (1991). Dimensions of social competence: Personality and coping style correlates. *Personality and Individual Differences, 12,* 955–964.

Moffit, T. E., & Silva, P. A. (1987). WISC-R verbal and performance IQ discrepancy in an unselected cohort: Clinical significance and longitudinal stability. *Journal of Consulting and Clinical Psychology, 55,* 708–774.

Morrisby, J. R. (1955). *Compound Series Test.* London: National Foundation for Educational Research.

Morrison, A., MacIntyre, D., and Sutherland, J. (1965). Teachers' personality ratings of pupils in Scottish primary schools. *British Journal of Educational Psychology, 35,* 306–319.

Prentky, R. A. (1980). *Creativity of Psychopathology.* New York: Praeger.

Rabin, A. I. (1965). Diagnostic use of intelligence tests. In: B. B. Wolman, (Ed.), *Handbook of Clinical Psychology,* 477–497. New York: McGraw-Hill.

Rawlings, D., and Carnie, D. (1989). The ineraction of EPQ extraversion with WAIS subtest performance under timed and untimed conditions. *Personality and Individual Differences, 10,* 453–458.

Redd, W. H., Porterfield, A. L., and Anderson, B. L. (1979). *Behavior Modification.* New York: Random House.

Ridding, L. W. (1967). An investigation of the personality measures associated with over and under achievement in English arithmetic. *British Journal of Educational Psychology, 37,* 397–398.

Robinson, D. L. (1982a). Properties of the diffuse thalamocortical system and the human personality: a direct test of Pavlovian–Eysenckian theory. *Personality and Individual Differences, 3,* 1–16.

Robinson, D. L. (1982b). Properties of the diffuse thalamocortical system, human intelligence and differential versus integrated modes of learning. *Personality and Individual Differences, 3,* 393–405.

Robinson, D. L. (1985). How personality relates to intelligence test performance: Implications for a theory of intelligence, ageing research and personality assessment. *Personality and Individual Differences, 6,* 203–216.

Robinson, D. L. (1986). The Wechsler Adult Intelligence Scale and personality assessment: Towards a biologically-based theory of intelligence and cognition. *Personality and Individual Differences, 7,* 153–159.

Rushton, J. (1966). The relationship between personality characteristics and scholastic success in 11-year-old children. *British Journal of Educational Psychology, 36,* 178–184.

Saklofske, D. H. (1985). The relationship between Eysenck's major personality dimensions of simultaneous and sequential processing in children. *Personality and Individual Differences, 6,* 429–433.

Saklofske, D. H., & Kostura, D. D. (1990). Extraversion–Introversion and intelligence. *Personality and Individual Differences, 11,* 547–551.

Saltz, E. (1970). Manifest anxiety: Have we missed the data? *Psychological Review, 77,* 568–573.

Sarton, A. (1969). *L'intelligence Efficace.* Paris: Centre d'Etude et de Promotion de la Lecture. Savage, R. D. (1966). Personality factors and academic attainment in junior school children. *British Journal of Educational Psychology.*

Saville, P. (1978). A critical analysis of Cattell's model of personality. Brunel University: Unpublished Ph.D. thesis.

Siegman, A. W. (1956a). Cognitive, affective and psychopathological correlates of the Taylor Manifest Anxiety Scale. *Journal of Consulting Psychology, 20,* 137–141.

Siegman, A. W. (1956b). The effect of manifest anxiety in a concept formation task, a non-directed learning task, and on timed and untimed intelligence tests. *Journal of Consulting Psychology, 20,* 176–178.

Spearman, C. (1927). *The Abilities of Man.* London: Macmillan.

Spielberger, C. (1958). On the relationship between manifest anxiety and intelligence. *Journal of Consulting Psychology, 22,* 220–224.

Spielberger, C. (1962). The effects of manifest anxiety on the academic achievement of college students. *Mental Hygiene, 46,* 420–426.

Sternberg, R. J. (1985). *Beyond IQ.* Cambridge: Cambridge University Press.

Sternberg, R. J., & Wagner, R. K. (Eds.). (1986). *Practical Intelligence.* Cambridge: Cambridge University Press.

Taylor, J. A. (1953). A personality scale of manifest anxiety. *Journal of Abnormal and Social Psychology, 48,* 285–290.

Turner, R. G., & Horn, J. M. (1976). MMPI item correlates of WAIS subtest performance. *Journal of Clinical Psychology, 32,* 583–594.

Upmanyu, V. V., & Kaur, K. (1986). Diagnostic utility of word association emotional indicators. *Psychological Studies, 32,* 71–78.

Walker, R. E., and Spence, J. T. (1964). Relationship between Digit Span and anxiety. *Journal of Counselling Psychology, 28,* 220–223.

Walker, R. E., Neilsen, M. K., & Nicolay, R. (1965). The effects of failure and anxiety on intelligence test performance. *Journal of Clinical Psychology, 21,* 400–402.

Walker, R. E., Sannito, T. C., & Firetto, A. C. (1970). The effect of subjectively reported anxiety on intelligence and performance. *Psychology in the Schools, 7,* 241–243.

Wallach, M. A., & Kogan, N. (1965). *Modes of thinking in young children.* New York: Holt, Rinehart & Winston.

Wankowsky, J. A. (1973). *Temperament, Motivation and Academic Achievement.* Birmingham: University of Birmingham Educational and Counselling Unit.

Ward, P. B., McConaghy, N., & Catts, S. V. (1991). Word association and measurement of psychosis-proneness in university students. *Personality and Individual Differences, 12,* 473–480.

Warrington, E. K., James, M., & Maciejewski, C. (1986). The WAIS as a lateralising and localising diagnostic instrument. *Neuropsychologia, 24,* 223–239.

Watson, C. G., Davis, W. E., & McDermott, M. T. (1976). MMPE–WAIS relationship in organic-schizophrenic patients. *Journal of Clinical Psychology, 32,* 539–540.

Wechsler, D. (1940). Non-intellectual factors in general intelligence. *Psychological Bulletin, 37,* 444–445.

Wechsler, D. (1958). *The Measurement and Appraisal of Adult Intelligence.* 4th Edition. Baltimore: Williams & Wilkins.

Weinman, J., Elithorn, A., & Cooper, R. (1985). Personality problem-solving: The nature of individual differences in planning, scanning and verification. *Personality and Individual Differences, 6,* 453–460.

Whitlock, R. V. (1961). A further study of the effects of emotional arousal in learning. University of London: Unpublished Ph.D. thesis.

Wilson, J. A. (1972). Personality and attainment in the primary school. II. Personality structure and attainment in 10-year-olds. *Research in Education, 7,* 1–10.

Woodcock, R. W. (1977). *Woodcock–Johnson Psycho-Educational Battery: Technical Report.* Boston: Teaching Resources.

Woody, E., and Claridge, G. (1977). Psychoticism and thinking. *British Journal of Social and Clinical Psychology, 16,* 241–248.

2 Intelligence, personality, and prudence

Nick Haslam and Jonathan Baron

In this paper we propose a broad concept of intelligence, which includes intellectual personality traits that help people to achieve their goals. These traits can be described as constituting a more comprehensive trait of prudence. We thus revive the evaluative concept of character as part of the study of personality. The line between the study of personality and the study of intelligence disappears. Character itself can be evaluated as more or less intelligent. Our approach would lead personality psychology to concentrate on asking what traits people should have and how these traits can be encouraged. We review relevant work from a number of domains.

We thus propose the concept of "prudence" as a bridge between intelligence and personality, and we attempt to demonstrate the capacity of the concept to encompass and enrich many existing theoretical and empirical traditions, as well as rendering several neglected areas of study germane to this volume's purpose. In addition to performing a useful synthetic service, the concept of prudence offers a distinctive perspective on the intersections of intelligence and personality.

We will present our account of prudence in three parts. In the first part, we describe an account of intelligence and practical rationality based on the work of one of us (Baron) over an extended period. We present a normative account of intelligent behavior, paying particular attention to the nature, addition, and trading-off of goals, and we review descriptive violations of this normative theory. This section draws out several of the continuing themes and grounding assumptions of that work, and indicates desiderata for a theory of intelligent character.

The second part introduces the concept of prudence, historically and in its recent developments, and demonstrates numerous theoretical points of contact between it and the themes and preoccupations of Baron's account of intelligence and rationality. More specifically, prudence is demonstrated to involve the balanced pursuit of longer-term ends or goals, to compose a faculty of good judgment in the face of uncertainty, and to be focally concerned with overcoming impulsive or short-sighted choices.

In the third part, we illustrate the integrative sweep of the concept of prudence with discussions of recent empirical work in the psychology of personality. (Baron, 1982, reviews earlier literature in a similar spirit, and we will not repeat that review here.) Areas of research discussed include work on goal concepts in personality, particularly goal-setting, conflict among and tradeoffs between goals; work on practical everyday cognition; work on self-defeating behavior and cognitive strategies; and work on time-perspective and self-control. This final part attempts to demonstrate how the prudential concerns that organize one account of intelligence and practical rationality can be followed into contemporary personality research. We attempt to show that this way of connecting the two domains of work offers mutual benefit, and represents a useful theoretical advance.

Character and intelligence

Character is the collection of acquired habits and rules that each person follows. These rules and habits affect our social behavior, our work, the behavior that affects our health (eating, drinking, and physical activity), our responses to negative events, our behavior as citizens, and – overlapping many of these other categories – our thinking. We focus on acquired habits and rules because we are interested in the implications of personality theory for the training of character, through child rearing, education, psychotherapy, or self-planning.

The kind of personality theory that we need for this enterprise has three parts: normative, descriptive, and prescriptive (Baron, 1988). Normative theory concerns the ideal. It is the ultimate standard that we use to evaluate character. Descriptive theory concerns character as it is. By comparing character as it is to the normative standard, we can determine where character is subject to improvement, and we can experiment with various methods of training. The body of advice that we develop in this way is the prescriptive theory of character. Prescriptive theory tells parents, teachers, therapists, and everyone what they need to strive for in order to develop better character. Prescriptive theory can include contingencies based on individual differences; the prescription for improvement might be contingent on measures of such differences. We shall use the term "rational" for general prescriptive rules that will probably help to do best according to the normative standard.

We shall focus here on decision making, broadly construed. Decision making is the thinking, or lack of thinking, that determines what we do when we are faced with more than one option about what to do and when we have time to think. In general, thinking consists of some sort of search process plus some inference that we draw from what the search has found. In decision making, the search is for alternative options, evidence bearing on the advantages and disadvantages of each option, and goals, which are criteria by which we evaluate the options in the light of the evidence. Decisions are typically made according to rules or habits, without much thinking. But the creation of these rules and habits results from earlier decisions, and thinking can come into play at several points in the formation of these rules and habits. It is at these points where character can be influenced most easily. For example, what we eat for breakfast is usually a matter of habit, but it can be influenced by suggestions from others, things we read, or our own thinking. (By contrast, eating dinner in a restaurant typically involves a conscious decision each time.)

Normative theory

Normative theory is developed in general, by philosophical analysis and reflection (Baron, 1993). It tells us what kind of goals to consider, but not what goals. It must be adapted to the individual case, and the version we endorse allows wide but not unlimited variation. Alternative approaches to intelligence and personality make tacit normative assumptions, e.g., that individual happiness (for personality) or ability to contribute to societal welfare (for intelligence) are ultimate evaluative criteria. We seek to make our criteria more explicit. In doing this, we open ourselves to challenge in ways that other psychological theorists have not. We welcome substantive challenges, for these can lead to improvements. But we are less patient with assertions that normative theory "can't be done" from those who then proceed to do it implicitly.

We take the normative theory of character to derive from the idea of maximizing goal achievement, or, to use a venerable but poorly chosen expression, maximizing utility. The best habits and rules to follow are those that maximize the achievement of your goals. If your goal is to be healthy and live a long life, you are well advised to follow certain rules: exercise regularly; don't smoke; don't get in trouble with the Mafia.

Uncertainty. Of course, following these rules does not guarantee a long life. They just increase its probability. Uncertainty is endemic. Therefore, when we say that the normative theory is to maximize utility, we really mean expected utility. This has a formal definition (Baron, 1988), which is not relevant here. But the fact that life is uncertain has some important general implications. One is that we cannot always evaluate the quality of a decision by evaluating its outcome (although we tend to do this even when we should not – see Baron & Hershey, 1988). Good decisions can have bad outcomes, and vice versa. Another implication is that "calculated risks" are sometimes normatively correct, even when they involve the risk of life itself. Boris Yeltsin's defiance of the attempted Soviet coup in August, 1991, was, arguably, a normatively correct decision even had it failed.

Tradeoffs. Goals conflict. Those who risk their lives for a cause need not desire to live any less than anyone else. Tradeoffs among goals occur even in the absence of uncertainty. Taking a vacation satisfies the goal of having a break in routine, etc., but impugns the goal of saving money. In making a decision, we must weigh the effects on all relevant goals, normatively. That is, when we evaluate a decision or a method of making decisions, we must take into account all goals. Other things equal, if one option is best in achieving a limited set of goals and another option is best in achieving all of a person's goals taken together, the second option is normatively better. If some practical method of decision making leads consistently to the choice of options like the second one, that method is prescriptively better than a method that does not do so. In particular, we might expect that single-minded pursuit of goals – neglecting other goals – is a dangerous way to live. This may occur, for example, in aspiring athletes who neglect their studies.

to selfish goals. Altruistic goals are goals for the achievement of the goals of others – perhaps only certain others or certain goals. Altruistic goals range from the desire for a child's welfare to a desire to prevent famines in Africa. They are contingent on the existence of relevant goals in relevant others and directed toward the achievement of those goals. Altruistic goals can concern both acts and omissions. The desire not to harm others through acts is perhaps the most widespread type of altruistic goal in this sense; the goal of helping others through acts (not to hurt them through omissions) is apparently less common (Spranca, Minsk, & Baron, 1991).

Moralistic goals concern outcomes that affect the achievement of the goals of others, but without regard to whether such achievement is helped or hindered. Although few real goals are purely selfish, altruistic, or moralistic, examples that come close to pure moralism are various standards concern etiquette, physical beauty, fashion, ritual cleanliness, piety, and sexual restraint. These goals are applied to outcomes that affect others, whether those affected hold the same goals, no comparable goals, or the opposite goals.

We have reason to encourage altruistic goals and rules that promote altruism. When we support social norms for altruism, and when people behave altruistically as a result of these norms, we benefit individually because people are altruistic toward us, if only because they refrain from hurting us. Support for social norms is expressed through rewards and punishments, modeling (following the norms so as to set an example for others), explicit instruction, moral reproach, and gossip (Sabini & Silver, 1982). Some of these norm-supporting activities are sufficiently costless that it is worth our while to engage in them simply for the selfish benefits that we reap, although commitment to altruistic or moralistic goals also serves to motivate us. Part of good character, then, is an attitude of support for social norms – not all norms, to be sure, but those that help us all achieve our goals.

A second reason for adoption of altruistic goals is that these goals will help one to achieve our individual long-term goals, since helping (and not hurting) others leads to such benefits as being welcomed into cooperative communities, being trusted, being given responsible (and highly rewarded) positions, being liked, and so on, as many scholars have recently argued (Frank, 1985). It is therefore rational for a person to adopt altruistic goals almost regardless of her other long-term goals. So it is rational, in general, for individuals to try to develop altruistic goals in themselves. The same cannot be said for moralistic goals in general.

Goals for one's own future.   Altruism toward others is closely analogous to concern for our own futures. You can think of "yourself" as a series of separate people, each existing over a short interval of time (Parfit, 1984), tied together by common memories, plans, and goals, some more closely than others, just as members of a family or community are tied together. Some of your reasons for caring about your "own" future derive from your present goals, but other reasons are more like altruism toward a somewhat different person, the person you will become. In general, it is rational for most people to adopt goals for the welfare of these future selves, because such goals are congruent with their other goals. It is also rational for others to convince you to look out for your own future, for this is a way of achieving their altruistic goals toward your future selves. Parents try to do this for their children.

In sum, altruistic goals and goals for one's own future are synergistic in several ways. Altruism helps one have a better long-term future. A desire for a good future for oneself is a kind of altruism, and an attitude of prudent concern with one's own long-term future could spill over into a concern for others. In addition, both kinds of goals are served by the same kinds of abilities (as we shall discuss), particularly the ability to restrain impulses and the intellectual abilities to discover truth in a manner uncontaminated by one's desires or prior beliefs.

Descriptive theory

People depart from the normative theory in all sorts of ways, but some of them are systematic and possibly widespread. One of these is shortsightedness or myopia, the tendency to neglect the future (Baron, 1988). This occurs in several forms. It may occur with respect to selfish goals (as in smoking or underinvestment) or altruistic goals (as in neglect of long-term trends such as population growth). Myopia can occur through lack of thought or through failure to exercise self-control. It may occur through consistent underweighing of the future, or through a kind of dynamic inconsistency. An example of dynamic inconsistency is the decision of a child on Tuesday at 4:59 PM, offered a choice between one piece of candy Tuesday at 5 PM or two pieces Wednesday at 5 PM. The child might well take the one piece on Tuesday, but, if offered the same two options (Tuesday vs. Wednesday) on Monday at 5 PM, the child might switch. Here, the child's goals do not change. If the Tuesday option achieves the child's goals better than the Wednesday option, then that must be true regardless of the time the choice is made. Of course, we are considering the child as an ongoing being with constant goals, or as a series of beings about which we have equal concern. But from the Monday child's point of view, the Tuesday and Wednesday children are somewhat different people. We shall discuss the consequences of myopia.

Another common departure from the normative standard is single-mindedness (Baron, 1988) or the making of decisions on the basis of a single goal, neglecting other goals. Thoughtless decisions often have this character, as when an adolescent has sex without contraception or begins smoking in order to be like his friends.

A third example of a general departure is wishful thinking or motivated self-deception (Kunda, 1990). When people want to believe that they have made a good decision, they search for evidence that their decision was good and fail to search as much for evidence that other options might have been better. When they find such evidence, they make inferences from it without taking into account the fact that it was the result of a biased search, so they become more convinced that their decision was good. This conviction prevents them from modifying their decision. In this way, people stick to self-destructive plans or habits, such as gambling (Gilovich, 1983). Religious conviction might operate in the same way.

Biased search and inference operate more generally, even when it is not clear that wishful thinking is involved. People with strong moral beliefs, for example, about capital punishment, work harder to discredit evidence against their beliefs than to question evidence in their favor (Kuhn, 1989), so that presentation of evidence on both sides can lead to strengthening of belief rather than moderation (Lord, Ross, & Lepper, 1979). Even when people make predictions or answer questions about matters of fact, an initial answer seems to bias the search for further evidence; people find evidence in favor of their initial answer more readily than they find evidence against it (Kuhn, 1989; Perkins, 1989). This kind of "myside bias" leads to overconfidence in the initial answer, which can be corrected by telling people to think of evidence on both sides (Anderson, 1982; Hoch, 1985; Koriat, Lichtenstein, & Fischoff, 1980).

The stronger such biases are, the more likely it is that people will form erroneous beliefs. When decisions are made on the basis of such beliefs, goals are less likely to be achieved than if the beliefs were more accurate, other things equal. If we are going to think about something, we simply waste time if we think in a way that leads to a foregone conclusion.

"Myside bias" occurs in both search and inference. Individual differences in the *search* component can be measured by asking people simply to list the reasons that occur to them as they think about some question. Perkins (1989; see also Perkins, Bushey, & Faraday, 1986) asked subjects to respond to questions about public policy, such as whether a state should have a law requiring all bottles to be returnable. He found that people tended to produce far more "myside" reasons than "otherside" reasons. Prodding to think of more reasons on both sides produces few more reasons on the subject's initial side but many more on the other side; this result indicates that the initial bias was not due to ignorance. Perkins also found that, while the number of myside reasons was correlated with a vocabulary test, the number of otherside reasons was not. Finally, a course designed to teach active open-mindedness (willingness to consider alternatives, counterevidence, and additional goals – in the sense of Baron, 1988) succeeded in increasing the number and quality of otherside reasons.

Another measure that seems to tap a component of active open-mindedness is the measure of "integrative complexity" used recently by Tetlock (e.g., 1983, 1985). It is based on separate scores for "differentiation" and "integration." Differentiation seems to amount to whether a person brings up reasons on the other side of the case she is making (if only to rebut them), and it is therefore similar to the measure used by Perkins. Integration is less clear, but, in fact, it plays little role in accounting for the results obtained with the integrative-complexity measure. Tetlock (1985) finds more differentiation when goals conflict, e.g., when a conservative thinks about the military draft (strong defense vs. personal liberty), but he also finds consistent individual differences across cases, unrelated to political ideology.

Baron (1991, 1989) has argued that myside bias (in both search and inference) arises in part from beliefs about the nature of good thinking itself. People who show this bias more (in measures like those used by Perkins) are more likely to evaluate other people's one-sided thinking as better than two-sided thinking, even when its conclusion is opposite to their own. These erroneous beliefs about what makes for good thinking could arise from training by cultural and religious institutions (whose survival prospects are enhanced by unquestioning loyalty of their members) and by parents (who find it easier to control unquestioning children). Schools do little to correct these beliefs; for example, high-school students can earn high grades on essays that present only one side of a controversial issue (e.g., "backing up their conclusion").

In addition to these biases in favor of prior conclusions or desired conclusions, some people tend simply to think too little. Baron, Badgio, and Gaskins (1986) tested a group of students in a private elementary school for children with reading disabilities. Although most of these students did learn to read in a couple of years, they continued to have academic difficulty, in part because of what teachers perceived to be a maladaptive cognitive style. Part of the problem was a rigidity of the sort just discussed. But another part was, apparently, a simple unwillingness to think enough about problems given, and to persist in carrying out an extended task. If thinking is search plus inference, then not only was their search and inference biased toward initial conclusions but, also, their search was too brief. Children differed in this sort of impulsiveness. Those judged by their teachers to be particularly impulsive also tended to spend less time on each problem in a test of logic and arithmetic problems and to make more errors.

An 8-month training program was instituted, in which an experimental group was trained to be less impulsive, less rigid, and more persistent. Compared to a control group, teacher ratings showed the training to be effective in all three areas, and those students who graduated and went on to other schools did better (controlling for IQ) according to ratings from new teachers who were not told about the experiment. In the logic and arithmetic tasks, all students in the experimental group took longer on each problem. But only some students made fewer errors, in particular, those students rated by their teachers as being particularly impulsive. It therefore seems that many of these students were already spending as much time on the problems as they could benefit from. The training may have helped them by reducing their rigidity and increasing their persistence, but it seems that some of the students did not benefit from the training to slow down and search longer.

So it is not the case that everyone thinks too little. Even many of these learning-disabled students were not making this mistake. Still, when people do think too little, this leads to error. Therefore, thinking too little is something that people should be taught to avoid.

Putting this all together, we suggest that a major problem with human thinking is that people's level of confidence is often not matched to the amount and quality of

thinking that they have done, so that they take major steps, or set
for themselves, on the basis of inadequate search, and then they f
their decisions, as though they had made them with justified con
examples are the kinds of political and religious conflicts we see a
Those on each side are absolutely certain that they are right, but neit
trouble to try to see through the eyes of the other. Although often one side *is* in the
right, both sides cannot be, so the existence of overconfident error is clear. Although
the problem of overconfident error is not universal, it is, however, a major contributor
to erroneous decisions, personal as well as social, and it is something that people
should all be warned against in their education.

Intelligence

We have just been discussing intelligence, although those who think of that term as
referring to the scores on IQ tests might not have noticed. IQ tests cannot define
intelligence. Even if our only interest is in the measurement of intelligence, we need
a way to evaluate whether a new IQ test measures intelligence, other than correlating
it with other tests. If the concept is nothing but a test, is has no theoretical status. We
can study the test, but we cannot generalize about what we have learned. Moreover,
our interest in intelligence might not be just to test it. We might regard it as something
that we should try to promote in individuals (Baron, 1985a). If so, we need to know
what to try to promote, and why.

Intelligence clearly refers to *abilities*, properties of performance that can be evaluated along a continuum from better to worse. Thus, many personality measures are
excluded. It is not clear – except to extroverts, perhaps – that extroversion is better
than introversion. A qualification is needed here. Certain personality traits, as we shall
discuss, can be thought of as virtues, so they do seem to be subject to ordering on an
evaluative continuum. But, beginning with Aristotle, many have thought that most
virtues were best practiced in moderation. Courage is a virtue because most people
are too timid, but if one moves from timidity to courage and continues moving in the
same direction, one can become foolhardy. Courage represents an optimal point on
a continuum. Likewise, if people are too inclined to defend their initial conclusions,
it is a virtue to question these and to consider alternatives. But too much of this can
lead to paralysis. So active open-mindedness is also a virtue best practiced in moderation. In what sense is it an ability, then? With other abilities, like mental speed, one
can never have too much (at least if one is a computer). The answer is that we can
redefine the ability in terms of a departure from the optimum (as done by Baron,
Badgio, and Ritov, 1991). The important part of an ability is that it is an evaluation,
and this part is retained by this definition.

Not all abilities should count as part of intelligence, as we think of it. The abilities
in question should be *general*. That is, they should be defined so that we can make
up tests of them, or discover how to cultivate them, in anyone, regardless of the

son's culture, and regardless of the person's perceptual and motor limitations (except when these are nearly total). If we count abilities that are less general as parts of intelligence, then we will not be able to measure them or cultivate them for some people. So "ability to memorize" would count, but "ability to memorize visual patterns" would not. We might use visual patterns to test memory, of course, but we would be clear that this is what we were doing, so that we could devise an alternative test for a blind person. This limitation to general abilities is not accepted by some students of intelligence, and it is not a necessary part of the study of intelligence. We include it in our concept because it focuses us on certain theoretical questions that might otherwise be neglected.

Beyond these criteria, the theory we have developed places a further potential restriction on what we might count as part of intelligence. We might want to say that intelligence consists of those abilities that help people achieve their goals. Now this criterion is nearly redundant with the idea that the abilities are evaluative dimensions, because we generally think that abilities are good exactly because they do help people to achieve their goals. But, by making this restriction explicit, we can see more clearly just why we might be interested in intelligence as something to measure or promote, and we can also focus on those abilities that are most important. We take this relation between intelligence and goal achievement as being the main reason for being interested in intelligence in the first place. It is also what ties together, as we argue here, the study of more traditional "intellectual" abilities and the study of the kinds of virtues that we discuss in this paper.

We see no reason to restrict the definition further. Importantly, we see no reason to restrict intelligence to abilities that are unmodifiable or uncontrollable. The kinds of traits of persistence and nonrigidity that Baron et al. (1986) sought to influence are therefore candidate abilities that might constitute part of intelligence. It is irrelevant (although true) that they correlated with scores on IQ tests. Likewise, any character traits that help people to achieve their goals are parts of intelligence.

Intelligence, then, can be taken to include the virtues of good thinking. In particular, good thinking is "actively open-minded." Good thinkers avoid the common errors described in the last section, because they consider alternatives to the options they favor, they look for goals that might be subverted by decisions they are about to take, and they seek evidence against a favored option as well as for it. Moreover, when they do not do these things – for whatever reasons – they do not have confidence in their tentative conclusions. Active open-mindedness is a major part of the prescriptive theory of thinking. Its absence is, we think, a major source of human folly.

Baron (1985a) has suggested that the benefits of active open-mindedness are often in the distant future, while the costs – in time, effort, and in the pain of discovering that one's initial idea might be wrong – are typically immediate. Poor thinking, then, would be caused by a general tendency to neglect the future relative to the immediate present. Moreover, poor thinking might also *cause* people to neglect the future, because future effects of options are probably the ones they are less likely to think of first. A teenager in the throes of passion, for example, is less likely to think about the possibility of pregnancy than about the passion. Only actively open-minded attention to the "still small voice" will lead to the consideration of alternative options, such as the use of contraceptives. In sum, the virtue of active open-mindedness is both caused by and a cause of neglect of the future. Attention to the future is a central element of prudence.

Prudence

The preceding section has spelled out the distinctive elements of a general account of intelligent cognition and behavior which attempts to connect them with broader issues and concerns within psychology. Several of these elements should now be noted. First, this account emphasizes that intelligent action is defined with respect to personal goals, the achievement of which is construed in utility–theoretic terms. Intelligence is a matter of maximizing the satisfaction of multiple goals, among which trade-offs must be made, in the presence of constrained opportunities. Utility is not merely hedonic, nor is it concerned simply with adaptive functions common to all people. Rather, goals are temporally extended prospective aims or ends which may conflict and which vary in their reflective merit. Second, intelligent behavior is placed squarely within the realm of everyday practical thinking, problem solving, and decision making. Practical cognition is understood to vary in the degree to which it can be expected to meet a person's goals, and aspects of cognitive style are assumed to play an important role in accounting for this variation. Third, intelligent behavior is considered to be subject, in principle, to comparison with normative models of cognition drawn from decision theory. This normative exercise is driven by the very practical need to develop prescriptive models for the improvement of practical cognition. A theory of intelligence, in other words, needs a theory of character, or of intellectual virtues to which everyday thinking should aspire.

   This synopsis of critical issues in the study of intelligence corresponds closely in its concerns with the ancient concept of prudence (Haslam, 1991), which we will discuss mostly in an Aristotelian context. Prudence is one translation of the term *phronesis,* which is alternatively translated as "practical reason" or "practical wisdom." The former of these alternative translations tends to be employed when the emphasis is placed on prudence as a faculty or process, the latter when a body of procedural or tacit knowledge is implied. "Prudence," on the other hand, is intended to encompass both senses, and at the same time add the connotation of virtue that the concept also carries. Prudent conduct is held up as conduct based on cognitive excellence, and reflects evaluatively on the actor. Further, it reflects on the aptness of the actor's goals, and on their farsightedness. The temporal aspect of prudence is paramount, and prudent conduct takes into fair account its temporally remote consequences. It is thus opposed to shortsighted conduct that fails, through lack of foresight, planning, or self-control, to consider the future adequately. A more thorough introduction to the concept of prudence follows.

Goals and ends

An account of prudence is particularly compatible with a theory of intelligence that emphasizes not a standard bundle of abilities but rather the practical achievement of personal goals, plans, and intentions. To refer to behavior as prudent is to make a claim about its advisability with respect to the person's longer-term interests. Although a cognitive virtue is implied, its merit is derived from its expected consequences, rather than from its mechanisms and processes. (As is true for contemporary decision theory, the internal structure of prudent cognition is not a central question.) The pertinent consequences are delayed consequences for the person's goals, although as Robinson (1989) points out, these goals tend to draw their meaning from the social context, and may in fact involve consequences for others.

According to Aristotle, prudence demands not only the farsighted pursuit of personal goals, but also a deliberative concern for the rationality of these goals themselves. Some goals or ends, which Aristotle identified as virtuous, are superior to others in providing intrinsic and developing satisfactions, and should be distinguished from other goals whose pursuit is motivated extrinsically and tends to degenerate. This approach to practically wise behavior is clearly distinct from an economic, or Humean, conception of rationality as the instrumentally efficient pursuit of goals about which theory should be agnostic. Earlier, however, we suggested that the choice of goals can itself be seen as a decision, to be evaluated in much the same way as other decisions are evaluated in terms of present goals. This suggestion could help to bridge the gap between Aristotelian and Humean views of rationality.

A further aspect of the prudential account of personal goals is the emphasis it places on the mutual achievement of goals. Prudence consists in the achievement of harmony among personal goals, and in the successful "co-satisfiability" of them (Charles, 1984), the degree to which they do not conflict and their respective demands are successfully balanced. For Aristotle, the ideal of harmonized ends is represented by the concept of *eudaimonia,* or human flourishing, which consists in an integrated vision of the good life as an extended unity in time. We attempted to incorporate this idea into our earlier suggestion about the rationality of choice of goals.

Although our modern concept of prudence is essentially based on long-run self-interest, Aristotle did not think of it that way. The distinction between self-interest and morality is, arguably, a more recent invention (Parfit, 1984). For Aristotle, concern for others and concern for oneself in the long run were fully harmonious goals, even in an imperfect world (Sherman, 1989).

Practical intelligence

As the alternative translations attest, prudence refers broadly to thinking in practical contexts, rather than in specifically intellectual domains. The kind of intelligence implicit in prudence is distinguished from technical or procedural skill and from abstract theoretical or philosophical cognition. Rather, it is characterized by a flexible and applied concern for the practical contingencies of behavior, especially in the face of uncertainty. Prudence is marked by a cautious attitude to risk and a moderate attitude toward aspiration. It allows a degree of rule-governedness for behavior, but emphasizes the need for flexibility in mediating between rules and the particularities of cases. This flexibility is a matter of deliberation. Prudence thus amounts in large part to a faculty of good judgment.

Prudence and impulsiveness

Prudence plainly refers to an ideal of thinking and behaving which is taken to be good in itself and worthy of emulation. It is taken to have an ethical dimension, and it is listed as one of the virtues. Its principal prescriptive recommendation is that it enables the person's resistance to a variety of forms of impulsive ("incontinent") and intemperate behavior, and in its fullest development the person is not even drawn towards these irrationalities. The discrepancy between the prudential norm and the reality of incontinence suggests that the main target of prescriptive efforts is weak-willed or impulsive behavior. Prudence carries prescriptive weight because of this basic self-regulatory deficiency, as well as its derivative consequences for other people, who suffer from the person's unpredictability and impulsiveness. For Aristotle, impulsive behavior is identified with antisocial vice.

Note that the concept of impulsiveness that we refer to here is different from, yet related to, two other concepts. In one sense, impulsive behavior simply involves too little thought. Kagan (1966) measured impulsivity by looking at individual differences in speed and accuracy on problem-solving tasks. Impulsives were those who were fast and inaccurate, compared to others. ("Reflectives" were slow and accurate.) Baron et al. (1986) argued that Kagan's concept was implicitly evaluative, and Baron et al. made the evaluation explicit by defining impulsiveness as thinking less than the optimal amount. Baron et al. (1991) attempted to show how, at least in principle, this kind of impulsiveness could be measured by calculating an optimum amount of thinking for each subject in each of several anagram tasks.

A second sense of "impulsiveness" is identical to temporal myopia or lack of concern for the future. This is typically measured by tasks in which subjects must decide between immediate and delayed rewards. Impulsiveness is defined either as a tendency to choose the immediate reward, relative to one's peers (Mischel, Shoda, & Rodriguez, 1989), or as the kind of dynamic inconsistency described earlier (Ainslie & Haendel, 1983; Solnick, Kanneberg, Eckerman, & Waller, 1980).

The sense of "impulsiveness" that we take as crucial here is an inability to control impulses, that is, an inability to inhibit an initial tendency to act (or to refrain from action). The ability to control impulses is at the heart of self-control, for we do not need self-control in order to live from moment to moment. Self-control makes it possible for us to think about what to do, so it is a precondition for reflectiveness in Kagan's sense. Likewise, it makes it possible for us to delay gratification for the sake of a later and larger reward, or for the sake of conformity to a moral principle or social norm. But we are not claiming that self-control is a fundamental, unanalyzable, trait. Thought itself may contribute to self-control (Ainslie, 1991).

Prudence is motivated by the avoidance and overcoming of failures of self-control and of precipitant giving-in to temptations. These forms of peremptory behavior have in common a failure to adhere to a longer-term plan in the interest of a competing shorter-term opportunity. But prudence also refers to a concern for long-term ends rather than present-centered consequences. It is not enough for people to be free from weakness of will; they must also care about their extended personal futures, have delayed goals that they take into due account in their practical thinking, and think of themselves as beings continuous in time. These requisites amount to having a coherent life-plan. In sum, although self-control is necessary for prudence, it is not sufficient.

Personality

Now that we have sketched a theory of intelligence and an account of a concept that matches that theory's concerns, it is important to attempt to show how these concerns, refracted through the concept of prudence, relate to matters of concern to personality psychologists. In several respects, prudence does appear to represent an intermediate step between intelligence and personality. For instance, by drawing intelligence out of the circumscribed domain of narrow cognitive abilities and into the domain of goal satisfactions, it becomes more closely linked to more general behavioral dispositions. Similarly, the extension of intelligence into the preserve of "hot" cognition or motivated irrationality promises a rapprochement with a more clinical approach to cognitive traits. However, we hope to argue that prudence serves more than a way-station role between intelligence and personality, but rather defines a new way of approaching both.

Goal concepts in personality

There has been considerable recent interest in goal concepts in personality (Pervin, 1989), and many attempts to import purposive concepts into the field (e.g., Frese and Sabini, 1985). This focus on goals represents a shift away from a dispositional view of personality, towards a more cognitive perspective on the processes and strategies used to express dispositions (Cantor, 1990). Goal concepts surface in many forms, including personal projects (Little, 1983), possible selves (Markus and Nurius, 1986), life tasks (Cantor, Norem, Niedenthal, Langston, & Brower, 1987), personal strivings (Emmons, 1986), and current concerns (Klinger, 1975). This family of approaches shares a strong commitment to future-oriented models of motivation and an understanding of people as more or less deliberate constructors of their own ends.

This trend within the field of personality opens up several compelling possibilities from the point of view of a theory of practical intelligence. Most importantly, it aligns the study of personality with a conception of utility as goal achievement, thus permitting personality to be analyzed in terms of decision making. Variant forms of personality organizations and process could potentially be compared for their capacity to yield durable goal achievement. This problem could be pursued in at least four directions.

First, different goals could be compared for their capacities to yield extended satisfactions, and different dimensions of goal setting could be examined in similar fashion. Aristotle's account of prudence would allow that some goals are more specious or shortsighted than others. For example, Freudians often speak of "love and work" as the two most important criteria of mental health. Are those who neglect these goals in favor of others such as sex or wealth (unrelated to work) demonstrably less satisfied in the long run? Do they judge their own lives to be less worthwhile?

Second, the internal organization of goals could be compared in terms of their harmony or conflict, their "co-satisfiability" in prudential terms. Can we find people who suffer from incompatible goals? Are such people more likely to be found seeking psychotherapy or counseling than are others otherwise like them? We might expect many effects of incompatibility to be noticed immediately. Longitudinal investigation is not required.

Third, the processes by which goals are traded off and conjointly pursued could be compared with normative models, and evidence for the operation of known cognitive biases involving single-mindedness and tradeoff aversion could be sought. Can we find people who sacrifice some goals irrationally for the sake of others? Almost any kind of commitment requires sacrifice of some goals. Does the ability to see a commitment through depend on an understanding of what is lost (as suggested by Janis and Mann, 1977)?

Finally, the process of goal revision could be examined. What happens to people who undergo religious conversions? What happens when people have children or enter law school? How does the aspiring poverty lawyer wind up doing corporate tax law?

These possible lines of inquiry will be examined in turn. In general, although we are able to find some relevant research, most of the important questions have no clear answers yet.

Comparison of goals. The possibility that goals might differ in their expected or intrinsic yields of satisfaction or utility is not contrary to our intuitions, but the psychology of personality has paid it little or no heed. However, Ainslie (1991) has suggested that many of the goals that we identify as immoral or immature, and which he calls "sell-outs," are those whose yield of rewards are particularly prone to decline over time, and whose pursuit is therefore shortsighted. With respect to aspects or dimensions of goals, the prospects for normative analysis are brighter, as there exists a large body of work, much of it outside of personality psychology, on the processes of goal setting (e.g., Locke and Latham, 1990), in complex (simulated) work-like environments. Often in combination with examinations of self-regulatory processes (e.g., Bandura and Cervone, 1983), which we shall discuss in a later section, this literature demonstrates the salutary effects on motivation and achievement of challenging and specific goals. Absent, vague, or undemanding goals adversely affect performance on a wide variety of tasks (Tubbs, 1986).

One noteworthy piece of research that brings a goal-setting approach to the study of broad, personally significant goals is reported by Palys and Little (1983), who found that low life satisfaction in a student sample was associated with the pursuit of more difficult personal projects, and those projects with a longer-term focus. Interestingly, in view of this finding, Ahrens (1987) suggests that high self-evaluative standards may predispose people to depression. Palys and Little suggested that the relative dissatisfaction of students pursuing more deferred and difficult projects may have been due to the perceived remoteness of project fruition, the perceived lack of instrumentality of the present efforts in achieving those projects, or to the incapacity of the students to break down longer-term projects into meaningful short-term goals. Although this study is important, from a normative point of view short-term life satisfaction indices are inappropriate measures of utility. As Palys and Little point out, goal achievement and life satisfaction over extended periods must be known for normatively relevant conclusions to be drawn. Similarly, momentary measures of life satisfaction in no way demonstrate the practical rationality of the cognitive processes governing goal achievement.

In this connection, Taylor and Brown (1988) and others (e.g., Seligman, 1991) have argued that biased and self-serving thinking performs a self-protective function and is therefore prescriptively valuable if not normatively correct. Along with other goals, people have a goal of being "happy," that is, the goal of believing that their other goals are being achieved. If they can convince themselves – even through self-deception – that their goals are being achieved, then they achieve one of their goals, the goal of happiness. Such self-deception has costs; first, the benefits of accurate beliefs are likely to be greater in the long run than they are immediately. Short-term happiness can be achieved through self-deception, but the long-run costs go unnoticed. Second, actively open-minded thinking, thinking that tries to be fair to both sides (Baron, 1988) is a valuable tool that habits of self-deception may dull. We would also suggest that the tradeoff is not as stark as the Taylor and Brown (1988) argument would suggest. The two options of being happy or achieving one's long-term goals are not the only options. People can also adjust their goals and their plans. If your goal is to be liked by everyone, so that you will be unhappy if you think that some people don't like you, then wishful thinking can increase your happiness. But if you adjust your goal so that you can be happy with less than perfection, you will not need to deceive yourself.

Internal organization of goals.   If the comparative study of goals and goal dimensions is not very far advanced within personality psychology, neither is the study of the organization of goals. Nevertheless, two studies have demonstrated some evidence for the importance of the co-satisfiability of goals. In these studies, subjects are asked to list their personal projects (temporally extended, concrete or abstract, personally construed goals or incentives) and strivings (objectives that they are typically trying to accomplish or obtain). Palys and Little (1983) found more conflictual organizations of personal projects in students with low life satisfaction, and Emmons and King (1988) demonstrated that conflict among personal strivings was associated with stable patterns of negative affectivity and a variety of negative health outcomes.

Making tradeoffs. A third direction in which a theory of prudence might inform a goal-oriented psychology of personality concerns the ways in which people's pursuit of goals falls prey to cognitive biases that normatively impair goal achievement. To our knowledge, no studies of this kind have been performed, although, we would suggest, such an approach has several precedents in other psychological domains. In the general domain of decision making and problem solving, single-minded attention to one goal or attribute and aversion to tradeoffs among goals have been documented (see Baron, 1988, for a review). Furthermore, research in related domains suggests systematic deviations from optimal allocation of effort or time to multiple goals or tasks. Tulga and Sheridan (1980) had subjects do a simulated time-management computer game where only one "task" could be worked on at a time and points were awarded for task completion. In this test of "supervisory control" there were considerable differences in optimality among Ss.

Time-management practices, moreover, appear to be important components of educational achievement over and above conventional measures of scholastic aptitude. Britton and Tesser (1991) used a time-management questionnaire to predict (prospectively) grade averages in college students. Two of the three factors in the questionnaire (called short-range planning and time attitudes—which referred to feelings of being in charge of one's time) predicted grades better than SAT scores (and in addition to them). The cognitive processes enabling the coordination among multiple goals would appear to be a promising domain of study in the field of personality.

Goal revision. A similarly promising but unstudied domain concerns the revision and addition of goals. Although the study of personality continuity and transitions is well developed (Caspi and Bem, 1990), little attention has been paid to qualitative or quantitative changes of goals, projects, or strivings. It is possible, for instance, that there is a general tendency for goals to be either too readily abandoned or irrationally persistent, in similar fashion to the well-researched persistence of belief. The normative analysis of goal revision is in its early stages of development (Baron, 1993) compared to the Bayesian account of belief revision, but in some cases at least the imprudent persistence of goals may be grounded in the imperviousness of a belief. The persistence of a goal to be a championship basketball player, for instance, may simply be due to a misguided and motivated probability estimate of the likelihood of that possibility (Frank, 1990).

Personality and practical cognition

The approach to personality psychology elaborated in this chapter places everyday cognition at its center. Prudence has always been opposed to purely abstract or technical cognition, and held to refer to the effective, harmonious and farsighted conduct of practical affairs. The theoretical shift away from a primarily dispositional account of personality to one based on local strategies and goals represents a movement towards practical cognition, just as does the recent attention paid to "practical intelligence" (Sternberg and Wagner, 1986) in the field of intelligence. A prudential account attempts to bridge this narrowing gap by specifying the decisional components and normative dimensions of goal achievement.

Three fundamental aspects of decision making are the evaluation of consequences, the assessment of likelihoods (or confidence), and the consideration of the temporal dimension of delay and behavioral allocation. The last of these three will be treated in a later section, on account of its centrality to the theoretical concerns of prudence. A smaller amount of theory and research on the application of the former two decisional aspects to personality psychology has accumulated.

A concern for the consequences of actions and for the range of alternative courses of action towards desired goals is a basic aspect of prudent behavior. Klemp and McClelland (1986), for instance, emphasize the importance of cause–effect reasoning and the capacity to anticipate the implications of events in the practically intelligent functioning of senior managers. Similarly, recent work on the concept and measurement of "hope" (Snyder et al., 1991) demonstrates that, in addition to a self-perception of successful agency, hope seems to involve the perceived capacity to generate successful alternative plans or "pathways." From a very different line of inquiry, Kreitler and Kreitler (1990) show that one of the elementary semantic components of the trait of impulsivity (in the sense of rash and precipitous behavior), which we take to be a fundamental cause of imprudence, is a lack of concern for the consequences of actions. Prudent personality would seem to require a developed capacity for causal and implicative reasoning, and a capacity to evaluate actions by their concrete and alternative outcomes.

Very little work has explored the connections between personality and the assessment of probabilities and confidence, although the concept of prudence is centrally concerned with judgment in the face of uncertainty, and implies a particular attitude to risk. Taylor and Brown (1988) review considerable research suggesting systematic overconfidence and self-serving estimates of the likelihood of positive and negative events, in a manner clearly antithetical to prudential prescriptions. Early research into the association between personality dispositions and probabilistic thinking (Wright and Phillips, 1979) found few associations for measures of dogmatism, authoritarianism, conservatism, and intolerance of ambiguity. More recent work (Wolfe and Grosch, 1990), however, finds a consistent pattern of small associations between confidence in judgment and measures of positive and negative affectivity, and several "cognitive/social" variables such as self-monitoring and need for cognition. These findings support Taylor and Brown's (1988) claim that self-enhancing illusions are associated with signs of good adjustment. As before, however, we would argue that self-deception has serious adverse consequences and does not constitute good prescriptive advice, whatever its weak associations with short-term indices of mental health. Certainly, deficits in probabilistic thinking and the acceptance of uncertainty appear to be associated with negative consequences such as accidents (Dahlback, 1991).

Before moving on to another aspect of the prudential approach to personality, we should mention one prominent direction of contemporary personality research pertinent to practical cognition. Epstein and Meier's work (1989) on constructive thinking explicitly acknowledges developments in the study of practical intelligence, and their constructive thinking measure was based directly on a sampling of everyday and automatic constructive and destructive thinking. The measure yielded superior prediction of a variety of criteria of success in living such as physical and psychological symptoms, love and work satisfaction, and self-discipline problems. This more ecological approach to personality assessment appears to have a great deal of promise.

The prescriptive approach to personality

Although Baron (1989) has argued the need for a prescriptive theory of intelligent character, psychologists have not studied personality from a prescriptive stance. Character has principally been entertained as a structural or taxonomic concept by psychoanalytic writers (e.g., Fenichel, 1945), and nonanalytic personality psychologists have taken an exclusively descriptive approach to their subject matter. The closest such an approach comes to having prescriptive implications is in studies that correlate personality variables with indices of subjective well-being or life success (e.g., Emmons and Diener, 1986), and in studies of "self-defeating" behavior (e.g., Baumeister and Sher, 1988). We have argued that the former kind of evidence is insufficient since it lacks an explicit normative model, tends to be based on potentially spurious and short-term measures of "happiness," and does not yield clear prescriptive implications. Work on self-defeating behavior, similarly, does not specify on what normative grounds behavior is defined thus, but rather selects it on a priori considerations.

One recent trend in the psychology of personality, however, holds more promise for a prescriptive approach to personality. In this line of work, personality is conceptualized in terms of cognitive strategies in the service of goal achievement (e.g., Showers and Cantor, 1985). Goals may be multiple and conflictual, such as goals involving the regulation of mood and self-esteem and goals involving adaptive mastery of the environment. Strategies, such as vigilance, self-handicapping, optimism, and defensive pessimism, are recognized in this emerging literature to incur costs as well as benefits, and to involve tradeoffs in their everyday exercise (Cantor, 1990). An exemplary analysis of the costs and benefits of defensive pessimism has been carried out by Norem and Cantor (1990), who found that defensive pessimism was beneficial in terms of providing anticipatory coping and motivation to succeed but has costs in anxiety concerning unlikely events, and in side-effects on personal health and life stress, as well as occasional weakened intrinsic motivation. Although this work has yet to perform an explicit normative examination of cognitive strategies, such an examination seems fully practicable and would have clear prescriptive implications for the practice of cognitive therapies. The strategic approach, then, promises the possibility of a prescriptive account of personality.

The subjective future and self-control in personality.

Perhaps the most important and distinctive elements of the concept of prudence are its concern for long-term considerations and the associated focus on the self-control of impulse. From a prudential point of view, the various forms of behavioral myopia are the principal traps of practical intelligence. Imprudent behavior will generally fail either to take more temporally remote consequences or goals into adequate consideration, by failure of foresight or motivation, or it will fail to hold to a prudent plan of action on account of inadequate impulse control. We shall treat these two related aspects of imprudent personality separately.

The subjective future.   Investigations of people's orientation to the future have had a continuing but neglected presence in personality psychology. A wide variety of temporal variables have been invoked in the study of personality, most notably a family of dispositional variables concerning "future time perspective" or "future orientation" (e.g., Nuttin, 1985). These variables refer to the temporal extent, density, and organization of habitual ways of thinking about the future, and have most frequently been used to predict academic achievement and motivation (deVolder & Lens, 1982; Van Calster, Lens, & Nuttin, 1987). They therefore concern the extent to which longer-term goals govern behavior, an important dimension of practical intelligence according to Wagner and Sternberg (1986), and the degree to which the future is planfully and purposively anticipated. A related formulation due to Bond and Feather (1988) brings this element of perceived temporal structure further into the foreground, and demonstrates the capacity of a measuring instrument to predict a broad spectrum of life-success indices. Bond and Feather's work brings the study of time perspective usefully close to work on time-management skills (e.g., Britton and Tesser, 1991).

In a different direction, Baumeister and Sher's (1988) account of self-defeating behavior suggests that a wide variety of maladaptive behaviors and cognitive strategies are based on a failure to weigh more remote goals against proximal goals. Haslam (1990) used a variety of related temporal personality variables to predict a global measure of self-defeating behavior and a measure of physical-health outcomes, demonstrating moderate and predictable associations of both, comparable to and independent of established predictors such as negative affectivity. With its explicit focus on planfulness and goal concepts, future-time perspective appears to be an important and under-researched dimension in a prudential approach to the study of personality.

However, future-time perspective does not exhaust the range of important temporal personality variables. One such variable is "action identification" (Vallacher and Wegner, 1985). Vallacher and Wegner (1989) demonstrate that people who habitually identify their actions in more global and extended terms are less impulsive, planful, and behaviorally consistent than those employing more temporally restricted units. Another personality variable concerning the temporal dimension of behavior and experience is perceived personal continuity. Ball and Chandler (1989) found that suicidal adolescents had a focal inability to reason about their personal identity over time. Prudent concern for the personal future would seem to be contingent on envisaging a meaningfully connected continuity of the self.

Self control. Weighing future goals and events adequately would appear to be a crucial underpinning of practical rationality. However, an equally fundamental basis for prudent behavior is the capacity to discipline behavior to meet farsighted goals. This capacity may be referred to as self-control or self-regulation, and has been well explored by a variety of writers in the field of personality, some of whom have documented its cognitive components.

We have good reason to suppose that self-control is an especially critical problem for prudent behavior. First, there is strong evidence that elementary motivational processes describable by Herrnstein's matching law (Herrnstein, 1961; Ainslie, 1991) dispose people and lower animals to shortsighted impulsivity. The fundamental nature of the temporal discounting of rewards appears to require efforts of self-control to prevent systematic failures of maximization. Second, individual differences in impulsivity have been conjectured to underlie a variety of maladaptive and imprudent behaviors, from various forms of psychopathology (Kirschenbaum, 1987) to criminality (Gottfredson and Hirschi, 1990), and predict levels of negative affect (Emmons and Diener, 1986).

Self-control has received a considerable measure of attention in the study of personality, if not always by that name, and such work tends to support its centrality to any account of practically intelligent behavior. Bandura's extensive writings on self-regulation (e.g., 1989), for instance, although not explicitly recognizing that goal-directed behavior faces intrinsic impulsivity, concern ways in which goal achievement can be maximized by judicious self-management. Bandura's self-evaluative processes, self-efficacy judgments, and goal-setting practices all involve mechanisms for overcoming short-term obstacles to motivation and persistence.

Another tradition of work pertinent to self-control refers to the related concepts of ego strength, ego control, and ego resiliency. In a several longitudinal studies, measures of these concepts have yielded strong association with a variety of measures of life success. Felsman and Vaillant (1987), for example, measured life success at age 47 by a rating of life stage (in an Eriksonian sense), by a general rating of mental health, by an index of maturity of defenses (after Vaillant), and by a measure of object relations (i.e., quality and development of social relationships). This was predicted by a measure of boyhood competency (at age 11 to 16), which Felsman and Vaillant take to be a measure of "ego strength," as well as by IQ and parental SES. The ego strength measure outperformed both in predicting middle-adulthood outcomes.

Funder, Block, and Block (1983) correlated delay of gratification at age 4 with personality at 3, 4, 7, and 11, and found that delay predicted Q-sort ratings such as *independent, resourceful, competent, deliberative, reasonable, attentive, coopera-tive,* and *able to modulate impulse.* Funder et al. explain these results in terms of ego control and resiliency. Similarly, Mischel, Shoda, and Peake (1988) demonstrated associations between preschool delay of gratification and a range of adolescent social and cognitive competencies. For example, Rodriguez, Mischel, and Shoda (1989) found that preschool delay was correlated with measures of IQ, attention deployment (distraction), and delay-rule knowledge in a group of 11-year-olds at risk for a variety of negative outcomes.

Mischel and his colleagues (e.g., Mischel, Shoda, and Rodriguez, 1989) have also shown that children's developing knowledge of delay tactics bears an important relation to delay success. This tactical approach allows self-control to be understood as a matter of cognitive skill and practical intelligence, amenable to a prescriptive analysis after the fashion of the strategic approach to personality (Cantor, 1990). A more elaborate taxonomy of self-control tactics with implications for clinical and personality psychology has been proposed by Ainslie (e.g., Ainslie and Haslam, 1991a), and a tentative prescriptive analysis for clinical therapeutic practice is pre-sented in Ainslie and Haslam (1991b).

Conclusion

We have attempted to show that emerging but dispersed trends in the psychology of personality combine to yield an integrated account of behavior. That account cor-responds in a variety of ways with a theory of intelligence and practical rationality. It emphasizes the practical, goal-directed, cognitive and strategic dimensions of behavior, and is amenable to a normative analysis in the service of prescriptive ends. The concept of prudence summarizes the convergences of a variegated body of work, and, we think, bridges the theoretical divide between the study of intelligent behavior and personality. In doing so, we believe, it helps to bring both intelligence and personality into the world of everyday cognition.

Some questions and ambiguities remain, of course. Prominent among these is the matter of the domain- or situation-specificity of prudent behavior. Little evidence is germane to this question, although the evidence supports only moderate consistency of prudent behaviors in the field of preventive health and in self-defeating behavior more generally (e.g., Haslam, 1990). Nevertheless, our claim is not that prudence represents a psychometrically coherent trait, readily amenable to valid measurement, but rather that it represents a way of conceptualizing personality in adaptive and cognitive terms.

A second matter of concern is the abstract and formalistic nature of our account of prudence, which provides the account with a broad sweep and a normative dimension, but leaves substantive questions on the nature of cognitive processes involved only weakly specified. However, we are confident that continuing work in the field of personality will flesh out some of these formal analyses. We hold particular hopes for the emerging work on cognitive strategies (e.g., Cantor, 1990) and on practical intelligence (Sternberg & Wagner, 1986).

Our approach has implications for education, in a broad sense that includes child rearing by families. Parents seek to give their children good characters, but they receive little systematic guidance from psychology. Such advice as psychologists give is likely to emphasize appropriate rules of discipline and the importance of parental concern, but without any kind of coherent theory of how parents can help their children live better lives, and why some methods might achieve this end better than others. Schools do a great deal of what used to be called character education, but mostly through a "hidden curriculum" of disciplinary rules and unstated practices. Calls for more self-conscious character education in the U.S. have come from the political Right, but these calls often advocate blind adherence to "traditional virtues," especially those of sexual restraint. Blind adherence to such traditions is not what we are advocating here. Rather, we think psychology should seek a deeper understanding of intelligent character as something to be promoted. Such an understanding would justify our practices in terms of their ultimate effects, and it would justify these effects in terms of a coherent theory of the good life.

References

Ahrens, A. H. (1987). Theories of depression: The role of goals and the self-evaulation process. *Cognitive Therapy and Research, 6,* 665–680.

Ainslie, G. (1991). *Picoeconomics: The interaction of successive motivational states within the individual.* New York: Cambridge University Press.

Ainslie, G., & Haendel, V. (1983). The motives of the will. In E. Gottheil, K. A. Druley, T. E. Skoloda, & H. M. Waxman (Eds.), *Etiologic aspects of alcohol and drug abuse.* Springfield, IL: Thomas.

Ainslie, G., & Haslam, N. (1991a). Self-control. In G. Loewenstein (Ed.), *Intertemporal choice.* New York: Russell Sage Foundation.

Ainslie, G., & Haslam, N. (1991b). *Psychotherapy and other methods to improve self-control.* Unpublished manuscript. Veterans Administration Medical Center, Coatesville, PA.

Anderson, C. A. (1982). Inoculation and counterexplanation: Debiasing techniques in the perseverance of social theories. *Social Cognition, 1,* 126–139.

Ball, L., & Chandler, M. (1989). Identity formation in suicidal and nonsuicidal youth: The role of self-continuity. *Development and Psychopathology, 1,* 257–275.

Bandura, A. (1989). Self-regulation of motivation and action through internal standards and goal systems. In L. A. Pervin (Ed.), *Goal concepts in personality and social psychology.* Hillsdale, NJ: Erlbaum.

Bandura, A., & Cervone, D. (1983). Self-evaluative and self-efficacy mechanisms governing the motivational effects of goal systems. *Journal of Personality and Social Psychology, 45,* 1017–1028.

Baron, J. (1982). Personality and intelligence. In R. J. Sternberg (Ed.), *Handbook of human intelligence*. New York: Cambridge University Press.

Baron, J. (1985a). *Rationality and intelligence*. New York: Cambridge University Press.

Baron, J. (1985b). What kinds of intelligence components are fundamental? In S. F. Chipman, J. W. Segal, & R. Glaser (Eds.), *Thinking and learning skills. Vol. 2: Research and open questions*. Hillsdale, NJ: Erlbaum, pp. 365–390.

Baron, J. (1988). *Thinking and deciding*. New York: Cambridge University Press.

Baron, J. (1989). Why a theory of social intelligence needs a theory of character. In R. S. Wyer and T. K. Srull (Eds.), *Advances in social cognition, Vol. 2: Social intelligence and cognitive assessments of personality*. Hillsdale, NJ: Erlbaum.

Baron, J. (1991). Beliefs about thinking. In J. F. Voss, D. N. Perkins, & J. W. Segal (Eds.), *Informal reasoning and education*, pp. 169–186. Hillsdale, NJ: Erlbaum.

Baron, J. (1993). *Morality and rational choice*. Dordrecht: Kluwer.

Baron, J. (1989). *Actively open-minded thinking versus myside bias: Causes and effects*. Paper presented at Fourth International Conference on Thinking, San Juan, Puerto Rico, August, 1989.

Baron, J., Badgio, P. C., & Gaskins, I. W. (1986). Cognitive style and its improvement: A normative approach. In R. J. Sternberg (Ed.), *Advances in the psychology of human intelligence, Vol. 3*. Hillsdale, NJ: Erlbaum.

Baron, J., Badgio, P., & Ritov, Y. (1991). Departures from optimal stopping in an anagram task. *Journal of Mathematical Psychology, 35*, 41–63.

Baron, J., & Hershey, J. C. (1988). Outcome bias in decision evaluation. *Journal of Personality and Social Psychology, 54*, 569–579.

Baumeister, R., & Sher, S. (1988). Self-defeating behavior patterns among normal individuals: Review and analysis of common self-destructive tendencies. *Psychological Bulletin, 104*, 3–22.

Bond, M. J., & Feather, N. T. (1988). Some correlates of structure and purpose in the use of time. *Journal of Personality and Social Psychology, 55*, 321–329.

Britton, B. K., & Tesser, A. (1991). Effects of time-management practices on college grades. *Journal of Educational Psychology, 83*, 405–410.

Cantor, N. (1990). From thought to behavior: "Having" and "doing" in the study of personality and cognition. *American Psychologist, 45*, 735–750.

Cantor, N., Norem, J. K., Niedenthal, P. M., Langston, S. A., & Brower, A. M. (1987). Life tasks, self-concept ideals, and cognitive strategies in life transitions. *Journal of Personality and Social Psychology, 53*, 1178–1191.

Caspi, A., & Bem, D. J. (1990). Personality continuity and change across the life course. In L. A. Pervin (Ed.), *Handbook of personality: Theory and research*. New York: Guilford.

Charles, D. (1984). *Aristotle's philosophy of action*. London: Duckworth.

Dahlback, O. (1991). Accident-proneness and risk-taking. *Personality and Individual Differences, 12*, 79–85.

deVolder, M. L., & Lens, W. (1982). Academic achievement and future time perspective as a cognitive-motivational concept. *Journal of Personality and Social Psychology, 42*, 566–571.

Elster, J. (1983). *Sour grapes: Studies of the subversion of rationality*. New York: Cambridge University Press.

Emmons, R. A. (1986). Personal strivings: An approach to personality and subjective well-being. *Journal of Personality and Social Psychology, 51*, 1058–1068.

Emmons, R. A., & Diener, E. (1986). Influence of impulsivity and sociability on subjective well-being. *Journal of Personality and Social Psychology, 50*, 1211–1215.

Emmons, R. A., & King, L. A. (1988). Conflict among personal strivings: Immediate and long-term implications for psychological and physical well-being. *Journal of Personality and Social Psychology, 54*, 1040–1048.

Epstein, S., & Meier, P. (1989). Constructive thinking: A broad coping variable with specific components. *Journal of Personality and Social Psychology, 57*, 332–350.

Felsman, J. K., & Vaillant, G. E. (1987). Resilient children as adults: A 40-year study. In E. J. Anthony & B. J. Cohler (Eds.), *The invulnerable child*. New York: Guilford.

Fenichel, O. (1945). *The psychoanalytic theory of neurosis*. New York: Norton.

Frank, R. H. (1985). *Passions within reason: The strategic role of the emotions.* New York: Norton.

Frank, R. H. (1990). Personal communication.

Frese, M., & Sabini, J. (Eds.) (1985). *Goal directed behavior: On the concept of action in psychology.* Hillsdale, NJ: Erlbaum.

Funder, D. C., Block, J. H., & Block, J. (1983). Delay of gratification: Some longitudinal personality correlates. *Journal of Personality and Social Psychology, 44,* 1198–1213.

Gibbard, A. (1990). *Wise choices, apt feelings: A theory of normative judgment.* Cambridge, MA: Harvard University Press.

Gilovich, T. (1983). Biased evaluation and persistence in gambling. *Journal of Personality and Social Psychology, 44,* 1110–1126.

Gottfredson, M. R., & Hirschi, T. (1990). *A general theory of crime.* Stanford: Stanford University Press.

Haslam, N. (1990). *Temporal personality variables, self-defeating behavior, and health.* Unpublished manuscript. Department of Psychology, University of Pennsylvania.

Haslam, N. (1991). Prudence: Aristotelian perspectives on practical reason. *Journal for the Theory of Social Behaviour, 21,* 151–169.

Herrnstein, R. (1961). Relative and absolute strengths of response as a function of frequency of reinforcement. *Journal of the Experimental Analysis of Animal Behavior, 4,* 267–272.

Hoch, S. J. (1985). Counterfactual reasoning and accuracy in predicting personal events. *Journal of Experimental Psychology: Learning, Memory, and Cognition, 11,* 719–731.

Janis, I. L., & Mann, L. (1977). *Decision making: A psychological analysis of conflict, choice, and commitment.* New York: Free Press.

Kagan, J. (1966). Reflection-impulsivity: The generality and dynamics of conceptual tempo. *Journal of Abnormal Psychology, 71,* 17–27.

Kirschenbaum, D. (1987). Self-regulatory failure: A review with clinical implications. *Clinical Psychology Review, 7,* 77–104.

Klemp, G. O., & McClelland, D. C. (1986). What characterizes intelligent functioning among senior managers? In R. J. Sternberg and R. K. Wagner (Eds.), *Practical intelligence: Nature and origins of competence in the everyday world.* Cambridge: Cambridge University Press.

Klinger, E. (1975). Consequences of commitment to and disengagement from incentives. *Psychological Review, 82,* 1–25.

Koriat, A., Lichtenstein, S., & Fischoff, B. (1980). Reasons for confidence. *Journal of Experimental Psychology: Human Learning and Memory, 6,* 107–118.

Kreitler, S., & Kreitler, H. (1990). *The cognitive foundations of personality traits.* New York: Plenum.

Kuhn, D. (1989). Children and adults as intuitive scientists. *Psychological Review, 96,* 674–689.

Kunda, Z. (1990). The case for motivated reasoning. *Psychological Bulletin, 108,* 480–498.

Little, B. R. (1983). Personal projects: A rationale and method for investigation. *Environment and Behavior, 15,* 273–309.

Locke, E. A., & Latham, G. P. (1990). *A theory of goal-setting and performance.* Englewood Cliffs, NJ: Prentice-Hall.

Lord, C. G., Ross, L., & Lepper, M. R. (1979). Biased assimilation and attitude polarization: The effects of prior theories on subsequently considered evidence. *Journal of Personality and Social Psychology, 37,* 2098–2109.

Markus, H., & Nurius, P. (1986). Possible selves. *American Psychologist, 41,* 954–969.

Mischel, W., Shoda, Y., & Peake, P. K. (1988). The nature of adolescent competencies predicted by pre-school delay of gratification. *Journal of Personality and Social Psychology, 54,* 687–696.

Mischel, W., Shoda, Y., & Rodriguez, M. L. (1989). Delay of gratification in children. *Science, 244,* 933–938.

Norem, J. K., & Cantor, N. (1990). Cognitive strategies, coping and perceptions of competence. In R. J. Sternberg & J. Kolligian, Jr. (Eds.), *Competence considered.* New Haven, CT: Yale University Press.

Nuttin, J. (1985). *Future time perspective and motivation.* Hillsdale, NJ: Erlbaum.

Palys, T. S., & Little, B. R. (1983). Perceived life satisfaction and the organization of personal project systems. *Journal of Personality and Social Psychology, 44,* 1221–1230.

Parfit, D. (1984). *Reasons and persons.* Oxford: Oxford University Press.

Perkins, D. N. (1989). Reasoning as it is and could be: An empirical perspective. In D. Topping, D.

Crowell, & V. Kobayashi (Eds.), *Thinking across cultures: The third international conference on thinking*. Hillsdale, NJ: Erlbaum.

Perkins, D. N., Bushey, B., & Faraday, M. (1986). *Learning to reason*. Unpublished manuscript, Harvard Graduate School of Education, Cambridge, MA.

Pervin, L. (Ed.) (1989). *Goal concepts in personality and social psychology*. Hillsdale, NJ: Erlbaum.

Robinson, D. N. (1989). *Aristotle's psychology*. New York: Columbia University Press.

Rodriguez, M. L., Mischel, W., & Shoda, Y. (1989). Cognitive person variables in the delay of gratification of older children at risk. *Journal of Personality and Social Psychology, 57*, 358–367.

Sabini, J., & Silver, M. (1982). *Moralities of everyday life*. New York: Oxford University Press.

Seligman, M. E. P. (1991). *Learned optimism*. New York: Knopf.

Sen, A. (1987). *The standard of living*. Cambridge: Cambridge University Press.

Sherman, N. (1989). *The fabric of character: Aristotle's theory of virtue*. Oxford: Oxford University Press.

Showers, C., & Cantor, N. (1985). Social cognition: A look at motivated strategies. In M. Rosenweig & L. W. Porter (Eds.), *Annual Review of Psychology*. Palo Alto, CA: Annual Reviews.

Snyder, C. R., Harris, C., Anderson, J. R., Holleran, S. A., Irving, L. M., Sigmon, S. T., Yoshinobu, L., Gibb, J., Langelle, C., & Harney, P. (1991). The will and the ways: Development and validation of an individual-differences measure of hope. *Journal of Personality and Social Psychology, 60*, 570–585.

Solnick, J. V., Kanneberg, C. H., Eckerman, D. A., & Waller, M. B. (1980). An experimental analysis of impulsivity and impulse control in humans. *Learning and Motivation, 11*, 61–77.

Spranca, M., Minsk, E., & Baron, J. (1991). Omission and commission in judgment and choice. *Journal of Experimental Social Psychology, 27*, 76–105.

Sternberg, R. J. (1986). Intelligence is mental self-government. In R. J. Sternberg & D. K. Detterman (Eds.), *What is intelligence?: Contemporary viewpoints on its nature and definition*. Norwood, NJ: Ablex.

Sternberg, R. J., & Wagner, R. K. (Eds.) (1986). *Practical intelligence: Nature and origins of competence in the everyday world*. Cambridge: Cambridge University Press.

Taylor, S. E., & Brown, J. D. (1988). Illusion and well-being: A social psychological perspective on mental health. *Psychological Bulletin, 103*, 193–210.

Tetlock, P. E. (1983). Cognitive style and political ideology. *Journal of Personality and Social Psychology, 45*, 118–126.

Tetlock, P. E. (1985). A value pluralism model of ideological reasoning. *Journal of Personality and Social Psychology, 50*, 819–827.

Tubbs, M. E. (1986). Goal-setting: A meta-analytic examination of the empirical evidence. *Journal of Applied Psychology, 71*, 474–483.

Tulga, M. K., & Sheridan, T. B. (1980). Dynamic decisions and work load in multitask supervisory control. *IEEE Transactions on Systems, Man, and Cybernetics, 10*, 217–232.

Vallacher, R. R., & Wegner, D. M. (1985). *A theory of action identification*. Hillsdale, NJ: Erlbaum.

Vallacher, R. R., & Wegner, D. M. (1989). Levels of personal agency: Individual variation in action identification. *Journal of Personality and Social Psychology, 57*, 660–671.

Van Calster, K., Lens, W., & Nuttin, J. R. (1987). Affective attitudes towards the personal future: Impact on motivation in high school boys. *American Journal of Psychology, 100*, 1–13.

Wagner, R. K., & Sternberg, R. J. (1986). Tacit knowledge and intelligence in the everyday world. In R. J. Sternberg and R. K. Wagner (Eds.), *Practical intelligence: Nature and origins of competence in the everyday world*. Cambridge: Cambridge University Press.

Wolfe, R. N., & Grosch, J. W. (1990). Personality correlates of confidence in one's decisions. *Journal of Personality, 58*, 515–534.

Wright, G. N., & Phillips, L. D. (1979). Personality and probabilistic thinking: An exploratory study. *British Journal of Psychology, 70*, 295–303.

Part II

Personality development and intelligence

3   A life-span perspective on the interface between personality and intelligence

Anna G. Maciel, Jutta Heckhausen, and Paul B. Baltes

In this chapter, we want to first articulate four mutually complementary propositions about life-span changes at the interface of personality and intelligence. The first proposition is that adaptive development is reflected in whether and to what extent individuals attain, extend, and maintain performance at their personal optimum in domains selected for growth or effective functioning. The second proposition is that development across the life span is not a unitary process but constituted by multi-dimensional and multidirectional components and processes of change. The third proposition is that adaptive mastery of developmental gains and losses is character-ized by general processes of selection, optimization, and compensation. The fourth proposition is that intellectual and personality capacities, as well as their interface, are regulated by three streams of influence; age-graded, history-graded, and non-nor-mative.

In the first part of the chapter we will begin with a characterization of these principles, which many life-span scholars view as essential for their conceptual enterprise. In the second part of the chapter, we illustrate this propositional frame-work, or parts thereof, for the personality–intelligence realm with a number of research examples. Because of the complexity of the subject matter, we will not be able to do this in a comprehensive manner. In the third part of the chapter we will develop some specific life-span developmental issues at the interface of intelligence and personality in more detail.

Human development from a life-span developmental perspective

The scope and potential for ontogenetic change in humans is larger than in any other species. This ontogenetic potential brings about both sizeable flexibility within an individual's life course and much variability between individuals. The relative open-ness of the human species for change has been a cornerstone of life-span theory (P. B. Baltes, 1987, 1993; Brim & Kagan, 1980; Dannefer, 1989; Dannefer & Perlmutter, 1990; Featherman, 1983; Lerner, 1984). Humans hold a broad potential to acquire within their individual life-course knowledge, skills, values, motives, and beliefs.

As anthropologists and cultural psychologists argue (e.g., Cole, 1990; Durham, 1990; Shweder, 1990), the scope of human potential is so large because humans' "capacity for culture" is unrivaled, and because human development is conditioned by two streams of "inheritance": genetic and cultural. Aside from the genetically based capacity for culture, the sources for high levels of personal and cognitive functioning lie in cultural contexts and the societally arranged goals and means of activation and specialization. At the same time, whatever is achieved is limited by the constraints of the current state of civilization and its historical conditions.

Life-span research and theory in psychology since its inception (e.g., P. B. Baltes, 1983; Riegel, 1976; Tetens, 1777), has struggled with the complexity and dynamic of the relationship between ontogenetic and societal change. One resulting theoretical orientation has been that of contextualism and systemic analysis (P. B. Baltes, 1987; Elder, 1991; Featherman, 1983; Lerner, 1991; Thomae, 1979). To understand life-span development implies, in addition to biological–genetic perspectives (Plomin & Thompson, 1988), the identification of the personal and societal contexts of life and of the interrelationships among the systems or domains (physical, mental, and social) of human functioning. The search for the nature of the coordination between intelligence and personality, therefore, is a conceptual imperative for life-span work.

Toward optimal development

It is beyond the scope of this chapter to identify the criteria for a theory of optimal development and its individual, social, and cultural variations (e.g., Brandtstädter, 1984; Dannefer, 1989; Shweder, 1990). Here, we can focus only on some of the essential properties of this approach. It is part of life-span theory to search for the biological and psychological conditions that permit individuals to maximize their potential (plasticity) into old age. Bringing this perspective of optimization into focus is necessary because societal expectations about the second half of life and especially old age are, on average, fairly negative or pessimistic, and more so for some subgroups (e.g., social class) than others. At present, civilization has not yet resulted in a "culture" of the second half of life that is close to what one could characterize as an ideal set of development-enhancing conditions. In this sense, aging is the most underdeveloped stage of life, paradoxically from a civilization point of view, old age is "young" (P. B. Baltes, 1991).

Our first proposition concerns a multitude of criteria for "successful" life-span development: length of life, physical health, mental health, autonomy, sense of personal control, and cognitive efficacy, to name but a few (Baltes & Baltes, 1990). On a general level, it is the question whether and to what extent individuals "optimize" their potential as intellectual problem solvers, as personal entities, and as social agents. Personal and cognitive development requires a coalition. For example, the extent to which individuals attain their personal optimum largely hinges on their mental and physical abilities. The other major component of adaptiveness is the individual's motivation to act and exert control over his or her environment, without which no action would be issued. Action motivation, in turn, depends on interests in the potential action goal and, most importantly, on the confidence that it can be achieved (see review in H. Heckhausen, 1991). Hence, the realization of one's personal potential depends on abilities and on core features of the self, such as self-ascribed capacities and perceived personal control (Baltes & Baltes, 1986; Bandura, 1986; Sternberg & Kolligian, 1990).

These general observations on the interface between intellectual and personality functioning are likely to be true for any approach to ontogenetic development. What, then, is special about a life-span view? First, a life-span view is expected to offer a general framework for the specification of the domains of mind and personality that need consideration, and how their interrelationship is likely to change as people live their lives. Second, a life-span view can be expected to identify new domains of functioning (both in personality and intelligence) as well as contextual conditions that may deserve attention as people move into the last periods of life. Not everything in old age, for example, may represent a simple continuation or maintenance of earlier life characteristics. Third, because of the relative novelty of old age as a high-frequency event in industrialized societies, a life-span view may alert us to new scenarios and opportunities that may gain in prominence as more and more people reach old age (P. B. Baltes & Mittelstraß, 1992; Riley & Riley, 1989).

Multidirectionality and multidimensionality throughout the life-span

A second theme in life-span work is the recognition that ontogenetic development is not unidimensional and unidirectional. Traditional perspectives view development as a unidirectional process towards improvement, both within and across domains of functioning. Such a conception reflects the longstanding emphasis in developmental psychology, which used to be almost exclusively concerned with infancy and childhood, during which developmental gains appear more salient than developmental losses.

The challenge to such a predominantly growth-oriented conception began when, during the 18th and 19th centuries (e.g., Carus, 1808; Quetelet, 1835; Tetens, 1777; see review in P. B. Baltes, 1983), and particularly in the second half of the 20th century, developmental psychologists included adulthood and old age as important periods of development. Recent and dramatic changes in population demographics towards an increasing proportion of elderly triggered an increasing interest in developmental changes during old age, both in the general public and in scientific psychology. This meant that not only age-related growth but also decline, believed to be the characteristic for old age, were now commonly conceived as developmental phenomena.

The treatment of the growth–decline dynamic resulted not only in an expanded conception of development. Life-span scholars, struggling with differential change trends for different domains of functioning, also attempted to attain a synthetic view of the dynamic between developmental gains and losses at each stage and throughout the life span (P. B. Baltes, 1987). Developmental change throughout the life span is conceived to be associated with positive and negative changes in human capacity. Even within the same category of functioning (e.g., intelligence), a given age change may entail advances and losses. Moreover, on a systemic level, as would be true for the personality–intelligence interface, one domain may exhibit advances while another may demonstrate a reduction in capacity.

More recently, Paul Baltes (1987; see also Labouvie-Vief, 1981) took the multidimensionality and multidirectionality argument one step further. He argued that the gain–loss view applies also to a single developmental change event. With a view for the consequences of each change event, the argument advanced was that development is *never* pure gain in adaptivity.

Language development in early childhood might serve as an example. While most of us would conceive of language development as pure growth, this developmental gain is only possible by a concurrent loss with regard to the range of possible vocalizations. Children can only acquire their native language by selecting out those sounds that are part of it, at the expense of the ability to utter other sounds possibly relevant for other languages (Levelt, 1992). Similarly, as children acquire the capacity to reason abstractly, they may at the same time lose some of their ability for fantasy.

Even more fundamentally, the gain–loss dynamic reflects the nature of early brain development. During the first three years of life, the functional maturation of the cerebral cortex is attained by means of a 50% loss of neurons (Huttenlocher, 1979). It is the *selective* strengthening of relevant neuronal connections at the expense of irrelevant ones that brings about the rapid increase in brain functioning (Greenough, Black, & Wallace, 1987; Singer, 1987).

Life-span development as selective optimization with compensation

A third proposition of life-span theory stems from the view of development as a process of canalization or specialization (Gottlieb, 1991; Waddington, 1975). According to this view, the ontogenetic movement toward higher levels of functioning (progress) requires selection and elaboration of some pathways at the expense of others.

This trade-off between options might appear as an unfortunate feature of human development. However, the gain–loss dynamic is an indispensable condition for any human functioning, and all the more for human ontogenetic development. Not only is there no development without loss, in addition, throughout a lifetime resources in terms of time and energy are far too scarce to follow up on every possible developmental course. On a psychological level of analysis, similar features are part of general models of development as a process of differential and cumulative learning with associated factors of positive vs. negative transfer (Gagné, 1968). More recently, the expertise model (Ericsson & Smith, 1991) has equally emphasized the view that ontogenetic advances, particularly when high (peak) levels of functioning are considered (Ericsson, 1990), imply strong effects of selection and extensive commitments in time and energy.

If this conception of development as a process of canalization is combined with the notion of aging-correlated losses in adaptive capacity (plasticity), a new view of life-span development results. As we move our perspective to adulthood and old age it becomes apparent that a "new component" becomes more and more relevant in the process of human adaptation: compensation (Baltes & Baltes, 1990; Bäckman & Dixon, 1992). Because of aging-correlated losses in plasticity and cumulative effects of a lifetime of specialization, the developmental potential for gains and losses is not equally distributed across the life course (P. B. Baltes, 1987; J. Heckhausen, Dixon, & P. B. Baltes, 1989). Instead, with increasing age the ratio between possible gains and losses gradually shifts towards higher risks for decline relative to the potential for growth – a process predominantly based on biological aging, the occurrence of accidents and illness, but possibly also on the negative transfer of past specializations which are no longer adaptive to the tasks of later life. This life-span process is also modulated by factors and processes of social differentiation (Dannefer, 1984). Sooner or later in their lives, individuals are confronted with functional limits prohibiting maintenance of performance levels in the selected domains of specialization and advances into new domains of functioning.

In order to maintain high levels of performance the individual can use several strategies (Baltes & Baltes, 1990; Brandtstädter, 1989; Brim, 1988, 1992; Frey & Ruble, 1990). One option is to further narrow or transform the fields of mastery, thus sharpening the selectivity of resource investment and goal-oriented optimization. A second option is to increasingly refrain from new tasks of adaptation. The third option is to use compensatory strategies in order to maintain previous levels of performance or to be able to approach new tasks.

Hence, and as shown in Figure 3.1, life-span development can be seen as a process of selective optimization with compensation (Baltes & Baltes, 1990). This process is universal in its basic characteristics (selection, optimization, and compensation). Its phenotypic expression, however, is assumed to vary widely by individuals, periods of life, subgroups, and cultures. For the topic of the present chapter, it is also obvious that the processes involved comprise a close coordination between personality and intelligence.

Development in context: age-graded, history-graded, and non-normative influences and tasks

A fourth proposition in life-span theory deals with the search for an adequate taxonomy of the biological and contextual sources of life-span development (P. B. Baltes, 1987). A contextual view not only addresses the constraints and influences on gains and losses in select domains of functioning, it also characterizes the fact that contexts are not domain-specific. The influences and tasks of personality and intelligence are not part of independent streams. Rather, the major contexts of develop-

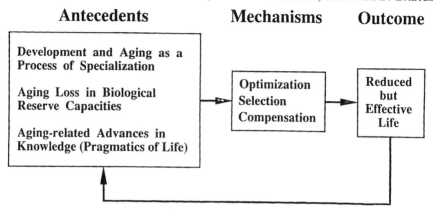

Figure 3.1. The ongoing life-span developmental dynamics of selective optimization with compensation (from Baltes & Baltes, 1990).

ment are likely to display correlated but not always synergistic impacts on personality and intelligence.

One example of this approach is the trifactor model which distinguishes between three kinds of biological and environmental influences and tasks: age-graded, history-graded, and non-normative (P. B. Baltes, 1987; P. B. Baltes, Reese, & Lipsitt, 1980; Riley, 1990). These sources of tasks and influences also show marked interindividual differences, by genetic and social conditions, such as social class and ethnicity (Dannefer, 1984; P. B. Baltes & Nesselroade, 1984).

Age-graded factors represent those specific biological features and social contexts that show much invariance in terms of occurrence and age sequencing, irrespective of membership to a certain birth cohort. History-graded influences are those biological and environmental factors that are ordered by historical time. In general, they are of two forms. The first is period-specific. For example, the impact of the fall of the Berlin Wall on Berlin residents vividly demonstrates how historical events can affect a society and thus life ecologies for individuals. A second concerns long-term processes of genetic and societal development. Major changes in fertility patterns, migration rates, historical changes in the legal system, work environments, health- and child-care systems, income conditions, and a host of other life domains can provide radically different contexts for life-span development of successive generations in a given society. This is illustrated by the existence of period and cohort effects in such areas as level of intellectual functioning (Schaie, 1983), length of life (Fries, 1990), or historical changes in fertility, work participation, and career patterns of women (Elder, 1985; Mayer, 1990).

The third category of influences, factors, and processes are non-normative, and also involve biological and environmental conditions. Their characteristic feature is that their occurrence, timing, and patterning is relatively unique (Brim & Ryff,

1980). For example, a major win in a lottery, a major inheritance, loss of a job, illness, or other sudden, unexpected life events would be considered non-normative contexts or constellations of development (Bandura, 1982).

A major challenge of life-span theory and research is the dynamic interaction between these three streams of influence and the "developmental goals and tasks of adaptation or mastery" resulting from their interaction. A comprehensive treatment of this topic is beyond the scope of this chapter.

In the present discussion, influences and tasks originating in the structure of the life course will receive greatest attention. Such structure is provided by age-graded opportunities and constraints, and by implication includes both the role of biological and environmental factors. In other words, how societies constitute the structure of the life course is the outcome of a particular constellation of what, at a given point in history, is biologically and environmentally possible, if not desirable. Thus, the life course is structured in an age-normative and age-sequential way.

Social institutions (e.g., the state and the educational system), consensual normative conceptions, as well as ontogenetic (including biological) factors, together provide a network of cornerstones and guidelines about age-related timing and proper sequencing of developmental events (Hagestad & Neugarten, 1985; Hagestad, 1990; Havighurst, 1952; J. Heckhausen, 1990; Mayer, 1986; Neugarten, Moore, & Lowe, 1965). School entry and timing of marriage, for example, are regulated by age norms provided by state law or consensual conceptions. Moreover, most higher careers involve certain pre-set sequences of education and employment, and most people continue to conceive of marriage preceding childbirth as more appropriate than childbirth preceding marriage. Finally, there are biological constraints on the timing of events as, for example, on childbearing, which for women can only occur during a specific age span. This fourth proposition on contextualism in life-span research and theory, then, offers further evidence for the conclusion that there is a close nexus in the ontogeny of personality and intelligence.

A life-span perspective on personality and intelligence

Contrary to the dominant perspectives of life-span theory and research, personality and intelligence theory and research have historically each followed, for the most part, their own separate tradition, focusing on their own set of variables (Heim, 1970). From a systemic perspective of life-span development, this dichotomy is largely a function of the pragmatics of research specialization involved in dealing with a complex set of interrelationships in human functioning, rather than based on theoretical distinctions between different biological, ontogenetic, or structural processes. In the next section, we will illustrate the life-span perspective for personality and intelligence separately, summarizing findings in each area to illustrate our lines of argument. In a closing section, we will attempt to highlight issues that are more central to the interface between personality and intelligence.

Stability and change in personality functioning

Much of the work in personality research concerned the degree to which personality changes or remains stable across the course of life (McCrae & Costa, 1984; Bengtson, Reedy, & Gordon, 1985). The evaluation of the evidence hinges on what criteria to accept (e.g., objective vs. subjective indicators), what aspect of change and stability is considered (e.g., level of functioning vs. rank order of inter- as well as intraindividual differences), what amount is seen as demonstration of stability vs. change, and whether the measures used are sensitive to change in the first place (Nesselroade, 1989).

We cannot deal with all these issues here. For the present purpose, we decided to focus on the recently emerging distinction between "concurrent" self-report data and those based on perception or attributions of life-span change. In general, when subjects are asked at a given age to describe themselves at that period in time, there is much evidence for developmental stability in level and rank order. When subjects, on the other hand, are asked to characterize processes of age change, there is more evidence for ontogenetic variance, at least in level of functioning.

Personality assessment at different ages. Evidence from personality assessment in longitudinal, cross-sectional, and cross-sequential research designs suggests that, on a global level, personality remains remarkably stable (Block, 1971, 1981; Costa & McCrae, 1980, 1985, 1988; Gough, 1987; Haan, Millsap, & Hartka, 1986; Leon, Gillum, Gillum, & Gouze, 1979; Schaie & Parham, 1976; Siegler, George, & Okun, 1979; Woodruff & Birren, 1972).

Costa and McCrae (1985, 1988; McCrae & Costa, 1984, 1987) for example, on the basis of longitudinal research on major dimensions of personality (i.e., neuroticism, extraversion, openness to experience, agreeableness, and conscientiousness) argued that there is little evidence to suggest major age-related differences in level and rank order (interindividual consistency). While this line of research is based on factor-analytically derived personality scales, some of the studies mentioned above, which use different assessments, have come to similar conclusions.

Stability was found not only with self-report measures, but also with respect to observers' judgments of functioning at a given age. For example, a study with adjective checklists in peer and spouse ratings over a 25-year span (Conley, 1985) indicated stable patterns. Using data from several extensive longitudinal studies, Block (1971) showed that data derived from observers' ratings of natural behavior and from self-report questionnaires displayed much consistency over long time spans. Correlations between personality characteristics over time ranged from −.51 to .76, with a mean of 7.30 for the entire sample.

Finally, ipsative stability, that is, the relative rank-ordering of personality aspects within persons, as assessed by means of the California Q-Sort (Block, 1978), is also impressive when correlates from junior high school to the mid-forties are considered for the Berkeley Growth Sample (Block, 1971, 1981). Single correlations that are not corrected for attenuation, for example, range between −.42 and .76 with a mean of .30 for a sample of 146 subjects on 90 personality variables. Given unreliability of measurement, these values could only be expected to be lower-bound estimates of true stability (Block, 1981). Taken together, with Costa and McCrae's (1985, 1988; Costa & McCrae, 1992) results, these findings do suggest that, on average in adults, close to half of the interindividual variance in trait-like measures is stable over fairly long age spans.

Aside from the counterpart fact that about half of the inter- and intraindividual variance in trait-like measures is subject to change (see also Brim & Kagan, 1980; Nesselroade, 1991), does this evidence suggest that people's "behavior" is also stable over age-contexts and developmental tasks, and that personality stability contradicts assumptions about development-related change? The answer is a complex one, but we will put forth a few arguments which buttress the view that a strong continuity position (as is suggested by Costa and his colleagues) is not the only conclusion to be drawn.

First, intraindividual personality stability on a molar level of analysis does not mean that behaviors across contexts and situations remain consistent (see also, e.g., Helson & Mitchell, 1978; Jackson & Paunonen, 1980; Mischel, 1977; Nesselroade, 1991). But it can mean that predictability or coherence may emerge in what appears to be different behavior at different times (Bowers, 1977; Endler, 1981; Kagan, 1980; Magnusson & Endler, 1977). This argument does not resolve the debate about qualitatively different stages of development versus continuity, but it can provide a perspective for thinking about different behavioral manifestations in different age contexts and at different periods during the life-span.

Second, when the focus of attention is shifted from a more "dispositional" perspective to a larger contextual view, the question becomes one of adaptability to changing age-graded, history-graded, and non-normative contexts. A life-span perspective that is sensitive to such influences and tasks suggests that development is best described and explained in a framework of "developmental contextualism" (Featherman & Lerner, 1985). An analysis of six global personality components (based on 73 individual characteristics) over a 50-year span with the Oakland Growth and Guidance samples supports contextual notions, suggesting that stability is to some extent a function of changing life contexts (Haan, Millsap, & Hartka, 1986). For example, while greatest individual stability and predictability was found for childhood and adolescent periods, the transition from adolescence to adulthood was the most unstable period, followed by the adult years.

Over and above an impressive degree of stability, the relative instability during adult years suggests that individuals adapt and change when faced with normative and non-normative experiences of serious consequence. In addition, some components of personality appear to be more stable than others. While the commitment to cognitive problem solving, dependability, and outgoingness, for example, were the most stable dimensions across the life course, self-confidence, warmth, and assertiveness were found to be more reactive to the hazards and opportunities of experience.

Third, there might be factors involved in subjective assessment of personality that promote a bias towards stability rather than change (Filipp & Klauer, 1986). There is some evidence, for example, that consistency of self-concept is preferred to inconsistency. Moreover, different reference frames for intra- versus interindividual assessment of change might be involved in apparent stability of personality. The latter issue will be discussed in greater detail in a later section.

Personality in life-span context. What is necessary, then, is a fuller exploration of the life-span contextualism or domain-relatedness argument. This can take two general forms. The first is a more explicit focus on questions of personality-related adaptive competence. The second is the search for personality processes and traits that reflect the unique task demands and growth perspectives of adulthood (e.g., Ryff, 1991). Neugarten and her co-workers (Neugarten, Moore, & Lowe, 1965) have proposed the notion of changing contexts that determine age-graded social and cultural appropriateness and timing of life events. A process of successful adaptation to age-graded life events, such as school entry, occupational transitions, or retirement, includes mastery of novel challenges as well as shaping one's environment so that it becomes suitable to the existing behavioral repertoire. Normative and non-normative events and contexts, to the extent that they influence personality functioning, can give direction to reorientation and potential growth.

Individuals differ in the degree to which they adapt successfully to such challenges (Caspi, Bem, & Elder, 1989; Elder, 1986; Liker & Elder, 1983), and in that sense personality dispositions shape and influence optimal development. Some specific insights on this point are provided by another study on an Oakland Growth and Guidance sample (Block, 1981). For men, for example, two distinct character and behavioral dispositions emerged, the "ego-resilient" and the "ego-controlled." Over a 35-year span, the ego-resilient group was characterized as well integrated, and exhibited a pattern of mastery of life's challenges, flexible adjustment, and independent thinking. They were described by others in glowingly positive terms, such as being dependable, productive, ambitious, bright, likable, poised, straightforward, sympathetic, introspective, warm, socially perceptive, and reasonably satisfied with themselves. This group appears to integrate challenges successfully and to react with resilience and flexibility to life transitions and events. In contrast, the ego-controlled group was less well adjusted.

Flexibility in personality style, especially in later life, appears to be another key variable not only for adjusting to changes in life contexts, but also for mental functioning (Schaie, 1984; Schaie, Dutta, & Willis, 1991). Those people who exhibit flexible attitudes and behaviors in mid-life, also showed greater maintenance of cognitive and intellectual functioning into old age. In addition, the degree to which people believe they are in control of their lives influences a positive outlook in general. Individuals who perceive themselves to be in greater control, also perceive turning points in their lives as more positive than those who are more anxious and depressed (Baltes & Baltes, 1986; George, 1978).

Subjective perception of personality change. Another avenue toward implementing a life-span contextual perspective in research on adult personality development is pursued by the stream of research that asks subjects to describe their view of age-related change (see Ahammer & P. B. Baltes, 1972; Ryff & P. B. Baltes, 1976; Woodruff & Birren, 1972; for precursor studies). When subjects of the same or of different ages are asked to describe their own past or future standing on personality traits, much larger age differences are obtained than when subjects at a given period in time are asked to describe themselves. This approach may best be illustrated by the work of Ryff and her colleagues (Ryff, 1982, 1984, 1991; Ryff & Heincke, 1983; Ryff & Migdal, 1984). A key part of their argument is that personality scales that were not designed on the basis of life-span theory may not be sensitive to aging issues. Following suggestions by Havighurst (1952) and Erikson (1959), and the view that there can be select growth into old age (P. B. Baltes, 1987), the Ryff group developed a battery of new measures of adult personality.

Employing dimensions based on adult developmental theory (i.e., Erikson, 1959; Neugarten, 1977), these investigators (Ryff, 1984; Ryff & Heincke, 1983) proposed a taxonomy of developmental personality scales, which are reproduced in Table 3.1. The generativity and integrity dimensions were drawn from Erikson's theory of psychosocial development, while the complexity and interiority dimensions were based on Neugarten's work (1973; see also Bühler, 1933; Jung, 1933). These dimensions figure prominently in middle-age and later life, with generativity and complexity viewed as key issues confronting middle-aged adults, and integrity and interiority as those important for older individuals. Generativity refers to having a sense of guidance and responsibility for the younger generation, and integrity highlights the successful integration of triumphs and disappointments of the past as meaningful and appropriate. Complexity emphasizes an active engagement in a multifaceted environment with multiple demands, while interiority describes a tendency towards turning inward with a lessening concern towards external environments and stimulation.

A comparison of young, middle-aged, and old individuals revealed interesting patterns in the expected direction with regard to self-perceptions of change on the dimensions complexity, generativity, integrity, and interiority. Generativity, for example, was rated as most prominent in midlife by all age groups, including anticipations by the young, the current assessments of the middle-aged, and the retrospective reports of the older individuals. Similarly, both middle-aged and old adults rated themselves as prospectively and currently higher in older age. At the same time, control scales considered not particularly pertinent to life-span issues (i.e., abasement, impulsivity, and order), did not reveal age-related differences. Thus it appears that dimensions which are meaningful in light of age-graded contexts do reflect reorientations in value systems and similar changes in psychosocial domains.

A related approach is research on subjective conceptions of life-span development. J. Heckhausen, Dixon, and P. B. Baltes (1989) investigated young, middle-aged, and old adults' normative (i.e., regarding "most other people") conceptions about devel-

Table 3.1. *Definitions of developmental personality scales (adapted from Ryff & Heincke, 1983)*

Scales	Definitions (Examples)
Complexity	
High scorer	Is actively engaged in a complex environment; involved in elaborate planning and scheduling of work and personal activities; feels in command and has a sense of growth and achievement in multiple spheres.
Low scorer	Feels bored and uninterested in daily routines; has empty time on hands; lacks a sense of growth or expansion; feels powerless in the face of a complex environment.
Generativity	
High scorer	Expresses concern in establishing and guiding the next generation; possesses awareness of responsibilities to children or those younger in age; views self as a norm-bearer and decision maker.
Low scorer	Views self as having little impact on others; shows little interest in sharing knowledge or experience with others; reveals excessive self-concern and self-preoccupation.
Integrity	
High scorer	Adapted to triumph and disappointments of being; accepts personal life as something that had to be; views past life as inevitable, appropriate, and meaningful; is emotionally integrated.
Low scorer	Fears death; has feelings of disgust and despair regarding past life; is concerned with shortness of remaining time; fails to accept previous life as meaningful and appropriate; disappointed with choice made.
Interiority	
High scorer	Is inward in orientation; invests less of self in outside life; freely relinquishes signs of external status and obligatory social roles; reflective; contemplative; more individuated and expressive.
Low scorer	Outward in orientation; emotionally invested in persons and events in external world; prefers interacting with others to being alone; avoids solitude; concerned with maintaining status in external world; unable to enjoy time with self.

opmental change throughout adulthood. Out of a large number of psychological attributes 41% were consensually perceived as change-sensitive, that is involving either life-span growth or decline. Adults at all three age levels also agreed on the age timing of developmental change in terms of onset and closing age. For more advanced age levels the expected gain–loss ratio increasingly shifted towards a predominance of losses. This pattern reflects a view of aging as decline, although some growth was expected throughout the life course, even in advanced old age. Moreover, desirable and late-life developmental changes were expected to be less controllable than desirable changes which predominate in earlier adulthood (J. Heckhausen & P. B. Baltes, 1991). The finding of decrease in perceived controllability at higher age levels converges with other research in this area (Brandtstädter, 1989).

Is this pattern of expected change and age-related shifts in the gain–loss ratio (P.

B. Baltes, 1987), which is found for normative conceptions about development, also reflected in developmental conceptions for the self? J. Heckhausen and Krueger (1993) compared self- and other-related conceptions about development, endorsed by the same adult subjects. Figure 3.2 gives ratings of expected change (increases and decreases) in desirable and undesirable attributes for seven decades of the adult life span (i.e., 20's, 30's, . . . , 80's) separately for the self and "most other people."

As can be seen in Figure 3.2, self-related and other-related conceptions about change were largely congruent. As expected from life-span theory on a shifting ratio between gains and losses, both for others and for the self, subjects expected fewer gains and an increasing number of losses at higher age levels. Only with regard to old age, self-related expectations were somewhat more optimistic than developmental prospects ascribed to "most other people" (a finding discussed in a section below). This study, thus, suggests that self- and other-related subjective conceptions about life-span development involve substantial change, and that this expected change is both systematic and consensual.

One possible explanation for the substantial consensus between individuals and the congruence in conceptions about developmental change between self and other would be that these subjective images simply reflect a nondifferentiated negative aging stereotype. This raises the question whether subjective conceptions about change also reflect multidimensionality and dimension-specific multidirectionality.

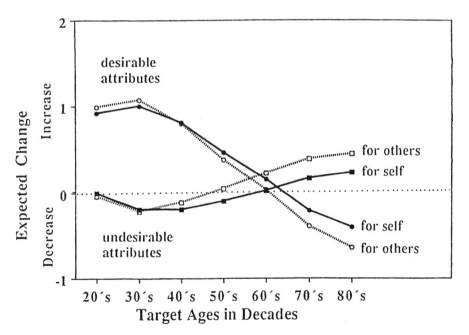

Figure 3.2. Developmental changes in desirable and undesirable attributes expected for the self and "most other people" across the adult life span (from J. Heckhausen & Krueger, 1993).

Krueger and J. Heckhausen (1993) investigated self-related developmental conceptions pertaining to psychological attributes associated with the Big Five personality
factors (Norman, 1963). The five panels of Figure 3.3 display perceived developmental change in desirable and undesirable aspects of the five personality dimensions: extraversion, agreeableness, conscientiousness, emotional stability, and intellectual functioning.

While a pattern of decreasing growth and increasing decline is found for most
dimensions, the specific trajectories reveal clear differences. Extraversion and intellectual functioning were associated with most change, and also most clearly
reflected the decline pattern. Desirable and undesirable aspects of agreeableness, in
contrast, reflected very little life-span change.

Self-report versus perception of age change: an integration.   These initial findings
suggest that the thrust of age-related findings on personality assessment based on
self-report and on expectations of change are far from similar. When subjects are
asked to indicate their perceptions of change (in themselves and in others), major age
differences emerge.

How can the apparent contradiction between assessed stability and "subjectively
perceived" change be resolved (P. B. Baltes, 1991)? One explanatory framework integrating findings from both concurrent self-reports and attributed change as
sources of evidence is the "shifting reference scale hypotheses" (J. Heckhausen & P.
B. Baltes, 1991; Krueger & J. Heckhausen, 1993; Ryff, 1991). In "objective" and
"subjective" assessments of change, people may employ different reference groups
on which to predicate their judgments. When, in trait-oriented ("objective") studies
of personality, people describe their psychological functioning at the current time, it
is reasonable to assume that the basis for those judgments is a reference group similar
to themselves in age (Harris & Associates, 1975, 1981; Schulz & Fritz, 1988). One
could argue, therefore, that the thrust of work such as that by Costa and McCrae
(1992) is dependent at least in part on the fact that a continuously shifting standard
of comparison (such that it always involves one's own age cohort) is stable. People's
ratings of themselves, relative to selected and continuously shifting reference groups,
might convey a picture of stability. (This does not imply, however, that the behaviors
themselves have the same property.)

A test of this "shifting-reference-scale hypothesis" is reported by Krueger and J.
Heckhausen (1993). In addition to asking the adult subjects to rate their beliefs about
change across the life span both for the self and for "most other people," ratings of
themselves at their current age were collected. If the shifting-reference-scale hypothesis is correct, ratings of perceived change should be congruent for self and other,
while cross-sectional comparisons of self-descriptions at various age levels should
indicate cross-age stability. This pattern of findings was actually discovered. While
all adults endorsed salient personality change both for self and most others, the same
adults' concurrent self-descriptions reflected cross-sectional stability in level.

In conclusion, as we consider the personality–intelligence interface during adult-

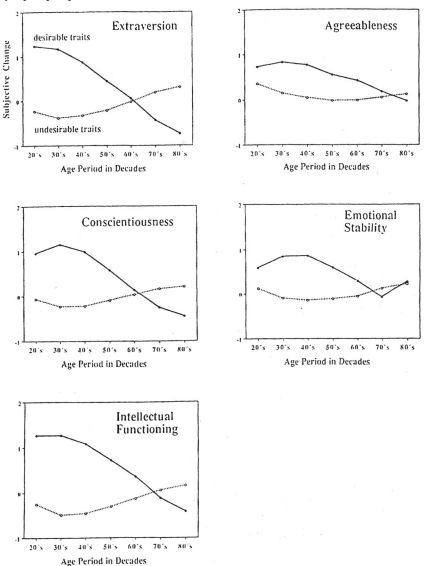

Figure 3.3. Expected developmental change for the self on desirable and undesirable attributes for the dimensions Extraversion, Agreeableness, Conscientiousness, Emotional Stability, and Intellectual Functioning across the adult life span (from Krueger & J. Heckhausen, 1993).

hood, it would be inappropriate to proceed from the dominant view that personality (its structure and level of functioning) is largely fixed by early adulthood and that investment of personality into the mastery of subsequent age periods is primarily the application of that foundation. Certainly, there is some continuity in personality dispositions, especially if measured by concurrent self-report. The acknowledgement, for instance, that personality dispositions such as ego strength, ego investment, and flexibility are facilitative of continued adaptive competence illustrates this view.

However, recent research has added to this picture a view that highlights two perspectives. First, as shown by the work of Ryff and her colleagues, there is a need to translate life-span contextualism and life-span growth models into a new set of personality constructs. Second, as shown by research on subjective conceptions and perceptions of change, there is definite evidence for major and systematic life-span changes even in personality traits that are generally found to be stable under conditions of self-report. The challenge for these newly emerging research lines is to establish their predictive validity and usefulness, including that for the study of the personality-intelligence interface.

Gains and losses in cognition and intelligence

In our evaluation, the evidence on adult intelligence and cognitive aging provides a clearer picture than that for the area of personality. When traditional measures of psychometric intelligence are used (e.g., Schaie, 1983), there is (perhaps even more so than is true for personality traits) much interindividual stability in rank order, and high measurement invariance across 14–21 years of longitudinal observation (Hertzog & Schaie, 1988). Also, there is systematic evidence on age trends (Salthouse, 1991).

A special emphasis in research on cognitive aging is the importance of making a clear distinction between average level of functioning and potential or range (plasticity) of functioning. It has become increasingly recognized that in order to attain a comprehensive picture of the aging mind it is necessary to study both interindividual variability and intraindividual plasticity, including their age-associated changes. For example, despite sizeable plasticity there is definite evidence that in those facets of the aging mind that are essentially instantiations of biologically based speed and accuracy of information processing, there is an age-correlated loss in functioning. If there are advances in functioning, these are restricted to specific domains in which old age harbors special knowledge-based opportunities. The study of and research for possible advances need to be based on a contextual and functionalist conception of intelligence (Berg & Sternberg, 1985; Dittmann-Kohli & P. B. Baltes, 1990; Dixon & Baltes, 1986; Sternberg & Detterman, 1986).

Multidimensionality and multidirectionality. The perhaps best-known case for multidimensional and multidirectional life-span change is the dual process model of fluid and crystallized intelligence, originally proposed by Cattell and Horn (Cattell, 1971; Horn, 1982). An analogous conception of the fluid "mechanics" and crystallized and knowledge-based "pragmatics" of intelligence, respectively, was introduced subsequently (P. B. Baltes, 1993; P.B. Baltes, Dittmann-Kohli, & Dixon, 1984). The fluid mechanics of intelligence (perhaps comparable to the idea of mental hardware) refer to basic processing operations, such as sensory-information input, motor and visual memory, and elementary processes of categorization and discrimination. In contrast, the pragmatics of intelligence (perhaps comparable to mental software) include the content-rich, culturally shared, and practical aspects of knowledge, as well as those idiosyncratic bodies of procedural and factual knowledge accumulated by the individual during his/her life. It is in the domain of cognitive pragmatics, then, where contextual and cultural characteristics of intelligence are paramount (Dittmann-Kohli & P. B. Baltes, 1990; Staudinger, Smith, & P. B. Baltes, 1992; Sternberg, 1986). Any intellectual activity is assumed to be a joint function of both.

The life-span perspective proposes that the developmental trajectories for the two major categories of the mind are dramatically different. This conclusion is based on theoretical and empirical grounds. Theoretically, the argument is that the fluid mechanics of intelligence are primarily regulated by biological–genetic factors. Because the biology of aging involves essentially an age-associated loss in functioning, the life-span trajectory for intelligence mechanics reflects an increase during childhood and adolescence, stability through young adulthood, and decline during middle adulthood and old age (see Figure 3.4). Conversely, because the crystallized prag-

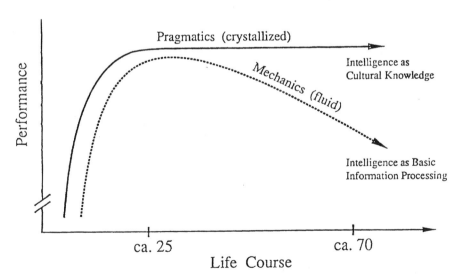

Figure 3.4.   Idealized model of the developmental trajectories of mechanics and pragmatics in intellectual functioning (after P. B. Baltes, 1987).

matics of intelligence are assumed to be based primarily on culture and its associated bodies of factual and procedural knowledge, their theoretical life-span trajectory should be reflective of how societies allocate knowledge-based resources, skills, and practice to people across the life span. An idealistic conception of societal functioning would suggest that the pragmatics of intelligence, under favorable conditions (health and life experiences), can be expected to be maintained late into adulthood or undergo even select advances up into old age (Alexander & Langer, 1990; P. B. Baltes, 1993; Featherman, Smith, & Peterson, 1990; Labouvie-Vief, 1985; Staudinger, Smith, & P. B. Baltes, 1992). Examples of possible areas of peak functioning are professional experience, social intelligence, and wisdom (Sternberg, 1990).

This general theoretical scenario finds some support in empirical work. Historically, the first evidence was the distinction between nonverbal (fluid) and verbal measures. Since, age-comparative studies have consistently found a marked age decline in measures of fluid intelligence (Salthouse, 1986, 1991). In tests of crystallized, pragmatic intelligence (such as in tasks of vocabulary or wisdom), older healthy adults (up to age 70 or so) show no or little decline and can be in the top range of performers. Also, in tests of professional expertise and wisdom, older adults can function in the top range (Smith, Staudinger, & Baltes, in press; Staudinger, Smith, & P. B. Baltes, 1992). How long in the life course, and in how many facets of cognitive pragmatics older adults can possibly function in top ranges, however, is unknown and subject to much current research.

Toward the study of the range of plasticity. In addition to this general differential pattern, the life-span approach also asserts that the study of "descriptive" age functioning is but part of the story. An added consideration is the exploration of latent potential. In fact, cognitive training research has demonstrated that there is substantial developmental plasticity, that is, intraindividual variability and modifiability in developmental change (P. B. Baltes & Willis, 1982; Keil, 1981; Kliegl, Smith, & P. B. Baltes, 1990; Lerner, 1984; Willis, 1987). In fact, such plasticity was demonstrated with regard to diverse aspects of the mechanics of intelligence, such as figural reasoning, inductive reasoning, or memory for words (serial learning), for example (P. B. Baltes & Lindenberger, 1988; Kliegl, Smith, & P. B. Baltes, 1990; Schaie & Willis, 1991). Following training, older subjects were able to improve their performance up to levels of young adults' normal functioning without training (Schaie & Willis, 1991). Does this imply unlimited plasticity in cognitive functioning, or are there functional limits to developmental reserve capacity which eventually do distinguish between young and old adults? The theoretical rationale for intelligence mechanics and their close association with biological–genetic factors as well as the empirical evidence on age decline in fluid intelligence would suggest that this is not so.

Indeed, cognitive-training research – especially when considered in the framework of a peak-performance approach – has identified definite age losses in the mechanics of the mind. One approach which systematically examines the boundaries of cognitive plasticity is known as the "testing-the-limits" paradigm (P. B. Baltes, 1987, 1993; M. M. Baltes & Kindermann, 1985; Coper, Jänicke, & Schulze, 1986; Kliegl & P. B. Baltes, 1987; Kliegl, Mayr, & Krampe, in press; Wiedl, 1984). Cognitive-training research on the fluid mechanics and its upper boundaries shows that developmental differences are most pronounced near maximum levels of performance and after extended periods of practice (P. B. Baltes & Kliegl, 1992; Carlson & Wiedl, 1980; Kliegl, Smith, & P. B. Baltes, 1989, 1990; Wiedl, 1984). When the research focus is the search for the upper limits of performance potential in cognitive mechanics (i.e., fluid intelligence), negative age differences are maximized to such a degree that there are few if any older adults who can function near the average of young adults in tests of fluid mechanics. The primary component processes accounting for the aging loss seems to involve a reduction in speed and in accuracy of working-memory processing (P. B. Baltes & Kliegl, 1986; Kliegl, Mayr, & Krampe, in press; Mayr & Kliegl, in press).

Aging-related decline in basic processes of intellectual functioning confronts the individual with the need to compensate when requisite cognitive resources decline. Compensation can be achieved by several different types of strategies: increased selectivity of effort, time investment, and task-specific compensatory pursuits (Bäckman & Dixon, 1992; Baltes & Baltes, 1990). While cognitive-training research demonstrates the effectiveness and limits of increasing effort and time, studies on naturally acquired expertise demonstrate the functioning of task-specific compensation (Ericsson & Smith, 1991). Salthouse (1984, 1991), for instance, was able to show that older expert typists can compensate for loss of speed by reading farther ahead in the text to be typed, and by planning for things to come in advance, in order to maintain performance levels comparable to those of their younger colleagues.

These examples of naturally or professionally acquired expertise demonstrate in an indirect manner the role of personality and motivational factors in achieving and maintaining peak performance. As proffered by Sternberg's (1985) triarchic theory of intelligence and made most explicit in life-history research on expertise (Ericsson, 1990), the mechanics of cognition are only part of the process. For levels of performance to reach levels of expertise, an ensemble of other performance factors are required to guarantee the sizeable effort that is required. In experts, intelligence and personality contexts are bound to form a coalition of synergistic forces.

Crystallized pragmatics. The focus on the coalition between intelligence, personality, and life-span contexts becomes most conspicuous with regard to the crystallized pragmatics of intelligence. As mentioned before, the life-span developmental approach proposes that despite aging losses in the mechanics there can be practice- and experience-based increases in some bodies of knowledge, both quantitatively and qualitatively (Alexander & Langer, 1990; P. B. Baltes, 1987; P. B. Baltes, Dittmann-Kohli & Dixon, 1984; Labouvie-Vief, 1981, 1985; Sternberg, 1990). A prototypical example of knowledge-based expertise attainable in late life is wisdom (P. B. Baltes

& Smith, 1990; Baltes & Staudinger, 1993; Sternberg, 1990) which will be discussed in more detail below. Qualitative shifts in the cognitive domain in later life have received increased attention in recent years (c.f., Perlmutter, 1988), and experience-based perspectives on cognition in later life are beginning to demonstrate stability and possible growth in select domains such as social, emotional, and practical aspects of intelligence (e.g., Blanchard-Fields, 1986; Cornelius & Caspi, 1987; Denney, 1984; Staudinger, Smith, & P. B. Baltes, 1992). A functional approach to cognitive development has also taken increases in life-knowledge aspects into consideration in discussions of life review and reminiscence (Butler, 1963; Staudinger, 1989), and autobiographical memory (e.g., Berger, 1963; Molinari & Reichlin, 1985). A further example is professional knowledge or artistic potential (Charness, 1985; Ericsson & Smith, 1991; Simonton, 1988).

A systemic approach to development in general and specifically late-life performance requires integration of the two traditionally separate areas of cognition and personality. The study of cognitive performance across the life span now pays increased attention to life contexts in which such performance occurs (e.g., Cornelius & Caspi, 1987; Dixon & P. B. Baltes, 1986; Sternberg, 1985; Sternberg & Berg, 1986). Taking social, affective, practical, and everyday life contexts into consideration, intellectual competence itself has thus undergone redefinition. Intelligence is not only a multidimensional system. Its contexts and ensemble of solution strategies are likely to undergo changes as well.

A focus on contextual demands and a dynamic perspective involving the interacting subcomponents of intelligence can, thus, complement a comprehensive analysis of functioning. The life-span system of intellectual change is a complex process with (1) differing trajectories, (2) biologically determined losses in the range of plasticity of the mechanics of the mind, (3) the need for recomposition or even new development of skills to permit compensation, (4) attention to new tasks, contexts, and opportunities (age-graded, history-graded, and non-normative) associated with the structure of the adult life course, and (5) the opportunity for growth in those domains, such as wisdom, where living longer may have an advantage and where knowledge can compensate for decline in intelligence mechanics.

Such a dynamic scenario involving the mechanics and pragmatics of the mind is a major challenge for human functioning. As individuals attempt, for instance, to manage their changing gain/loss ratio, personality characteristics such as traits and values are important.

A life-span approach to the personality–intelligence interface

In the last part of this chapter we will examine the set of conditions that are relevant for how the personality–intelligence dynamic operates across life with a particular focus on adulthood and old age. The emphasis chosen is on how individuals' representations of life-span reality and action resources guide and mediate whether and to what extent they are able to activate their potential and achieve desired levels of functioning. In the context of the four life-span propositions described earlier, this topical focus permits us to highlight some issues at the interface of personality and intelligence. First, we will examine some principles and empirical findings in the belief system surrounding motivation, which can enhance or impede a person's aspiration to achieve a personal optimum level of functioning. Second, we will consider the importance of beliefs about control over resources and one's own efficacy for actual performance. Third, we will examine some select strategies for maintaining a positive self-image despite age-associated losses. Last, the sample case of wisdom will be used as an illustration for a social prototype of successful aging integrating personality and intellectual functioning.

Motivation: aspiration to achieve personal optimum

The degree to which an individual's ability and potential are manifested in performance hinges on the motivation to achieve high standards in the respective domain. High levels of motivation promote a process of selective optimization in the chosen domain of functioning, which implies that personal resources (e.g., effort, time, finances, and social support) are selectively invested and refined in a given domain at the expense of other nonchosen domains. Research demonstrates that selective investment, as for example in artistic or athletic careers, promotes high performance levels (Ericsson & Smith, 1991), but at the same time brings with it the danger of reduced flexibility for goal adjustment (Raynor, 1980).

Moreover, increasingly unfavorable gain–loss ratios in cognitive and physical domains, as well as changing contextual demands at different life stages, call for compensatory efforts in domains considered particularly relevant for the self. Such compensation can be achieved, for instance, by sharpening the selective investment of effort and other personal resources in particular chosen goals. Selecting a viable goal in favor of other less attractive and more difficult ones, or not selecting unrealistic goals in light of one's reserve capacities and opportunities can thus be one strategy to maximize one's potential in spite of aging-related loss.

Aspiring to peak performances or one's personal "optimum" across the life span requires the *anticipation* of increasing and decreasing opportunities and constraints in middle-range and long-term developmental and life planning. Most individuals attempt to exert personal control over their own development (Brandtstädter, 1984, 1986, 1989; Brandtstädter & Renner, 1990). Which developmental goals and projects are selected for which period of the life span will depend on the individual's beliefs about the feasibility of attaining these goals at the respective age period (J. Heckhausen, 1989).

Research on normative conceptions about development and the life course has demonstrated, however, that there is a high level of consensus with regard to the nature and timing of life-span changes (J. Heckhausen & P. B. Baltes, 1991; J. Heckhausen et al., 1989). Young, middle-aged, and old adults share ideas about which developmental gains and losses typically occur in a given period during the life span for a great variety of psychological dimensions and about their controllability. Until very old age, on the whole, expected gains outnumber perceived losses. Even in very old age, a small number of gains are expected. The later in life developmental changes are expected the less desirable and less controllable they are perceived to be (Brandtstädter, 1986; J. Heckhausen & P. B. Baltes, 1991). Thus, whatever their age, individuals anticipate fewer opportunities for intentionally regulating development for later periods of the life span. Selection of appropriate goals at a given life period is only one adaptive strategy for optimization of potential.

A second issue is that, after a particular goal has been chosen, it is necessary to set one's aspiration level within an appropriate range of what can be achieved (Bandura, 1990; Sternberg & Kolligian, 1990). Severe over- or underestimation would seem less optimal since excessive or insufficient effort might be expended to achieve the chosen goal. Thus, a reasonable degree of "accuracy" of perceptions about one's own ability is critical. However, it has been suggested that normal as opposed to depressed individuals usually overestimate their capacities and the likelihood of success in future action (e.g., Alloy & Abramson, 1979). Taylor characterizes such "positive illusions" as "creative self-deceptions of the healthy mind," and regards them as prerequisites of normal mental functioning (Taylor, 1989). In convergence with this view, achievement-motivation research has demonstrated that aspiration levels slightly above the previous performance are most frequently selected by success-motivated individuals, and are most conducive to performance improvements (H. Heckhausen, 1991).

Indeed, in the context of the processes of acquisition and development, moderate overestimations of one's own performance potential might be particularly appropriate. Strictly realistic conceptions and aspirations would, in fact, probably hinder developmental progress and the utilization of reserve capacity.

Consideration of three aspects of reserve capacity, which have been addressed in the context of cognitive-plasticity research (P. B. Baltes, 1987; Kliegl & P. B. Baltes, 1987), may be helpful in understanding the impact of beliefs about potential on subsequent behavior and development. First, *current reserve capacity* designates the highest previously attained level of performance and demarcates the limits of performance potential under presently optimal conditions. Second, *current learning-reserve capacity* affords a wide range of potential improvement in the course of the acquisition processes (Brown & French, 1979; Ferrara, Brown, & Campione, 1986; Guthke, 1982). Finally, *developmental reserve capacity* (P. B. Baltes, 1987; Kliegl & P. B. Baltes, 1987), with its focus on future conditions of optimization, opens an even wider range of potential improvement (or decrement) of performance. The degree to which individuals hold proper or unrealistic beliefs about their current or future levels of reserve capacities, has a major impact on their initiation of development-enhancing behavior.

In the first half of life, the general pattern of beliefs most likely is oriented toward enhancement. During life-span periods of rapid developmental growth, such as in early childhood, new motor skills and mental capacities become accessible within brief intervals of time because of processes of physical growth and new environmental opportunities. This fact is part of our general belief about this age period. Thus, substantial overestimation of one's own competence is likely to turn out to be a realistic forecast of imminent developmental gains. In contrast, during later life-span periods, such as in advanced old age, the evidence is less clear. In general, there is a critical attitude toward the widely held negative age bias because it may suggest less reserve capacity than is available. At the same time, the general developmental directionality of capacity reserves described earlier calls for more cautious and even decreasing levels of aspiration. What was possible today may be out of reach tomorrow. Thus, in very old age expectations about one's performance must continuously be adjusted downward and below previous performance levels. In this manner, aspirations to achieve one's personal optimum need to reflect age-related shifts in developmental opportunities and constraints without, however, reaching into levels that are below one's actual capacity reserves.

With increasing age the expected scope of self-initiated developmental plasticity wanes (J. Heckhausen & P. B. Baltes, 1991; J. Heckhausen et al., 1989). When the scope of direct or primary control (Rothbaum, Weisz, & Snyder, 1982) over development is reduced, how does the individual cope with impending aging-related losses? A set of "secondary control" strategies directed at the inner mental world of the self (e.g., emotions, goals, self-evaluations, and causal attributions) are probably crucial for maintaining a sense of control and a positive self-image (J. Heckhausen & Schulz, 1993; Schulz, J. Heckhausen, & Locher, 1991).

Beliefs about personal control

People's beliefs about their own competence and effectiveness have implications for present performance and the direction of future development. Self-efficacy and control beliefs in particular are important mediators between ability and performance (Baltes & Baltes, 1986; Bandura, 1977, 1982, 1990; Sternberg & Kolligian, 1990). People's beliefs about their own effectiveness influence their choice of activities, the amount of effort they expend, and their persistence on tasks. These factors in turn, mediate specific task performance. Thus, a sense of agency and self-efficacy is crucial for whether individuals can change their level of performance towards maximizing their true potential. Individuals with similar potentials may evidence differences in performance because they differ in beliefs about what they are able to achieve.

Role of life-span contexts and domains.   Life-span research on control beliefs (Baltes & Baltes, 1986; Fry, 1988) suggests several lines of investigation. For example, because of changes in the contexts and tasks of life and changes in their cognitive representation, it is necessary to consider the possibility that categorizations of the attributed causes for phenomena may change (Dittmann-Kohli, in press). Furthermore, as life unfolds, it is increasingly necessary to pay particular attention to multidimensionality and multidirectionality in development. Research by Lachman

(1986a) is a good illustration. College students and elderly adults were compared cross-sectionally on Levenson's multidimensional (internal, powerful others, and chance) locus-of-control measure (Levenson, 1973) separately for three domains of functioning: health, intelligence, and generalized. While there were no age differences with regard to the generalized measures, control beliefs for the intelligence and health domains showed age trends. Old adults exhibited higher external control beliefs in both domains than their young counterparts (Lachman, 1986b, 1991). In addition, those older adults with external control attributions also showed poorer performance on intelligence measures than those with internal control orientations. This pattern of findings was partially replicated by a five year longitudinal study of elderly persons (Lachman & Leff, 1989), and is consistent with work by Reker, Peacock, and Wong (1987).

Overall, Lachman's research suggests that generalized measures of control beliefs may be insensitive to age-related differences, and domain-specific measurement instruments need to be developed (Lachman, 1986b). A recent study lends further support to this argument (Lachman, 1991). It addressed domain-specific age differences and the finding was that control beliefs did not differ for three age groups (young, middle, and old adults) for the interpersonal or political domains, but, as in earlier work, age differences did emerge for the domains of health and intellectual aging. For example, older adults had lower internal control and higher external control beliefs than young and middle-aged adults, particularly with regard to beliefs about memory performance.

Agency (efficacy) and means–ends (causality) beliefs. Beliefs about causal agency and causal mechanisms of control would thus seem to be critical mediators, not only for selection of goals and effort investment, but also for choosing compensatory strategies for perceived losses. In recognition that beliefs about personal control over resources would hinge on specific attributions, a further distinction was introduced in terms of "self-agency" and "means-ends" beliefs as two conceptually orthogonal components of control beliefs (Skinner, Chapman, & P. B. Baltes, 1988). Means–ends beliefs are beliefs about causality and controllability in general; that is, which factors and causes are held by individuals to be relevant to which outcomes, irrespective of who is the agent. In contrast, efficacy and self-agency beliefs address the question about personal access to outcome-producing means and resources. The importance of this distinction has been demonstrated with research on children. For example, in the intelligence domain self-agency (efficacy) more than means–ends beliefs mediate performance. Whether and to what degree individuals attribute to themselves personal agency with regard to effort, ability, change, or powerful others is related to objective achievement (Levenson, 1974; Oettingen, Little, Lindenberger, & P. B. Baltes, in press; Paulhus, 1983; Skinner, Chapman, & P. B. Baltes, 1988).

Children who think they have personal access to various causal factors (e.g., ability and luck) involved in school performance attain higher school grades than those who perceive less personal agency (Oettingen, Little, Lindenberger, & P. B. Baltes, in press). This model has not been employed in research with adults, but because of the high degree of similarity between efficacy and agency beliefs, research on those topics (e.g., Baltes & Baltes, 1986; Bandura, 1990; Sternberg & Kolligian, 1990) can be assumed to indicate related processes. The pioneering work of Rodin and Langer (1980), and many subsequent studies, suggest that the impact of these efficacy and control-related phenomena is important in research on adult development and old age. The aging-research program by Lachman (1983, 1986a, 1986b, 1991) is especially interesting. Lachman's (1986b) results, for example, show that internal and generalized beliefs (i.e., those about ability and means–ends beliefs) remain relatively stable. Beliefs about access to external resources and self-agency, however, may change with changing contingencies across the life span. Older adults may correctly perceive greater limitations on internal (e.g., physical) resources, but adapt effectively by placing greater weight on the development of external resources. Successfully dealing with greater physical frailty, for example, can mean developing greater knowledge about good medical support and how best to access existing supportive institutions. Similarly, successful older managers develop support structures in personnel organization such that responsibilities can be delegated to younger co-workers without the sense of loss of personal control (e.g., Klemp & McClelland, 1986).

That control-and agency-related beliefs are paramount in the second half of life is also supported by data mentioned earlier. J. Heckhausen and P. B. Baltes (1991) identified a life-span script of age-related decrease in controllability of those phenomena that subjects perceive as undergoing aging-related decline. In general, therefore, older adults can be expected to have to deal with tasks of adaptation, for which expected controllability is much reduced. Therefore, it seems reasonable that this age-associated context of reduced controllability is a risk factor and that generally observed relationships in research on efficacy, control, and agency (e.g., Bandura, 1990) increase in importance. For example, individuals who believe that a perceived cognitive loss is subject to personal control are more likely to attempt remedial efforts in an attempt to compensate. Similarly, the individual with a high self-estimate of ability is likely to use more effort and to be less distracted by feelings of self-doubt, while the reverse is true for the person with a low estimate of ability. In addition, a declining sense of efficacy may result in individuals' curtailing specific activities (Bandura, 1981; Kuypers & Bengtson, 1973), which then, for lack of practice, may result in actual decline of performance as well as in loss of motivation. Because of the increase in incidents of decline and the fact that, on average, old-age change events are expected to be less controllable than life-span change in earlier periods of life, research on the interface between cognitive performance and control- and action-related beliefs has attracted much attention in recent work. Such research, for instance, has demonstrated that beliefs about one's own competence are important for understanding cognitive performance in older adults on a variety of tasks (e.g., Cavanaugh & Green, 1990; West & Graziano, 1989; Hertzog, Dixon, & Hultsch, 1990).

Compensatory strategies for maintaining a positive self-image

In the previous two sections we have shown how individuals can strive for peak performances including their personal optimum, but also have to acknowledge age-related constraints in functioning, especially at later stages in the life span. The next question to be considered is how an aging individual can maintain and foster a stable and positive self-image despite inevitable decline.

One of the most striking findings in aging research is that in spite of aging-related decline, subjective well-being and self-esteem (P. B. Baltes, 1991; Bengtson, Reedy, & Gordon, 1985; Blazer, 1989; Brandtstädter & Greve, in press; Filipp & Klauer, 1986), as well as general beliefs about personal control (Lachman, 1986b; Lachman & Leff, 1989), on average, remain stable and fairly positive throughout the life span. This finding is puzzling because radical aging-related decline would lead one to expect corresponding negative shifts in self-esteem and subjective well-being. It is less puzzling, however, when, in addition to selection mechanisms, specific self-regulatory mechanisms are interpreted as compensatory. We will examine three strategies of personal adjustment in this context, which appear to serve the purpose of compensation for experienced loss and anticipated decline: adjustments of aspiration level, adjustment of goal hierarchy, and strategic social comparison (Baltes & Baltes, 1990; Brim, 1988, 1992; J. Heckhausen & Schulz, 1993, Lawton, 1989). These strategies can also be viewed as part of the ensemble of mechanisms associated with selective optimization with compensation (see above).

Adjustments of aspiration level. When coping with aging-related loss, levels of aspiration have to be lowered in order to be functional. A strategy optimally suited for avoiding disappointment would not only involve adjustment in response to experienced losses, but also in anticipation of expected future decline. Such a strategy can, however, easily overshoot its goal and lead to relinquishment of control and dependent behavior. Observational research in caregiving institutions for the elderly, for instance, demonstrates that the process of negative adjustments of aspirations for independence is enhanced by corresponding dependency-reinforcing behavior of the social environment such as professional caregivers (M. M. Baltes, 1988, in press; M. M. Baltes & Wahl, 1987; M. M. Baltes, Wahl, & Reichert, 1991).

Adjustment of aspiration level, however, may often not be sufficient to deal with the realization that some goals are no longer attainable. Developmental goals, for instance, may simply move out of reach, unless they are attained at a certain age. Thus, it is functional for the individual to disengage from these goals and pursue others (Klinger, 1975), thereby redefining goals and adjusting the goal hierarchy.

Adjusting and transforming goals and the goal hierarchy

A second general strategy is to identify new goals and reorganizing goal hierarchies (Brim, 1992). The identification of new goals is, of course, part and parcel of the notion of developmental tasks and developmental transitions. If properly constituted by society, old age includes new goals (e.g., in retirement) that are attainable. Another related strategy involves adjustments within a framework of generally or personally accepted structures, when resources become limited. Brandtstädter and Renner (1990) have addressed this process in their distinction between assimilative and accommodative coping. While assimilative coping attempts to adjust "life circumstances to personal preferences," accommodative coping adapts "personal preferences and goal orientations to given situational forces and constraints" (Brandtstädter & Renner, 1990, p. 58). These investigators developed a measurement instrument for capturing assimilative coping as a tendency for tenacious goal pursuit, and accommodative coping as a tendency to flexibly adjust one's goals.

In a large cross-sectional study of 34–63-year-old adults, tenacious goal pursuit was found to gradually decrease across middle adulthood, while flexible goal adjustment exhibited a marked increase during the same age period (Brandtstädter & Renner, 1990). Both tendencies were positively related to subjective well-being, perceived attainment of developmental goals, and positive outlook on one's future development. In addition however, flexible goal adjustment substantially moderated the detrimental effect of unattained developmental goals on life satisfaction. Those adults who were willing to flexibly adjust their life goals to developmental circumstances were more satisfied than those who did not.

Strategic social comparison. Another strategy for buffering negative effects of uncontrollable aging-related losses on one's self-image is strategic social comparison, including age-based "handicapping" (Brim, 1992). Developmental decline appears less threatening for the self-image if evaluated in the context of "downward social comparison" (Wills, 1981; Wood, 1989). In situations that are severely threatening to one's self-esteem, comparing oneself to those who are even worse off can enhance self-esteem. "Downward social comparison" (Wills, 1981) was found to be a common response to threats on self-esteem, as in severe disability (Schulz & Decker, 1985), illness (Taylor & Lobel, 1989; Taylor, Wood, & Lichtman, 1984), and crime-victimization (Burgess & Holmstrom, 1979).

When age is conceived as a potential threat to positive self-image, strategic downward comparison might serve a similar purpose (Schulz & Fritz, 1988). Large U.S. cross-national surveys support this assumption; older adults hold much more positive views about their own life circumstances, health, and subjective well-being than they attribute to most other old people (Harris & Associates, 1975, 1981). J. Heckhausen and Krueger (1993; J. Heckhausen, 1992) compared self-related conceptions about adult development with conceptions about most other people's development. While self- and other-related expected trajectories were congruent for young and middle adulthood, expectations for old age diverged. Expectations for the self in old age included less decline and more growth when compared to expectations for "most other people." This self-enhancing pattern of expectations was especially pronounced in the old adults, who presumably are most imminently threatened by aging-related decline.

These findings are in accordance with O'Gorman's (1980) domain-specific analysis of national survey data (Harris & Associates, 1975, 1981) which uncovered a characteristic pattern of social comparative strategies. The worse off a respondent was with regard to a particular domain (e.g., health, financial problems, or loneliness), the more negative was his image of most other old people's situation in this respect. Paradoxical as it may seem, negative aging stereotypes appear to serve an adaptive function in buffering old people's self-image by providing a negatively contrasting social reference frame. Compared to the downgraded reference group of most other old people, elderly individuals perceive themselves as positive exceptions who have come up against the stream of aging (see review in J. Heckhausen, 1990; Thomas, 1981).

Wisdom as a sample case

In this last section we would like to consider a specific example, namely wisdom, as an illustration for a prototype of "mindful personality functioning," which can serve as a guidepost of successful aging for individual development (P. B. Baltes & Smith, 1990; Baltes & Staudinger, 1993). Wisdom is well suited for this purpose for a number of reasons.

First, wisdom appears to be one of the few positive attributes associated with later life, and therefore can provide a positive and desirable goal one can aspire to achieve. While in early and middle adulthood positive attributes abound, lay people believe that positive characteristics associated with later life are few and far between. In a study of naive theories of aging involving more than 100 personality attributes, only "wise" and "dignified" were both associated with a later-life phase and regarded as highly desirable characteristics (J. Heckhausen et al., 1989), as shown in Figure 3.5.

Approaching or achieving the goal of being "wise" or "dignified," however, may not easily be possible, let alone by many. It could be that what people have in mind when they talk about wisdom is in fact an idealized version of reality, and in that sense may be a true prototype in the Roschian sense (Rosch, 1978). The actual value of such an ideal virtue could be that it sets an aspiration level towards which people can strive to reach their own personal optimum. With such motivation, a given individual might reach greater intellectual and personal maturity. The scientific study of wisdom may serve a similar purpose. While it is possible that a definitive answer may never be achieved, in the course of studying an ideal aspect of late-life growth, some important forms of potentials and accomplishments might be uncovered (Maciel & Staudinger, in press).

Second, the study of wisdom appears to provide one framework for an integrative approach to cognition and personality from a life-span perspective in that it transcends traditional paradigmatic boundaries. While the study of lay conceptions about wisdom has contributed to an understanding of the content of the category, scientific theories have also considered developmental processes. Studies of naive and formal theories will be briefly considered in turn.

Systematic examination of what the common folk believe to be essential characteristics of wisdom has proceeded in two ways. One was to study the internal structure of the category and to distill its major components (Brent & Watson, 1980; Clayton

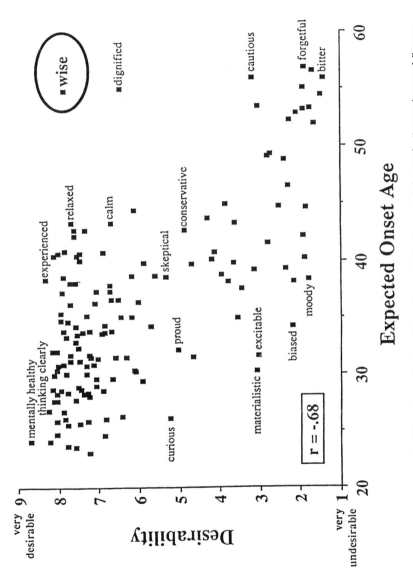

Figure 3.5. Desirability and perceived age timing of expected developmental changes for "most other people" across the adult life span (from J. Heckhausen, Dixon, & P. B. Baltes, 1989).

& Birren, 1980; Maciel, Sowarka, Smith, & P. B. Baltes, 1993; Sowarka, 1989), and the other was to demarcate overlapping attributes such as *"wise," "intelligent," "creative," "perceptive," "shrewd,"* and *"spiritual"* (Chandler & Holliday, 1990; Holliday & Chandler, 1986; Sternberg, 1986). The former studies showed that the internal structure of this domain comprises a unique blend of cognitive, interpersonal, social, and personality attributes as illustrated in Table 3.2. The latter approach showed that the concept of wisdom is unique in the sense that its features do not fully overlap with "creativity," "old age," or "intelligence," and that it represents constraints akin to a conceptual prototype (Rosch, 1978).

Approaches to wisdom have emerged from both personality and cognitive traditions, and tend to emphasize either personality (e.g., Erikson, 1959; Kohut, 1977; Jung, 1953; Orwoll & Perlmutter, 1990) or cognitive and knowledge aspects (e.g.,

Table 3.2. *Naive theories of wisdom: characteristics of exceptional adult competence based on general studies*

First cluster: Exceptional knowledge about the self and the pragmatics of life

Comprehends the nature of human existence (e.g., mortality, vulnerability and emotionality)
Recognizes the limits of his/her own knowledge
Knows that the importance of difficult life-domains changes during the life span
Thinks before acting or making decisions
Is a clear and careful thinker
Uses common sense
Is able to see things within a broader context
Is able to consider/see all points of view
Sees the essence of situations
Knows when to give/withhold advice
Can read between the lines
Can offer solutions on the side of right and truth

Second cluster: Exceptional personality and interpersonal skills

Is introspective
Is a good listener
Is a person whose advice one would solicit for difficult life problems
Is capable of empathy in difficult life problems
Is open-minded, empathetic, and reflective
Is not afraid to admit mistakes
Is mature
Is curious
Is intuitive, insightful, and foresighted
Knows self best
Has exceptional understanding of other's feelings and motives
Is experienced
Is able to learn from experience

Sources: Clayton & Birren, 1980; Holliday & Chandler, 1986; Maciel, Sowarka, Smith, & Baltes, 1993; Sowarka, 1989; Sternberg, 1986.

Arlin, 1990; P. B. Baltes & Smith, 1990; Kitchener & Brenner, 1990; Labouvie-Vief, 1985). However, what they share is the view that wisdom as a unique accomplishment may require an integrative perspective between cognition, emotion, and personality.

A person of exceptional personal maturity has achieved wisdom as a result of successfully negotiating the final conflict between integrity versus despair (Erikson, 1959), as a result of progressively deeper confrontation with aspects of the self (Jung, 1953), or as a result of transcendence of a narcissistic preoccupation with one's self (Kohut, 1978). From a more cognitive perspective, wisdom is regarded as a form of postformal and dialectical thought (Rybash, Hoyer, & Rodin, 1986), a kind of integrative thought process that embraces paradox and transformation (Labouvie-Vief, 1990), awareness about the limits of one's own personal knowledge (Meacham, 1990), knowledge that effectively integrates emotional and cognitive components (Blanchard-Fields, 1986; Clayton & Birren, 1980; Kramer, 1990) such as expert knowledge about the fundamental pragmatics of life (P. B. Baltes & Smith, 1990).

Empirical demonstration of these characteristics in wise people and respective developmental progress is still scarce. In a first attempt to study wisdom in a life-span framework, P. B. Baltes and Smith (1990) defined this form of competence as "expert knowledge involving good judgment and advice in the domain fundamental pragmatics of life" (p. 95). Based on the dual-process view of intelligence presented earlier, their assumption is that wisdom is a function of life-long growth in knowledge-based life pragmatics, a form of expertise that is truly rare, and an accomplishment exceedingly difficult to attain. In order to operationalize this expertise, a family of five criteria was developed (i.e., rich factual knowledge, rich procedural knowledge, life-span contextualism, relativism, and the ability to understand and manage uncertainty), which serve as guidelines for examining the degree to which individuals evidence this aspect of wisdom (for a more detailed discussion, see also Smith & P. B. Baltes, 1990; Staudinger, Smith, & P. B. Baltes, 1992).

What about the interface between wisdom and measures of intelligence versus personality? In one study of 126 professional women (young, middle, and older), wisdom-related knowledge was investigated in addition to traditional measures of intelligence and personality (Maciel, Smith, & P. B. Baltes, 1993; Staudinger, Smith, & Baltes, 1992). The purpose of the study was to examine the extent to which standard individual-difference variables would contribute to wisdom-related knowledge. The results indicated that individual-difference measures of personality and intelligence accounted for about 22% of the variance in global wisdom-related knowledge (Maciel, Staudinger, Smith, P. B. Baltes, 1991). Fluid but not crystallized intelligence was important, but played a lesser role in contrast to personality. Over and above fluid intelligence, openness to experience and introversion were the strongest predictors of wisdom-related knowledge; accounting for more than twice the variance.

In sum, there is substantial convergence in scientific and laypersons' conceptions about wisdom. Both psychological and common-sense approaches integrate personality aspects and intellectual abilities into a prototypical ideal of successful life-span development. The study of wisdom, then, is one instantiation of the special emphases that may evolve as researchers turn their attention to the interface between personality and intelligence during adult development and aging. It also illustrates that human development across life continues to strive for advances, even though the biology of the aging individual may suggest otherwise. In this sense, it is the special challenge for a culture of old age to outwit the limitations of biology. In our case, the biological limitations of old age are most directly expressed in the fact that the mechanics of the aging mind show decline. Culture- and knowledge-based processes of intelligence and personality, however, are the foundation for continued adaptivity and self-maintenance (P. B. Baltes, 1993).

Summary

Four major propositions about the interface of personality and intelligence in life-span development are presented. The first proposition states that adaptive development depends on whether and to what extent individuals extend and maintain their potential and optimum across the life course into old age. Second, life-span development is conceived as a multidimensional and multidirectional process, and as a dynamic involving a changing matrix of gains and losses. In the second half of life, this dynamic change of realized and anticipated gains and losses changes increasingly toward a less positive balance. The third proposition captures the gain–loss dynamic of life-span development as a process of continued optimization based on selection and compensation. Finally, life-span development, that is, development of personality and intellectual capacities, is regulated by three types of influences: age-graded, history-graded, and non-normative.

Our treatment of the personality–intelligence interface is preceded by a condensed presentation of major findings on adult change in personality and intelligence. This presentation aims at a characterization of the major themes that need consideration as we examine interrelationships among the two domains.

With regard to personality, the long-standing debate on stability versus change is discussed. Two perspectives are introduced. The first is the importance of considering personality in context. Much personality research is based on context-invariant dispositions and, therefore, may possibly not be sensitive enough to the special circumstances deriving from the changing goals and contexts of adult life. Only recently has there been a stronger concern with developing constructs (such as generativity and wisdom) that are explicitly geared towards personality change during adulthood. The second perspective concerns the distinction between concurrent and time-sensitive measurement of change. While cross-sectional and longitudinal studies of concurrent self-report personality measures indicate much overall stability in level and inter-individual differences, investigations of subjectively perceived or attributed change suggest substantial personality change. The shifting-reference-scale hypothesis integrates these seemingly contradictory findings. It is assumed that concurrent self-report measures reflect a peer-based interindividual reference scale, which shifts according to age-related changes in individuals' age cohorts. As a consequence, what is reported in the concurrent self reports, is not likely to be a good indicator of "objective" personality functioning. Assessments of subjectively perceived change, by contrast, emphasize time-ordered processes.

The evidence on life-span development in intellectual functioning reflects more closely the four propositions outlined. The life-long potential of human intelligence is reflected in continued plasticity and the possibility of advances in select bodies of knowledge such as professional expertise and wisdom. The losses are most evident in measures of fluid aspects of intelligence ("mechanics") and at limits of developmental reserve capacity. The selective optimization with compensation proposition is demonstrated by the fact that losses in fluid functioning can be slowed down through increased practice and, more importantly, through compensatory effects involving technology- and knowledge-related factors.

Four key mediators of the interface of personality and intelligence are discussed in view of a life-span approach. The first mediator regards the motivation for attaining select goals, which determines the amount of personal resources invested. The basic assumption is that individuals strive to approach personal levels of peak or optimal functioning, and adjust their expectations and aspiration levels in accordance with their prospective developmental potential. It would therefore be adaptive if developmentally attenuated aspiration levels would reflect overestimations in earlier parts of the life span. The situation in later life is less clear. On the one hand, the widely held negative age bias would suggest a change in the direction of a more positive view of the potential of old age so that development-enhancing behaviors are initiated. On the other hand, these beliefs need to reflect at the same time the fact of age-associated constraints and losses.

Second, beliefs about personal control are also crucial mediators for effort investment. Research on children and adults has suggested that beliefs about personal control are multidimensional and differ by domain. Beliefs about self agency are more closely related to achievement outcomes, and need to be differentiated from general beliefs about causal relations between means and ends. Moreover, older adults seem to have control-related beliefs largely similar to those of young adults, except for some select domains of decline, such as memory and health.

Third, self-regulatory strategies involving selection and compensation are essential for maintaining a positive self-image in spite of objective aging-related decline. Three common and prototypical strategies are discussed: adjustment of aspiration level, adjustment of the goal hierarchy, and strategic social comparison. Normal (i.e., nonpathological) adults skillfully employ these strategies to protect their self-esteem and hopefulness, in an effort to maintain motivational resources for active (primary) control and continued engagement in strategies of successful development such as selective optimization with compensation.

Fourth, wisdom represents a conceptual prototype of successful life-span development, which could serve as a culturally shared guidepost for "successful" integration of the interface between intelligence and personality. Indeed, both scientific and common-sense conceptions view wisdom as such a special combination and coalition. In a sense, wisdom is a sample case that reflects the joint operation of the four propositions that were used to characterize the direction and dynamics of life-span development.

References

Ahammer, I. M., & Baltes, P. B. (1972). Objective vs. perceived age differences in personality: How do adolescents, adults, and older people view themselves and each other? *Journal of Gerontology, 27,* 46–51.

Alexander, C., & Langer, E. (Eds.). (1990). *Higher stages of human development: Perspectives on adult growth.* New York: Oxford University Press.

Alloy, L. B., & Abramson, L. Y. (1979). Judgement of contingency in depressed and non-depressed students: Sadder but wiser? *Journal of Experimental Psychology, 108,* 441–485.

Arlin, P. K. (1990). Wisdom: The art of problem finding. In R. J. Sternberg (Ed.), *Wisdom: Its nature, origins, and development* (pp. 230–243). New York: Cambridge University Press.

Bäckman, L., & Dixon, R. A. (1992). Psychological compensation: A theoretical framework. *Psychological Bulletin, 112,* 259–283.

Baltes, M. M. (1988). The etiology and maintenance of dependency in the elderly: Three phases of operant research. *Behavior Therapy, 19,* 301–319.

Baltes, M. M. (in press). Dependency in old age: Gains and losses. *Current Directions in Psychological Science.*

Baltes, M. M., & Baltes, P. B. (Eds.). (1986). *The psychology of control and aging.* Hillsdale, NJ: Erlbaum.

Baltes, M. M., & Kindermann, T. (1985). Die Bedeutung der Plastizität für die klinische Beurteilung des Leistungsverhaltens im Alter. [The significance of plasticity for the clinical assessment of competence in later life.] In D. Bente, H. Coper & S. Kanowski (Eds.), *Hirnorganisches Psychosyndrom im Alter* (Vol. 2, pp. 171–184). Berlin: Springer-Verlag.

Baltes, M. M., & Wahl, H.-W. (1987). Dependence in aging. In L. L. Carstensen & B. A. Edelstein (Eds.), *Handbook of Clinical Gerontology* (pp. 204–221). New York: Pergamon.

Baltes, M. M., Wahl, H.-W., & Reichert, M. (1991). Institutions and successful aging for the elderly? *Annual Review of Gerontology and Geriatrics, 11,* 311–337.

Baltes, P. B. (1983). Life-span developmental psychology: Observations on history and theory revisited. In R. M. Lerner (Ed.), *Developmental psychology: Historical and philosophical perspectives* (pp. 79–111). Hillsdale, NJ: Erlbaum.

Baltes, P. B. (1987). Theoretical propositions of life-span developmental psychology: On the dynamics between growth and decline. *Developmental Psychology, 23,* 611–626.

Baltes, P. B. (1991). The many faces of human aging: Toward a psychological culture of old age. *Psychological Medicine, 21,* 837–854.

Baltes, P. B. (1993). The aging mind: Potential and limits. *Gerontologist, 33,* 580–594.

Baltes, P. B., & Baltes, M. M. (Eds.). (1990). *Successful aging: Perspectives from the behavioral sciences.* New York: Cambridge University Press.

Baltes, P. B., Dittmann-Kohli, F., & Dixon, R. A. (1984). New perspectives on the development of intelligence in adulthood: Toward a dual-process conception and a model of selective optimization with compensation. In P. B. Baltes & O. G. Brim, Jr. (Eds.), *Life-span development and behavior* (Vol. 6, pp. 33–76). New York: Academic Press.

Baltes, P. B., & Kliegl, R. (1986). On the dynamics between growth and decline in the aging of intelligence and memory. In K. Poeck, H. J. Freund, & H. Gänshirt (Eds.), *Neurology* (pp. 1–17). Heidelberg: Springer-Verlag.

Baltes, P. B., & Kliegl, R. (1992). Further testing of limits of cognitive plasticity: Negative age differences in a mnemonic skill are robust. *Developmental Psychology, 28,* 121–125.

Baltes, P. B., & Lindenberger, U. (1988). On the range of cognitive plasticity in old age as a function of experience: 15 years of intervention research. *Behavior Therapy, 19,* 283–300.

Baltes, P. B., & Mittelstraβ, J. (Eds.). (1992). *Zukunft des Alterns und gesellschaftliche Entwicklung* [Future of aging and societal change] (pp. 408–436). Berlin: De Gruyter.

Baltes, P. B., & Nesselroade, J. R. (1984). Paradigm lost and paradigm regained: Critique of Dannefer's portrayal of life-span developmental psychology. *American Sociological Review, 49,* 841–847.

Baltes, P. B., Reese, H. W., & Lipsitt, L. P. (1980). Life-span developmental psychology. *Annual Review of Psychology, 31,* 65–110.

Baltes, P. B., & Smith, J. (1990). Toward a psychology of wisdom and its ontogenesis. In R. J. Sternberg (Eds.), *Wisdom: Its nature, origins, and development* (pp. 87–120). New York: Cambridge University Press.

Baltes, P. B., & Staudinger, U. M. (1993). The search for a psychology of wisdom. *Current Directions in Psychological Science, 2,* 75–80.

Baltes, P. B., & Willis, S. L. (1982). Plasticity and enhancement of intellectual functioning in old age: Penn State's Adult Development and Enrichment Project (ADEPT). In F. I. M. Craik & S. E. Trehub (Eds.), *Aging and cognitive processes* (pp. 353–389). New York: Plenum.

Bandura, A. (1977). Self-efficacy: Toward a unifying theory of behavioral change. *Psychological Review, 84,* 191–215.

Bandura, A. (1981). Self-referent thought: A developmental analysis of self-efficacy. In J. Flavell & L. Ross (Eds.), *Social cognitive development.* New York: Cambridge University Press.

Bandura, A. (1982). Self-efficacy mechanism in human agency. *American Psychologist, 122,* 122–147.

Bandura, A. (1986). *Social foundations of thought and action. A social cognitive theory.* Englewood Cliffs, NJ: Prentice-Hall.

Bandura, A. (1990). Conclusion: Reflections on nonability determinants of competence. In R. J. Sternberg & J. Kolligian, Jr. (Eds.), *Competence considered* (pp. 315–362). New Haven: Yale University Press.

Bengtson, V. L., Reedy, M. N., & Gordon, C. (1985). Aging and self-conceptions: Personality processes and social contexts. In J. E. Birren & K. W. Schaie (Eds.), *Handbook of the psychology of aging* (pp. 544–593). New York: Van Nostrand Reinhold.

Berg, C. A., & Sternberg, R. J. (1985). A triarchic theory of intellectual development during adulthood. *Developmental Review, 5,* 334–370.

Berger, P. L. (1963). *Invitation to sociology: A humanistic perspective.* Garden City, NY: Doubleday.

Blanchard-Fields, F. (1986). Reasoning on social dilemmas varying in emotional saliency: An adult developmental perspective. *Psychology and Aging, 1,* 325–333.

Blazer, D. (1989). Depression in late life: An update. *Annual Review of Gerontology and Geriatrics, 9,* 197–215.

Block, J. (1971). *Lives through time.* Berkeley, CA: Bancroft Books.

Block, J. (1978). *The Q-Sort Method in personality assessment and psychiatric research.* Palo Alto, CA: Consulting Psychologists Press.

Block, J. (1981). Some enduring and consequential structures of personality. In A. I. Rabin (Ed.), *Further explorations in personality.* New York: Wiley.

Bowers, K. S. (1977). There's more to Iago than meets the eye: A clinical account of personal consistency. In D. Magnusson & N. S. Endler (Eds.), *Personality at the crossroads* (pp. 65–81). Hillsdale, NJ: Erlbaum.

Brandtstädter, J. (1984). Personal and social control over development: Some implications of an action perspective in life-span developmental psychology. In P. B. Baltes & O. G. Brim (Eds.), *Life-span development and behavior* (Vol. 6, pp. 1–32). New York: Academic Press.

Brandtstädter, J. (1986). Personale Entwicklungskontrolle und entwicklungsregulatives Handeln: Überlegungen und Befunde zu einem vernachlässigten Forschungsthema [Personal control and regulative action in development: Thoughts and findings on an underrated issue of research]. *Zeitschrift für Entwicklungspsychologie und Pädagogische Psychologie, 18,* 316–334.

Brandtstädter, J. (1989). Personal self-regulation of development: Cross-sequential analyses of development-related control beliefs and emotions. *Developmental Psychology, 25,* 96–108.

Brandtstädter, J., & Greve, W. (in press). The aging self: Stabilizing and protective processes. *Developmental Review.*

96 ANNA G. MACIEL, JUTTA HECKHAUSEN, AND PAUL B. BALTES

Brandtstädter, J., & Renner, G. (1990). Tenacious goal pursuit and flexible goal adjustment: Explication and age-related analysis of assimilative and accommodative strategies of coping. *Psychology and Aging, 5,* 58–67.

Brent, S. B., & Watson, D. (1980). *Aging and wisdom: Individual and collective aspects.* Paper presented at the meeting of the Gerontological Society of America, San Francisco, CA.

Brim, O. G., Jr. (1988). Losing and winning. *Psychology Today, 9,* 48–52.

Brim, O. G., Jr. (1992). *Ambition.* New York: Basic Books.

Brim, O. G., Jr., & Kagan, J. (Eds.). (1980). *Constancy and change in human development.* Cambridge, MA: Harvard University Press.

Brim, O. G., Jr., & Ryff, C. D. (1980). On the properties of life events. In P. B. Baltes & O. G. Brim, Jr. (Eds.), *Life-span development and behavior* (Vol. 3, pp. 367–388). New York: Academic Press.

Brown, A. L., & French, L. A. (1979). The zone of potential development: Implications for intelligence testing in the year 2000. *Intelligence, 3,* 255–273.

Bühler, C. (1933). *Der menschliche Lebenslauf als psychologisches Problem.* [The human life course as psychological problem.] Leipzig: Hirzel.

Burgess, J. M., & Holmstrom, L. L. (1979). Adaptive strategies and recovery from rape. *American Journal of Psychiatry, 136,* 1278–1282.

Butler, R. N. (1963). The life-review: An interpretation of reminiscence in the aged. *Psychiatry, 26,* 65–76.

Carlson, J. S., & Wiedl, K. H. (1980). Application of a dynamic testing approach in intelligence assessment: Empirical results and theoretical formulations. *Zeitschrift für differentielle und diagnostische Psychologie, 1,* 303–318.

Carus, F. A. (1808). *Psychologie. Zweiter Theil: Specialpsychologie* [Psychology: Part Two: Special Psychology]. Leipzig: Barth & Kummer.

Caspi, A., Bem, D. J., & Elder, G. H., Jr. (1989). Continuities and consequences of interactional styles across the life course. *Journal of Personality, 57,* 375–406.

Cattell, R. B. (1971). *Abilities: Their structure, growth and action.* Boston: Houghton Mifflin.

Cavanaugh, J. C., & Green, E. E. (1990). I believe, therefore I can: Self-efficacy beliefs in memory aging. In E. A. Lovelace (Ed.), *Aging and Cognition: Mental processes, self-awareness, and interventions.* Amsterdam: Esevier.

Chandler, M. J., & Holliday, S. G. (1990). Wisdom in a postapocalyptic age. In R. J. Sternberg (Ed.), *Wisdom: its nature, origins, and development.* New York: Cambridge University Press.

Charness, N. (Ed.). (1985). *Aging and human performance.* Chichester, GB: John Wiley & Son.

Clayton, V., & Birren, J. E. (1980). The development of wisdom across the life span: A re-examination of an ancient topic. In P. B. Baltes & O. G. Brim (Eds.), *Life span development and behavior* (Vol. 3). New York: Academic Press.

Cole, M. (1990). Cultural psychology: A once and future discipline? In *Nebraska Symposium on Motivation, 38,* 279–335.

Conley, J. J. (1985). Longitudinal stability of personality traits: A multitrait-multimethod-multioccasion analysis. *Journal of Personality and Social Psychology, 49,* 1266–1282.

Coper, H., Jänicke, B., & Schulze, G. (1986). Biopsychological research on adaptivity across the life-span of animals. In P. B. Baltes, K. L. Featherman, & R. M. Lerner (Eds.), *Life-span development and behavior* (Vol. 7, pp. 207–233). Hillsdale, NJ: Erlbaum.

Cornelius, S. W., & Caspi, A. (1987). Everyday problem solving in adulthood and old age. *Psychology and Aging, 2,* 144–153.

Costa, P. T., & McCrae, R. R. (1980). Still stable after all these years: Personality as a key to some issues in adulthood and old age. In P. B. Baltes & O. G. Brim, Jr. (Eds.), *Life-span development and behavior* (Vol. 3, pp. 65–102). New York: Academic Press.

Costa, P. T., & McCrae, R. R. (1985). *The NEO personality inventory manual.* Odessa, FL: Psychological Assessment Resources.

Costa, P. T., Jr., & McCrae, R. R. (1988). Personality in adulthood: A six-year longitudinal study of self reports and spouse ratings on the NEO personality inventory. *Journal of Personality and Social Psychology, 54,* 853–863.

Costa, P. T., Jr., & McCrae, R. M. (1992). Trait psychology comes of age. In T. B. Sonderegger (Ed.),

Nebraska Symposium on Motivation: Psychology and Aging. Lincoln, NE: University of Nebraska Press.

Dannefer, D. (1984). Adult development and social theory: A paradigmatic reappraisal. *American Sociological Review, 49*, 100–116.

Dannefer, D. (1989). Human action and its place in theories of aging. *Journal of Aging Studies, 3*, 1–20.

Dannefer, D., & Perlmutter, M. (1990). Development as a multidimensional process: Individual and social constituents. *Human Development, 33*, 108–137.

Denney, N. W. (1984). A model of cognitive development across the life span. *Developmental Review, 4*, 171–191.

Dittmann-Kohli, F. (in press). Das persönliche Sinnsystem. *Ein Vergleich zwischen frühem und spätem Erwachsenenalter.* [The personal meaning system. A comparison of early and late adulthood.] Göttingen: Hogrefe.

Dittmann-Kohli, F., & Baltes, P. B. (1990). Toward a neofunctionalist conception of adult intellectual development: Wisdom as a prototypical case of intellectual growth. In C. Alexander & E. Langer (Eds.), *Higher stages of human development: Perspectives on adult growth* (pp. 54–78). New York: Oxford University Press.

Dixon, R. A., & Baltes, P. B. (1986). Toward life-span research on the function and pragmatics of intelligence. In R. J. Sternberg & R. K. Wagner (Eds.), *Practical intelligence* (pp. 203–234). New York: Cambridge University Press.

Durham, W. H. (1990). Advances in evolutionary culture theory. *Annual Review of Anthropology, 19*, 187–210.

Elder, G. H. (1985). *Life-course dynamics: Trajectories and transitions 1968–1980*. Ithaca, NY: Cornell University Press.

Elder, G. H., Jr. (1986). Military times and turning points in men's lives. *Developmental Psychology, 22*, 233–245.

Elder, G. H. (1991). The life course. In Borgatta , E. F. & Borgatta , M. L. (Eds.), *The encyclopedia of sociology*. New York: Macmillan.

Endler, N. S. (1981). Persons, situations, and their interactions. In A. I. Rabin, J. Aronoff, A. M. Barclay, & R. A. Zucker (Eds.), *Further Explorations in Personality* (pp. 114–151). New York: Wiley.

Ericsson, K. A. (1990). Peak performance and age: An examination of peak performance in sports. In P. B. Baltes & M. M. Baltes (Eds.), *Successful aging: Perspectives from the behavioral sciences* (pp. 164–195). New York: Cambridge University Press.

Ericsson, K. A., & Smith, J. (Eds.). (1991). *Toward a general theory of expertise*. New York: Cambridge University Press.

Erikson, E. (1959). Identity and the life cycle. *Psychological Issues, 1*, 18–164.

Featherman, D. L. (1983). The life-span perspective in social science research. In P. B. Baltes & O. G. Brim, Jr. (Eds.), *Life-span development and behavior* (Vol. 5, pp. 1–59). New York: Academic Press.

Featherman, D. L., & Lerner, R. M. (1985). Ontogenesis and socio-genesis: Problematics for theory and research about development and socialization across the lifespan. *American Sociological Review, 50*, 659–676.

Featherman, D. L., Smith, J., & Peterson, J. G. (1990). Successful aging in a post-retired society. In P. B. Baltes & M. M. Baltes (Eds.), *Successful aging: Perspectives from the behavioral sciences* (pp. 50–93). New York: Cambridge University Press.

Ferrara, R. A., Brown, A. L., & Campione, J. C. (1986). Children's learning and transfer of inductive reasoning rules: Studies of proximal development. *Child Development, 57*, 1087–1099.

Filipp, S.-H., & Klauer, T. (1986). Conceptions of self over the life span: Reflections on the dialectics of change. In M. M. Baltes & P. B. Baltes (Eds.), *The psychology of control and aging* (pp. 167–205). Hillsdale, NJ: Erlbaum.

Frey, K. S., & Ruble, D. N. (1990). Strategies for comparative evaluation: Maintaining a sense of competence across the life span. In R. S. Sternberg & J. Kolligian, Jr. (Eds.), *Competence considered* (pp. 167–189). New Haven: Yale University Press.

Fries, J. F. (1990). Medical perspectives upon successful aging. In P. B. Baltes & M. M. Baltes (Eds.), *Successful aging* (pp. 35–49). New York: Cambridge University Press.

Fry, P. S. (Ed.). (1988). *Psychological perspectives of helplessness and control in the elderly.* Amsterdam: North-Holland.

Gagné, R. (1968). Contributions of learning to human development. *Psychological Review, 75,* 177–191.

George, L. K. (1978). The impact of personality and social status factors upon levels of activity and psychological well-being. *Journal of Gerontology, 33,* 840–847.

Gottlieb, G. (1991). Experiential canalization of behavioral development: Theory. *Developmental Psychology, 27,* 4–13.

Gough, H. G. (1987). *Manual for the California Psychological Inventory.* Palo Alto, CA: Consulting Psychologists Press.

Greenough, W., Black, J., & Wallace, C. (1987). Experience and brain development. *Child Development, 58,* 539–559.

Guthke, J. (1982). The learning test concept – an alternative to the traditional static intelligence test. *The German Journal of Psychology, 192,* 3–17.

Haan, N., Millsap, R., & Hartka, E. (1986). As time goes by: change and stability in personality over fifty years. *Psychology and Aging, 1,* 220–232.

Hagestad, G. O. (1990). Social perspectives on the life course. In R. Binstock & L. George (Eds.), *Handbook of Aging and the Social Sciences* (pp. 151–168). New York: Academic Press.

Hagestad, G. O., & Neugarten, B. L. (1985). Age and the life course. In R. H. Binstock & E. Shanas (Eds.), *Handbook of aging and the social sciences* (pp. 35–61). New York: Van Nostrand Reinhold.

Harris, L., & Associates (1975). *The myth and reality of aging in America.* Washington, DC: National Council on the Aging.

Harris, L., & Associates (1981). *Aging in the Eighties: America in transition.* Washington, DC: National Council on the Aging.

Havighurst, R. J. (1952). *Developmental tasks and education.* New York: McKay.

Heckhausen, H. (1991). *Motivation and action.* New York: Springer.

Heckhausen, J. (1989). Normatives Entwicklungswissen als Bezugsrahmen zur (Re)konstruktion der eigenen Biographie [Knowledge about development as a framework for reconstructing one's own biography]. In P. Alheit & E. Hoerning (Eds.), *Biographisches Wissen: Beiträge zu einer Theorie lebensgeschichtlicher Erfahrung* (pp. 202–282). Frankfurt: Campus.

Heckhausen, J. (1990). Erwerb und Funktion normativer Vorstellungen über den Lebenslauf: Ein entwicklungspsychologischer Beitrag zur sozio-psychischen Konstruktion von Biographien [Acquisition and function of normative conceptions about the life course: A contribution for the socio-psychological construction of biographies]. In K.-U. Mayer (Ed.), *Kölner Zeitschrift für Soziologie und Sozialpsychologie, 31,* 351–373. Opladen: Westdeutscher Verlag.

Heckhausen, J. (1992). Adults' expectancies about development and its controllability: Enhancing self-efficacy by social comparison. In R. Schwarzer (Ed.), *Self-efficacy: Thought control of action* (pp. 107–126). Washington: Hemisphere.

Heckhausen, J., & Baltes, P. B. (1991). Perceived controllability of expected psychological change across adulthood and old age. *Journal of Gerontology: Psychological Sciences, 46,* 165–173.

Heckhausen, J., Dixon, R. A., & Baltes, P. B. (1989). Gains and losses in development throughout adulthood as perceived by different adult age groups. *Developmental Psychology, 25,* 109–121.

Heckhausen, J., & Krueger, J. (1993). Developmental expectations for the self and most other people: Age-grading in three functions of social comparison. *Developmental Psychology, 29,* 539–548.

Heckhausen, J., & Schulz, R. (1993). Optimization by selection and compensation: Balancing primary and secondary control in life-span development. *International Journal of Behavioral Development, 16,* 287–303.

Heim, A. (1970). *Intelligence and Personality.* Baltimore: Penguin Books.

Helson, R., & Mitchell, V. (1978). Personality. *Annual Rev. Psych., 29,* 555–585.

Hertzog, C., Dixon, R. A., & Hultsch, D. F. (1990). Relationships between metamemory, memory predictions, and memory task performance in adults. *Psychology and Aging, 5,* 215–227.

Hertzog, C., & Schaie, K. W. (1988). Stability and change in adult intelligence: 2. Simultaneous analysis of longitudinal means and covariance structures. *Psychology and Aging, 3,* 142–165.

Holliday, S. G., & Chandler, M. J. (1986). *Wisdom: Explorations in human competence.* New York: Karger.

Horn, J. L. (1982). The theory of fluid and crystallized intelligence in relation to concepts of cognitive psychology and aging in adulthood. In F. I. M. Craik & S. E. Trehub (Eds.), *Aging and cognitive processes* (pp. 847–870). New York: Plenum.

Huttenlocher, P. (1979). Synaptic density in human frontal cortex-developmental changes and effects of aging. *Brain Research, 163,* 195–205.

Jackson, D. N., & Paunonen, S. V. (1980). Personality structure and assessment. *Ann. Rev. Psych., 31,* 503–551.

Jung, C. G. (1933). *Modern man in search of a soul.* New York: Harcourt, Brace & World.

Jung, C. G. (1953). *Two essays on analytical psychology.* New York: Pantheon Books.

Kagan, J. (1980). Perspectives on continuity. In O. G. Brim, Jr., & J. Kagan (Eds.), *Constancy and change in human development* (pp. 26–74). Cambridge, MA: Harvard University Press.

Keil, F. C. (1981). Constraints on knowledge and cognitive development. *Psychological Review, 88,* 187–227.

Kitchener, K. S., & Brenner, H. G. (1990). Wisdom and reflective judgment: Knowing in the face of uncertainty. In R. J. Sternberg (Ed.), *Wisdom: Its nature, origins, and development* (pp. 212–229). New York: Cambridge University Press.

Klemp, G. O., Jr., & McClelland, D. C. (1986). What characterizes intelligent functioning among senior managers? In R. J. Sternberg & R. K. Wagner (Eds.), *Practical intelligence: Nature and origins of competence in the everyday world* (pp. 31–50). New York: Cambridge University Press.

Kliegl, R., & Baltes, P. B. (1987). Theory-guided analysis of mechanisms of development and aging through testing-the-limits and research on expertise. In C. Schooler & K. W. Schaie (Eds.), *Social structure and individual aging processes.* Norwood, NJ: Ablex.

Kliegl, R., Mayr, U., & Krampè, R. T. (in press). Time-accuracy functions for determining process and person differences: An application to cognitive aging. *Cognitive Psychology.*

Kliegl, R., Smith, J., & Baltes, P. B. (1989). Testing-the-limits and the study of adult age differences in cognitive plasticity of a mnemonic skill. *Developmental Psychology, 25,* 247–256.

Kliegl, R., Smith, J., & Baltes, P. B. (1990). On the locus and process of magnification of age differences during mnemonic training. *Developmental Psychology, 26,* 894–904.

Klinger, E. (1975). Consequences of commitment and disengagement from incentives. *Psychological Review, 82,* 1–25.

Kohut, H. (1977). *Restoration of the self.* New York: International Universities Press.

Kohut, H. (1978). Forms and transformations of narcissism. In P. Ornstein (Ed.), *The search for the self* (pp. 427–460). New York: International Universities Press.

Kramer, D. A. (1990). Conceptualizing wisdom: The primacy of affect-cognition. In R. J. Sternberg (Ed.), *Wisdom: Its nature, origins, and development* (pp. 279–313). New York: Cambridge University Press.

Krueger, J., & Heckhausen, J. (1993). Personality development across the adult life span: Subjective conceptions versus cross-sectional contrasts. *Journal of Gerontology: Psychological Sciences, 48,* 100–108.

Kuypers, J. A., & Bengtson, V. L. (1973). Social breakdown and competence: A model of normal aging. *Human Development, 16,* 181–201.

Labouvie-Vief, G. (1981). Proactive and reactive aspects of constructivism: Growth and aging in life-span perspective. In R. M. Lerner & N. A. Busch-Rossnagel (Eds.), *Individuals as producers of their development* (pp. 197–230). New York: Academic Press.

Labouvie-Vief, G. (1985). Intelligence and cognition. In J. E. Birren & K. W. Schaie (Eds.), *Handbook of the psychology of aging* (2nd ed., pp. 500–530). New York: Van Nostrand Reinhold.

Labouvie-Vief, G. (1990). Wisdom as integrated thought: Historical and developmental perspectives. In R. J. Sternberg (Ed.), *Wisdom: Its nature, origins, and development* (pp. 52–83). New York: Cambridge University Press.

Lachman, M. E. (1983). Perceptions of intellectual aging: Antecedent or consequence of intellectual functioning? *Developmental Psychology, 19,* 482–498.

Lachman, M. E. (1986a). Personal control in later life: Stability, change and cognitive correlates. In M. M. Baltes & P. B. Baltes (Eds.), *The psychology of control and aging* (pp. 207–236). Hillsdale, NJ: Erlbaum.

Lachman, M. E. (1986b). Locus of control in aging research: A call for multidimensional and domain-specific assessment. *Psychology and Aging, 1,* 34–40.

Lachman, M. E. (1991). Perceived control over memory aging: Developmental and intervention perspectives. *Journal of Social Issues, 47,* 159–175.

Lachman, M. E., & Leff, R. (1989). Perceived control and intellectual functioning in the elderly: A 5-year longitudinal study. *Developmental Psychology, 25,* 722–728.

Lawton, M. P. (1989). Behavior-relevant ecological factors. In K. W. Schaie & C. Schooler (Eds.), *Social structure and aging: Psychological processes* (pp. 57–78). Hillsdale, NJ: Erlbaum.

Leon, G. R., Gillum, B., Gillum, R., & Gouze, M. (1979). Personality stability and change over a 30-year period – middle age to old age. *Journal of Consulting and Clinical Psychology, 47,* 517–524.

Lerner, R. M. (1984). *On the nature of human plasticity.* New York: Cambridge University Press.

Lerner, R. M. (1991). Changing organismic-context relations as the basic process of development: A developmental contextual perspective. *Developmental Psychology, 27,* 27–32.

Levelt, W. J. M. (1992). *Speaking: From intention to articulation.* Cambridge, MA: MIT Press.

Levenson, H. (1973). Perceived parental antecedents of internal, powerful others, and chance locus of control orientations. *Developmental Psychology, 9,* 260–265.

Levenson, H. (1974). Activism and powerful others: Distinctions within the concept of internal-external control. *Journal of Personality Assessment, 38,* 377–383.

Liker, J. K., & Elder, G. H., Jr. (1983). Economic hardship and marital relations in the 1930's. *American Sociological Review, 48,* 343–359.

Maciel, A. G., Sowarka, D., Smith, J., & Baltes, P. B. (1993). Prototypical attributes of wise people. *Resources in Education, ED 354421.*

Maciel, A. G., Staudinger, U. M. (in press). What became of the prophecy of senescence? A view from life-span psychology. In K. W. Schaie & A. Achenbaum (Eds.), *Social structure and aging: Historical perspectives.* Hillsdale, NJ: Erlbaum.

Maciel, A.G., Staudinger, U. M., Smith, J., & Baltes, P. B. (1991, August). *Which factors contribute to wisdom? Age, Intelligence, or Personality?* Poster presented at the 99th annual meeting of the American Psychological Association, San Francisco, CA.

Magnusson, D., & Endler, N. S. (1977). Interactional psychology: Present status and future prospects. In D. Magnusson & N. S. Endler (Eds.), *Personality at the crossroads* (pp. 3–31). Hillsdale, NJ: Erlbaum.

Mayer, K. U. (1986). Structural constraints on the life course. *Human Development, 29,* 163–170.

Mayer, K.-U. (Ed.). (1990). *Kölner Zeitschrift für Soziologie und Sozialpsychologie, Special issue: 31,* Lebensverläufe und sozialer Wandel [Life-histories and social change]. Opladen: Westdeutscher Verlag.

Mayr, U., & Kliegl, R. (in press). Sequential and coordinative complexity: Age-based processing limitations in figural transformations. *J. Exp. Psych.: Learning, Memory, and Cognition.*

McCrae, R. P., & Costa, P. T., Jr. (1984). *Emerging lives, enduring dispositions: Personality in adulthood.* Boston: Little Brown.

McCrae, R. R., & Costa, P. T., Jr. (1987). Validation of the five-factor model of personality across instruments and observers. *Journal of Personality and Social Psychology, 52,* 81–90.

Meacham, J. A. (1990). The loss of wisdom. In R. J. Sternberg (Ed.), *Wisdom: Its nature, origins, and development* (pp. 181–211). New York: Cambridge University Press.

Mischel, W. (1977). The interaction of person and situation. In D. Magnusson & N. S. Endler (Eds.), *Personality at the crossroads* (pp. 333–352). Hillsdale, NJ: Erlbaum.

Molinari, V., & Reichlin, R. E. (1985). Life review reminiscence in the elderly: A review of the literature. *International Journal of Aging and Human Development, 20,* 81–92.

Nesselroade, J. R. (1989). Adult personality development: Issues in addressing constancy and change. In A. I. Rabin, R. A. Zucker, R. A. Emmons, & S. Frank (Eds.), *Studying persons and lives* (pp. 41–85). New York: Springer.

Nesselroade, J. R. (1991). The warp and the woof of the developmental fabric. In Downs, Liben, & Palermo (Eds.), *Visions of development, aesthetics, and the environment: The legacy of Joachim F. Wohlwill.* Hillsdale, NJ: Erlbaum.

Neugarten, B. L. (1973). Personality change in late life: A developmental perspective. In C. Eisdorfer &

M. P. Lawton (Eds.), *Psychology of adult development and aging* (pp. 311–335). New York: Academic Press.

Neugarten, B. L. (1977). Personality and aging. In J. E. Birren & K. W. Schaie (Eds.), *Handbook of the psychology of aging* (pp. 626–649). New York: Van Nostrand Reinhold.

Neugarten, B. L. (1987). Kansas City studies of adult life. In G. L. Maddox (Ed.), *The encyclopedia of aging* (pp. 372–373). New York: Springer.

Neugarten, B. L., Moore, J. W., & Lowe, J. C. (1965). Age norms, age constraints, and adult socialization. *American Journal of Sociology, 70,* 710–717.

Norman, W. T. (1963). Toward an adequate taxonomy of personality attitudes: Replicated factor structure in peer nomination personality ratings. *Journal of Abnormal and Social Psychology, 66,* 574–583.

Oettingen, G., Little, T. D., Lindenberger, U., & Baltes, P. B. (in press). Causality, agency, and control beliefs in East versus West Berlin children: A natural experiment on the role of context. *Journal of Personality and Social Psychology.*

O'Gorman, H. J. (1980). False consciousness of kind: Pluralistic ignorance among the aged. *Research on Aging, 2,* 105–128.

Orwoll, L., & Perlmutter, M. (1990). The study of wise persons: integrating a personality perspective. In R. J. Sternberg (Ed.), *Wisdom: Its nature, origins, and development* (pp. 160–177). New York: Cambridge University Press.

Paulhus, D. (1983). Sphere-specific measures of perceived control. *Journal of Personality and Social Psychology, 44,* 1253–1265.

Perlmutter, M. (1988). Cognitive potential throughout life. In J. E. Birren & V. Bengtson (Eds.), *Emergent theories of aging* (pp. 247–268). New York: Springer.

Plomin, R., & Thompson, L. (1988). Life-span developmental behavioral genetics. In P. B. Baltes, D. L. Featherman, & R. M. Lerner (Eds.), *Life-span development and behavior* (Vol. 8, pp. 1–31). Hillsdale, NJ; Erlbaum.

Quetelet, A. (1835). *Sur l'homme et le developpement de ses facultes* [On man and the development of his faculties]. Paris: Bachelier.

Raynor, J. O. (1980). Motivation and career striving. In J. W. Atkinson, & J. O. Raynor (Eds.), *Motivation and achievement* (pp. 173–180). Washington, DC: Winston & Sons.

Reker, G.T., Peacock, E. J., & Wong, P. T. P. (1987). Meaning and purpose in life and well-being: A life-span perspective. *Journal of Gerontology, 42,* 44–49.

Riegel, K. F. (1976). The dialectics of human development. *American Psychologist, 31,* 689–700.

Riley, M. W. (1990). The influence of sociological lives: Personal reflections. *Annual Review of Sociology, 16,* 1–25.

Riley, M. W., & Riley, J. W., Jr. (Eds.). (1989). The quality of aging: Strategies for interventions. *Annals of the American Academy of Political and Social Sciences, Special issue: 503.*

Rodin, J., & Langer, E. (1980). Aging labels: the decline of control and the fall of self-esteem. *Journal of Social Issues, 36,* 12–29.

Rosch, E. (1978). Principles of categorization. In E. Rosch & B. B. Lloyd (Eds.), *Cognition and Categorization* (pp. 27–48). Hillsdale, NJ; Erlbaum.

Rothbaum, F., Weisz, J. R., & Snyder, S. S. (1982). Changing the world and changing the self: A two-process model of perceived control. *Journal of Personality and Social Psychology, 42,* 5–37.

Rybash, J. M., Hoyer, W. J., & Rodin, P. A. (1986). *Adult cognition and aging.* New York: Pergamon.

Ryff, C. D. (1982). Self-perceived personality change in adulthood and aging. *Journal of Personality and Social Psychology, 42,* 108–115.

Ryff, C. D. (1984). Personality development from the inside: The subjective experience of change in adulthood and aging. In P. B. Baltes & O. G. Brim, Jr. (Eds.), *Life-Span Development and Behavior, 6,* 243–279.

Ryff, C. D. (1991). Possible selves in adulthood and old age: A tale of shifting horizons. *Psychology and Aging, 6,* 286–295.

Ryff, C. D., & Baltes, P. B. (1976). Value transitions and adult development in women: The instrumentality–terminality sequence hypothesis. *Developmental Psychology, 12,* 567–568.

Ryff, C. D., & Heincke, S. G. (1983). The subjective organization of personality in adulthood and aging. *Journal of Personality and Social Psychology, 44,* 807–816.

Ryff, C. D., & Migdal, S. (1984). Intimacy and generativity: Self-perceived transitions. *Signs: Journal of Women in Culture and Society, 9,* 470–481.

Salthouse, T. A. (1984). The skill of typing. *Scientific American, 250,* 128–135.

Salthouse, T. A. (1986). Perceptual, cognitive, and motoric aspects of transcription typing. *Psychological Bulletin, 99,* 303–319.

Salthouse, T. A. (1991). Expertise as the circumvention of human processing limitations. In K. A. Ericsson & J. Smith (Eds.), *Toward a general theory of expertise* (pp. 286–300). Cambridge: Cambridge University Press.

Schaie, K. W. (1983). The Seattle Longitudinal Study: A twenty-one year exploration of psychometric intelligence in adulthood. In K. W. Schaie (Ed.), *Longitudinal studies of adult psychological development* (pp. 64–135). New York: Guilford.

Schaie, K. W. (1984). Midlife influences upon intellectual functioning in old age. *International Journal of Behavioral Development, 7,* 463–478.

Schaie, K. W., Dutta, R., & Willis, S. L. (1991). Relationships between rigidity, flexibility, and cognitive abilities in adulthood. *Psychology and Aging, 6,* 371–383.

Schaie, K. W., & Parham, I. A. (1976). Stability of adult personality: Fact or fable? *Journal of Personality and Social Psychology, 34,* 146–158.

Schaie, K. W., & Willis, S. L. (1991). *Adult development and aging.* New York: Harper.

Schulz, R., & Decker, S. (1985). Long-term adjustment to physical disability: The role of social support, perceived control, and self-blame. *Journal of Personality and Social Psychology, 48,* 1162–1172.

Schulz, R., & Fritz, S. (1988). Origins of stereotypes of the elderly: An experimental study of the self-other discrepancy. *Experimental Aging Research, 13,* 189–195.

Schulz, R., Heckhausen, J., & Locher, J. L. (1991). Adult development, control, and adaptive functioning. *Journal of Social Issues, 47,* 177–196.

Shweder, R. (1990). *Thinking through cultures.* Cambridge, MA: Harvard University Press.

Siegler, I. C., George, L. K., & Okun, M. A. (1979). Cross-sequential analysis of adult personality. *Developmental Psychology, 15,* 350–351.

Simonton, D. K. (1988). Age and outstanding achievement: What do we know after a century of research? *Psychological Bulletin, 104,* 251–267.

Singer, W. (1987). Activity-dependent self-organization of synaptic connections as a substrate of learning. In J.-P. Changeux & M. Konishi (Eds.), *The neural and molecular bases of learning* (pp. 301–336). New York: Wiley.

Skinner, E. A., Chapman, M., & Baltes, P. B. (1988). Control, means–ends, and agency beliefs: A new conceptualization and its measurement during childhood. *Journal of Personality and Social Psychology, 54,* 117–133.

Smith, J., & Baltes, P. B. (1990). A study of wisdom-related knowledge: Age/cohort differences in responses to life planning problems. *Developmental Psychology, 26,* 494–505.

Smith, J., Standinger, U. M., & Baltes, P. B. (in press). Setting facilitating wisdom-related knowledge: The sample case of clinical psychologists. *Journal of Consulting and Clinical Psychology.*

Sowarka, D. (1989). Weisheit und weise Personen: Common-Sense-Konzepte älterer Menschen [Wisdom and wise persons: Common sense concepts in older people]. *Zeitschrift für Entwicklungspsychologie und Pädagogische Psychologie, 21,* 87–109.

Staudinger, U. M. (1989). *The study of life review: An approach to the investigation of intellectual development across the life span.* Berlin: Edition Sigma.

Staudinger, U. M., Smith, J., & Baltes, P. B. (1992). Wisdom-related knowledge in a life review task: Age differences and the role of professional specialization. *Psychology and Aging, 7,* 271–281.

Sternberg, R. J. (1985). *Beyond IQ: A triarchic theory of human intelligence.* New York: Cambridge University Press.

Sternberg, R. J. (1986). Implicit theories of intelligence, creativity, and wisdom. *Journal of Personality and Social Psychology, 49,* 607–627.

Sternberg, R. J. (Ed.). (1990). *Wisdom: Its Nature, origins, and development.* New York: Cambridge University Press.

Sternberg, R. J., & Berg, C. A. (1986). Quantitative Integration: Definitions of Intelligence: A comparison of the 1921 and 1986 Symposia. In R. J. Sternberg & D. K. Detterman (Eds.), *What is Intelligence?* (pp. 155–162). Norwood, NJ: Ablex.

Sternberg, R. J., & Detterman, D. K. (Eds.). (1986). *What is Intelligence?* Norwood, NJ: Ablex Publishing Corp.

Sternberg, R., & Kolligian, J., Jr. (Eds.). (1990). *Competence considered.* New Haven, CT: Yale University Press.

Taylor, S. E. (1989). *Positive illusions: Creative self-deception and the healthy mind.* New York: Basic Books.

Taylor, S. E., & Lobel, M. (1989). Social comparison activity under threat: Downward evaluation and upward contacts. *Psychological Review, 96,* 569–575.

Taylor, S. E., Wood, J. V., & Lichtman, R. R. (1984). Attributions, beliefs about control, and adjustment to breast cancer. *Journal of Personality and Social Psychology, 46,* 489–502.

Tetens, J. N. (1777). *Philosophische Versuche über die menschliche Natur und ihre Entwicklung* [Philosophical essays on human nature and its development]. Leipzig: Weidmanns Erben und Reich.

Thomae, H. (1979). The concept of development and life-span developmental psychology. In P. B. Baltes & O. G. Brim, Jr. (Eds.), *Life-span development and behavior* (Vol. 2, pp. 282–312). New York: Academic Press.

Thomas, W. C., Jr. (1981). The expectation gap and the stereotype of the stereotype: Images of old people. *The Gerontologist, 21,* 402–407.

Waddington, C. H. (1975). *The evolution of an evolutionist.* Edinburgh: Edinburgh University Press.

West, S. G., & Graziano, W. G. (1989). Long-term stability and change in personality: An introduction. *Journal of Personality, 57,* 175–193.

Wiedl, K. H. (1984). Lerntests: Nur Forschungsmittel und Forschungsgegenstand? [Tests of learning: only a strategy and topic of research?]. *Zeitschrift für Entwicklungspsychologie und Pädagogische Psychologie, 16,* 245–281.

Willis, S. L. (1987). Cognitive training and everyday competence. In K. W. Schaie (Ed.), *Annual review of gerontology and geriatrics* (Vol. 7, pp. 159–188). New York: Springer.

Wills, T. A. (1981). Downward comparison principles in social psychology. *Psychological Bulletin, 90,* 245–271.

Wood, J. V. (1989). Theory and research concerning social comparison of personal attributes. *Psychological Bulletin, 106*(2), 231–248.

Woodruff, D. W., & Birren, J. E. (1972). Age changes and cohort differences in personality. *Developmental Psychology, 6,* 252–259.

4 Toward an integrative model of personality and intelligence: a general framework and some preliminary steps

Chi-yue Chiu, Ying-yi Hong, and Carol S. Dweck

Intuitively, intelligence and personality may seem like different things. When we use the two words, we typically have different referents in mind. We will propose that distinguishing the two constructs makes sense, but only when the psychological processes making up each construct are in their latent, inert form. We will propose that whenever either set of processes is activated and put to use in any way whatever, intelligence and personality become inextricably intertwined. This argument will form the basis of the present chapter.

We will begin by addressing the construct of intelligence. Here we will describe three levels of mental processes and their functioning that have all been termed intelligence by various theorists: (a) basic mental operations, (b) collections of skills and knowledge, and (c) the processes as they are actualized and brought to bear on a particular task to produce more adaptive or less adaptive behavior.

Next, we will define what we mean by personality processes and will describe three levels that are analogous to the ones described for intelligence: (a) basic motivational and affective processes, (b) knowledge structures and belief systems, and (c) the processes as they are actualized in patterns of more or of less adaptive behavior.

The reader will notice the striking similarity between the intellectual and personality processes at the second and third levels, and this will form the crux of our argument that (a) intellectual and motivational/personality processes are never activated and utilized in isolation from each other – they always co-occur, and (b) once they are activated and utilized, there is no way to separate their processes or evaluate their separate contributions.

The major part of the chapter will be devoted to a discussion of research from our own laboratory and we will place that research in the context of the proposal described above, illustrating the joint action of intelligence and personality. We will show how in three domains – intellectual, social, and moral – individuals' core beliefs influence their judgments and behaviors in ways that affect the rationality of their judgments and the adaptiveness of their behavior.

We conclude by exploring the implications of our position for the understanding and study of intellectual and personality processes. Which distinctions between personality retain their utility? Which distinctions have clouded our judgment and are best left behind?

Three levels of intellectual functioning

Psychologists interested in human intelligence typically view intelligence as involving one or more of these three levels of functioning: (1) fundamental mental operations involved in knowledge acquisition, (2) the level of knowledge and skills available, and (3) the ability to adapt to new situations (see Matarazzo & Denver, 1984). In this section, we briefly survey how these three levels of intellectual functioning are understood in the literature. Later, we argue that, although fundamental mental operations conceptually can be distinguished from basic personality (e.g., motivational/affective) processes, the boundary between intelligence and personality becomes less clear when intelligence is referred to as a repertoire of knowledge and skills or as adaptive behavior, because (1) the kinds of knowledge and skills that make up intelligence are not distinct from those that make up personality, and (2) the kind of adaptive behaviors that interest psychologists studying intelligence also interest personality psychologists and vice versa. Indeed, both psychologists studying intelligence and personality psychologists have come to recognizing a huge overlap in the phenomena each side studies and the need and potential for an interface between intelligence and personality variables in explaining these phenomena (e.g., Cantor, 1990; Cantor & Kihlstrom, 1989; Sternberg & Wagner, 1989).

Basic mental operations

Psychologists studying intelligence who subscribe to the information-processing perspective have referred to intelligence as the basic mental operations or fundamental cognitive processes that are responsible for the acquisition of knowledge, and for the formulation and monitoring of problem-solving behavior (e.g., Carroll, 1982; Keating, 1984; Sternberg, 1985; see Sternberg, 1990 for review). For them, individual differences in performance on intellectual tasks are typically seen as manifestations of individual differences in basic mental processes.

What do psychologists studying intelligence consider these basic mental operations to be? Recently, Sternberg (1984, 1985, 1987, 1988) proposed a list of basic mental operations individuals apply in task performance for reaching a solution. They include (a) metacognitive processes used for planning, executing, monitoring, and evaluating task performance, (b) performance processes used in problem analysis, and (c) knowledge acquisition, retention, and transfer processes involved in learning and storing new information. In a similar vein, Carroll (1982) has suggested that performance on mental tests can be explained in terms of a small set of basic mental operations, ranging from attention–encoding–apprehension, to perceptual integration–problem representation, comparison–transformation, and execution–monitoring.

If intelligence is defined by basic mental operations, it follows that individual differences in intelligence may also be understood in terms of individual differences in how these processes are carried out. Advocates of this viewpoint (e.g., Eysenck, 1967) proposed that the primary sources of individual differences in intelligence are individual differences in the power or efficiency of the information-processing system. More recently, Hunt (1983) has suggested that individual differences in lexical access, in how information is manipulated in working memory, and in problem representation give rise to individual differences in mental functioning. Similarly, Sternberg (1990) reasoned that, if intelligence consists of component processes (such as those named above), then individual differences in the number of component processes used in problem solving, in how these processes are combined and ordered, and in the accuracy and efficiency of the processes should contribute to individual differences in intellectual performance.

Skills and knowledge

Intelligence has also been referred to as the level of skills and knowledge currently available for problem solving. This view has a long tradition. For example, early associationists, such as Thorndike, Bergman, Cobb, and Woodyard (1926) defined intelligence as the number of associations individuals have as a result of previous learning. More recently, psychologists such as Cattell (1987) and Horn (1968, 1986) have asserted that one important kind of intelligence – crystalized intelligence – consists of a repertoire of skills and knowledge learned under the aegis of a particular institution (e.g., a school). Similarly, Glaser (1986) has suggested that an important aspect of intelligence is proficiency in the knowledge acquired through schooling or socialization.

Recent developments in artificial intelligence have stimulated a new wave of theorizing in the psychology of intelligence. One result of this is the characterization of intelligence as expertise, or, the repertoire of knowledge used in problem-solving (Anderson, 1983). Anderson views this knowledge repertoire as consisting of both declarative knowledge and procedural knowledge. Interestingly, declarative knowledge includes factual information as well as beliefs and attitudes. Procedural knowledge includes the rules, skills, and strategies available for acquiring, manipulating, storing, and retrieving declarative knowledge.

One aspect of this wave of theorizing is particularly noteworthy for our purposes. Beliefs and attitudes are usually a central construct in personality psychology. By including them as a constituent of a person's knowledge base or expert system, psychologists studying intelligence are making the intelligence–personality boundary a fuzzy one. Other current intelligence theorists include such factors as part of intelligence as well. For example, Sternberg and Wagner (1989) believe that an important constituent of intelligence is the individual's beliefs about people, situations, events, and the self. Thus, although traditionally psychologists have regarded personal values, beliefs, and constructs primarily as personality constructs, cognitive psychologists interested in intelligence are beginning to view them also as parts of the intelligence system.[1]

Indeed, the boundary between intelligence and personality was not very clear from the inception of the psychology of intelligence. That is, early theorists tended to view individuals' world views, attitudes, and beliefs as part of general intelligence (e.g., Binet & Simon, 1916; Wechsler, 1944, 1949). Only later were such factors banished from the study of "pure" intelligence, but, as noted above, they are finding their way back (see also Piaget & Garcia, 1989).

Adaptive problem-solving behavior

As early as 1916, Binet and Simon (1916) singled out adaptation as one of the defining criteria of intelligence. The notion of intelligence as adaptation is also central to Piaget's (1972) theory of cognitive development. For modern cognitive theorists who view intelligent behavior as adaptive problem-solving behavior, the adaptiveness of a cognitive system is evaluated primarily by whether the system can make maximal use of the available information (Barlow, 1983, 1987), whether it can function to achieve the organism's goals (Sternberg, 1985, 1988), and whether it permits the organism to meet the demands of a changing environment (Anastasi, 1986; Berry, 1986).

A definition as broad as this has practically removed any conceivable distinction between intelligence and personality functioning. As we shall show in the next section, the concept that personality is an individual's modes of adjustment to the environment is found in a wide spectrum of personality theories. Traditionally, psychologists studying intelligence have concentrated on the study of adaptive behavior in academic areas, whereas personality psychologists have concentrated on the study of adaptive behavior in nonacademic or social contexts. As long as both sides keep to their traditionally defined territories, a distinction may still be made between intelligence and personality. However, as psychologists studying intelligence become interested in everyday problem-solving behavior, this distinction may fade. For example, Sternberg and Wagner (1989) have extended the scope of intelligent behavior to include adaptive problem-solving behavior in daily life, and their research has shown that what gives rise to such intelligent behavior is not the factual knowledge needed in answering IQ test questions, but rather practical knowledge about how to self-regulate, how to work with others, and how to get one's work done (Sternberg & Wagner, 1989; Wagner, 1987; Wagner & Sternberg, 1985).

Furthermore, as we will show shortly, personality researchers are also studying the processes underlying adaptive problem-solving behavior in academic areas and are finding that many of these processes are analogous to those underlying adaptive problem-solving behavior in nonacademic areas. This would further blur the distinction between the two fields of study.

Summary

Modern cognitive psychologists have used the term intelligence to refer to one or more of the three levels of mental functioning: basic mental operations, the knowledge base, and adaptive problem-solving behavior. In this section, we argued that only at the level of basic mental operations can a clear distinction be made between intellectual processes and personality processes. At the level of the knowledge base, factors that have traditionally been classified as personality factors are being included as part of the expert system. At the actualized behavioral level, there is great overlap in the basic phenomena studied by psychologists studying intelligence and those studied by personality psychologists. It is true that psychologists studying intelligence have concentrated on the study of problem solving in academic areas whereas personality psychologists have concentrated on the study of problem solving in social contexts. However, this distinction becomes blurred as more psychologists studying intelligence are extending their scope of analysis to problem-solving behavior in the daily world. And the distinction will become even more obscure when we show later that many of the processes that generate adaptive behavior in the academic and nonacademic domains do not differ in kind.

Three levels of personality processes

Personality theorists have endowed the term personality with so many different meanings that there are almost as many definitions of personality as there are personality psychologists. In 1937, Allport (1937) conducted an exhaustive review of the literature and extracted almost fifty different definitions of personality. By 1952, personality was elected by Eysenck (1957) as the most general and ill-defined term in psychology. The diversity in the definitions of personality was captured by Hall and Lindsay (1957, 1970, 1978) when they declared in their now classic personality textbook that no substantive definition of personality can be applied with any generality, and that personality can be defined only by the particular empirical concepts personality theorists developed in their theory.[2]

However, this state of theoretical plurality is less disheartening than it appears to be, for a survey of the major personality constructs presented in dominant personality theories reveals that most of them can be grouped into one of the three levels analogous to the ones described for intelligence: (a) basic motivational and affective processes, (b) knowledge structures and beliefs, and (c) adaptive problem-solving behavior.[3] In this section, we describe different core personality constructs presented in various personality theories that fall into these three categories.

Basic motivational and affective processes

Basic motivational and affective processes have been referred to as the "hot" processes in psychological functioning, in contrast to the "cold" basic mental operations (Zajonc, 1980, Zajonc & Markus, 1985). We focus on them as the basic personality processes because they provide the greatest contrast with basic cognitive processes and hence provide the strongest case for the potential separability between intelligence and personality.

Personality theories have customarily assigned basic motivational and affective processes crucial roles in personality. In fact, it is extremely difficult, and may even be impossible, to find a personality theory that does not contain any assumption, implicit or explicit, about what motivates behavior. Even radical behaviorist theories of personality, which tried to exile "inner forces" from formal psychological theorizing, had to postulate basic hedonic motivational processes to account for reinforcement effects (see Herrnstein, 1977).

Indeed, a question that sits at the center of personality psychology has not been whether or not motivational processes affect behavior but *what* motivates behavior. Answers to this question form an important part of the classical personality theories. Psychodynamic theorists contributed much to the enrichment of motivational vocabulary in personality psychology, although the scientific status of the motivational constructs they proposed has been widely called into question. Among others, Freud (1940/64) underscored the role of basic motivational and affective processes in personality. For him, the basic motivational processes involved trying to satisfy the biologically based instincts of the id while at the same time minimizing punishment and guilt (Maddi, 1968). Much of the individuals' ideation and actual behavior were thought to be largely determined by how these inner conflicts were resolved.

One motif in the neo-Freudian movement was to explore other fundamental motives. From this came Alder's striving for superiority (1929, 1939), Frankl's striving for meaning (1969), Murray's psychogenic needs (1938), Erikson's (1968) epigenetic drive, Sullivan's (1953) need for interpersonal contact and Mahler, Pine, and Bergman's (1975) need for autonomy.

The neo-Freudians' recognition of prosocial motives and the need for self-development foreshadowed the emphasis on growth needs by humanistic personality psychologists. Maslow (1954) and Rogers (1951), among others who were active in the Third Force Movement in personality psychology, singled out self-actualization as the master motive. They posited that the individuals' modes of cognition, affect, and behavior can be understood by studying how the environment facilitates or frustrates the inborn tendency towards growth.

We may consider these classical motivational personality theories as attempts to systematize the relations between motivation on the one hand and cognition–affect–behavior systems on the other hand. These theories suggested the possibility that human cognition (or all human functioning) is shaped by or organized around human motives, a possibility that most psychologists studying intelligence have not deeply explored. However, two aspects of these theories have seriously undermined their heuristic value in contemporary personality research. First, most motivational constructs in these theories are formulated at a highly abstract level. As such, they are difficult to operationalize (see Popper, 1963), although they might be useful as a general framework that can potentially be addressed empirically. Second, many of these constructs are derived from highly value-laden metatheoretical assumptions (see Vitz, 1977). Consequently, questions concerning which motives are fundamental can usually be answered only by referring to the theorists' personal conviction about what image of humans *should* be portrayed in personality theorizing (see Harré, 1983; Shotter, 1975).

Contemporary personality psychologists have sought motivational constructs that can be more precisely defined, operationalized, and assessed, but still can potentially offer a unified framework for considering both cognition and affect, and are useful for conceptualizing personality coherence and adaptive functioning. The concept of goal seems to be a promising candidate in meeting these desiderata, and accordingly is rapidly gaining currency within personality psychology (Baron, 1989; Baumeister, 1989; Cantor & Kihlstrom, 1989; Dweck & Leggett, 1988; Emmons & King, 1989; Pervin, 1989; Read & Miller, 1989; for empirical examples, see Elliott & Dweck, 1988; Emmons & King, 1988; Palys & Little, 1983).

One immediate consequence of these formulations is that personality functioning can be conceptualized as the display of relatively stable tendencies to pursue particular goals and to pursue them in particular ways. They also allow for domain-specific personality patterns in a way that broad motives did not, and accordingly allow us to understand better the organization of an individual's behavior within and across situations (see Dweck & Leggett, 1988). Moreover, using goal constructs, personality psychologists are now better equipped to conduct more dynamic, moment-to-moment analyses of the impact of particular goals on the cognition–affect–behavior systems. For example, as we will see later, Elliott and Dweck (1988) explained how setting different achievement goals affects children's cognition, affect, and behavior when they met with failures in problem-solving tasks. Specifically, they found that although children in different experimental conditions did not differ in performance before failure was introduced, those who were experimentally induced to set a performance goal (of documenting their ability) tended to display more negative self-cognitions, more negative affect, and more deterioration in their problem-solving strategies under failure, compared to children who were oriented towards a learning goal (of increasing their ability).

Interaction between basic motivational/affective processes and basic mental operations. Let us digress for a moment from our examination of the three levels of personality to ask: What are the relations between basic motivational/affective processes (e.g., goal-related processes) and basic mental operations? Customarily, basic mental operations have been regarded as a set of "cold" processes that operate independent of affect (see Fiske, 1982; Zajonc, 1980; Zajonc & Markus, 1985). In contrast, goal-related processes are typically viewed as "hot." That is, affect is associated with the motivational process of approaching or moving away from a goal (N. E. Miller, 1951) and with goal-related cognitions and behavior (see Pervin, 1983).

However, basic motivational and affective processes suffuse basic mental operations when these operations are set into action and brought to bear on a task (Anderson, 1983; Klinger, 1989). There are several ways in which motivational/affective processes suffuse cognitive processing. First, cognitive processes cannot invigorate themselves. They need some kind of motivational/affective processes to fuel them, and even "goal-less" thought would need affect to sustain it. Also, it is being increasingly recognized that cognitive processes are generally activated in the service of certain goals (Anderson, 1983; Emmons & King, 1989; Newell & Simon, 1972).

Second, evidence suggests that goals can influence the nature of cognitive processing: the way individuals conceptualize and categorize objects (Barsalou, 1983; see also Murphy & Medin, 1985), how causal explanations are formulated (e.g., J. G. Miller, 1984), and how the results of these cognitive processes, such as factual knowledge, learned skills and problem-solving strategies, are organized (Baumeister, 1989; Linville & Clark, 1989).

In fact, once motivational and affective processes suffuse cognitive processes, it is difficult to ascribe the product solely to the quality of the basic mental operations. Indeed, almost every example of distinguished accomplishment in art and science in history speaks to this point. For instance, if Einstein, given his talent, had not shown the immense interest in and fascination with one area of physics, it is doubtful that the quality of his thinking would have been as exceptional. When Einstein derived his mass–energy equation, he was not just applying logical–mathematical operations. More than that, he was applying logical–mathematical operations *to answer a question that had fascinated him for a long time.* Mozart, great though his talent was, turned out early compositions that were amateurish and trite. How much of his subsequent level of functioning was a result of "obsessive" devotion to his craft? In each of these cases, both motivational processes and cognitive processes had to be there to generate this high level of cognitive processing, because without one or the other these operations probably would not have been carried out, at least not by Einstein or Mozart. Thus, there is no way we can isolate the motivational processes from the cognitive processes and evaluate the relative contribution of each.

In short, goals combine with cognitive processes to shape and suffuse the acquisition of knowledge, skills, and beliefs. The idea that basic motivational/affective processes and basic mental operations are so fully blended that no line of demarcation can be discerned gives rise to the integrative model of psychological functioning illustrated in Figure 4.1.

Toward an integrative model: a further digression. Figure 4.1 depicts the relations between processes that are customarily labeled as intellectual processes and personality processes at the levels of basic processes, intermediate processes, and empirical phenomena. When psychological processes are reduced to their most basic level and conceptualized in the form of latent processes, it is conceivable that they may fall into two distinct behavior-generating systems: the cognitive system that processes information, and the motivational/affective system that plays a role in energizing and directing behavior. Traditionally, we have called the cognitive system "intelligence" and the motivational/affective processes part of "personality."

Figure 4.1 also shows that basic mental operations and basic motivational/affective processes always co-occur in the genesis and development of both factual and

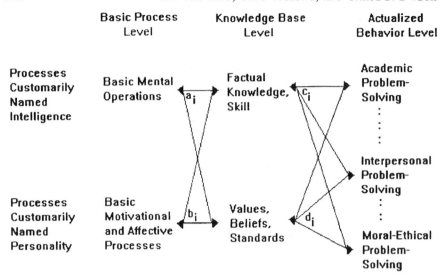

Figure 4.1.   An integrative model of psychological functioning.

nonfactual knowledge at the intermediate level (processes denoted by aî, bî). Here, the blending is so thorough that there is no way to separate them or to evaluate their independent contributions. Moreover, once knowledge and beliefs are formed, they can feed back to the basic processes and affect future cognitive processing (see Note 1) and goal selection.

Finally, both factual and nonfactual knowledge are activated and utilized in problem-solving behavior at the actualized behavioral level in various domains (processes denoted by arrows cî, dî). We will further explicate this model as we proceed.

Knowledge structures and beliefs

We turn now to the second level of personality processes: knowledge structures and beliefs. Instigated by the cognitive revolution in the seventies, many investigators have focused on the "mid-level" cognitive units of analysis within personality psychology (Dweck & Leggett, 1988; Epstein, 1990; Higgins, 1987; Markus & Nurius, 1986; Mischel, 1973, 1990; Rokeach, 1973; see Cantor & Zirkel, 1990 for a review).

Most of these constructs can be classified as certain kinds of nonfactual knowledge structures. For example, the implicit theories postulated by Dweck and Leggett (1988) or personal theories of reality postulated by Epstein (1990) are beliefs, and the self-guides postulated by Higgins (1987) and possible selves postulated by Markus and Nurius (1986) are standards.

One of the strengths of the current theories of beliefs and standards, compared to the overly broad constructs in early personality theories, is that they allow theorists to specify and empirically test the conditions that may give rise to these structures, as well as the impact of these structures on goal choice and pursuit. In fact, beliefs and standards played an important role in early personality theories. For instance, the Freudian notions of ego-ideal and conscience can be interpreted as a set of ethical standards, with the ego-ideal representing what an individual would ideally like to be and the conscience representing what an individual ought to be (see Morrison, 1983; Piers and Singer, 1953; see also Hong & Chiu, 1992). The notion of self-structure in Rogers's (1951) theory refers to an individual's values and beliefs about himself or herself. As he put it, the self is "what the individual recognizes, interprets, and values as his very own" (p. 498). Finally, the central construct in Kelly's (1955) cognitive theory of personality – the personal construct – is a belief an individual entertains to organize events and to anticipate future events. These constructs have been useful in providing a general perspective for us to think about how we can better understand human psychological functioning by using constructs such as beliefs, standards, and values. However, like the motivational constructs in early personality theories, these constructs tend to be so broadly defined that they generally do not specify how beliefs, standards, and values affect an individual's goal choice, goal pursuit, or the resultant cognition, affect, and behavior.

In contrast, the constructs of beliefs, values, and standards in current personality theories tend to be much more fine-tuned. For instance, Higgins's self-discrepancy theory demonstrates specific relationships between particular standards (e.g., ideal standards versus ought standards) and particular emotional responses (e.g., dejection versus agitation). As we will see later in the discussion of our own empirical work, using particular beliefs, we show clear specific prediction to domain-specific patterns of goal-directed behavior and the resultant affect and cognition.

Another noteworthy trend is that, as psychologists studying intelligence have begun to regard nonfactual knowledge as part of the knowledge base, personality psychologists are paying increasing attention to factual knowledge as part of the knowledge base. That is, although many of the postulated cognitive constructs are nonfactual knowledge structures, many personality theories now recognize the importance of factual knowledge (e.g., skills and expertise) in personality functioning. For example, in Linville and Clark's (1989) formulation, solving problems in a social context requires a repertoire of coping skills. As an individual's social problem-solving skills develop with practice, they are compiled into a set of procedural rules. This procedural knowledge is what underlies the individual's subsequent coping style.

Other investigators have tried to spell out the interaction between factual and nonfactual knowledge. For example, Higgins's (1987) self-discrepancy theory hypothesizes another kind of interaction between factual and nonfactual knowledge. He presents evidence that emotional vulnerabilities can be predicted by how factual knowledge about oneself stands in relation to one's standards or self-guides. Emotional vulnerabilities are present when there is a discrepancy between individual's factual (or actual) self and their standards.

Another way to look at the relation between factual and nonfactual knowledge is represented by Dweck and her associates (Bergen & Dweck, 1989; Dweck & Leggett, 1988). They consider factual knowledge or skills as a pool of mental resources individuals may draw on to formulate problem-solving strategies. However, individuals' nonfactual knowledge (such as beliefs and values) imposes constraints on the factual knowledge or skills that are actually mobilized and used in problem solving.

In summary, new kinds of knowledge structures have been proposed. Unlike the overly broad constructs in early personality theories, these constructs allow investigators to specify more precisely and test empirically how these structures are generated and organized, and how they affect goal choice, goal pursuit, and problem-solving behavior in different contexts. In addition, while psychologists studying intelligence are beginning to acknowledge the role of nonfactual knowledge, factual knowledge is finding its way in models of personality. However, this convergence does not necessarily mean that a distinction cannot be made between intellectual variables and personality variables. If the phenomena studied by intelligence researchers and personality researchers are different, one can still argue that the knowledge needed in intelligent behavior is different from that needed in adaptive personality functioning, although they are both knowledge. But what if the phenomena studied in these two fields are often quite similar? We turn now to an examination of this possibility.

Problem-solving behavior

As with intelligence, it is within the tradition of personality psychology to evaluate personality functioning in terms of individual adaptiveness. Allport, for example, defined personality as the "consistent and stable modes of an individual's adjustment to his environment" (Allport & Odbert, 1936, p. 26). Similarly, behavioral psychologists have used the extent to which individuals' learned behavior fits in with their environmental milieu as the defining criterion of personality functioning (e.g., Skinner, 1953). Not surprisingly, how individuals adjust to or cope with daily problems or life problems has been a major topic in personality research (e.g., Lazarus & Folkman, 1984).

With increasing emphasis on goal concepts has come a broadening concept of what constitutes adaptive problem-solving behavior. Earlier, the analysis of adaptive behavior was largely restricted to individuals' *reactive* problem-solving strategies in the face of stressful events. Now, many investigators believe that every goal individuals pursue creates a set of problems to be solved, because it requires them to formulate plans and strategies and to pursue these goals persistently even in the face of frustration or temptation (Dweck, 1990; Mischel, Shoda & Rodriguez, 1990; Pervin, 1989). The challenge for the field is thus to identify empirically which problem-solving approaches are adaptive for goal attainment and which are not. Some of the adaptive versus maladaptive problem-solving approaches that have been successfully identified in empirical research are the mastery-oriented versus helpless pattern (Diener & Dweck, 1978, 1980), mindfulness versus mindlessness (Langer, 1989), and high-level versus low-level action identification (Vallacher & Wegner, 1987).

Are the problem-solving approaches that characterize adaptive personality functioning different from those that characterize intelligent behavior? Conceptually, the answer is no. First, functionally speaking, both of them are designed to increase the probability of goal attainment. Moreover, intelligent behavior and adaptive personality problem solving have much in common (Dweck & Wortman, 1982). For example, both entail better utilization and deeper processing of information (Barlow, 1983, 1987; Langer, 1989) and the organization of action around higher-order goals (Anderson, 1983; Vallacher & Wegner, 1987).

Of course, as noted above, one can argue that the knowledge or problem-solving strategies used in the pursuit of goals in the intellectual domain may not be applicable to the pursuit of goals in the personality–social domain, and vice versa. Therefore, it may still be meaningful to draw a line between intelligent behavior and adaptive personality functioning. However, research in our laboratory strongly suggests (1) that many of the psychological processes underlying adaptive problem-solving behavior in the academic domain are directly analogous to the psychological processes underlying adaptive problem-solving behavior in the personality–social domain, and (2) that both are associated with the similar beliefs about valued attributes in their respective domains. We will elaborate this argument presently.

Conclusion

To conclude, our selective review of the current intelligence and personality literature suggests an integrative model of psychological functioning. This model, as illustrated in Figure 4.1, highlights the following points.

1. Intelligence and personality can be distinguished conceptually as two independent causal systems when the former refers to the set of latent basic mental operations and when the latter refers to the set of basic motivational/affective processes in their inert form. However, any attempt to make a clear separation between intelligence and personality beyond this level would be difficult and perhaps misleading. This argument is supported by the following observations.

2. There is now evidence that the acquisition and organization of knowledge results from the intertwined actions of the basic mental operations and basic motivational/affective processes. Thus, the acquisition of the knowledge base itself can be called an intellectual process or a personality–motivational process, depending on what one prefers to call it.

3. Both psychologists studying intelligence and those studying personality agree that the knowledge base of interest in their fields contains both factual knowledge and nonfactual knowledge (beliefs, values, and standards), and that both factual and nonfactual knowledge are involved in problem solving. Thus, granted that an investigator agrees that the individual's knowledge base constrains problem-solving

behavior, that investigator may describe this process as an intellectual process or as a personality process, depending on which term he or she prefers.

4. The psychology of intelligence and personality psychology often have the same object of study, particularly at the level of actualized behavior. Both are concerned with adaptive problem-solving behavior. Although, customarily, psychologists studying intelligence are primarily interested in academic problem solving whereas personality psychologists are mainly interested in social problem solving, the line of demarcation is less distinguishable now as psychologists studying intelligence start to extend their scope of analysis to practical problem solving (Wagner, 1987; Wagner & Sternberg, 1985) and to moral problem solving (Gibbs, Widaman, & Colby, 1982), while at the same time, some personality psychologists have extended their scope of analysis to academic problem solving (Cantor & Kihlstrom, 1989; Diener & Dweck, 1978, 1980; Henderson & Dweck, 1990; Hong & Dweck, 1993; Mischel, Shoda, & Rodriguez, 1989; Shoda, Mischel, & Wright, 1991). Thus, many of the same behavioral phenomena can be called intelligent behavior or adaptive personality functioning. What they are called is often a matter of preference.

Furthermore, studies in our laboratory show that many of the psychological processes underlying adaptive problem solving in the academic domain are directly analogous to those underlying adaptive problem solving in the social and moral domains. This implies that important aspects of adaptive functioning in these different domains can potentially be described by a unified theory of psychological functioning.

Illustrative research examples

Overview

In this section, we summarize the research programs in our laboratory that illustrate some aspects of the integrative model of psychological functioning depicted in Figure 4.1. Our work concentrates on how beliefs affect goal choice, goal pursuit and adaptive behavior. It thus illustrates how an individual's knowledge/belief base feeds back to the basic motivational processes and feeds forward to adaptive behavior.

We argue that similar psychological processes may affect an individual's adaptiveness in the intellectual, social, and moral domains. We start with a description of the common features of the adaptive versus maladaptive psychological patterns that we have documented in these various domains. We then move on to show that individuals' adaptiveness in these domains can be predicted by their core beliefs (or implicit theories) about the domain in question. These theories, which we view as part of people's personal epistemology, allow individuals to "understand" their reality, to choose appropriate goals, and to plan their action in that domain.

Specifically, in the intellectual domain, we will examine people's theories of intelligence; in the social domain, their theories of personality; and in the moral domain, their theories about the world and people's morality. For each, we identify people's beliefs about the basic nature of that attribute, particularly its malleability. They can either believe that the attribute is malleable – subject to instrumental control by the individual ("incremental theory") – or they can believe that the attribute is not under the control of the individual – being fixed or unpredictable ("entity theory"). An incremental theory assumes that a reality can be altered, developed, or shaped by the individual whereas an entity theory assumes a rigid or unresponsive reality and obliges the individuals to operate within it.

Having laid out this theoretical framework, we present evidence from research in our laboratory showing that, in any given domain, entity theorists, compared to incremental theorist, often display less adaptive or effective psychological functioning. Indeed, there are quite striking parallels in the features of the adaptive versus maladaptive response patterns across the three domains.

Intellectual achievement

Adaptive versus maladaptive patterns.   Our previous research (Diener & Dweck, 1978, 1980; Elliott & Dweck, 1988; Heyman, Dweck, & Cain, 1992; Licht & Dweck, 1984; see Dweck, 1990) has identified two patterns of response to challenges and obstacles in the pursuit of intellectual goals. The *mastery-oriented pattern* is characterized by the seeking and enjoyment of challenge, as well as by persistence and the generation of effective problem-solving strategies in the face of obstacles. This pattern appears to be adaptive because it allows individuals to maintain a commitment to their valued goals and increases the probability of goal attainment in the long run. In contrast, the *helpless response pattern* is characterized by risk avoidance, as well as by self-denigrating thoughts, negative affect, lack of persistence and performance deterioration following failure.

Our research has identified these patterns in populations ranging from preschool-aged children through college-aged individuals. It is important to note at the outset that individuals displaying the two patterns do not differ in actual ability (particularly in the grade-school years, where much of this work has been conducted). On both general measures of ability (e.g., IQ tests) and on task-specific measures of problem-solving ability prior to failure, the two groups are typically identical. Only in the face of impending or actual failure does their achievement tend to diverge. Thus, as will be seen, our studies begin with individuals identical in ability and often end with individuals who sharply differ in the level of skill they have acquired or can display.

These two distinctive patterns of responses were first extensively analyzed by Diener and Dweck (1978, 1980). In their experimental paradigm, the participants (late-grade-school children) were first given an attributional measure, shown by previous research (Dweck, 1975; Dweck & Reppucci, 1973) to be predictive of helpless and mastery-oriented behavior (e.g., persistence) in the face of failure. Some time later, the children participated in the experimental situation in which they worked on concept-formation problems. In order to monitor various aspects of their response to failure, after successfully solving the first eight problems, children were given another four problems that were too difficult for children of their age to solve. To monitor reported affect and cognitions, several trials before the failures began, the investigators asked the participants to verbalize their thoughts. They also monitored the strategies the participants used and measured their prediction of future performance before and after the failure trials. Before the onset of failure, the mastery-oriented children and the helpless children used equally sophisticated strategies and were equally interested in the task. This suggests that there was *no* ability difference between mastery-oriented children and helpless children before the onset of failure. However, after the onset of failure, two distinct patterns emerged.

First, the helpless children quickly began to engage in self-denigrating thoughts, attributing their failure to deficiency in global intellectual attributes (e.g., memory and intelligence). Moreover, despite their repeated success only moments before, they no longer expected success once failure was experienced. In striking contrast, the mastery-oriented children did not engage in self-denigrating thoughts. In fact, they did not seem to have viewed the unsolved problems as failures. Rather, they instructed themselves to exert effort or to concentrate, engaged extensively in formulating hypothesis-testing strategies and maintained high expectations for future success.

Second, the helpless children expressed boredom with the problems, aversion to the task, or anxiety over their performance, whereas the mastery-oriented children maintained their interest in and positive affect toward the task. Some even became enthusiastic about the opportunity for learning and mastery.

Finally, the helpless children, compared to the mastery-oriented children, reported task-irrelevant thoughts (often of a diversionary or self-aggrandizing nature), perhaps attempting to bolster their image in other ways instead of concentrating their resources on attaining success. Consistent with this, most helpless children showed a clear decrement in the level of problem-solving strategy, often falling into completely unproductive strategies. In contrast, most mastery-oriented children maintained or even increased the sophistication of their strategies. The latter actually taught themselves more developmentally-advanced strategies over the failure trials.

Implicit theories of intelligence. What orients individuals toward a particular pattern of problem-solving behavior? Our recent work suggests that how individuals conceive of intelligence may play a pivotal role in their behavior during difficult tasks (Henderson & Dweck, 1990; Dweck & Bempechat, 1983; see Cain & Dweck, 1989; Dweck & Leggett, 1988). Bandura and Dweck (1985) proposed that some individuals would conceive of intelligence as a relatively static entity over which they had no control ("entity theory"), whereas others would regard it as a malleable, dynamic quality that could be developed through their efforts ("incremental theory"). Different theories of intelligence were predicted to have different implications for achievement goals and their attainment. To begin with, when individuals believe that intelligence (a highly valued attribute) is a nonmalleable or fixed trait, their focal concern will be to document their intelligence. Thus, at any given moment, they will ask, "Is my ability adequate?" In contrast, if individuals conceive of intelligence as an increasable quality, they will be concerned with how they can develop their ability or achieve mastery.

Accordingly, entity theorists and incremental theorists should pursue different goals, with entity theorists more concerned with documenting their ability ("performance goals") and incremental theorists more concerned with increasing their ability ("learning goals"). Second, entity and incremental theorists should interpret and react to the same situation in different ways. For entity theorists, failures should more readily be seen as documenting a lack of ability and therefore should more readily precipitate a helpless response. This should be the case especially for entity theorists who have low confidence in their intellectual ability to begin with, because, for them, the negative feedback would provide confirmatory evidence for their "intellectual deficiency."

Our research findings support these hypotheses. First, entity theorists and incremental theorists appear to pursue different goals in the intellectual domain, with entity theorists preferring tasks that document ability and incremental theorists preferring tasks that promote learning. For example, Leggett (see Dweck & Leggett, 1988) measured junior high school students' theories of intelligence by means of a questionnaire asking them to agree or disagree with such statements as, "Your intelligence is something very basic about you that you can't really change." She then related the participants' theories to their preference for performance versus learning goals. These goals were embodied in three different kinds of tasks they could choose to work on: (a) a challenging performance task, (b) an easy performance task (that assured nonfailure), and (c) a challenging learning task (that risked performance failure). The latter two tasks sharply distinguished the entity and incremental theorists. Half of the entity theorists, but only about 10% of the incremental theorists, chose to work on easy problems that would not reflect poorly on their intelligence. In contrast, incremental theorists were far more likely than entity theorists to choose to work on challenging problems that would provide an opportunity for learning but by no means assured good performance (60.9% versus 18.2%). The important point here is that entity theorists sacrificed the opportunity for new learning when it carried a risk of poor performance, and often avoided challenge entirely for the "safety" of an easy task with no potentials for errors. In terms of long-term adaptation to one's environment, turning away from learning opportunities and challenges would limit the acquisition of skills and knowledge that would maximize future successes.

In another study, Dweck, Tenney, and Dinces (see Dweck & Leggett, 1988) manipulated children's theories of intelligence by asking children to read a passage that espoused an entity or incremental theory. Again, the results indicated that an incremental theory of intelligence is more consistently associated with a learning goal choice in the domain of intellectual achievement. Specifically, children who read the incremental passage, compared to children who read the entity message, were significantly more likely to choose challenging learning tasks and less likely to choose tasks that assured positive or avoided negative judgment. These results are consistent with the assertion depicted in Figure 4.1 that beliefs, after they are formed, can shape further goal pursuit. However, does entity versus incremental theory predict adaptive versus maladaptive problem solving at the actualized behavioral level?

Recent studies by Cain (1990) with grade-school children, Henderson and Dweck (1990) with junior high-school students, and Hong and Dweck (1993) with college students, linked individuals' theories of intelligence directly to the mastery-oriented versus helpless pattern. Specifically, Hong and Dweck (in preparation, Study 1) measured college students' theories of intelligence and their intellectual confidence and used them to predict the participants' reactions to programmed feedback on a conceptual-ability test about one week later.

Before presenting the main findings of this study, we want to underscore once again that the actual performance for entity and incremental theorists on the conceptual ability test did *not* differ. Thus, any differences between entity and incremental theorists in their response to feedback cannot be attributed to ability differences.

In this study, the investigators found that entity theorists displayed a more helpless pattern than incremental theorists. First, in terms of cognitive appraisal, when entity theorists were told that they had done poorly on the test they were more likely than incremental theorists to attribute their poor performance to lack of ability or skill. Incremental theorists, however, were more likely than the entity theorists to attribute their poor performance to lack of effort. Second, in terms of behavioral persistence, fewer entity theorists than incremental theorists chose to work on the same task after receiving the failure feedback.

In another experiment, Hong and Dweck (1993, Study 1) found that, compared to incremental theorists, entity theorists showed a much sharper change in response latency to ability-related words (but not to control words) after experiencing a failure. This again suggests that failures have greater implications for one's ability when one views intelligence as a fixed trait.

In another study, Henderson and Dweck (1990) assessed children's implicit theories of intelligence and their intellectual confidence and used these measures to predict their academic performance in junior high school. They reasoned that because the work, the pace, and the grading in the typical grade school are relatively unthreatening compared to those in the typical junior high school, the transition from grade school to junior high school may create conditions for the helpless pattern, just as the transition from initial success to failure created conditions for the helpless pattern in the Diener and Dweck study. As predicted, when they were in the seventh grade, children holding an incremental theory tended to show the mastery-oriented pattern. Overall, they matched or exceeded their projected grade point in seventh grade. In contrast, children holding an entity theory showed the helpless pattern. They displayed pronounced decline in their relative standing in seventh grade, compared to sixth grade. Overall, entity theorists who had had poor grades in the sixth grade remained low achievers and many of those who had been high achievers in sixth grade were now among the lowest achievers. Debilitation was most pronounced among high-confidence entity theorists, possibly because the confusion of the transition was most threatening to those who believe that intelligence is fixed and have been accustomed to thinking of themselves as having it.

The groups also showed predicted attributional and affective differences. On a measure that asked students what they would attribute poor grades to, entity theorists reported that they would attribute poor grades to lack of ability significantly more than incremental theorists did. In contrast, incremental theorists made significantly more strategy and more effort attributions than entity theorists did. Finally, entity theorists with low confidence reported significantly higher school anxiety than other groups. In summary, in the domain of intellectual achievement, implicit theories appear to set up and organize different patterns of behavior.

To summarize thus far, our research findings have consistently shown that individuals' theories of intelligence are systematically associated with adaptive versus maladaptive responses to failures on intellectual tasks. Incremental theorists are more likely than entity theorists to pursue learning goals and to display the mastery-oriented pattern in the face of obstacles, in real world situations as well as in laboratory situations.

Comments.   Predicting achievement outcomes in the intellectual domain has customarily been the subject matter of the psychology of intelligence. Thus, we may label the mastery-oriented response pattern intelligent behavior and the helpless pattern unintelligent behavior. However, the "unintelligent" response pattern is constituted partly by negative and often erroneous self-beliefs and self-attributions and by negative affect, which are phenomena studied primarily by personality psychologists (e.g., Tesser & Campbell, 1983).

Moreover, even if we could artificially decompose the adaptive versus maladaptive pattern into its respective "intellectual" elements (problem-solving strategies or academic performance being a good candidate) and "personality" elements (such as self-beliefs or self-attributions), the overall phenomenon would lose its psychological meaning, because, as our research suggests, at least some of the time, personality variables such as beliefs can predict level of problem-solving strategies and academic achievement better than measures of intellectual ability (Licht & Dweck, 1984). That is, measures of intellectual ability often do not appear to be good predictors of academic achievement under stress or failure. Indeed, in a study by Licht and Dweck (1984), IQ was *negatively* correlated with mastery of new material following failure for fifth grade girls. In contrast, students' beliefs were significant predictors of intellectual performance. What is called for then is an interface between "intelligence" and "personality" as conventionally defined in the explanation of adaptive academic behavior.

Social interaction

Adaptive versus maladaptive patterns.   As mentioned earlier, analogous mastery-oriented and helpless patterns have been found in the domain of social interaction.

Goetz and Dweck (1980) adapted the experimental paradigm used by Diener and Dweck (1978, 1980) to study grade-school children's responses to social rejection. In this study, the participants who were likely to display the helpless pattern were identified based on their responses to an attributional measure. They blamed their personal social competence for social rejection, whereas other children blamed either a negative attribute of the rejector, the unpredictable mood of the rejector, or a misunderstanding. The children then tried out for a pen pal club three weeks after the administration of the attributional measure. They communicated a sample getting-to-know-you letter to a peer evaluator who represented the pen pal acceptance committee. The evaluator initially expressed uncertainty about admitting the child into the club, but allowed the child the opportunity to compose a second letter. The letters composed before and after rejection were coded and compared.

The results were analogous to those in the Diener and Dweck studies. Again, helpless children did not differ from other children in their skills at the task: Children in different groups showed comparable performance prior to rejection in that the first letter produced by different groups did not differ in length and quality. However, clear differences between the helpless children and other children emerged in the letter that followed rejection. The differences provide a striking parallel to the difference between helpless children and mastery-oriented children in the intellectual achievement domain. For example, following rejection, helpless children, compared to other children, were far more likely to show task aversion, defensive self-aggrandizement, and disruption in performance. Specifically, about 40% of them showed initial refusal to try again after rejection or verbatim repetition of the first unsuccessful message. They also included less new information in the second message. In summary, the helpless children in the social-rejection study displayed point for point the aspects of the maladaptive pattern displayed in the intellectual-failure studies.

Implicit theories of personality.   Can these analogous adaptive versus maladaptive patterns be predicted by analogous cognitive–personality variables, that is, by implicit theories about the malleability of the core attribute in that domain? A recent study conducted by Erdley, Dumas-Hines, Loomis, Cain, Olshefsky and Dweck (1991, Study 1) supports this possibility. Erdley *et al.* reasoned that the individual's personality is typically a valued attribute in the social domain. Therefore, holding a theory that one's personality is a nonmalleable trait should heighten the individual's concern about obtaining a positive evaluation of that trait. For these individuals, having their advances rejected may be interpreted as evidence of deficiencies in their personality. Accordingly, they may engage in negative self-attributions. Entity theorists, then, particularly those with low confidence in their social skills, were predicted to blame their lack of ability to make friends as a reason for social failure. Further, following rejection, because entity theorists may believe that they lack the necessary attributes for success and any further efforts may simply set them up for additional failures, they may display the other aspects of the helpless pattern.

In contrast, children who enter a challenging social situation with an incremental theory of personality should be more concerned with developing and acquiring social skills. Thus, they may interpret initial failure as resulting from a lack of effort or an erroneous strategy, and may continue to try again with new strategies and tactics.

To test these predictions, Erdley *et al.* measured late-grade-school students' implicit personality theory using a questionnaire that asked them to agree or disagree with statements such as "You have a certain personality, and it is something that you can't change very much." They also measured their confidence in social ability. Each item consisted of a pair of contrasting statements, and the children were asked to choose the one that was more like them, e.g., "When I meet new people I am not sure if they will like me" versus "When I meet new people I think that they will like me." Based on these two measures, the children were divided into four groups: the entity–high confidence, entity–low confidence, incremental–high confidence, and incremental–low confidence. Approximately one week later, each child was seen individually and administered the Goetz and Dweck pen-pal paradigm. The predicted results emerged.

First, as revealed in the similar length and content of the prerejection letter across the four theory–confidence groups, the groups appeared to be equally skilled at the pen-pal task prior to rejection. However, following the rejection, incremental theorists included significantly more information in their second letter than entity theorists. Incremental theorists also made more positive self-evaluations in their letters than entity theorists did. Finally, also as predicted, low-confidence entity theorists tended to blame their failure on lack of ability at making friends more than any of the other groups did.

In both the domain of intellectual achievement and the domain of social interaction, we have seen that entity theorists tend to make global self-judgments, and to underutilize information for their self-development. Do these phenomena apply to their perception and judgments of others? In another series of studies, Erdley and Dweck (1991) showed that children who hold an entity theory of other people's personality are more prone to make global, rigid judgments of peers than children who hold an incremental theory. In these studies, children watched a slide show of a target child engaging in a series of negative behaviors (e.g., a new boy in school telling white lies, cheating a little, and stealing some examination materials in order to do well on his first day) and were later asked to make judgments about the target's current and future behavior. The behaviors engaged in by the target child were portrayed as stemming in part from situational pressures (e.g., being eager to make a good impression), were engaged in somewhat reluctantly, and were never malicious or harmful to others. Nevertheless, entity theorists, compared to incremental theorists, made more long-term negative predictions, more global negative judgments (endorsing superordinate traits like "bad" and "mean") and maintained many of their negative judgments even when they were exposed to direct counter-information. They also expressed less sympathy for the target child's plight and recommended harsher punishment. In summary, not unlike entity theorists in the intellectual domain, entity theorists in the social domain tend to display more global self and other judgments. Also not unlike entity theorists in the intellectual domain, who do not efficiently use incoming information to revise their problem-solving strategies, entity theorists in the social domain also tend to underutilize relevant information to update their social strategies or their judgment of others.

Summary and comments.   To summarize the information thus far, we have found parallel patterns in adaptive versus maladaptive responses in the domains of intellectual achievement and social interaction, and shown that adaptive versus maladaptive behavior patterns in both domains can be predicted by analogous cognitive–personality variables, namely, the belief in the malleability of the core attributes in the respective domains. This suggests that important aspects of adaptive functioning in the intellectual domain (generally regarded as "intelligent behavior") and adaptive functioning in the social domain (generally regarded as "adaptive personality functioning") may potentially be understood within one theoretical framework.

In both domains, adaptive problem-solving involves utilization of previously learned skills and knowledge. However, individuals also bring their prior beliefs into a challenging intellectual or social situation. These beliefs, as we have seen, structure the way individuals seek out information and the way they interpret information, which in turn affect their cognition, affect, and problem-solving strategies. These intricate interactions between "intelligence" and "personality" need to be acknowledged and studied directly in order to do justice to the phenomena in question.

Morality

Adaptive versus maladaptive patterns and implicit theories.   Are there analogous patterns of adaptive versus maladaptive responses to moral outcomes, and if so, can these patterns be predicted by analogous psychological processes? A recent set of studies by Chiu and Dweck (1991) suggests that the answer is an affirmative one. They hypothesized that implicit theories would predict mastery-oriented versus helpless responses to injustice.

Specifically, they reasoned that since injustice emanates from conditions of the world and people's morality, whether these conditions are conceived of as malleable or not should have important implications for the individual's responses to injustice. When individuals believe that they live in a world of fixed or uncontrollable givens ("entity theorists"), they may accept the injustice as unalterable and hence display helpless responses. In contrast, those who believe that they live in a world that can be shaped and changed ("incremental theorists") should perceive the injustice as a problem to solve and hence tend to be mastery-oriented in the face of injustice.

To test these hypotheses, Chiu and Dweck (1991) used questionnaires to measure college students' implicit theories about the world and other people's morality. On these questionnaires, the participants were asked to agree or disagree with statements such as "Our world has its basic and ingrained dispositions, and you really can't do much to change it" and "Whether a person is responsible and sincere or not is deeply ingrained in their personality. You can't change them very much." Based on their scores on these measures, the participants were classified as "entity theorists" (i.e., had entity theories about the world and people's morality), or as "incremental theorists" (i.e., had incremental theories about the world and people's morality).

Then, the investigators assessed the participants' reactions to injustice in two ways. First, they presented a chronicle of the Tienanmen Massacre that happened in China in June, 1989. The chronicle described how unarmed Chinese students and civilians were massacred and arrested by the Chinese government during and after a peaceful prodemocracy demonstration in Beijing. The participants' recommended reactions to the portrayed injustice were assessed. Second, they described an injustice in which students did not get the grade they were promised in an introductory calculus class because the professor in that class went back on his word. The participants were asked to imagine, as they read, that this had happened to them, and then to indicate how they would react to this situation.

The results showed that, in the Tienanmen Massacre scenario, entity theorists were significantly more likely than incremental theorists to endorse resigned (helpless) responses, e.g., "There is not much people in China could do" and "the Chinese democrats could only hope that the old Communist leaders would die soon." In addition, incremental theorists were significantly more likely than entity theorists to assert that the Chinese democrats had the right to change the system.

Next, in their response to the personal injustice, although entity theorists and incremental theorists did not differ in the likelihood of reporting some kind of action, incremental theorists reported significantly more persistence than entity theorists if their action was not initially successful. Moreover, entity theorists and incremental theorists who intended to take action had different goals. Whereas the entity theorists' goal was to release their anger, the incremental theorists' goal was to persuade the professor to adhere to a moral principle.

Finally, entity theorists and incremental theorists who did not plan to take action offered different reasons for their decision. Entity theorists justified their inaction by saying either that there was not much they could do about it or that they thought that confronting the professor would be too costly or too much trouble. In contrast, incremental theorists who did not intend to take action believed that the class was meant to learn and not to achieve a grade. Thus, the mastery-oriented versus helpless patterns were revealed in the face of injustice. Entity theorists, compared to incremental theorists, were more pessimistic and resigned, less persistent, and less concerned with rectifying an injustice.

In this study to examine the discriminant validity of theory measures in different domains, the investigators also measured the participants' entity versus incremental theories about intelligence. They found that only implicit theories about the world and people's morality, but not implicit theories about intelligence, predicted the participants' mastery-oriented versus helpless pattern to injustice. This suggests that an individual's belief–action system may be domain-specific; that is, behavioral patterns in a particular domain are best predicted by beliefs in the same domain.

In another study, Gervey, Chiu, and Dweck (1991) investigated how entity and incremental theorists in the moral domain utilized information in making juridical judgments. They found that, as in the intellectual and social domains, entity theorists, relative to incremental theorists, did not utilize relevant information effectively, and hence were more prone to making erroneous or biased judgments. Specifically, when making a juridical judgment (of guilt and sentence duration in a murder case), entity theorists gave substantial weight to peripheral, essentially crime-irrelevant information, such as the respectability of the defendant's clothing, whereas incremental theorists gave no weight to such information and focussed instead on the evidence that spoke directly to the probability of guilt.

One interpretation, supported by additional data in this study, is that entity theorists used this peripheral information to judge the defendant's overall moral character. This may then have mediated their differential judgments.

In summary, in the moral domain, entity theorists, compared to incremental theorists, displayed more helpless versus mastery-oriented responses to injustice, and tended to overuse peripheral information to make sweeping juridical judgments.

Summary and comments.   Taken together, findings from our research program suggest that there are parallel patterns of adaptive versus maladaptive behavior across different domains. We have also documented that these parallel patterns are characterized by analogous psychological processes. Accordingly, different patterns of adaptive versus maladaptive behavior may potentially be understood within a general theoretical framework. This possibility raises a number of interesting theoretical issues, and in the next section we will discuss two issues that have direct bearing on the relations between intelligence and personality. These issues are: What are the common denominators of adaptive functioning across various domains and what are the levels of explanation of adaptive functioning that are most appropriate or illuminating?

Toward a general model of adaptive functioning

Common denominators of adaptive functioning

The possibility of a general theory of psychological functioning raises the issue of how we should define adaptive functioning across various domains. Dweck (1990) proposed three criteria in defining adaptive psychological functioning that may be useful in dealing with this issue. First, in contrast to a maladaptive pattern that puts an individual's basic goals in conflict, an adaptive pattern should render individuals' basic needs compatible with each other. Second, whereas a maladaptive pattern reduces the probability of attaining self-chosen goals, an adaptive pattern should promote the attainment of valued goals. Finally, an adaptive pattern should allow an individual to make fuller use of the information available. In contrast, a maladaptive pattern leads an individual to traffic excessively in fictions instead of realities. These proposed common denominators of adaptive functioning have been documented in our research in the domains of intellectual achievement, social interaction and morality. We will address each of them in turn.

First, in the academic domain, the basic goals are performance and learning. In this domain, the entity-helpless pattern focuses individuals' attention on moment-to-moment performance evaluation, the effect of which is to curtail individuals' motivation to learn. In contrast, the incremental–mastery pattern focuses individuals on constructive mastery efforts, the long-term effect of which is greater learning and improvement in performance. Thus, the incremental theory fosters coordination and attainment of both goals.

The same applies in the social domain. As far as interpersonal interactions are concerned, basic goals are to maintain positive social judgments from relevant others, to develop and maintain relationships, and to acquire social skills. Again, the entity–helpless pattern may heighten individuals' concerns about social judgment, which is often incompatible with acquiring new skills and developing relationships, especially in the face of obstacles. The incremental–mastery pattern, in contrast, fosters information utilization and the generation of effective strategies, which in turn may lead to positive social judgments and better relationships.

Finally, in the moral domain, the goals of responses to injustice are to restore the social or interpersonal inequity caused by the injustice (e.g., to get even) and to prevent future injustices from occurring. The goals of both restoring social and interpersonal inequity and preventing future injustice are more compatible in the incremental system than in the entity system. For example, in the incremental system, once the perpetrators are persuaded to go back to an ethical principle, the interpersonal inequity will be rectified and the probability of future injustice will be reduced. In contrast, entity theorists' responses to injustice, such as resignation and retaliation, reduce the probability of attaining both goals or put these two goals in conflict. Take retaliation as an example. Its purpose is to get even. However, once the victims have gotten even, the perpetrators may perceive the situation as equitable and hence will not see any need to change their behavior or to work out an alternative social arrangement that would prevent future injustice from occurring.

The second common denominator of adaptive functioning is whether the probability of goal attainment will be enhanced or reduced. Our research shows that, in the face of obstacles, an entity system reduces the probability of attaining self-chosen goals, whereas an incremental system tends to enhance it. Granted that the self-chosen goals within an entity framework are often to foster positive self-evaluations in the intellectual and social domains, and to restore social and interpersonal equity in the moral domain, we have seen how the entity system leads to the demise of effective striving, which in turn reduces the probability of achieving these goals. For example, in the intellectual and social domains this demise of effective striving results in debilitation and consequently lowers the probability of maintaining positive self-evaluation. In the moral domain, the resigned coping strategies used by entity theorists might in the long run operate to stabilize injustices instead of restoring equity.

Finally, our research has documented that, across all domains, entity theorists relative to incremental theorists, did not utilize information effectively in making judgments. They tended either to under-utilize information or to utilize irrelevant information when making a judgment, oftentimes resulting in judgments that were overgeneralized, rigid, and even erroneous. For example, in the intellectual and social domains, their self-judgments of ability, particularly in the face of difficulty, were often a very inaccurate reflection of their actual abilities. In the social and moral domains, their judgments about others were often global, rigid, and overgeneralized.

In summary, by the three criteria specified (i.e., minimizing goal conflict, maximizing goal attainment, and effective information utilization), incremental theorists appear to exhibit more adaptive functioning.

Levels of explanation

Having identified a set of meaningful empirical phenomena that can be used to distinguish adaptive functioning from maladaptive functioning, the next question would be how to explain them. Subsumed under this issue are the issues of how many levels of explanation do we need and which level of explanation is most psychologically meaningful. Throughout this chapter, we have tried to separate three levels of psychological processes. At the first level are basic mental operations and basic motivational/affective processes. At the intermediate level is the individual's knowledge base which is comprised of factual knowledge, skills, values, standards, and beliefs. The third level is a set of empirical phenomena that we term (mal)adaptive problem-solving behavior.

We have concentrated our research effort on spelling out the relationship between individuals' knowledge base and adaptive problem solving. In this respect, individuals bring with them previously acquired skills and factual knowledge into every problem-solving situation. This factual knowledge base forms a resource pool. That is, this knowledge can potentially be used by individuals to solve the problems they are facing. Thus, how large this pool is will have an important bearing on the adaptiveness of individuals' problem-solving responses. However, our research has also shown that, controlling for the level of prior factual knowledge and skills, individuals' beliefs remain a significant predictor of adaptive problem solving. It appears that what knowledge is actually used in problem solving is often constrained by individuals' belief systems.

However, this does not imply that psychologists should concentrate all their research effort on individuals' beliefs and factual knowledge. Indeed, as Figure 4.1 implies, more microanalyses of cognitive processing and of the various ways that motivational/affective states affect cognitive processes (e.g., Bower, 1981; Simon, 1967) are critically important to our understanding (1) the acquisition of the knowledge base, (2) the contents and organization of the knowledge base and, (3) the application of the skills and knowledge to problem solving. Thus different levels of analysis remain essential to our understanding of adaptive psychological functioning and its underpinnings.

Some final comments on the distinction between intelligence and personality

Earlier we argued that investigators can call the psychological processes involved in the intermediate (knowledge base) and third (actualized behavior) levels intelligence or personality, depending on their preference. However, we do not wish to imply that these processes should be studied *either* as an intellectual process *or* as a personality process. We can use different names, but one way or another, we cannot capture these processes by referring to either the intellectual processes or the personality (e.g., motivational) processes alone. In fact, we caution against naming these processes as "intelligence" *or* "personality." We are particularly concerned about naming all processes "intelligence" because, traditionally, intelligence research has focused primarily on an individual's performance on intellectual tasks and how this reflects the individual's underlying cognitive processes; that is, motivational and affective processes have been generally neglected. Although current cognitive theories of personality (such as Cantor and Kihlstrom's social intelligence model) have maintained a fairly balanced emphasis on both cognitive and motivational aspects of personality, our concern is that if investigators choose to call all processes involved in the intermediate and third levels "intelligence," once the metaphor is lost the motivational and affective aspects of adaptive psychological functioning might be neglected. Thus, it appears that a more satisfactory treatment of the issue is (1) to retain the distinction between intelligence and personality at the basic process level, (2) to be wary of distinction between intelligence and personality at the second and third levels, and (3) to keep in mind that, as Figure 4.1 shows, the processes and phenomena in the second and third levels always result from the joint action of the basic intellectual processes and basic personality processes.

Conclusion

In this chapter, we described three levels of psychological processes that are customarily called intellectual processes and personality processes: the level of basic processes, the intermediate level of knowledge base, and the level of adaptive problem solving. We argued, with evidence from our own research, that the distinction between intelligence and personality can be clearly made only at the level of basic processes when the processes that comprise each construct are in their latent, inert form. However, when these basic processes are in action, they never work in isolation. Once the basic mental operations (intellectual processes) and basic motivational/affective processes (personality processes) are blended together, there is no way to draw a line of demarcation between them. Moreover, evidence from our laboratory suggests that important aspects of adaptive responding in the intellectual, social, and moral domains have similar cognitive–affective–behavioral manifestations, and may share similar psychological underpinnings. Thus, adaptive functioning across various domains may potentially be understood within a broadened and integrated framework of psychological functioning.

Notes

1 The introduction of artificial intelligence models into the psychology of intelligence has also heightened investigators' attention to the interaction between basic mental operations and the knowledge base. Clearly, basic mental operations shape the acquisition, retention, and transfer of knowledge and skills. However, as an individual's knowledge base is enlarged or modified, new metacognitive understandings may be created (Butterfield, 1986) and the workings of the basic mental operations may themselves be modified (see Anderson, 1983).
2 In fact, the state of theoretical plurality in personality psychology also characterizes the state of the art in the psychology of intelligence (see Sternberg & Detterman, 1986).
3 However, this does not imply that most theorists define personality by constructs at only one of these levels. Indeed, most personality theories recognize that personality functioning involves coordination of constructs at different levels.

References

Alder, A. (1929). *Problems of neurosis.* New York: Harper Torchbooks.

Alder, A. (1939). *Social interest.* New York: Putnam.

Allport, G. W. (1937). *Personality: A psychological interpretation.* New York: Holt.

Allport, G. W., & Odbert, H. S. (1936). Trait names: A psycho-lexical study. *Psychological Monographs, 47,* (No. 211).

Anastasi, A. (1986). Intelligence as a quality of behavior. In R. J. Sternberg & D. K. Detterman (Eds.), *What is intelligence? Contemporary viewpoints on its nature and definition* (pp. 19–21). Norwood, NJ: Ablex.

Anderson, J. R. (1983). *The architecture of cognition.* Cambridge, MA: Harvard University Press.

Bandura, M. M., & Dweck, C. S. (1985). *The relationship of conceptions of intelligence and achievement goals to achievement-related cognition, affect and behavior.* Unpublished Manuscript. Harvard University.

Barlow, H. B. (1983). Intelligence, guesswork, language. *Nature, 304,* 207–209.

Barlow, H. B. (1987). Intelligence: The art of good guesswork. In R. L. Gregory (Ed.), *The Oxford companion to the mind* (pp. 381–383). Oxford: Oxford University Press.

Baron, J. (1989). Why a theory of social intelligence needs a theory of character? Social intelligence and cognitive assessments of personality. In R. S. Wyer, Jr. & T. K. Srull (Eds.), *Social intelligence and cognitive assessments of personality* (pp. 61–70). Hillsdale, NJ: Erlbaum.

Barsalou, L. W. (1983). Ad hoc categories. *Memory and Cognition, 11,* 211–227.

Baumeister, R. F. (1989). Social intelligence and the construction of meaning in life. In R. S. Wyer, Jr. & T. K. Srull (Eds.), *Social intelligence and cognitive assessments of personality* (pp. 71–80). Hillsdale, NJ: Erlbaum.

Bergen, R., & Dweck, C. S. (1989). The functions of personality theories. In R. S. Wyer, Jr. & T. K. Srull (Eds.), *Social intelligence and cognitive assessments of personality* (pp. 81–92). Hillsdale, NJ: Erlbaum.

Berry, J. W. (1986). A cross-cultural view of intelligence. In R. J. Sternberg & D. K. Detterman (Eds.), *What is intelligence? Contemporary viewpoints on its nature and definition* (pp. 35–38). Norwood, NJ: Ablex.

Binet, A., & Simon, T. (1916). The development of intelligence in children (The Binet–Simon Scale). (E. S. Kite, Trans.). Baltimore: Williams & Wilkins.

Bower, G. H. (1981). Emotional mood and memory. *American Psychologist, 36,* 129–148.

Butterfield, E. C. (1986). Intelligent action, learning, and cognitive development might be explained with the same theory. In R. J. Sternberg & D. K. Detterman (Eds.), *What is intelligence? Contemporary viewpoints on its nature and definition* (pp. 45–49). Norwood, NJ: Ablex.

Cain, K. M. (1990). *Children's motivational patterns and conceptions of intelligence: A study of the developmental relationship between motivation and cognition.* Unpublished doctoral dissertation, University of Illinois.

Cain, K. M., & Dweck, C. S. (1989). The development of children's conceptions of intelligence: A theoretical framework. In R. J. Sternberg (Ed.), *Advances in the psychology of human intelligence* (Vol. 8, pp. 47–82). Hillsdale, NJ: Erlbaum.

Cantor, N. (1990). From thought to behavior: "Having" and "doing" in the study of personality and cognition. *American Psychologist, 45,* 735–750.

Cantor, N., & Kihlstrom, J. F. (1989). Social intelligence and cognitive assessments of personality. In R. S. Wyer, Jr. & T. K. Srull (Eds.), *Social intelligence and cognitive assessments of personality* (pp. 1–59). Hillsdale, NJ: Erlbaum.

Cantor, N., & Zirkel, S. (1990). Personality, cognition, and purposive behavior. In L. A. Pervin (Ed.), *Handbook of personality: Theory and research* (pp. 135–164). New York: Guilford.

Carroll, J. B. (1982). The measurement of intelligence. In R. J. Sternberg (Ed.), *Handbook of human intelligence* (pp. 29–120). Cambridge: Cambridge University Press.

Cattell, R. B. (1987). *Intelligence: Its structure, growth and action.* New York: Elsevier.

Chiu & Dweck (1991). *A meaning-action system approach to justice and moral beliefs.* Unpublished Manuscript.

Diener, C. I., & Dweck, C. S. (1978). An analysis of learned helplessness: Continuous changes in performance, strategy and achievement cognitions following failure. *Journal of Personality and Social Psychology, 36,* 451–462.

Diener, C. I., & Dweck, C. S. (1980). An analysis of learned helplessness: 2. The processing of success. *Journal of Personality and Social Psychology, 31,* 940–952.

Dweck, C. S. (1975). The role of expectations and attributions in the alleviation of learned helplessness. *Journal of Personality and Social Psychology, 39,* 674–685.

Dweck, C. S. (1990). Self-theories and goals: Their role in motivation, personality, and development. *Nebraska Symposium on Motivation, 1990* (pp. 199–235). Lincoln: University of Nebraska Press.

Dweck, C. S., & Bempechat, J. (1983). Children's theories of intelligence. In S. Paris, G. Olsen, & H. Stevenson (Eds.), *Learning and motivation in the classroom* (pp. 239–256). Hillsdale, NJ: Erlbaum.

Dweck, C. S., & Leggett, E. L. (1988). A social-cognitive approach to motivation and personality. *Psychological Review, 95,* 256–273.

Dweck, C. S., & Reppucci, N. D. (1973). Learned helplessness and reinforcement responsibility in children. *Journal of Personality and Social Psychology, 25,* 109–116.

Dweck, C. S., & Wortman, C. B. (1982). Learned helplessness, anxiety, and achievement motivation. In H. W. Krohne & L. Laux (Eds.), *Achievement, stress, and anxiety* (pp. 93–125). Washington, DC: Hemisphere.

Elliott, E. S., & Dweck, C. S. (1988). Goals: An approach to motivation and achievement. *Journal of Personality and Social Psychology, 54,* 5–12.

Emmons, R. A., & King, L. A. (1988). Personal striving conflict: Immediate and long-term implications for psychological and physical well-being. *Journal of Personality and Social Psychology, 54,* 1040–1048.

Emmons, R. A., & King, L. A. (1989). On the personalization of motivation. In R. S. Wyer, Jr. & T. K. Srull (Eds.), *Social intelligence and cognitive assessments of personality* (pp. 111–122). Hillsdale, NJ: Erlbaum.

Epstein, S. (1990). Cognitive–experiential self-theory. In L. A. Pervin (Ed.), *Handbook of personality: Theory and research* (pp. 165–192). New York: Guilford.

Erdley, C. A., Dumas-Hines, F., Loomis, C. C., Cain, K. M., Olshefsky, L. M., & Dweck, C. S. (1991). *Social-cognitive mediators of children's responses to social failure.* Unpublished Manuscript.

Erdley, C. A., & Dweck, C. S. (1991). *Children's implicit personality theories as predictors of their social judgments.* Unpublished Manuscript.

Erikson, E. H. (1968). *Identity: Youth and crisis.* New York: Norton.

Eysenck, H. J. (1952). Personality. *Annual Review of Psychology, 3,* 151–174.

Eysenck, H. J. (1967). Intelligence assessment: A theoretical and experimental approach. *British Journal of Educational Psychology, 37,* 81–98.

Fiske, S. T. (1982). Schema-triggered affect: Applications to social perception. In M. S. Clark & S. T. Fiske (Eds.), *Affect and cognition: The 17th annual Carnegie symposium on cognition* (pp. 55–78). Hillsdale, NJ: Erlbaum.

Frankl, V. E. (1969). *The will to meaning: Foundations and applications of logotherapy.* New York: New American Library.

Freud, S. (1940/1964). New introductory lectures on psychoanalysis. In J. Strachey (Ed. and Trans), *The standard edition of the complete psychological works of Sigmund Freud* (Vol. 23, pp. 139–207). London: Hogarth Press.

Gervey, B. M., Chiu, C., & Dweck, C. S. (1991). *Implicit theories as a predictor of what constitutes evidence in juridical judgments.* Unpublished raw data.

Gibbs, H. C., Widaman, K. F., & Colby, A. (1982). *Social intelligence: Measuring the development of sociomoral reflection.* Englewood Cliffs, NJ: Prentice-Hall.

Glaser, R. (1986). Intelligence as acquired proficiency. In R. J. Sternberg & D. K. Detterman (Eds.), *What is intelligence? Contemporary viewpoints on its nature and definition* (pp. 77–83). Norwood, NJ: Ablex.

Goetz, T. E., & Dweck, C. S. (1980). Learned helplessness in social situations. *Journal of Personality and Social Psychology, 39,* 246–255.

Hall, C. S., & Lindsay, G. (1957). *Theories of personality.* New York: Wiley.

Hall, C. S., & Lindsay, G. (1970). *Theories of personality* (2nd Ed.). New York: Wiley.

Hall, C. S., & Lindsay, G. (1978). *Theories of personality* (3rd Ed.). New York: Wiley.

Harré, R. (1983). *Personal being: A theory for individual psychology.* Oxford: Basil Blackwell.

Henderson, V., & Dweck, C. S. (1990). Adolescence and achievement. In S. Feldman & G. Elliott (Eds.), *At the threshold: Adolescent development.* Cambridge, MA: Harvard University Press.

Herrnstein, R. J. (1977). The evolution of behaviorism. *American Psychologist, 32,* 593–603.

Heyman, G. D., Dweck, C. S., & Cain, K. M. (1992). Young children's vulnerability to self-blame and helplessness: Relationship to beliefs about goodness. *Child Development, 63,* 401–415.

Higgins, E. T. (1987). Self-discrepancy: A theory relating self and affect. *Psychological Review, 94,* 319–340.

Hong, Y., & Chiu, C. (in press). A study of the comparative structure of guilt and shame. *Journal of Psychology, 126,* 171–179.

Hong, Y., & Dweck, C. S. (1993). *A test of implicit theory and self-confidence as predictors of self-inferences after failure.* Manuscript submitted for publication.

Horn, H. L. (1968). Organization of abilities and the development of intelligence. *Psychological Review, 75,* 242–259.

Horn, H. L. (1986). Some thoughts about intelligence. In R. J. Sternberg & D. K. Detterman (Eds.), *What is intelligence? Contemporary viewpoints on its nature and definition* (pp. 91–96). Norwood, NJ: Ablex.

Hunt, E. (1983). On the nature of intelligence. *Science, 219,* 141–146.

Keating, D. P. (1984). The emperor's new clothes: The "new look" in intelligence research. In R. J. Sternberg (Ed.), *Advances in the psychology of human intelligence* (Vol. 2, pp. 1–45). Hillsdale, NJ: Erlbaum.

Kelly, G. (1955). *The psychology of personal constructs.* New York: Norton.

Klinger, E. (1989). Goal orientation as psychological linchpin: A commentary on Cantor and Kihlstrom's "Social intelligence and cognitive assessment of personality." In R. S. Wyer, Jr. & T. K. Srull (Eds.), *Social intelligence and cognitive assessments of personality* (pp. 12–130). Hillsdale, NJ: Erlbaum.

Langer, E. J. (1989). *Mindlessness/Mindfulness.* Reading, MA: Addison-Wesley.

Lazarus, R. S., & Folkman, S. (1984). *Stress, appraisal, and coping.* New York: Springer.

Licht, B. G., & Dweck, C. S. (1984). Determinants of academic achievement: The interaction of children's achievement: The interaction of children's achievement orientations with skill area. *Developmental Psychology, 20,* 628–636.

Linville, P. W., & Clark, L. F. (1989). Production systems and social problem-solving: Specificity, flexibility, and expertise. In R. S. Wyer, Jr. & T. K. Srull (Eds.), *Social intelligence and cognitive assessments of personality* (pp. 131–151). Hillsdale, NJ: Erlbaum.

Maddi, S. (1968). *Personality theories: A comparative analysis.* Homewood, IL: Dorsey.

Mahler, M., Pine, F., & Bergman, A. (1975). *The psychological birth of the human infant: Symbiosis and individuation.* New York: Basic Books.

Markus, H., & Nurius, P. (1986). Possible selves. *American Psychologist, 41,* 954–969.

Maslow, A. H. (1954). *Motivation and personality.* New York: Harper & Row.

Matarazzo, J. D., & Denver, D. R. (1984). Intelligence measures. In R. J. Corsini & Ozaki, B. D. (Eds.), *Encyclopedia of psychology,* (Vol. 2, pp. 231–234). New York: Wiley.

Miller, J. G. (1984). Culture and the development of everyday explanation. *Journal of Personality and Social Psychology, 46,* 961–978.

Miller, N. E. (1951). Comments on theoretical models: Illustrated by the development of a theory of conflict behavior. *Journal of Personality, 20,* 82–100.

Mischel, W. (1973). Toward a cognitive social learning reconceptualization of personality. *Psychological Review, 80,* 252–283.

Mischel, W. (1990). Personality dispositions revisited and revised: A view after three decades. In L. A. Pervin (Ed.), *Handbook of personality: Theory and research* (pp. 111–134). New York: Guilford.

Mischel, W., Shoda, Y., & Rodriguez, M. L. (1990). Delay of gratification in children. *Science, 244,* 933–938.

Morrison, A. P. (1983). Shame, ideal self, and narcissism. *Contemporary Psychoanalysis, 19,* 295–318.

Murphy, G. L., & Medin, D. L. (1985). The role of theories in conceptual coherence. *Psychological Review, 92,* 289–316.

Murray, H. A. (1938). *Explorations in personality.* New York: Oxford University Press.

Newell, A., & Simon, H. A. (1972). *Human problem-solving.* Englewood Cliffs, NJ: Prentice-Hall.

Palys, T. S., & Little, B. R. (1983). Perceived life satisfaction and the organization of personal project systems. *Journal of Personality and Social Psychology, 44,* 1221–1230.

Pervin, L. A. (1983). The stasis and flow of behavior: Toward a theory of goals. In M. M. Page (Ed.), *Personality: Current theory and research.* Lincoln: University of Nebraska Press.

Pervin, L. A. (1989). Psychodynamic-systems reflections on a social-intelligence model of personality. Social intelligence and cognitive assessments of personality. In R. S. Wyer, Jr. & T. K. Srull (Eds.), *Social intelligence and cognitive assessments of personality* (pp. 153–161). Hillsdale, NJ: Erlbaum.

Piaget, J. (1972). *The psychology of intelligence.* Totowa, NJ: Littlefield Adams.

Piaget, J., & Garcia, R. (1989). *Psychogenesis and the history of science.* (F. Feider, Trans.). New York: Academic Press.

Piers, G., & Singer, M. B. (1953). *Shame and guilt: A psychoanalytic and a cultural study.* Springfield, IL: Charles C. Thomas.

Popper, K. R. (1963). *Conjectures and refutations: The growth of scientific knowledge.* New York: Harper and Row.

Read, S. J., & Miller, L. C. (1989). The importance of goals in personality: Toward a coherent model of persons. Social intelligence and cognitive assessments of personality. In R. S. Wyer, Jr. & T. K. Srull (Eds.), *Social intelligence and cognitive assessments of personality* (pp. 163–174). Hillsdale, NJ: Erlbaum.

Rogers, C. R. (1951). *Client-centered therapy: Its current practice, implications and theory.* Boston, MA: Houghton Mifflin.

Rokeach, M. (1973). *The nature of human values.* New York: The Free Press.

Shoda, Y., Mischel, W., & Wright, J. C. (1991). *The role of social intelligence and situational demands in behavior organization and personality coherence.* Unpublished Manuscript.

Shotter, J. (1975). *Images of man in psychological research.* London: Methuen.

Simon, H. A. (1967). Motivational and emotional controls of cognition. *Psychological Review, 74,* 29–39.

Skinner, B. F. (1953). *Science and human behavior.* New York: Collier-MacMillan.

Sternberg, R. J. (1984). Toward a triarchic theory of human intelligence. *Behavioral and Brain Sciences, 7,* 269–287.

Sternberg, R. J. (1985). *Beyond IQ: A triarchic theory of human intelligence.* Cambridge: Cambridge University Press.

Sternberg, R. J. (1987). Intelligence. In R. L. Gregory (Ed.), *The Oxford companion to the mind* (pp. 375–379). Oxford: Oxford University Press.

Sternberg, R. J. (1988). *The triarchic mind: A new theory of human intelligence.* New York: Viking.

Sternberg, R. J. (1990). *Metaphors of mind: Conceptions of the nature of intelligence.* New York: Cambridge University Press.

Sternberg, R. J., & Detterman, D. K. (Eds.). (1986). *What is intelligence? Contemporary viewpoints on its nature and definition.* Norwood, NJ: Ablex.

Sternberg, R. J., & Wagner, R. K. (1989). The fate of the trait: A reply to Cantor and Kihlstrom. In R. S. Wyer, Jr. & T. K. Srull (Eds.), *Social intelligence and cognitive assessments of personality* (pp. 175–185). Hillsdale, NJ: Erlbaum.

Sullivan, H. S. (1953). *The interpersonal theory of psychiatry.* New York: Norton.

Tesser, A., & Campbell, J. (1983). Self-definition and self-evaluation maintenance. In J. Suls & A. Greenwald (Eds.), *Social psychological perspectives on the self* (Vol. 2, pp. 1–31). Hillsdale, NJ: Erlbaum.

Thorndike, E. L., Bergman, E. O., Cobb, M. V., & Woodyard, E. I. (1926). *The measurement of intelligence.* New York: Teachers' College.

Vallacher, R.R., & Wegner, D. M. (1987). What do people think they are doing? Action identification and human behavior. *Psychological Review, 94,* 3–15.

Vitz, P. C. (1977). *Psychology as religion: The cult of self worship.* Herts, England: Lion.

Wagner, R. K. (1987). Tacit knowledge in everyday intelligent behavior. *Journal of Personality and Social Psychology, 52,* 1236–1247.

Wagner, R. K., & Sternberg, R. J. (1985). Practical intelligence in real-world pursuits: The role of tacit knowledge. *Journal of Personality and Social Psychology, 49,* 436–458.

Wechsler, D. (1944). *The measurement of adult intelligence.* Baltimore: Williams & Wilkins.

Wechsler, D. (1949). *Wechsler Intelligence Scale for Children: Manual.* New York: Psychological Corps.

Zajonc, R. B. (1980). Feeling and thinking: Preferences need no inferences. *American Psychologist, 35,* 151–175.

Zajonc, R. B., & Markus, H. (1985). Must all affect be mediated by cognition? *Journal of Consumer Research, 12,* 363–364.

Part III

Personality and the manifestations of intelligence

5 Social intelligence and personality: flexible life task pursuit

*Nancy Cantor and Robert E. Harlow**

A common theme emergent from various approaches to the study of intelligence is that intelligent behavior is both adaptive and goal directed. It is adaptive in that it allows the person to confront and meet challenges encountered either internally or externally, and goal directed in that the person wants more than just to "get by," but has its own agenda, which intelligent behavior is used to meet (Sternberg & Salter, 1982). In recent years several approaches to the study of intelligence have been proposed that place a premium on intelligent behavior as it is performed within specific contexts (Sternberg, 1984a, 1984b). Sternberg (1984a, 1984b) emphasizes the utility of these "contextual" approaches over psychometric ones, largely because intelligent behavior is applied to real-world problems in real-world settings and only rarely to the kinds of aptitude tests widely used as criterion measures in psychometric intelligence research.

The burgeoning interest in contextual theories of intelligence (see Sternberg, 1984a, 1984b) closely parallels the growing interest among personality and social psychologists in understanding behavior as growing out of an interaction between elements of both the person and the situation, as opposed to considering dispositional or situationist approaches in isolation (Snyder & Ickes, 1985). This interest has prompted new methods for examining person–situation interaction and the discovery of units of analysis that better reflect the links between behavior and its context (Buss & Cantor, 1989). Resulting efforts have underscored Lewin's famous dictum that it may not be optimal to examine person and situation variables as pristine elements unchanged by the process of interaction (Lewin, 1935). Rather, person and situation variables may best be understood not only as independent variables but also as dependent variables that influence each other in the dynamic transaction between the person and his or her environment (Cantor & Kihlstrom, 1982). In this regard, person and situation elements act not as catalysts that produce behavior and remain un- changed by the process of interaction, but rather as enzymes whose characteristics undergo change as behavior unfolds.

---

*The order of names is alphabetical. This chapter represents equal contributions from both authors.

137

With the above-mentioned concerns of contextualized measurement of intelligence and transactional models of behavior in mind, Cantor and Kihlstrom (1987) have advanced a cognitive theory of personality, a theory of *social intelligence*. Social intelligence represents the efforts of individuals to solve problems of daily life and work toward desired goals. Earlier theories of social intelligence were largely concerned with person perception and perceptiveness in social interactions (see Walker & Foley, 1973, for a review). Cantor and Kihlstrom's social-intelligence perspective differs from these earlier theories in having a scope that extends to all domains in which individuals work toward attaining goals and solving the problems of daily life. According to this perspective, behavior is guided by suggestions and demands emergent from situational, sociocultural, and personal–autobiographical contexts. Situational and cultural contexts suggest goals that are adopted by individuals in accord with their own experiences, beliefs, and desires (Cantor & Langston, 1989). Situational, sociocultural, and self demands thereby become merged by the person into *life tasks,* the contextual "demands construed as desires" (e.g., finishing a dissertation or finding a marriage partner; Cantor & Kihlstrom, 1987, p. 169; Reich & Zautra, 1983). These desires, or life tasks, become the problems that individuals work towards solving and that provide meaning and organization to day-to-day life (Klinger, 1977). As units of empirical analysis, life tasks seem well suited for investigations of the person behaving in specific contexts, reflecting not only "dispositions" but potentials for expressing those dispositions in daily-life contexts.

To meet the demands of daily life and to work on their self-constructed life tasks, individuals make use of their collection of problem-solving strategies and schemas that together constitute the personal social-intelligence repertoire. Schemas include concepts of the self, others, social situations, and social information, providing the *interpretive context* in which tasks are constructed, situations are defined, plans are made, and behavior is executed. Problem-solving strategies represent active attempts to work on life tasks. The social-intelligence approach places particular emphasis on the creativity and ingenuity with which schemas and strategies are fine tuned to meet the demands of daily life and to work on life tasks, allowing for successful adaptation to various settings (Cantor, 1990; see also Smith & Lazarus, 1990).

In this approach, therefore, schemas and strategies constitute cognitive *structures* of personality, while the *dynamics* of personality are represented in the processes of personally defining life-task goals, construing daily life events as opportunities for task pursuit, and regulating behavior in an effort to pursue those tasks. The "stylistic mark" of an individual's personality is reflected in part by his or her characteristic patterns in different life domains of interpreting normative tasks in personal ways and therefore seeing particular contexts as appropriate for doing those tasks. For example, each parent of an adolescent has his or her own way of interpreting the seemingly inevitable power struggles associated with the transition to adulthood of this period, and that interpretation is reflected in where and when and to whom and how discipline is used and freedom is allocated. The dynamics of personality are directed often toward answering questions of when, where, with whom, and how to address life tasks in everyday life (Cantor & Fleeson, 1991). In answering those questions, the person's "social intelligence" – schemas and strategies developed in relevant domains of the past – provides an interpretive context. For example, a person may be biased toward leniency when personal memories of ineffective threats in childhood are chronically accessible frames for present decisions (e.g., Higgins, 1990). To say this another way, personal style is carried in the *current* set of if–then relations whereby individuals routinely direct their efforts toward their life tasks in particular contexts and through particular strategies (Linville & Clark, 1989; Wright & Mischel, 1987).

As previous cognitive theories of personality (Kelly, 1955; Mischel, 1973, 1984; Bandura, 1977, 1986; Rotter, 1954) have recognized, cognition (broadly defined) is critically involved in situation definition (Kelly, 1955), the weighing of behavior alternatives (Rotter, 1954), motivation (Bandura, 1986) and behavior regulation (Mischel, 1973, 1984). The social-intelligence perspective borrows from and works to integrate these inherently interactionist perspectives in an effort to illustrate the function of cognition in the goal-directed behavior of daily life, imparting both choice and freedom to the construal of situations and tasks, and the endorsement of strategies. Fundamentally, this element of choice, imparted by the cognitive capacity to transform and construct anew, is where we see the locus of intelligence in personality (Cantor, 1990).

At the center of cognitive approaches to personality are these construal processes. As the interpretive context of task construction and goal-directed behavior, construal processes link the other units of personality. The idea that flexible construal is advantageous has been a hallmark of social cognitivism since its beginnings (Kelly, 1955) and it is still seen as a marker of optimal functioning allowing for adaptive response (Kobasa, 1979; Mischel, 1984). Beginning with Kelly, the social cognitivists demonstrated a concern with how individuals ascribe meaning to their environments. In his view, the person is a naive scientist constantly engaged in anticipating and explaining events on the basis of hypotheses derived from personal constructs, the dimensions on which the person evaluates factors about the self and the world (Kelly, 1955). It is these cognitive constructions that give meaning to the world: "Man looks at his world through transparent patterns or templates *which he creates and then attempts to fit over* the realities of which the world is composed" (1955, pp. 8–9; emphasis added).

There is considerable richness and variety in the content of personal constructs, and this variety allows for *constructive alternativism,* the notion that the same event may give rise to an infinite number of construals, or be "seen" in multiple ways. In this regard, Kelly locates considerable power in cognition and leaves the person much room for flexibility in the construal of social events: "All our present interpretations of the universe are subject to revision or replacement . . . [n]o one needs to paint himself in a corner, no one needs to be completely harnessed by circumstances" (Kelly, 1955, p. 15).

"Contextualizing" personality and intelligence

The study of personality and of intelligence historically share a common debate about the heuristic value of "decontextualizing" the person in an effort to get to the "purer" personal contribution to behavior or performance (see Sternberg, 1984a; Cervone, 1991). As assumption of the psychometric approach is that in the interest of measurement purity, intelligence can (and should) be measured without regard to the contexts in which intelligent behavior is manifested (Sternberg, 1984a), or at least with an eye toward separating analytic ability from specific knowledge of real-world domains (Baltes, 1987; cf. Cattell & Horn, 1978). In this manner, intelligence is and only can be, as Gould (1981) has argued, that which intelligence tests measure.

The comparable measurement tradition in personality (e.g., Cattell, 1943; see John, 1990) never really expected to be able to strip the person from the situation in rank-ordering individuals on personality-trait scales. However, the thrust of this effort has been directed toward perfecting the "personality" construct in ways that increase the span of situations over which aggregation can occur in the prediction of behavior (see Cantor & Kihlstrom, 1982). A large part of the compellingness of the "big five solution" to the nature of personality structure is its applicability across cultures, across the life-span, across the sexes, and so forth – all instances of aggregation across major variations in the life contexts of the target persons (McAdams, 1991; Cervone, 1991). The objective, therefore, is to be able to portray the essence of people detached as much as possible from the *particulars* of their living environments (cf. Veroff, 1983).

Although we do not eschew the value or feasibility of these abstract mapping enterprises in either domain, in order to see the contribution of social intelligence we believe that the units of analysis must more genuinely reflect the conditional links between behavior and context that comprise individuals' styles of goal pursuit (Bandura, 1986; Mischel, 1990). As Cervone (1991) notes in describing the units of analysis common to social–cognitive personality theories: "These units are inherently contextual; social and self-knowledge develop through interactions with the environment (particularly other people) and inherently pertain to aspects of oneself and that environment" (p. 372).

The central objective of the social-intelligence approach is to elucidate individuals' ways of interpreting normative tasks in personal terms by construing particular kinds of contexts as relevant to task pursuit, and endorsing particular kinds of strategies to work on those tasks in those contexts. This is not to say that people don't generalize their task pursuit across contexts or their strategies across tasks, but rather to underline the view that their *intelligence* is still tied to the costs and benefits of those particular patterns of generalization, and to the flexibility (or rigidity) with which they generalize. Therefore, it is essential to know about how they construe and treat contexts in their lives, and not to aggregate in the service of parsimony or predictability.

In this view, we also share with other "contextual" theories of intelligence a conviction that behavior cannot be deemed intelligent without a reference to the contexts in which behavior is performed (e.g., Berg, 1990). The social-intelligence perspective is not concerned with uncovering general abilities that transcend all domains of problem-solving activity, or a "social I.Q." Intelligent behavior is behavior that is efficacious in successful life-task pursuit and therefore can only be understood with reference to the domains and contexts in which it is exhibited and the life tasks it is designed to serve. It is therefore possible, according to this perspective, for a behavior performed in one domain (e.g., ingratiation directed at superiors at work) to be intelligent in that domain and unintelligent in another (e.g., ingratiation directed at an adolescent son or daughter). In the same respect, it is possible for a person to act quite intelligently in one domain (e.g., professional) and quite unintelligently in another (e.g., family relations), as social intelligence is largely dependent on expertise, which we can expect to exhibit considerable interdomain variability.

This analysis of social intelligence is structured around particular life tasks that individuals pursue, and the ways in which they interpret and pursue a task at a particular period in their life. The life task is a unit of analysis that is defined, therefore, only in context – it joins a person having a particular history and current repertoire with a life context of typical events, typical partners, and typical social groups and norms for behavior (Veroff, 1983). This bottom-up building of a portrait of individuals in context allows for some points of specificity or even inconsistency in people to come to light (e.g., the parent who interprets his or her parenting task as a "disciplinary" endeavor with an adolescent youngster may, at the same time, melt at the sight of a toddler grandchild willfully disobeying, especially if the grandparenting task is construed as one of generativity not authority). In fact, it is just those special patterns of interpretation and strategic behavior, selective as they may be for any given person, that provide an opening in which to study *intelligence* in personality.

The present discussion will briefly consider the "tools" (structure) of social intelligence and how these tools are used, and then focus more extensively on the dynamics of personality and intelligence, i.e., the *flexibility* individuals can exhibit in adapting to different settings and working on their life tasks.

A social-intelligence repertoire of schemas and strategies

Schemas

As a theory of problem solving about daily life, the social-intelligence perspective is initially concerned with the knowledge structures (i.e., schemas and strategies) in which social expertise resides. Cantor & Kihlstrom (1987) propose that social concepts are one basic set of cognitive units of personality. Social concepts organize our knowledge of the kinds of people, situations and events we encounter in everyday life. They thereby shape our experience of ourselves and the world, providing the interpretive context for intelligent behavior (Cantor, 1990). The content of these knowledge structures is organized around different aspects of a person's life and therefore these structures are brought to bear in relevant, domain-specific contexts.

Social concepts may include stereotypes about certain groups (Deaux & Lewis, 1984; Hamilton, 1981), personality types such as yuppies or computer hackers (Andersen & Klatzky, 1987; Cantor & Mischel, 1979), broad classes of social situations such as dates and parties (Cantor, Mischel, & Schwartz, 1982; Pervin, 1976), trait-based categories of social behavior such as dominance and extraversion (Buss & Craik, 1983; Hampson, 1982), interpersonal schemata capturing relationships with significant people in one's life (e.g., Andersen & Cole, 1990; Thorne, 1989; Read & Miller, 1989), and generic scripts for social interactions (Abelson, 1981; Forgas, 1982; Nelson, 1986; Tomkins, 1979). Social concepts across domains may be elaborated to different degrees. Knowledge in some domains may be so well elaborated that processing within them requires little concentrated effort. As with nonsocial expertise, social expertise is the product of experience with certain classes of information (Cantor & Kihlstrom, 1987; Laboratory of Comparative Human Cognition [LCHC], 1982). Well-elaborated knowledge structures provide considerable advantages in processing information, allowing for inferences that sometimes go beyond the information given (Bruner, 1957; Higgins & Bargh, 1987). They allow for convenient organization of information in memory and facilitate rapid encoding of new information (Bargh, 1982; Markus, Smith, & Moreland, 1985). The problem-solving efforts of individuals with varying degrees of expertise will be characterized by varying degrees of automaticity and, therefore, varying degrees of efficiency. The mechanisms allowing for such efficiency may, however, lead to biased judgments that are consistent with existing knowledge structures but not necessarily inclusive of all relevant incoming data (Duncan, 1976; Sagar & Schofield, 1980; Langer & Abelson, 1974). Cantor and Kihlstrom (1987) referred to this as the double-edged sword of social-knowledge expertise: it can be cognitively economical but personally and interpersonally expensive, especially if its ease of use fosters a "lazy" attitude toward the disconfirmation of theories of self and others (cf. Swann, 1987; Hilton & Darley, 1985).

This readiness to assimilate information into existing knowledge structures may also engender a lack of sensitivity to environmental subtleties, thereby promoting nondiscriminative (and maladaptive) responding. The "mindful" individual is sensitive to subtle environmental changes and not afraid to live without the certainty that absolute reliance on current constructions can provide (Langer, 1989). Such sensitivity can facilitate adaptive revision and replacement of existing knowledge structures. This is not to deny the utility of automatic processing, which can be an asset in the processing of familiar, often over-learned information. On the other hand, automatic processing can encourage us to miss the opportunities for goal pursuit if we always treat a routine event as an arena for the same "scripted" activity. Maximum utility in problem solving is realized when an individual is sensitive to *when* processing information automatically is beneficial and *what* situations call for a more reflective, careful approach to the data (Showers & Cantor, 1985).

In addition to social concepts, the social intelligence repertoire also contains procedural rules for processing social information (see Fiske & Taylor, 1991). As is the case in the processing of nonsocial information, some of these rules are explicit (Anderson, 1983) and some are more automatic (Banaji & Greenwald, 1991), including, for example, rules for categorization and stereotyping (Cantor & Mischel, 1979; Devine, 1989), for inferences concerning dispositional traits and emotional states (Jones & Davis, 1965; Shaver et al., 1987; Weiner, 1985), for evaluating likability (Anderson, 1974; Fiske & Pavelchak, 1986), for making social judgments (Nisbett & Ross, 1980; Kunda, 1987) and testing hypotheses (Skov & Sherman, 1986; Snyder, 1981a), and for identifying acts (Vallacher & Wegner, 1987). These rules are subject to considerable individual difference variability, as evidenced, for example, by research on attributional style and complexity (Fletcher, Danilovics, Fernandez, Peterson, & Reeder, 1986; Metalsky & Abramson, 1981), evaluative styles (Ostrom & Davis, 1979), attentional focus (Carver & Scheier, 1981), action identification styles (Vallacher & Wegner, 1989), and ways of coping (Lazarus & Folkman, 1984; Miller & Mangan, 1983). Individuals vary in the extent and nature of their implicit and explicit procedural knowledge, often falling back on a few well-learned "rules of thumb" that are so proceduralized as to be hard to change (Langer, 1989; Linville & Clark, 1989).

Self-schemas

Individuals also possess considerable knowledge about the self that is brought to bear in day-to-day living. Self-knowledge can be classified in the same manner as other knowledge: declarative and procedural. Declarative self-knowledge can further be divided into semantic self-knowledge, or self-concept, and episodic self-knowledge, or autobiographical memory (Kihlstrom & Cantor, 1984; Kihlstrom et al., 1988). The self-concept is the person's mental representation of his or her own personality. Because personality is multifaceted, several cognitive approaches to the study of the self suggest that it may not be possible to think of one unitary self that influences all life domains, but rather instead to consider many domain-specific selves (e.g., Markus, 1977), and representations of self-in-relationships and self-as-group-member (Markus & Cross, 1990). These selves may be broadened to include not only actual selves but ideal selves (Higgins, Klein, & Strauman, 1985) and desired and feared possible selves (Markus & Nurius, 1986). At any given time, only a subset of these selves guides processing, or is "activated" (the "working self-concept"; Markus & Nurius, 1986). Such activation may be the result of tasks made salient or of other contextual cues (Bargh, 1982; Cantor, Markus, Niedenthal, & Nurius, 1986).

Arguing for a multiplicity of selves is not the same as saying that the self is fragmentary or incoherent. The self is a family of selves related to each other through resemblance and feature overlap (Rosenberg & Gara, 1985). These shared features contribute to a sense of unity. Lewicki (1984) has suggested that there is a prototypical or basic-level self that anchors social interaction across domains and situations. Similarly, autobiographical memory provides a sense of continuity across the life span (Kihlstrom & Evans, 1979). Autobiographical memory constitutes the episodic content of the self-concept, serving as a record of previous events in a person's life. It is not, however, merely an objective record of events, but rather is subject to revision, accentuation, or "filling in" as individuals attempt to provide themselves with coherent, cohesive self-stories (Ross, 1989). Such revision and accentuation reflects current goals and concerns of the individual (Cohler, 1982; Greenwald, 1980). In this way, self-stories (along with self-concepts) guide the interpretation of new (and old) information, so that it is congruent with these stories (McAdams, 1989; McGuire, 1984). Self-concepts also influence both behavior direction and regulation. Knowledge of what we are like and what we are good at (or what we believe that we are like and we are good at) influences choices concerning the activities in which we will engage (Bandura, 1986; Snyder, 1981b). Our actions are also guided by knowledge of what we could be (Markus & Nurius, 1986; Wurf, 1988), what we ought or would ideally like to be (Higgins, Klein, & Strauman, 1985), what we think others will let us be (Schlenker & Weigold, 1989), and what we fear becoming (Markus & Nurius, 1986). In this "forward-looking" way, self-concepts act as cognitive frames for life-task definition (e.g., "I'm a high-anxiety type but I can imagine myself as more laid back; I'll try parenting without losing my cool") (Cantor et al., 1986).

Strategies

Problem-solving strategies are characteristic ways of working on life tasks. Consistent with theories of human problem solving (i.e., Anderson, 1983, 1987; Newell & Simon, 1972), the social-intelligence perspective assumes that these strategies are typically applied in specific domains and are characterized by different levels of expertise across these domains. When attempting to solve a problem, people do have both weak and strong strategies at their disposal (Anderson, 1983, 1987; Newell & Simon, 1972; Chase & Simon, 1973). Weak strategies are general strategies (e.g., generate and test, trial and error) that are applicable across a wide variety of domains, but at the cost of efficiency and accuracy (Simon, 1990). With experience, domain-specific "expert" strategies are developed. Such "dedicated" strategies are more apt to take into account relational properties specific to their domains – relations that go beyond general properties such as color, size, appearance, or quantity (for example, the cooperative relationship between a catcher and a pitcher in a game of baseball), and therefore lead to quicker and more accurate judgments. Expertise and dedicated strategy formation are products of exposure and experience within a domain, and will therefore be differentially elaborated across domains (Keil, 1984, 1986). Although investigations of problem solving have been largely concerned with problem solving in nonsocial domains (but cf. Ford & Tisak, 1983), the social-intelligence perspective assumes that social expertise is structured in much the same manner as nonsocial expertise and employed in addressing the problems of daily life.

The social intelligence perspective assumes that strategies involve more than behavioral plans, developing from complex appraisals of tasks and situations and, therefore, encompassing the motivational and emotional work that is associated with relevant life tasks and their typical contexts. Motivation, cognition, and affect work together in the service of reaching desired goals. Achievement strategies, for example, will reflect personal investment in achievement concerns and appraisals of achievement tasks (Price, 1982; Norem & Cantor, 1986); to the extent that achievement tasks implicate self-worth concerns, they may engender considerable stress and a vigilant reactive style (Price, 1982). On-line, achievement strategies may implicate subgoals pertaining to the regulation of arousal, anxiety, and/or positive affect, as these elements signal the individual to goal satisfaction possibilities, threats, and feedback (Klinger, Barta, & Maxeiner, 1980; Smith & Lazarus, 1990).

Life tasks: the integrative unit of analysis

The social-intelligence approach concentrates on how individuals define and pursue their current life tasks in their daily life contexts. This unit is an integrative one in which the person's *schemas* set the stage for adopting and defining certain life tasks, the *tasks* themselves connect the individual to his or her daily life *contexts,* and the person's preferred *strategies* are evoked in turn in these task–context conditions. A person who sees himself as socially anxious, for example, may invest special effort in "finding a steady mate" – an age-graded, normative task for young adults in this particular culture – but his construal of this task may deviate from others' in terms of his appraisal of the difficulty of the task, and the contexts in which he typically pursues intimacy (e.g., work settings rather than singles' bars and parties), and the strategy with which he attempts to master intimacy (e.g., a risk-averse, "wait and be courted strategy," Langston & Cantor, 1989).

We consider it important to cement the study of social intelligence in the normative, age-graded life tasks "presented" to individuals as they mature in particular cultures and social-group settings. Somewhat paradoxically, a purely idiographic approach to the analysis of personal goals and goal pursuit can easily lose sight of systematic patterns in the ways in which *one individual* construes and pursues his or her goals *differently* in line with the nature or content of each goal (e.g., flexibly addressing social tasks and rather rigidly taking on achievement tasks). Idiographic goal assessment systems facilitate the consideration of general characteristics of a person's unique goal system, such as amount of intergoal conflict in the system (e.g., Emmons & King, 1988), but they tend to lose sight of the particular goals or domains that contribute most (pain or pleasure) to particular individuals and/or groups in particular living environments (e.g., Cantor, Acker, & Cook-Flannagan, 1991).

Consideration of normative patterns in task adoption and pursuit seems wise in light of both the considerable consensus in the tasks that individuals in a particular life period and cultural milieu articulate as self-relevant (e.g., Havighurst, 1953), and the contingencies for social feedback and social comparison that are set against these standards of what a person *should* be doing at each point in the life-course (Helson, Mitchell, & Moane, 1984; Higgins & Parsons, 1983; Neugarten, 1968). Moreover, each living environment sets out certain normative patterns of task pursuit, for example, in the everyday contexts that are acceptable for "doing" a certain task (e.g., Argyle, 1981) and in the strategies considered appropriate for task pursuit (e.g., Jones & Pittman, 1982).

Nevertheless, the analysis of social intelligence in large part concerns personal deviations from those norms. Specifically, we focus on deviations in task appraisal, task–context links, and strategies associated by each person with particular tasks-in-contexts (Cantor & Langston, 1989). In this way, we stay focused on how individuals make choices in the pursuit of particular, commonplace tasks, by their construal of what the tasks mean and where and how to pursue them in day-to-day living.

Intelligent behavior: attunement and flexibility

Having discussed the "tools" of social intelligence, we now turn to a discussion of what constitutes intelligent use of this repertoire. Effective problem solving is in the service of providing adaptation, including goal satisfaction and the meeting of contextual demands. In our view, such behavior is enhanced by *attunement* – attunement to the consequences of one's actions, including social and emotional feedback, as well as implications of those consequences for other goals, and attunement to the goal-fulfilling potentials of different situations. Such attunement facilitates *flexibility* – flexibility to adjust behavior in light of feedback suggesting that problem-solving strategies are resulting in error, or in response to newly perceived demands emergent from the self, others, and changing contexts. Across discussions of adaptation from various viewpoints, flexibility is the virtue and rigidity is the vice. We would agree with this view and argue that a prerequisite for such flexibility is situational attunement.

Flexibility and attunement: the what, where, when, and how of task pursuit

Flexibility has previously been considered in investigations of problem solving as a facility to apply old learning to new problems in a sensitive manner (Anderson, 1981; Gick & Holyoak, 1983; Lesgold, 1988; Hellesnes, Raaheim, & Bengtsson, 1982). At the core of many of these lines of work is an interest in the ability to apply declarative or procedural knowledge from one domain to another, to facilitate seeing a problem in a new light, applying information from the past to new and different present circumstances. Such creativity is believed to be related to an individual's abilities of divergent production (e.g., Guilford, 1959). Although divergent thinking can enhance problem-solving efforts, it cannot alone determine successful adaptation, and is best taken advantage of when used in concert with other abilities, such as convergent thinking, or the capacity to evaluate ideas (Baron, 1982; Guilford, 1959; Hellesnes,

Raaheim, & Bengtsson, 1982). We can think of the "manic" as the ultimate divergent thinker, able to see a wide range of possibilities for the self. However, this thinking is not attuned to the goal fulfilling possibilities of the settings in which it is carried out, and is therefore of little value in adaptation.

Flexibility and attunement, in terms of social problem solving and social intelligence, involve "breaking set" in the course of daily life when doing so would enhance life-task pursuit. For example, changing contextual demands (e.g., as brought on by a life transition) can necessitate reconsideration of *what* tasks to pursue – often requiring leaving old tasks behind and constructing new ones that are responsive to new contextual demands and can take full advantage of new contextual opportunities. Day to day, different settings may provide opportunities for work on various tasks, and the "intelligent" individual is also attuned to *where* and *when* such opportunities are present, perhaps above and beyond more conventional ideas concerning what tasks to pursue in which settings. In addition, tasks themselves have many aspects, and *how* they are pursued should reflect a careful, accurate reading of these aspects; some task domains will be more structured than others, or perhaps more familiar than others. Moreover, task appraisals (e.g., importance and feelings of control) will vary from person to person and among tasks. Intelligent individuals are attuned to the various attributes of tasks and the subgoals they may involve, and are discriminating in their employment of strategies for work on life tasks.

In the sections that follow we will consider these different aspects of flexibility and attunement, drawing whenever possible on evidence from studies of individuals engaged in life-task pursuit in their day-to-day lives.

Flexibility and life-task definition: choosing what to pursue

Life tasks are not merely products of individual motives and perceived abilities, but are constructed in light of environmental and cultural suggestion (Cantor & Kihlstrom, 1987; see also Veroff, 1983). Individuals can display considerable flexibility of task pursuit in response to environmental changes. An example of such flexibility has recently been described by Brandtstadter and Renner (1990), who considered individuals' responses to situational constraints imposed by critical life crises and transitions. In such instances, where personal agency is sharply reduced (e.g., a move from a condominium to a nursing home), holding on to old (now unfeasible) goals may engender feelings of helplessness and depression (see also Janoff-Bulman & Brickman, 1982) as repeated efforts are met with failure. Brandtstadter and Renner suggest that individuals who are characteristically attuned to and flexibly adjust goals in accord with situational constraints are able to avoid these "hidden costs" of perceived control (e.g., helplessness and depression) and are more satisfied with their lives. In addition, flexible individuals tend to feel closer to attaining their (albeit more modest) goals, possibly imparting a sense of personal agency that will facilitate future goal-directed behavior (Bandura, 1982). Such flexibility is in sharp contrast to a steadfast refusal to relinquish unrealistic goals, a tendency that may have significant emotional costs (see Janoff-Bulman & Brickman, 1982 for a discussion of the "pathology of high expectations"). Brandtstadter and Renner suggest that the "onset, duration, and severity of depressive episodes depends not only on the degree of perceived control over personally important developmental domains . . . but as well on the ability to disengage from unfeasible goals and build up new commitments and developmental perspectives" (1990, p. 65). This statement highlights a potential downside to the normally more functional approach of "high-agency" individuals who tenaciously hang on to their goals in the face of obstacles (Vallacher & Wegner, 1989; Dweck & Leggett, 1988).

In addition to relinquishing unfeasible tasks in a new life setting, individuals should also be attuned to the changed meanings of tasks in different developmental phases. For example, consider the "meaning" of "being independent." This life task will entail different challenges across different developmental phases, as Zirkel (1992) has demonstrated in a longitudinal analysis of Honors College students making the transitions into and out of college. In her study, those who were particularly anxious about independence in college also associated this anxiety with their achievement pursuits (presumably reflecting a desire to prove one's worth to both parents and self and thereby establish independence through the achievement arena). However, after college, they "transferred" (as it were) this anxiety to the newly age-appropriate demand of "establishing a secure social network," retaining their heightened concerns about independence, but perhaps now playing them out in a different way, and no longer showing enhanced anxieties about professional or achievement pursuits. As Zirkel suggests, this shift of life-task concern is not necessarily inconsistent with their earlier concerns, but rather may reflect a *flexible redefinition* of what it means to be independent in the two different life transitions. In her words, being absorbed with independence may mean having a heightened concern for whatever is the most salient age-graded task of the life transition – i.e., academics in college and social networks in young adulthood. The students in her sample, concerned with demonstrating competence in each new domain, exhibited considerable attunement to what constituted the most salient contextual demands.

Attunement will also lead to differences in "readings" of a task, even within the same cohort, to the extent that individuals in that cohort are responding to different contextual demands. For example, Zirkel (1992) also found that the independence task took different meanings in different university subcultures and living environments. In one context, the Honors College at the University of Michigan (discussed above), establishing independence became infused with achievement concerns. For sorority women on the same campus, establishing independence was read differently, involving more of an interpersonal meaning of the separation from home and family. Accordingly, anxiety surrounding independence in this group was associated with a concern with demonstrating competence in the most salient task in this environment, establishing ties with sorority sisters and building social relationships, perhaps as a substitute for prior family relationships. These different living environments suggested different meanings of the task of being on one's own, which were reflected in the specific anxieties of those students struggling with independence in each setting. Presumably, the students in these different living environments also chose them in part because of a basic compatibility with the kinds of meanings imparted to such age-graded life tasks in each setting (Snyder, 1981b).

Determining when and where to pursue tasks

Attunement to task-pursuit opportunities in daily life. The literature on goal pursuit in a daily life context suggests that individuals may be quite attuned to goal-fulfilling opportunities in their daily routines (e.g., Tennen, Suls, & Affleck, 1991; Pervin, 1989). One measure of such attunement is the association between participation in daily events and the motivation to fulfill goals typically associated with such activities (Emmons & McAdams, 1991). When there is room for choice in daily activities, individuals find ways to spend time doing things that are consistent with their current goals. For example, McAdams & Constantian (1983) observed positive correlations between affiliation motive and participation in interpersonal activities among college students. This relationship is sometimes even observed when the activities themselves are experienced as difficult and negatively arousing. Zirkel and Cantor (1990) found such a pattern among a group of Honors College students who were relatively absorbed in and anxious about "being on their own, away from family": they spent relatively much time pursuing independence-related errands and chores, but were also more negatively aroused in such events, according to their reports of affect in an experience-sampling study.

Another, more indirect measure of attunement to the goal-fulfilling properties of everyday events is suggested by the emotional arousal and involvement associated with the relevance of a life task or current concern in daily life (Klinger, 1989). For example, Cantor et al. (1991) observed in a daily experience-sampling study with women living in a college sorority that the women were more affectively aroused or involved in a daily event when it was construed as relevant to at least one of their current life tasks (with relevance rated in nightly diaries and affect rated in daily event reports) than when it was not task-relevant at this time. This suggests a general level of attunement to potential goal fulfillment that fits with expectations for an intelligent system. Emmons (1991) observed a similar pattern of selective affective reactivity in line with individuals' particular salient strivings – for achievement-oriented individuals, positive affect was associated with successful achievement events and negative affect with unsuccessful achievement events, whereas for those with an affiliative orientation, affective reactivity was associated with the nature of affiliation events.

Klinger's (1977, 1989) programmatic work on current concerns and the engagement and disengagement of attentive processes in the flow of daily activity provides the most coherent support for this "intelligent" attunement of individuals to the goal-potential of routine events. According to Klinger's theory, current concerns set in motion a state of preparedness to react with emotional arousal to a variety of routine cues that are associated with those current goal concerns. The ensuing emotional reaction precipitates enhanced processing of those cues, directing attention and effort toward goal pursuit – whether it be to take advantage of an opening for pursuit or to waylay an obstacle in one's path (e.g., Klinger et al., 1980).

Whereas people may be quite well-attuned to the goal-fulfilling potential of daily events, there is considerably less evidence for attunement to one's own impact on the unfolding shape of those events. For example, in assessing another person's behavior, we rarely adjust for our own contribution to his or her behavior, typically ignoring the interpersonal press on behavior (Thorne, 1987, 1989). This asymmetry in attunement is captured in the extreme in the case of individuals who are highly sensitive to nuances of the situation in regulating their own behavior, but considerably less attuned to their impact in "creating" the situation itself. Such a case brings to mind the self-regulatory style of a high self-monitoring individual (Snyder, 1987).

Similarly, when we do take the opportunity to pursue a personal goal in an unusual setting, we frequently point to aspects of the context as critical precipitators of our pursuit (e.g., "I couldn't help but . . . at that time"). This is apparently true even when the behavior in question is quite exceptional at the time – for example, heroic acts are often "explained" away by the performer as practically mandated by the situation as if anyone would have done the same in that context (Eldar Shafir, personal communication). As Klinger (1989) observed, individuals may be intelligently attuned without being aware of the choices they make or the impact they have in everyday life, because much of their sensitivity to the self-relevant potential in a setting is quite automatically elicited.

Flexibility in construal.   Fleeson and Cantor (1991a) have turned recently to questions of flexibility in life-task pursuit in everyday life events, in order to address the core Kellyian proposition of constructive alternativism. How often, they asked, do people actually take the opportunity to flexibly construe a routine event as an opportunity to pursue a self-relevant life task that is not necessarily typical in the event context? How often do people pursue achievement at parties or affiliation in the classroom or at work? Can time spent alone be construed as relevant to affiliative tasks and time with others as relevant to achievement tasks? Do college students pursue "grades" on weekends and "friends" during the week, even when the culture presses toward a reverse pattern of temporal regulation of goal pursuit?

Working with daily-event reports obtained in an experience-sampling study with a sample of 54 sorority women, Fleeson and Cantor (1991a) observed systematic patterns of "atypical event construal" in which routine events of the day were construed in nightly diary reports as relevant to life tasks that were unusual for the event context (e.g., a session in the library as relevant to an intimacy life task). For example, in a 15 day period in which five events were randomly sampled per day per subject, the sorority women construed about 15% of the events that took place in social situations as relevant to the pursuit of "getting good grades; doing well academically" and about 36% of the events taking place in academic situations as relevant to "getting along with others; making friends." Whereas most of the time people pursue tasks that are highly normative or typical for the settings they are in, there were plenty of occasions for each subject in this sample when an atypical setting-task construal occurred. Moreover, these atypical construals were systematically associated with affective experiences in the events in a direction that reversed the typical experience in those settings. Thus, pursuing affiliation in the library or on weekdays or by oneself can go quite far – sometimes all the way, in fact, toward reversing the typical mood-deflating effect associated with these settings. These affect-reversal patterns emerged in analyses that considered each subject's experiences in each type of setting, across repeated instances when for that particular subject the task in question was and was not construed as relevant in events occurring in a particular kind of setting (with setting defined in three ways: situation, day of the week, and number of people with the person). Hence, not only did these data support flexible construal of routine events in the light of personal goals in highly "scripted" contexts, but this constructive alternativism was shown to be *meaningfully* associated with variations in the affective experience of daily life.

We view these kinds of data as critical support for flexible construal in daily life. Even so, the next step in such analyses is to consider the extent and nature of individuals' attunement to the costs and benefits accrued from such flexible task pursuit. How sensitively, for example, do people vary their task-relevant construals according to the likely variations in affective experience or in social feedback associated with such pursuit in specific contexts? We have some data from these experience-sampling studies suggesting that people are not routinely sensitive (i.e., intelligent) in this regard. Fleeson and Cantor (1991b), for example, considered whether college students for whom a particular life-task goal was especially important would regulate their task pursuit so as to do their "extra work" on the task at times that would most benefit their affective experience of daily life events. Considering the pursuit of "doing well academically" ("grades") and "getting along with others" ("friends") across days of the week, the answer was clearly no. That is, students for whom the "grades" task was especially important did pursue this task more frequently across their daily events (compared to those for whom this was a somewhat less important task), but they were just as likely to do their extra "grades" work on weekends as on weekdays, even though the pursuit of "grades" on weekends costs considerably more in terms of diminution of positive affect than does the pursuit during the week, even for these highly motivated individuals. This relative lack of wisdom in task-pursuit regulation was also evident for the inherently more "positive" life task of "getting along with others; making friends." Subjects for whom the "friends" task was especially important worked more on the task in general (than did those for whom this was a somewhat less motivating task), but they did not confine (or simply step up) their extra pursuit to the weekends when affiliative task pursuit was most strongly associated (even for them) with the experience of positive affect in routine events. At least in the context of temporal regulation of task pursuit, we may well be less sensitively calibrated to the costs and benefits for affective experience than is possible in light of our ability to demonstrate flexible construal and pursuit.

What about our sensitivity to the interpersonal costs of flexible goal pursuit? Perhaps temporal regulation is uniquely difficult as a test of attunement. Unfortunately, we do not foresee a more optimistic picture in terms of sensitivity to the interpersonal costs of "doing one's thing" in unusual settings. For example, in the experience-sampling study with college sorority women, Cantor, Fleeson, and Cook-Flannagan (1991) considered the case of women in the sample who relatively frequently pursued their "grades" task in interpersonal events (e.g., at parties, relaxing with others, or at meal time). Whereas these women experienced as much satisfaction in their academic pursuits (and performed as well academically) as did their peers who pursued "grades" in more typical contexts, they experienced a significant diminution in the quality of their social interactions and satisfaction with their social life, relative to their peers. Moreover, this was a particularly steep cost for them to pay since these particular women were actually quite interpersonally oriented, had a particularly intimate network of social confidants, and rated the intimacy life task as especially important at this time in their lives. In other words, given their own goal priorities, they could ill-afford the costs that seemed to be associated with their "out of context" pursuit of "grades" in social events.

Why did they experience these costs, and what cues might they have been missing? At this point we can only speculate, but we suspect that this is a similar phenomenon to one reported in the depression literature, in which nondepressed individuals do not like to be around depressed people in part because they "talk negative" (Coyne, 1976; Strack & Coyne, 1983). Norem (1989) suggests that "defensive pessimists" – individuals who carefully prepare for the worst despite their past successes – also annoy their friends and families as they strategically work to harness their anxieties. In a similar way, we suspect that not only was the pursuit of "grades" in social events mood deflating for these women in these social events (which we know to be the case from their experience-sampling reports), but it may also have deflated the atmosphere for their friends and acquaintances at the same time. When the women look back and rate the quality of their regular social interactions, their relative dissatisfaction may reflect some of this spill-over of the negativity of "grades" pursuit in otherwise enjoyable settings. If so, perhaps could they have been more sensitively attuned to the social cues from their friends and acquaintances in those events? The depression literature suggests that depressed individuals are strikingly insensitive to these social costs (or, at least unable to regulate interpersonal behavior more sensitively). Similarly, this pattern of nonattunement may be widespread. It may be more true and more costly than we imagine in the routines of daily life.

Discriminative facility and attunement to consequences of task pursuit

Thus far we have suggested that people are reasonably good at seeing opportunities for "doing their thing," but more poorly attuned to the wider array of costs sometimes associated with this persistent albeit creative task pursuit. In a sense, therefore, the construal mechanisms that allow for flexibility may potentially give rise to rigidity when goals are extensively, perhaps even indiscriminantly, construed as relevant across various settings. At the extreme, a person's set of personal constructs may be so simple or even monolithic that similar construals are ascribed to widely dissimilar events, engendering like responses to clearly different situational demands. As a result of this lack of attunement, different situations are seen as equivalent "ifs" of an "if-then" production sequence, and therefore, lead the individual to similar behavior tendencies (the "thens" of an "if-then" sequence) across situations (see Linville & Clark, 1989). As Walter Mischel (1968, 1984) vigorously asserted some time ago, flexible behavior implies more than indiscriminate responding; rather, it reflects a sensitivity to changing norms and contingencies for behavior, not just to changing opportunities for "doing one's preferred thing."

Flexible, adaptive behavior is a product of construal and behavioral processes that readily adapt to situational demands, a sensitivity that Mischel (1973) has termed *discriminative facility*. Discriminative facility refers to the capacity of the individual to be attuned to the environment and responsive to changes within it. A person who construes situations inflexibly cannot exhibit discriminative facility, because behavioral response grows out of construals and similar construals will therefore generate similar behaviors. Mischel endorsed Raush, Dittman, and Taylor's (1959) suggestion that social behavior becomes more responsive to situational influences with greater ego development.

Discriminative facility is "patterned variability in individuals' construals of situations" (Cantor & Kihlstrom, 1987, p. 7). Given the same "objective" situation or event, different people will see opportunities to work on different tasks (Cantor et al., 1991). Such interindividual variation is not random, but is a function of the importance individuals ascribe to their life tasks; more important life tasks are seen as relevant in a wider variety of situations than less important tasks (Bruner, 1951; Cantor et al., 1991). In moderation, such flexible construal can foster progress on life tasks. Indiscriminant processing, such that all (or no) situations are seen as relevant to a goal-related activity, however, can be detrimental. Consider, for example, the individual who inappropriately tries to find a mate at every social or work gathering, seemingly unable to discriminate when doing so would and would not most likely be effective (or countereffective; see Cantor & Fleeson, 1991 for a discussion of the role that consensual situation definition plays in facilitating goal attainment).

Such insensitivity to environmental changes and opportunities is seen in the day-to-day behavior of Type A individuals, characterized by competitive achievement striving and hostility and an excessive concern with achievement (Jenkins, 1975). It appears that in the case of Type A individuals, over-arching achievement-related goals become so strong as to confirm achievement-related hypotheses in inappropriate settings, to the end that many situations and stimuli are inappropriately seen as relevant to these goals. Work on tasks in inappropriate settings may undermine other goals (e.g., self-presentation). Consider, for example, the Type A who "works" on achievement and/or status goals while playing checkers with a 10-year old. Such inappropriateness underlines the importance of discriminative facility; the individual, to maximally fulfill his or her goals, must be sensitive to when circumstances can and cannot be used to bring about desired (goal-directed) outcomes, weighing the consequences that their behavior can have on other goals.

Construing settings as ideal for tasks that are nonconventional in those settings can, however, be advantageous (Cantor, Fleeson, & Cook-Flannagan, 1991). Cantor and her colleagues found that sorority women who construed the task of "finding intimacy" as relevant when working on school work tended to enhance the experience of this otherwise unenjoyable pursuit. This finding suggests that bringing enjoyable tasks to bear when working on tasks which one finds difficult but necessary can be adaptive. As noted earlier, however, Cantor and her colleagues also discovered another side to this flexible task pursuit. Other women in their sample chose to bring the task of "getting good grades" to bear in social situations. These women experienced a considerable trade-off as a result of their conversion of a consensually agentic task into a communal one, experiencing lower social satisfaction and less positive affect in social situations. Although working on the "grades" task in social settings may have had some advantage for these women, this advantage was not without cost as it was associated with diluted social satisfaction. Such goal trade-offs are not uncommon (Baumeister & Scher, 1988), and it may be the case that this diluted social satisfaction is a trifling cost compared to the consequences of not bringing the "grades" tasks to bear in social settings. What seems to distinguish successful from unsuccessful nonconventional construal is sensitivity to the implications that working on tasks in nonconventional settings has for progress on other tasks.

Just as indiscriminantly bringing tasks to bear in atypical settings can engender difficulties in adaptation, overapplication of the same "favored" constructions across dissimilar events may do so as well (e.g., Nasby & Kihlstrom, 1986). Smith and Rhodewalt (1986) have argued that Type As exhibit chronic time urgency because they construe environmental demands indiscriminantly. Such nondiscriminative construal may lead to perceptions of hostility and competition across situations (e.g., Harlow, Scotto, & Panter, 1989) and contribute to Type As' vigilant reactive style. In this sense, cross-situational consistency in use of problem-solving strategies or construal can be unintelligent. In the achievement domain, which the Type A strategy is used to serve, within-domain indiscriminant construal of environmental demands may actually impair performance (as a result of the increased arousal associated with the perception of a demanding environment and the performance impairment this arousal engenders; Harlow, 1991). In addition, indiscriminate construal of demands, such that demands are construed when they are nonexistent, may be one precipitant of the greater stress levels that Type As experience (Smith & Rhodewalt, 1986), and their lack of sensitivity to changes in demands (Harlow, 1991; Jenkins, 1975). There is a certain irony here in that a strategy that is undertaken to produce superior work actually undermines the goals it was set up to accomplish (see also Friedman & Rosenman, 1974; Price, 1982).

The generalized response style of the Type A individual within and outside the vocational domain may be sharply contrasted to the highly discriminative behavior in social settings by individuals who are high in self-monitoring. Self-monitoring refers to the tendency to exercise control over self-presentation (Snyder, 1979). High self-monitors are sensitive to the expression and self-presentation of others in social situations, and use these cues to guide their own self-presentation. Such attunement to situational cues (i.e., discriminative facility) and flexible regulation of behavior brings about considerable variability across situations. Low self-monitors, on the other hand, are not as responsive to situational cues and allow self-cues (affective states and attitudes) to regulate behavior. Given the considerable discriminative facility exhibited by high self-monitors in social situations, it is not surprising to find that they are more successful than low self-monitors with interpersonal tasks (Snyder, 1979). Given the attunement of this strategy to interpersonal cues and social norms, however, it is not necessarily the case that the high self-monitoring strategy would be associated with success in other, perhaps less socially regulated, domains.

Nonetheless, the combined "lesson" of the Type A's overgeneralized construal strategy and the high self-monitor's discriminative facility seems to point to some general benefits of situational attunement and construal flexibility. Being open to multiple perspectives can open doors to multiple behavioral plans (Langer, 1989). In contrast, when meanings remain fixed and categories and situations appear as absolutes, individuals close off potential routes of problem solving and adaptation (Langer, 1989; Kelly, 1955). Unfortunately, a critical part of taking a less rigid, more "conditional" perspective to events (Langer & Piper, 1987) is the willingness to relinquish a bit of personal control in the service of exploration and discovery. This may not be easy for some – for example, Harlow (1990) observed a hesitance on the part of a sample of Type A college students to engage in the (age-appropriate) consideration of multiple personal identities, separate from their achievement strivings. As Type A individuals are known for their high need for control (Glass, 1977), the exploratory stance of the typical late adolescent may have seemed somewhat threatening to them. (Of course, they also disguise their rigidity by making a supreme commitment to achievement success.) However, flexibility and exploration can be acquired skills, especially when particularly good models are observed in specific life domains (C. R. Snyder, 1991).

Flexibility and strategic choices: deciding how to pursue tasks

Individuals' plans and strategies, the routes people choose to get from one point to another, were the focus of much of Rotter's (1954) emphasis on personal control and flexibility. These strategies, the *"how"* of life-task pursuit, also play a central role in Cantor and Kihlstrom's theory of social intelligence. It is clear that although individuals may pursue similar tasks, they may work on these tasks in different ways (Cantor & Kihlstrom, 1987; Norem, 1989). For example, Norem and Cantor (1986) studied two different strategies that late adolescents employ to work on the task "getting good grades" – academic optimism and academic defensive pessimism. In approaching academic challenges, optimists tend to focus on past success, providing them with a (sometimes) illusory glow that imparts feelings of confidence in future performance. Defensive pessimists, on the other hand, consider the possibility of failure and set low performance expectations – despite comparable histories of past success – and play through worst-case scenarios that they then work hard to avoid. For defensive pessimists, such anticipatory coping appears to serve the purpose of harnessing anxiety that could otherwise interfere with performance. In spite of the extreme process differences, the strategies appear successful for both groups of individuals. Moreover, when defensive pessimists are encouraged by statements that they will do well, imparting the kind of confidence that seems to fuel the optimists, such encouragement appears to interfere with their strategy and yields performance impairments (Norem & Cantor, 1986). Because the different strategies involve different subgoals associated with different task appraisals, what may be useful for one group is not useful for the other (see also Norem & Cantor, 1990; Norem, 1989; Showers & Ruben, 1990).

More recently, Norem & Illingworth (1993) have clearly shown this difference in the pessimists' and optimists' subgoals in achievement tasks. They employed a multimethod analysis that included both laboratory tasks (thought listing and performance measures of anxiety and perceived control, and daily life-experience sampling with a quasiexperimental manipulation of whether or not the subjects considered their progress on central life tasks in each activity report. Across these diverse task settings and measures, the specificity and diagnosticity of these two strategic approaches emerged: for the defensive pessimists (who tend to be anxious prior to tasks despite their history of success), self-reflection and task reflection serve to bolster their perceived control, calm their anxieties, and facilitate performance; for the optimists (who typically feel less anxious anyway), such reflective activity is disruptive in all of these respects. These are two very different ways to intelligently tackle challenging achievement tasks, suited to the different individual "readings" of the tasks.

It seems valuable to consider strategy choice in terms of discriminative facility and flexibility. Strategies are chosen by the individual, although we would guess that individuals often do not realize their own role in choice or even that there are other strategies available or possible outside of their own "time-worn" strategies. Individuals exhibit considerable discriminative facility in this regard, often (though not always) choosing strategies that "fit" the "problems" presented by various contexts (Norem, 1989). For example, although there are individuals who engage in defensive pessimism in social domains, these are not usually the same individuals who are academic defensive pessimists, as the social and academic tasks typically require different competencies and evoke different "readings" for the individual. Such discriminative facility appears adaptive, and we would expect indiscriminant strategy use to undermine task success. In fact, those individuals who do apply the defensive-pessimism strategy in both domains exhibit considerable stress and life dissatisfaction, and Norem (1989) suggests that even "pan-domain" optimism may have its costs, blinding individuals perhaps too quickly to potential obstacles in the offing.

The discriminative facility with which the academic optimist and academic pessimist apply their characteristic strategies highlights the importance of examining multiple tasks separately in the investigation of personality and intelligence. Within individuals, different tasks are appraised differently. Obtaining overall measures of goal conflict or feelings of success removes the link to particular tasks and, therefore, precludes understanding of specific strategies applied to separate tasks (e.g., Emmons & King, 1988; Sternberg, 1984a; see also Zirkel, 1992). Across individuals, the same tasks (e.g., making friends) will have different feelings surrounding them (e.g., Langston & Cantor, 1989). What is threatening to one person may be exciting to another, and this aspect of tasks, in addition to the "objective" content, gives shape and meaning to the task (Klinger, Barta & Maxeiner, 1980). Therefore, to be effective, strategies must be tailored not only to objective task characteristics but also to the individualized meanings ascribed to them.

It is also important to consider the consequences of strategies as they impinge upon the pursuit of other tasks to which the person is committed. For example, Norem and Cantor (1986) demonstrated that although defensive pessimism can bring about successful academic outcomes, the anxiety engendered by this strategy has consequences for other life tasks. Such "strategy spill-over" has also been associated with the Type A behavior pattern, which is characterized by intense vocational efforts at the expense of other life tasks (Burke, Weir, & DuWors, 1979; Harlow, 1990). Life-task definition does not occur in a vacuum, and in addition to requiring a sensitivity to environmental and sociocultural opportunities for work on life tasks, individuals must be aware of the compatibility of their own tasks and strategies with each other. Tasks that evoke incompatible strategies, for example, may engender negative affect and psychosomatic complaints (Emmons & King, 1988), as individuals inhibit their own efforts towards these tasks. Successful functioning may in fact require a balancing of a person's tasks and strategies, taken as a whole.

Intelligence and personality: flexible life-task pursuit

The present approach places a great deal of emphasis on the variety of the context–life task–strategy links reflected in the routine ways that people try to accomplish their personal tasks in daily life (Read & Miller, 1989). In recent years, personality theorists have begun more fully to explore the grounding of behavior in such if-then relationships, based often on individuals' habitual (albeit idiosyncratic) patterns of behavior–contexts associations (e.g., Wright & Mischel, 1987) and interpersonal context–behavior associations (e.g., Thorne, 1989). We take a similar approach, emphasizing instead the pattern of a person's associations between tasks and even settings in daily life (Fleeson & Cantor, 1991a).

In so doing, we suggest that both the coherence of personality and the potential for socially intelligent behavior and change resides in individuals' proclivity to see the (often atypical) opportunities to pursue life tasks in commonplace, routine events of daily life. This frequently involves breaking set with social norms (norms of what is appropriate or even simply typical to pursue in a given setting) and/or relinquishing old routines and strategies for task pursuit. Since individuals typically have their preferred strategies for accomplishing different kinds of tasks (e.g., assertiveness for achievement and cooperativeness for intimacy), when a task is performed in an unusual context, even the strategic form of behavior changes (e.g., cooperative achievement in the family context). Therefore, flexibility in life task pursuit can come in the context of ordinary behavior in ordinary life circumstances, and can implicate the "wisdom" of individuals in "modifying their ways" without being incoherent in their motives (Baltes, Smith, & Staudinger, 1991).

Sometimes this flexibility in task pursuit comes with age and/or with the experience of a life change or life transition (e.g., Staudinger, Smith, & Baltes, 1992; Zirkel, 1992). However, as Kelly's (1955) constructive-alternativism postulate suggests, it may not be necessary to posit unusual conditions for flexibility to emerge. For example, Fleeson and Cantor's (1991a) analysis suggests that college students vary their task pursuit quite a bit, even in the highly regularized confines of a university environment. Of course, varying the event–task links does not always imply intelligent use of opportunities in daily life, as we noted earlier in the case of students pursuing "grades" as vigorously on weekends as on weekdays, and at parties as well as in the classroom. Nonetheless, there is potential for intelligent task pursuit if and when attunement and flexibility are combined in self-regulation.

Langston (1990) draws a useful analogy between this kind of intelligent self-regulation and the wise use of investment and withdrawal strategies in accounting. For example, he argues that some individuals are able to "save" up their "good events" in daily life (keeping a cognitive–affective bank account if you will) and then draw on that account when preparing for a taxing, negative event or in getting over such an experience (Steele, 1988; Linville, 19850. In the context of daily life events, this might translate into the following strategy for task pursuit: "work on a difficult (but important) life task that may be mood deflating when you have the cushion of a good mood already in reserve; work on a relatively easy and rewarding task after you have experienced a negative life event."

Langston (1990) tested this accounting metaphor for intelligent task pursuit, working with experience sampling and diary data gathered over a 15 day period with a group of 54 women in a college sorority (Cantor et al., 1991). Focusing on their diary reports of positive and negative events in the academic and social life-task domains, he was able to show systematic deviations in their subsequent activity in those domains (during the day and across to the next day) as a function of the quality of their experience in the day. When these women experienced a negative academic event, they withdrew effort in that domain (as compared to activity following positive events), whereas when they experienced a negative event in the social domain, they increased their subsequent task activity (as compared to comparable activity following positive events). Langston interprets these results in terms of his accounting metaphor as follows: "People seem to invest their time and energy in an 'economically' sensible fashion. In difficult domains (e.g., the academic life task) when things are going well people increase their activity perhaps to build upon their success. When things are going badly, people seem loath to throw good efforts after bad – to risk further investment where it does not seem to pay off. In a controllable domain (e.g., the social life task), negative events seem to engage attention perhaps because a small additional investment would be likely to pay off quite well." (1990, p. 68).

In contrast to this strategy, others might prefer to follow a more conservative but perhaps equally well-attuned strategy of task pursuit: "work on a deflating task only when you are already in a bad mood." In that case, for example, in light of the "blue Monday" effect on mood, college students might be advised to restrict their enhanced efforts at "grades" pursuit to weekdays when their mood is already likely to be "down" (cf. Fleeson & Cantor, 1991b). Or, those individuals who persist in pursuing "grades" at parties perhaps should only do so in the context of a "bad party," when their own and others' moods stand little to lose by the importation of achievement concerns into an otherwise affiliative context (cf. Cantor, Fleeson, & Cook-Flannagan, 1991). In each instance, intelligent task pursuit means attunement and flexibility – seeing opportunities for life task pursuit without missing the likely correlates of such activity.

Langston (1990) also coded the content of the individuals' reported responses to positive and negative daily life events, and observed that when these women "marked" a positive event (by seeking social contact or communicating about the event) rather than simply continuing with their daily routines, their positive affect and emotional involvement increased during the rest of the day. In the case of negative events, personal self-esteem played a moderating role, with high self-esteem individuals seeming able to benefit significantly from a "marking" response to a negative event. In this latter case, these high-self-esteem women may have been actively seeking social support in their marking responses. For positive events, Langston suggests a different function of marking – i.e., to keep the event memorable for the self and others. As a whole, therefore, these experience-sampling data shed considerable light on the flexibility of individuals in responding to task-relevant positive and negative daily life events. Not only do people respond differently in light of the nature of their beliefs about the specific life-task domains (e.g., social tasks as controllable and academic tasks as especially difficult), but they also utilize the same kind of strategic response for different purposes in different contexts (e.g., marking for memory sake and marking to evoke social support). This kind of domain-specificity and nonrigid responding is quite consistent with the discriminative facility that Mischel (1968, 1990) and others (Cantor & Kihlstrom, 1987) suggest as a critical feature of human intelligence and personality.

Of course, in many daily life contexts, intelligent behavior involves avoiding either extreme on a rigidity–flexibility continuum (Dweck & Leggett, 1988). On one hand, persistent, rigid task pursuit often reflects a breakdown in the system when a person faces situations in which he or she feels overwhelmed or overly taxed (Wright &

Mischel, 1987). On the other hand, flexibility in the extreme can reflect indiscriminate (rather than discriminative) strategy application with poor outcomes. It is best to have a variety of tasks and strategies – especially in the face of obstacles and unexpected "curveballs" (Norem, 1989) – and to pursue them in a variety of contexts and combinations, but not without care.

Capturing intelligence in personality

In keeping pace with the intelligence of individuals' personalities, a special burden is placed on the investigator to capture the rather specific patterning with which people construe their world, pursue their tasks, and regulate their behavior in day-to-day living. We think that this effort requires close attention to the domains of life in which people operate, and to the varying nature of the life tasks on which they work at any given time in life. Although it is certainly true that both intelligence and personality can be described effectively as an average capacity and/or dispositional style, it still seems likely that such a description will miss the within-person, domain-sensitive flexibility and attunement observed in the kinds of experience-sampling and behavioral-observation studies noted here (Fleeson & Cantor, 1991a; Langston, 1990; Norem, 1989; Zirkel, 1992; Shoda, Mischel, & Wright, 1992). At the least, we need some tools that monitor the intelligence of personality – that is, the individual's attunement to choice and opportunity in the routines of daily life, to varying construals, tasks, and strategies across these situations and over time in rewarding ways.

In so doing, we may need to enhance our understanding of the systematic but specific patterning of behavior-in-context (Wright & Mischel, 1987), by paying closer scrutiny, for example, to which tasks individuals pursue, and where, when, and how they pursue each sort (Cantor & Fleeson, 1991). In considering any particular cohort or sociocultural group, we need to map out the typical contexts in which they pursue particular kinds of tasks day to day, and the strategies typically employed to address those tasks in those contexts. With this normative map in hand, it is then possible to pursue the more idiographic route, understanding the systematic but idiosyncratic ways in which individuals construct task–context–strategy associations that depart in significant ways from those norms (i.e., we can portray the personality of the individual in the light of his or her own map of task–context–strategy relations). Finally, taking the next step, we can identify the points or regions of intelligence in each person's personality map at that point in life, identifying domains in which the person's task–context–strategy rules seem most flexible and well-attuned to the costs as well as the benefits of task pursuit.

How would one evaluate those regions of intelligence within a person's map? We have suggested assessment according to flexibility and attunement in the: what, where/when, and how of task pursuit within life-task domains that are brought to the fore by sociocultural demands at a particular time in a person's life. With regard to *what* tasks a person pursues, flexibility comes with changing settings and opportunities across the life course, and attunement reflects sensitivity to the particulars of the demands of a specific living environment (e.g., Zirkel, 1992). As to *where/when* a person pursues a task, flexibility is seen in the diversity of settings in which people construe opportunities for working on a task in the regularity of daily life (e.g., Fleeson & Cantor, 1991a). In contrast, in this case, attunement involves discrimination in the pursuit of tasks in selectively beneficial settings rather than indiscriminant pursuit across settings (e.g., Smith & Rhodewalt, 1986). And flexibility in *how* a task is pursued is revealed in the specific strategies that individuals employ in accord with their particular "reading" of the task; demonstrating the multiple routes that people take to succeed at everyday life tasks (e.g., Norem & Illingworth, 1993). People demonstrate strategic attunement by being discriminating in their use of these preferred strategies across their life tasks, and by carefully assessing the costs for one task of a strategic solution to another task. Unfortunately, such attunement to the costs of generalization of strategies across tasks – "strategy spillover" – is probably one of the most difficult facets of self-regulation to perform (Cantor & Norem, 1989).

Through such maps it should be evident that individuals vary as much within themselves in intelligence as they differ from others; people even change their domains of intelligence over the lifecourse (Baltes et al., 1991). We have outlined several facets of flexibility in task pursuit, each likely to be exhibited to different degrees by a person with regard to different tasks and life settings. For example, we can all point to individuals who are expertly tuned to the opportunities for task pursuit in professional and achievement settings, and well-calibrated to the costs of those pursuits in different settings and with different strategies. Yet many of those same people are clumsy at best in handling their personal and family relationships, and they seem downright inept in their failure to take care of their personal health. Indeed, theirs' is a very selective intelligence map with respect to the full array of their relevant life tasks. Therefore, the only sense in which it seems reasonable to even speak of their generalized level of social intelligence is in some assessment of how well they are balancing these various life task pursuits (Little, 1989). But even the notion of a metaskill at balancing life goals implicates careful attention to the specifics of each task that is pressing to be addressed, and awareness of the ever-evolving dynamics of task pursuit, such that an "intelligent" priority list at one time in life or in one living environment may quickly become a rather "stupid" solution with time and in new places (Brandtstadter & Renner, 1990). Thus, for example, the "whiz" at work may get away with shortchanging family and health in young adulthood, perhaps only to face the "consequences" of this decision in a midlife divorce and poor health in older adulthood (e.g., Whyte, 1963). Such events may be enough to precipitate a reshuffling of life task priorities, but the person is still more likely to be a "novice" than an "expert" in addressing these newly salient pursuits. Relatively speaking, we know little as to how well expertise fine-tuned, for example, in the workplace in early adulthood will transfer to intelligently tackling these new problems in a later life period and a new life setting (Baltes et al., 1991). Intelligence, then, is indeed a very difficult thing to precisely evaluate in a general or even stable way in the realms of social life at issue in the study of personality.

References

Abelson, R. (1981). Psychological status of the script concept. *American Psychologist, 36,* 715–729.

Anderson, J. R. (1981). *Cognitive psychology and its implications.* San Francisco: Freeman.

Anderson, J. R. (1983). *The architecture of cognition.* Cambridge, MA: Harvard University Press.

Anderson, J. R. (1987). Skill acquisition: Compilation of weak-method problem solutions. *Psychological Review, 94,* 192–210.

Anderson, N. H. (1974). Cognitive algebra: Integration theory applied to social attribution. In L. Berkowitz (Ed.), *Advances in experimental social psychology* (Vol. 7, pp. 1–101). New York: Academic Press.

Andersen, S. M., & Cole, S. W. (1990). "Do I know you?'" The role of significant others in general social perception. *Journal of Personality and Social Psychology, 59,* 384–399.

Andersen, S. M., & Klatzky, R. (1987). Traits and social stereotypes: Levels of categorization in person perception. *Journal of Personality and Social Psychology, 53*(2), 235–246.

Argyle, M. (1981). The experimental study of the basic features of situations. In D. Magnusson (Ed.), *Toward a psychology of situations: An interactional perspective* (pp. 63–83). Hillsdale, NJ: Erlbaum.

Baltes, P. (1987). Theoretical propositions of life-span developmental psychology: On the dynamics between growth and decline. *Developmental Psychology, 23,* 611–626.

Baltes, P. B., Smith, J., and Staudinger, U. M. (in press, 1991). Wisdom and successful aging. In Theo B. Sonderegger (Ed.), *Nebraska Symposium on Motivation* (Vol. 39, pp. 123–167). Lincoln, NB: University of Nebraska Press.

Banaji, M. R., & Greenwald, A. G. (1991). Measuring implicit attitudes. Invited symposium on The Unconscious, American Psychological Society, Washington, D.C.

Bandura, A. (1977). *Social learning theory.* Englewood Cliffs, NJ: Prentice-Hall.

Bandura, A. (1982). Self-efficacy mechanism in human agency. *American Psychologist, 37,* 122–147.

Bandura, A. (1986). *Social Foundations of thought and action: A social cognitive theory.* Englewood Cliffs, NJ: Prentice-Hall.

Bargh, J. A. (1982). Attention and automaticity in the processing of self-relevant information. *Journal of Personality and Social Psychology, 43,* 425–436.

Baron, J. (1982). Personality and intelligence. In R. Sternberg (Ed.), *Handbook of human intelligence* (pp. 3–28). Cambridge: Cambridge University Press.

Baumeister, R., & Scher, S. (1988). Self-defeating behavior patterns among normal individuals: Review and analysis of common self-destructive tendencies. *Psychological Bulletin, 104,* 3–22.

Berg, C. A. (1990). What is intellectual efficacy over the life course?: Using adults' conceptions to address the question. In J. Rodin, C. Schooler, & K. W. Schaie (Eds.), *Self-directedness: Cause and effects throughout the life course* (pp. 157–181). Hillsdale, NJ: Erlbaum.

Brandtstadter, J., & Renner, G. (1990). Tenacious goal pursuit and flexible goal adjustment: Explication and age-related analysis of assimilative and accommodative strategies of coping. *Psychology and Aging, 5*(1), 58–67.

Bruner, J. S. (1951). Personality dynamics and the process of perceiving. In R. R. Blake & G. V. Ramsey (Eds.), *Perception: An approach to personality* (pp. 121–147). New York: Ronald Press.

Bruner, J. S. (1957). Going beyond the information given. In H. Gruber, K. R. Hammond & R. Jesser (Eds.), *Contemporary approaches to cognition.* Cambridge, MA: Harvard University Press.

Burke, R. J., Weir, T., & DuWors, R. E. (1979). Type A behavior of administrators and wives' reports of marital satisfaction and well-being. *Journal of Applied Psychology, 64,* 57–65.

Buss, D. M., & Cantor, N. (Eds.), (1989). *Personality psychology: Recent trends and emerging directions.* New York: Springer-Verlag.

Buss, D. M., & Craik, K. H. (1983). The act frequency approach to personality. *Psychological Review, 90,* 105–126.

Cantor, N. (1990). From thought to behavior: "Having" and "doing" in the study of personality and cognition. *American Psychologist, 45*(6), 735–750.

Cantor, N., Acker, M., & Cook-Flannagan, C. (1991). *Conflict and preoccupation in the intimacy life task.* Unpublished manuscript, University of Michigan.

Cantor, N., & Fleeson, W. (1991). Life tasks and self-regulatory processes. In M. Maehr & P. Pintrich (Eds.), *Advances in motivation and achievement* (Vol. 7, pp. 327–369). Greenwich, CT: JAI Press.

Cantor, N., Fleeson, W., & Cook-Flannagan, C. (1991). *The flexible pursuit of life tasks in daily events.* Paper presented at the meetings of the American Psychological Society, Washington, D.C., June.

Cantor, N., & Kihlstrom, J. F. (1982). Cognitive and social processes in personality, In T. Wilson & C. Franks (Eds.), *Contemporary behavior therapy* (pp. 142–201). New York: Guilford.

Cantor, N., & Kihlstrom, J. F. (1987). *Personality and social intelligence.* Englewood Cliffs, NJ: Prentice-Hall.

Cantor, N., & Langston, C. A. (1989). "Ups and downs" of life tasks in a life transition. In L. A. Pervin (Ed.), *Goal concept in personality and social psychology* (pp. 127–168). Hillsdale, NJ: Erlbaum.

Cantor, N., & Mischel, W. (1979). Prototypes in person perception. In L. Berkowitz (Ed.), *Advances in experimental social psychology* (Vol. 12, pp. 3–52). New York: Academic Press.

Cantor, N., Mischel, W., & Schwartz, J. (1982). A prototype analysis of psychological situations. *Cognitive Psychology, 14,* 45–77.

Cantor, N., Norem, J., Langston, C., Zirkel, S., Fleeson, W., & Cook-Flannagan, C. (1991). Life tasks and daily life experience. *Journal of Personality,* Special issue on daily events and personality, *59*(3), 425–451.

Cantor, N., Markus, H., Niedenthal, P., & Nurius, P. (1986). On motivation and the self-concept. In R. M. Sorrentino & E. T. Higgins (Eds.), *Handbook of motivation & cognition: Foundations of social behavior* (pp. 96–121). New York: Guilford.

Carver, C. S., & Scheier, M. F. (1981). *Attention and self-regulation: A control-theory approach to human behavior.* New York: Springer-Verlag.

Cattell, R. B. (1943). The description of personality: Basic traits resolved into clusters. *Journal of Abnormal and Social Psychology, 38,* 476–506.

Cattell, R. B., & Horn, J. L. (1978). A check on the theory of fluid and crystallized intelligence with description of new subtest designs. *Journal of Educational Measurement, 15,* 189–264.

Cervone, D. (1991). The two disciplines of personality psychology. *Psychological Science, 2*(6), 371–376.

Chase, W. G., & Simon, H. A. (1973). Perception in Chess. *Cognitive Psychology, 4,* 55–81.

Cohler, B. (1982). Personal narrative and life course. In P. Baltes & O. Brim, Jr. (Eds.), *Life-span development and behavior* (Vol. 4, pp. 205–241). New York: Academic Press.

Coyne, J. C. (1976). Depression and the response of others. *Journal of Abnormal Psychology, 85*(2), 186–193.

Deaux, K., & Lewis, L. L. (1984). The structure of gender stereotypes: Interrelationships among components and gender label. *Journal of Personality and Social Psychology, 46,* 991–1004.

Devine, P. G. (1989). Stereotypes and prejudice: Their automatic and controlled components. *Journal of Personality and Social Psychology, 56,* 5–18.

Duncan, S. L. (1976). Differential social perception and attribution of intergroup violence: Testing the lower limits of stereotyping of blacks. *Journal of Personality and Social Psychology, 34,* 590–598.

Dweck, C. S., & Leggett, E. L. (1988). A social-cognitive approach to motivation and personality. *Psychological Review, 95*(2), 256–273.

Emmons, R. A. (1991). Personal strivings, daily life events, and psychological and physical well-being. *Journal of Personality, 59*(3), 453–472.

Emmons, R. A., & King, L. A. (1988). Conflict among personal strivings: Immediate and long-term implications for psychological and physical well-being. *Journal of Personality and Social Psychology, 54*(6), 1040–1048.

Emmons, R. A., & McAdams, D. P. (1991). Personal strivings and motive dispositions: Exploring the links. *Personality and Social Psychology Bulletin, 17*(6), 648–654.

Fiske, S. T., & Pavelchak, M. A. (1986). Category-based versus piecemeal-based affective responses: Developments in schema-triggered affect. In R. M. Sorrentino & E. T. Higgins (Eds.), *Handbook of motivation & cognition: Foundations of social behavior* (pp. 167–203). New York: Guilford.

Fiske, S. T., & Taylor, S. E. (1991). *Social cognition.* Reading, MA: Addison-Wesley.

Fleeson, W. W., & Cantor, N. (1991a). *Flexible construal, life tasks, and the affective experience of daily life.* Unpublished manuscript, University of Michigan.

Fleeson, W. W., & Cantor, N. (1991b). *Temporal Regulation of Long-Term Tasks: Choices and Costs.* Paper presented at the meetings of the Midwestern Psychological Association, Chicago, IL, May.

Fletcher, G., Danilovics, P., Fernandez, G., Peterson, D., & Reeder, G. (1986). Attributional complexity, an individual differences measure. *Journal of Personality and Social Psychology, 51*(4), 875–884.

Ford, M. E., & Tisak, M. S. (1983). A further search for social intelligence. *Journal of Educational Psychology, 75*(2), 196–206.

Forgas, J. (1982). Episode cognition: Internal representations of interaction routines. *Advances in Experimental Social Psychology, 15,* 59–101.

Friedman, M., & Rosenman, R. (1974). *Type A behavior and your heart.* New York: Knopf.

Gick, M. L., & Holyoak, K. J. (1983). Schema induction and analogical transfer. *Cognitive Psychology, 15,* 1–38.

Glass, C. D. (1977). *Behavior patterns, stress, and coronary disease.* Hillsdale, NJ: Erlbaum.

Gould, S. J. (1981). *The mismeasure of man.* New York: Norton.

Greenwald, A. G. (1980). The totalitarian ego: Fabrication and revision of personal history. *American Psychologist, 35,* 602–618.

Guilford, J. P. (1959). Three faces of intellect. *American Psychologist, 14,* 469–479.

Hamilton, D. L. (1981). *Cognitive processes in stereotyping and intergroup behavior.* Hillsdale, NJ: Erlbaum.

Hampson, S. E. (1982). *The construction of personality: An introduction.* London: Routledge & Kegan Paul.

Harlow, R. E. (1990). Type A behavior during the transition to college: Characteristic demand integration and disregard of identity negotiation. Unpublished Masters Thesis, University of Michigan.

Harlow, R. E. (1991). Social construal and evaluation apprehension effects. Unpublished Masters Thesis, Princeton University.

Harlow, R. E., Scotto, F., & Panter, A. T. (1989). *Person perception and the type A behavior pattern.* Unpublished manuscript, New York University.

Havighurst, R. J. (1953). *Human development and education.* New York: Longmans, Green.

Hellesnes, T., Raaheim, K., & Bengtsson, G. (1982). Attempts to predict intelligent behavior. III. The relative importance of divergent and convergent production. *Scandinavian Journal of Psychology, 23,* 263–266.

Helson, R., Mitchell, V., & Moane, G. (1984). Personality and patterns of adherence and nonadherence to the social clock. *Journal of Personality and Social Psychology, 46,* 1079–1096.

Higgins, E. T. (1990). Personality, social psychology, and person–situation relations: Standards and knowledge activation as a common language. In L. A. Pervin (Ed.), *Handbook of personality: Theory and research* (pp. 301–338). New York: Guilford.

Higgins, E. T., & Bargh, J. A. (1987). Social cognition and social perception. In M. R. Rosenweig & L. W. Porter (Eds.), *Annual Review of Psychology* (Vol. 38, pp. 369–425). Palo Alto, CA: Annual Reviews.

Higgins, E. T., Klein, R., & Strauman, T. (1985). Self-concept discrepancy theory: A psychological model for distinguishing among different aspects of depression and anxiety. *Social Cognition, 3,* 51–76.

Higgins, E. T., & Parsons, J. C. (1983). Social cognitions and the social life of the child: Stages as subcultures. In E. T. Higgins, D. N. Ruble, & W. W. Hartup (Eds.), *Social cognition and social development: A socio-cultural perspective* (pp. 15–62). New York: Cambridge University Press.

Hilton, J., & Darley, J. (1985). Constructing other persons: A limit on the effect. *Journal of Experimental Social Psychology, 21,* 1–18.

Janoff-Bulman, R., & Brickman, P. (1982). Expectations and what people learn from failure. In N. T. Feather (Ed.), *Expectations and action: Expectancy-value models in psychology* (pp. 207–272). Hillsdale, NJ: Erlbaum.

Jenkins, C. D. (1975). The coronary-prone personality. In W. D. Gentry & R. B. Williams (Eds.), *Psychological aspects of myocardial infarction and coronary care.* St. Louis: C. V. Mosby Co.

John, O. P. (1990). The "big five" factor taxonomy: Dimensions of personality in the natural language and in questionnaires. In L. A. Pervin (Ed.), *Handbook of personality: Theory and research* (pp. 66–100). New York: Guilford.

Jones, E. E., & Davis, K. E. (1965). From acts to dispositions: The attribution process in person perception.

In L. Berkowitz (Ed.), *Advances in experimental social psychology* (Vol. 2, pp. 219–266). New York: Academic Press.

Jones, E. E., & Pittman, T. S. (1982). Toward a general theory of strategic self-presentation. In J. Suls (Ed.), *Psychological Perspectives on the Self* (Vol. 1, pp. 231–262). Hillsdale, NJ: Erlbaum.

Keil, F. C. (1984). Transition mechanisms in cognitive development and the structure of knowledge. In R. Sternberg (Ed.), *Mechanisms of cognitive development* (pp. 81–99). San Francisco: Freeman.

Keil, F. C. (1986). The acquisition of natural kind and artifact terms. In W. Demopoulos & A. Marras (Eds.), *Language learning and concept acquisition* (pp. 133–153). Norwood, NJ: Ablex.

Kelly, G. A. (1955). *The psychology of personal constructs.* New York: Norton.

Kihlstrom, J. F., & Cantor, N. (1984). Mental representations of the self. In L. Berkowitz (Ed.), *Advances in experimental social psychology* (Vol. 17, pp. 1–47). New York: Academic Press.

Kihlstrom, J. F., Cantor, N., Albright, J. S., Chew, B. R., Klein, S. B., & Niedenthal, P. M. (1988). Information processing and the study of the self. In L. Berkowitz (Ed.), *Advances in experimental social psychology* (Vol. 21, pp. 145–180). New York: Academic Press.

Kihlstrom, J. F., & Evans, F. (1979). Memory retrieval processes in posthypnotic amnesia. In J. Kihlstrom & F. Evans (Eds.), *Functional disorders of memory* (pp. 179–218). Hillsdale, NJ: Erlbaum.

Klinger, E. (1977). *Meaning and void: Inner experience and the incentives in people's lives.* Minneapolis: University of Minnesota Press.

Klinger, E. (1987). Current concerns and disengagement from incentives. In F. Halisch & J. Kuhl (Eds.), *Motivation, intention and volition* (pp. 337–347). New York: Springer.

Klinger, E. (1989). Goal-orientation as psychological linchpin: A commentary on Cantor and Kihlstrom's "Social intelligence and cognitive assessments of personality." In R. S. Wyer, Jr., & T. K. Srull (Eds.), *Advances in social cognition* (Vol. 2, pp. 123–130). Hillsdale, NJ: Erlbaum.

Klinger, E., Barta, S. G., & Maxeiner, M. E. (1980). Motivational correlates of thought content frequency and commitment. *Journal of Personality and Social Psychology, 39*(6), 1222–1237.

Kobasa, S. C. (1979). Stressful life events, personality, and health: An inquiry into hardiness. *Journal of Personality and Social Psychology, 37*(1), 1–11.

Kunda, Z. (1987). Motivated inference: Self-serving generation and evaluation of causal theories. *Journal of Personality and Social Psychology, 53,* 636–647.

Laboratory of Comparative Human Cognition. (1982). Culture and intelligence. In R. Sternberg (Ed.), *Handbook of human intelligence* (pp. 3–28). Cambridge: Cambridge University Press.

Langer, E. J. (1989). *Mindfulness.* Reading, MA: Addison-Wesley.

Langer, E. J., & Abelson, R. P. (1974). A patient by any other name . . . : Clinician group difference in labeling bias. *Journal of Consulting and Clinical Psychology, 3.42,* 4–9.

Langer, E., & Piper, A. (1987). The prevention of mindlessness. *Journal of Personality and Social Psychology, 53*(2), 280–287.

Langston, C. A. (1990). *The dynamics of daily life: Responses to positive and negative events, life-task activity, mood and well-being.* Unpublished doctoral dissertation, University of Michigan.

Langston, C. A., & Cantor, N. (1989). Social anxiety and social constraint: When "making friends" is hard. *Journal of Personality and Social Psychology, 56*(4), 649–661.

Lazarus, R. S., & Folkman, S. (1984). *Stress, appraisal, and coping.* New York: Springer.

Lesgold, A. (1988). Problem solving. In R. J. Sternberg and E. E. Smith (Eds.), *The psychology of human thought* (pp. 188–213). Cambridge: Cambridge University Press.

Lewicki, P. (1984). Self-schema and social information processing. *Journal of Personality and Social Psychology, 47*(6), 1177–1190.

Lewin, K. (1935). *A dynamic theory of personality.* New York: McGraw-Hill.

Linville, P. (1982). Affective consequences of complexity regarding the self and others. In M. Clark & S. Fiske (Eds.), *Affect and cognition: The 17th annual Carnegie Symposium on Cognition* (pp. 79–109). Hillsdale, NJ: Erlbaum.

Linville, P. (1985). Self-complexity and affective extremity: Don't put all of your eggs in one basket. *Social Cognition, 3,* 94–120.

Linville, P. W., & Clark, L. F. (1989). Production systems and social problem solving: Specificity, flexibility, and expertise. In R. S. Wyer & T. K. Srull (Eds.), *Advances in social cognition* (Vol. 2, pp. 131–152). Hillsdale, NJ: Erlbaum.

Little, B. (1989). Personal projects analysis: Trivial pursuits, magnificent obsessions and the search for coherence. In D. M. Buss & N. Cantor (Eds.), *Personality psychology: Recent trends and emerging directions* (pp. 15–31). New York: Springer-Verlag.

McAdams, D. P. (1991). The five-factor model in personality: A critical appraisal. *Journal of Personality, 60*, 329–361.

McAdams, D. P., & Constantian, C. A. (1983). Intimacy and affiliation motives in daily living: An experience sampling analysis. *Journal of Personality and Social Psychology, 45*, 851–861.

McGuire, W. J. (1984). Search for the self: Going beyond self-esteem and the reactive self. In R. A. Zucker, J. Arnoff, & A. I. Rubin (Eds.), *Personality and the prediction of behavior* (pp. 73–120). New York: Academic Press.

Markus, H. (1977). Self-schemata and processing information about the self. *Journal of Personality and Social Psychology, 35*, 63–78.

Markus, H., & Cross, S. (1990). The interpersonal self. In L. A. Pervin (Ed.), *Handbook of personality: Theory and research* (pp. 576–608). New York: Guilford.

Markus, H., Smith, J., & Moreland, R. (1985). Role of the self-concept in the perception of others. *Journal of Personality and Social Psychology, 49*, 1495–1512.

Markus, H., & Nurius, P. (1986). Possible selves. *American Psychologist, 41*, 954–969.

Metalsky, G. I., & Abramson, L. Y. (1981). Attributional styles: Toward a framework for conceptualization and assessment. In P. C. Kendall & S. D. Hollon (Eds.), *Cognitive-behavioral interventions: Assessment methods*. New York: Academic Press.

Miller, S. M., & Mangan, C. (1983). Interacting effects of information and coping style in adapting to gynecologic stress: Should the doctor tell all? *Journal of Personality and Social Psychology, 45*, 223–236.

Mischel, W. (1968). *Personality and assessment*. New York: Wiley.

Mischel, W. (1973). Toward a cognitive social learning reconceptualization of personality. *Psychological Review, 80*, 252–283.

Mischel, W. (1984). Convergences and challenges in the search for consistency. *American Pathologist, 39*, 351–364.

Mischel, W. (1990). Personality dispositions revisited and revised: A view after three decades. In L. A. Pervin (Ed.), *Handbook of personality: Theory and research* (pp. 111–134). New York: Guilford.

Nasby, W., & Kihlstrom, J. F. (1986). Cognitive assessment of personality and psychopathology. In R. E. Ingram (Ed.), *Information Processing approaches to psychopathology and clinical psychology* (pp. 217–239). New York: Academic Press.

Nelson, K. (1986). *Event knowledge: Structure and function in development*. Hillsdale, NJ: Erlbaum.

Neugarten, B. L. (Ed.) (1968). *Middle age and aging*. Chicago: University of Chicago Press.

Newell, A., & Simon, H. A. (1972). *Human problem solving*. Englewood Cliffs, NJ: Prentice-Hall.

Nisbett, R. E., & Ross, L. (1980). *Human inference: Strategies and shortcomings in social judgment*. Englewood Cliffs, NJ: Prentice-Hall.

Norem, J. K. (1989). Cognitive strategies as personality: Effectiveness, specificity, flexibility, and change. In D. M. Buss & N. Cantor (Eds.), *Personality psychology: Recent trends and emerging directions* (pp. 45–60). New York: Springer-Verlag.

Norem, J. K., & Cantor, N. (1986). Defensive pessimism: "Harnessing" anxiety as motivation. *Journal of Personality and Social Psychology, 51*, 1208–1217.

Norem, J. K., & Cantor, N. (1990). Cognitive strategies, coping, and perceptions of competence. In R. J. Sternberg & J. Kolligian, Jr. (Eds.), *Competence considered* (pp. 190–204). New Haven: Yale University Press.

Norem, J. K., & Illingworth, K. S. S. (1993, in press). Strategy-dependent effects of reflecting on self and tasks: Some implications of optimism and defensive pessimism. *Journal of Personality and Social Psychology*.

Ostrom, T., & Davis, D. (1979). Idiosyncratic weighting of trait information in impression formation. *Journal of Personality and Social Psychology, 37*(11), 2025–2043.

Pervin, L. (1976). A free-response description approach to the analysis of person–situation interaction. *Journal of Personality and Social Psychology, 34*(3), 465–474.

Pervin, L. A. (Ed.) (1989). *Goal concepts in personality and social psychology.* Hillsdale, NJ: Erlbaum.

Price, V. (1982). *The type A behavior pattern: A model for research and practice.* New York: Academic Press.

Raush, H. L., Dittman, A. T., & Taylor, T. J. (1959). The interpersonal behavior of children in residential treatment. *Journal of Abnormal and Social Psychology, 58,* 9–26.

Read, S. J., & Miller, L. C. (1989). Inter-personalism: Toward a goal-based theory of persons in relationships. In L. Pervin (Ed.), *Goal concepts in personality and social psychology* (pp. 413–472). Hillsdale, NJ: Erlbaum.

Reich, J. W., & Zautra, A. J. (1983). Demands and desires in daily life: Some influences on well-being. *American Journal of Community Psychology, 1,* 41–58.

Rosenberg, S., & Gara, M. A. (1985). The multiplicity of personal identity. In P. Shaver (Ed.), *Review of personality and social psychology* (Vol. 6). Beverly Hills: Sage.

Ross, M. (1989). The relation of implicit theories to the construction of personal histories. *Psychological Review, 96,* 341–357.

Rotter, J. B. (1954). *Social learning and clinical psychology.* Englewood Cliffs, NJ: Prentice-Hall.

Sagar, H. A., & Schofield, J. W. (1980). Racial and behavioral cues in black and white children's perceptions of ambiguously aggressive acts. *Journal of Personality and Social Psychology, 39,* 590–598.

Schlenker, B. R., & Weigold, M. F. (1989). Goals and the self-identification process: Constructing desired identifies. In L. A. Pervin (Ed.), *Goal concepts in personality and social psychology* (pp. 243–390). Hillsdale, NJ: Erlbaum.

Shaver, P., Schwartz, J., O'Connor, C., Kirson, D., Marsh, C., & Fischer, S. (1987). Emotions knowledge: Further exploration of a prototype model. *Journal of Personality and Social Psychology, 52(6),* 1061–1086.

Shoda, Y., Mischel, W., & Wright, J. C. (1992). *The role of social intelligence and situational demands in behavior organization and personality coherence.* Manuscript in preparation.

Showers, C., & Cantor, N. (1985). Social cognition: A look at motivated strategies. *Annual Review of Psychology, 36,* 275–305.

Showers, C., & Ruben, C. (1989). Distinguishing defensive pessimism from depression: Negative expectations and positive coping. *Cognitive Therapy and Research, 14,* 385–399.

Simon, H. A. (1990). Invariants of human behavior. *Annual Review of Psychology, 41,* 1–9.

Skov, R. B., & Sherman, S. J. (1986). Information-gathering processes: Diagnosticity, hypothesis-confirmatory strategies, and perceived hypothesis confirmation. *Journal of Experimental Social Psychology, 22,* 93–121.

Smith, C. A., & Lazarus, R. S. (1990). Emotion and adaptation. In L. A. Pervin (Ed.), *Handbook of personality: Theory and research* (pp. 609–637). New York: Guilford.

Smith, T. W., & Rhodewalt, F. (1986). On states, traits, and processes: A transactional alternative to the individual difference assumptions in Type A behavior and physiological reactivity. *Journal of Research in Personality, 20,* 229–251.

Snyder, C. R. (1991). Reality negotiation: From excuses to hope and beyond. *Journal of Social and Clinical Psychology, 8,* 130–157.

Snyder, M. (1979). Self-monitoring processes. In L. Berkowitz (Ed.), *Advances in experimental social psychology* (Vol. 12, pp. 85–128). New York: Academic Press.

Snyder, M. (1981a). Seek, and ye shall find: Testing hypotheses about other people. In E. T. Higgins, C. P. Herman, & M. P. Zanna (Eds.), *Social cognition: The Ontario symposium on personality and social psychology* (Vol. 1, pp. 277–304). Hillsdale, NJ: Erlbaum.

Snyder, M. (1981b). On the influence of individuals in situations. In N. Cantor & J. Kihlstrom (Eds.), *Personality, cognition and social interaction* (pp. 309–329). Hillsdale, NJ: Erlbaum.

Snyder, M. (1987). *Public appearances/private realities.* New York: W. H. Freeman.

Snyder, M., & Ickes, W. (1985). Personality and social behavior. In G. Lindzey & E. Aronson (Eds.), *The handbook of social psychology* (3rd ed., Vol. 2, p. 883–948). New York: Random House.

Staudinger, U. M., Smith, J., & Baltes, P. B. (1992). Wisdom-related knowledge in a life-review task: Age differences and the role of professional specialization in clinical psychology. *Psychology and Aging, 7,* 271–281.

Strack, S., & Coyne, J. C. (1983). Social confirmation of dysphoria: Shared and private reactions to depression. *Journal of Personality and Social Psychology, 44*(4), 798–806.

Steele, C. (1988). The psychology of self-affirmation: Sustaining the integrity of the self. In L. Berkowitz (Ed.), *Advances in experimental social psychology* (Vol. 21, pp. 261–302). New York: Academic Press.

Sternberg, R. J. (1984a). Toward a triarchic theory of human intelligence. *The Behavioral and Brain Sciences, 7,* 269–315.

Sternberg, R. J. (1984b). A contextualist view of the nature of intelligence. In P. S. Fry (Ed.), *Changing conceptions of intelligence and intellectual functioning*. Amsterdam: North-Holland.

Sternberg, R. J., & Salter, W. (1982). Conceptions of intelligence. In R. Sternberg (Ed.), *Handbook of human intelligence* (pp. 3–28). Cambridge: Cambridge University Press.

Swann, W. B., Jr. (1987). Identity negotiation: Where two roads meet. *Journal of Personality and Social Psychology, 53*(6), 1038–1051.

Tennen, H., Suls, J., & Affleck, G. (1991). Personality and daily experience: The promise and the challenge. *Journal of Personality, 59*(3), 313–338.

Thorne, A. (1987). The press of personality: A study of conversations between introverts and extraverts. *Journal of Personality and Social Psychology, 53*(4), 718–726.

Thorne, A. (1989). Conditional patterns, transference, and the coherence of personality across time. In D. M. Buss & N. Cantor (Eds.), *Personality psychology: Recent trends and emerging directions* (pp. 149–159). New York: Springer-Verlag.

Tomkins, S. S. (1979). Script theory: Different magnification of affects. In H. E. Howe, Jr. & R. A. Dienstbier (Eds.), *Nebraska Symposium on Motivation* (Vol. 26, pp. 201–236). Lincoln: University of Nebraska Press.

Vallacher, R. R., & Wegner, D. M. (1987). What do people think they're doing? Action identification and human behavior. *Psychological Review, 94,* 3–15.

Vallacher, R. R., & Wegner, D. M. (1989). Levels of Personal Agency: Individual variation in action identification. *Journal of Personality and Social Psychology, 57*(4), 660–671.

Veroff, J. (1983). Contextual determinants of personality. *Personality and Social Psychology Bulletin, 9,* 331–343.

Walker, R. E., & Foley, J. M. (1973). Social intelligence: Its history and measurement. *Psychological Reports, 33,* 839–864.

Weiner, B. (1985). An attributional theory of achievement motivation and emotion. *Psychological Review, 92*(4), 548–573.

Whyte, W. H., Jr. (1963). The wives of management. In P. Olsen (Ed.), *America as a mass society*. New York: McGraw-Hill.

Wright, J. C., & Mischel, W. (1987). A conditional approach to dispositional constructs: The local predictability of social behavior. *Journal of Personality and Social Psychology, 53*(6), 1159–1177.

Wurf, E. (1988). *Negativity in the self-concept: Self-construal and feedback-seeking*. Unpublished doctoral dissertation, University of Michigan, Ann Arbor, MI.

Zirkel, S. (1992). Developing independence in a life transition: Investing the self in the concerns of the day. *Journal of Personality and Social Psychology, 62,* 506–521.

Zirkel, S., & Cantor, N. (1990). Personal construal of life tasks: Those who struggle for independence. *Journal of Personality and Social Psychology, 58*(1), 172–185.

6 Thinking styles: theory and assessment at the interface between intelligence and personality

Robert J. Sternberg

This chapter considers thinking styles–an interface between intelligence and personality. The chapter also considers the implications of thinking styles for testing. It is argued that whereas many in the field have sought to solve the problems of the inadequacy of standardized ability tests with so-called "authentic testing," such testing is no panacea. An important supplement would be the testing of an interface between abilities and personality, namely, thinking styles. In particular, the chapter argues that our approaches to testing inadvertently reward students who show certain profiles of thinking styles, while punishing students who show other profiles. Ideally, testing should involve converging operations that allow abilities and achievements to show through the various profiles of styles students may have.

The chapter opens with a general consideration of some issues and testing, after which the remainder of the article is divided into five main parts. The first is a consideration of the concept of styles. The second is a presentation of one theory of thinking styles – the theory of mental self-government. The third is a discussion of the interface between thinking styles and assessment, including an analysis of the implications of thinking styles for conventional assessment and a description of some measures of styles, based on the theory of mental self-government. The fourth is a description of some measures of styles, based on the theory. The fifth is an analysis of the implications of this theory for testing of abilities and achievement.

Both producers and consumers of psychological tests are always looking for panaceas. The panaceas never emerge. The result is that we see the pendulum of testing theory and practice swinging from one extreme to another, never finding any sensible middle ground. Instead of a dialectical process of "thesis–antithesis–synthesis," we move from thesis to antithesis to thesis and back to antithesis, with the result that new ideas sound strangely like old ones, or at least fail to build on the strengths of the old ones.

Nowhere is this more obvious today than in the area of testing. In the past, we relied heavily on so-called objective, multiple-choice testing formats for measuring abilities and achievement, thereby gaining objectivity of scoring and reliability at the expense of authenticity and ecological validity. In the past few years, there has been growing momentum to replace conventional standardized tests with unconventional ones that would gain authenticity and ecological validity, but at the expense of objectivity in scoring and reliability (see, e.g., Linn, Baker, & Dunbar, 1991; Stiggins, 1987; Wiggins, 1989). Whatever kinds of problems may be solved by the new tests, however, among them will not be problems of culture–fairness and mitigation of group differences. The new tests are at least as culturally biased as the old ones, if not more so, with their heavy emphasis on writing and, in general, on the organization of cultural information. Indeed, this emphasis is a "double-whammy," because not only do children from different backgrounds have differential relevant prior experience in writing, but the scoring of essays will inevitably reflect the cultural biases of the scorer. We are about to replace one inadequate kind of test with another.

I am not trying to criticize or defend any one particular type of testing, but rather to argue for the necessity of *converging operations* (Garner, Hake, & Erikson, 1956) in testing, that is, the use of multiple kinds of assessments, including both newer, more authentic ones, and older, more objectively scorable ones. Any single kind of testing is inadequate, because it does better with respect to some kinds of criteria than others. One maximizes on assessment when diverse kinds of assessments are used. The principle is actually the same as that of financial diversification. It can be shown that one maximizes return from a diversified financial portfolio (Malkiel, 1985), because each kind of investment helps compensate for the weaknesses of another kind.

When we think of the use of multiple testing strategies, we are most likely to think of the advantages of diversification in psychometric terms: for example, in terms of the tradeoff between objective scoring and ecological validity, or between reliability and diversity of skills measured. In this view, the advantage of diversification is essentially statistical – one cancels out various kinds of measurement errors. The goal of this chapter is to consider another kind of advantage, namely, a strictly psychological one. My main point is that in concentrating on the measurement of ability and achievement, we have neglected the role of a "moderator" variable, namely, styles of thinking. Styles of thinking are at the interface between abilities and personality. What kind of test will best display the abilities and achievements of a given individual will depend largely upon that individual's preferred thinking styles.

Objectively scorable, multiple-choice tests tend to benefit examinees with certain styles, but place other examinees at a disadvantage. The same is also true for "authentic" assessments. In other words, we may be going from a system that gives an unfair advantage to one group, to a system that gives an unfair advantage to another group.

The concept of thinking styles

The nature of styles

A thinking style is a preferred way of thinking. It is not an ability, but rather a preferred way of expressing or using one or more abilities. Two or more people at the same level of ability may nevertheless have very different styles. In order to make the notion of a style concrete, I will briefly review an example of styles as shown by three college roommates. I will consider here only that they differ in styles, and later, I will analyze what these styles are.

Three college roommates

Consider three college chums (all of them real people). The friends – Alex, Bob, and Charles (only one of the names is unchanged) – seemed to be remarkably similar intellectually when they entered college. All had almost identical Scholastic Aptitude Test scores, similar high school academic averages, and similar strengths and weaknesses in their intellectual abilities. For example, all three were more verbal than quantitative, and better in abstract inductive reasoning than in spatial ability. Thus, in terms of standard theories of intelligence, such as those of Spearman (1927) or Thurstone (1938), the three roommates seemed quite similar. Even in terms of more modern, diversified theories, such as those of Gardner (1983) or Sternberg (1985), the roommates would not have varied very much. Moreover, today, all three roommates are fairly successful in their jobs and have achieved some recognition for their work. Thus, one could not attribute differences among the three to motivational differences alone.

Yet, looking beyond the intellectual similarities of the three roommates, one cannot help but notice some salient variations that have profoundly affected their lives. Consider some of the differences among them.

Alex, today a lawyer, could be characterized (and would characterize himself) as fairly conventional, rule-bound, and comfortable with details and structure. He does well what others tell him to do, as a lawyer must, and has commented to me that his idea of perfection would be a technically flawless legal document or contract whereby those who sign on the dotted line are bound to the terms of the contract without loopholes, unless they want to pay extra legal fees. In a nutshell, Alex is a follower of systems, and follows them extremely well. Even in school, he showed the same tendencies. He was happiest when given assignments and tests that were well-structured and clearly circumscribed. He was less happy in his senior year when working on a senior project that he, rather than his teachers, had to structure, in which the boundaries of the assignment were only vaguely circumscribed.

Bob, today a university professor, is quite different stylistically from Alex. He is fairly unconventional, and unlike Alex, dislikes following or even dealing with other people's rules. Moreover, he has relatively few rules of his own. Although he has some basic principles that he views as invariants, he tends not to take rules very seriously, viewing them as conveniences that are meant to be changed or even broken as the situation requires. Bob dislikes details, and generally is comfortable working within a structure only if it is his own. He does certain things well, but usually only if they are things he really wants to do. His idea of intellectual perfection would be the generation of a great idea and a compelling demonstration that the idea is correct, or at least useful. In brief, Bob is a creator of systems, and has designed various psychological theories that reflect his interest in system creation. In school, as well, he was happiest with independent assignments and projects, and liked the least highly structured assignments and tests. The more freedom he was given to pursue his own interests and ways of doing things, the happier he was.

Charles, today a psychotherapist, is also fairly unconventional. Like Bob, he dislikes others' rules, but unlike Bob, he has a number of his own. He tends to be indifferent to details. He likes working within certain structures, which need not be his own, but the structures have to be ones that he has adjudged to be correct and suitable. Charles does well what he wants to do. His idea of perfection would be a difficult but correct psychological diagnosis, followed by an optimal psychotherapeutic intervention. In sum, Charles is a judge of systems. He showed his interest, perhaps passion, for judging early in his career, when, as a college student, he constructed a test (which we called the "Charles Test") to give to others – especially to dates – that judged the suitability of their values and standards. Charles was also editor of the college course critique, a role in which he took responsibility for the evaluation of all undergraduate courses at the college. In college, Charles was happiest doing analytical essays, especially those that allowed him to point out the strengths and weaknesses of various ways of approaching intellectual problems.

What we can see from these examples is that three students with almost identical levels and patterns of abilities nevertheless have very different preferred ways of expressing these abilities. They like to use their intellects in different ways, and the very kind of assignment or test that will be favored by one will not be favored by another. For example, given a certain set of material, Alex will be drawn to a structured multiple-choice test emphasizing recall of knowledge, Bob to an essay that allows creativity and going beyond the bounds of the knowledge that was learned, and Charles to either multiple-choice or essay questions that emphasize critical evaluation and analysis.

The differences among Alex, Bob, and Charles could be loosely defined as ones of "personality." But the differences are not really ones of static single personality traits such as aggressiveness or dominance or whatever, but rather ones of configurations of dispositions with regard to use of intellectual abilities. The differences are not those of cognitive functioning alone, nor are they those of personality functioning. Instead they're something in between – namely, thinking styles.

Capsule view of some alternative theories of styles

Many different theories of styles have been proposed, and it would not be possible to review them all here. Rather, I shall simply try briefly to summarize a few, in order to give readers a sense of the kinds of psychological phenomena that these theories address.

Myers (1980; Myers & McCaulley, 1985) has proposed a series of psychological types based upon Jung's (1923) theory of types. According to Myers, there are 16 types, resulting from all possible combinations of two ways of perceiving – sensing versus intuition; two ways of judging – thinking versus feeling; two ways of dealing with self and others – introversion versus extraversion; and two ways of dealing with the outer world – judgment versus perception. Gregorc (1985) has proposed four main types or styles, based upon all possible combinations of just two dimensions – concrete versus abstract and sequential versus random. Taking a more educationally oriented slant, Renzulli and Smith (1978) have suggested that individuals have various learning styles, with each style corresponding to a method of teaching: projects, drill and recitation, peer teaching, discussion, teaching games, independent study, programmed instruction, lecture, and simulation. Holland (1973) has taken a more job-related orientation and proposed six styles that are used as a basis for understanding job interests as revealed by the Strong-Campbell Interest Inventory (Strong, Campbell, & Hansen, 1985). Holland's typology includes six styles: realistic, investigative, artistic, social, enterprising, and conventional.

Other theories have not been of styles, in general, but of specific aspects of cognitive–stylistic functioning. For example, Kagan (1976) has dealt with the differences in children showing an impulsive versus a reflective style. Children (or adults, for that matter) with an impulsive style tend to be quick to say and do things without thinking through what they say or do, whereas children with a reflective style tend to say or do only after considering carefully their possible courses of action. Witkin (1978) has dealt with the respective styles of field dependence and field independence. The field-dependent person has trouble separating his perceptions from the context of those perceptions, whereas the field–independent person can make this separation, for example, seeing a figure embedded in a context that tends to obscure that figure. Other specific styles have been studied as well, of course (see Kogan, 1983, for a review).

These theories are all different, perhaps at least in part because they deal with slightly different phenomena. The Myers-Briggs theory is based upon a theory of personality, that of Jung. The theory of Gregorc is more cognitive. The theory of Renzulli and Smith is intended to apply primarily in educational settings, whereas the theory of Holland is intended to apply primarily in occupational settings. This difference in domain is not different from what would be encountered in theories of other psychological phenomena. For example, there is no real uniformity either in theorists' conceptions of intelligence, with the result that various theories of intelligence also tend to deal with somewhat different aspects of the phenomenon (Sternberg, 1990). The theory of mental self-government (see also Sternberg, 1988), as presented below, also deals with particular aspects of the interface between intellect and cognition.

Mental self-government: a theory of thinking styles

Introduction to the theory

At the heart of the theory of mental self-government is the notion that people need somehow to govern or manage their everyday activities, in school as well as outside.

There are many ways of doing so; whenever possible, people choose styles of managing themselves with which they are comfortable. Still, people are at least somewhat flexible in their use of styles and try, with varying degrees of success, to adapt themselves to the stylistic demands of a given situation. The flexible use of the mind for mental self-government accounts for a variety of thinking styles.

Styles, like abilities, are not etched in stone at birth. They are in large part a function of the environment, and they can be developed. An individual with one proclivity in one situation may have a different proclivity in another situation. Moreover, some individuals may have one preferred style at one stage of life and another preferred style at another stage. Styles are not fixed, therefore, but fluid.

People's proclivities toward certain styles must be distinguished from their ability to implement these styles. Someone may like doing things a certain way, but not be very good at it. For example, most of us have had students who want to express themselves creatively, but who seem not to have developed the creative talent to make these expressions all that the students (and we, as teachers) would like them to be. Or people may not want to capitalize on their most outstanding abilities because they do not feel comfortable while exercising them. For example, a potentially creative person may never realize her creativity for lack of a desire to stand out from a crowd. Thus, we must distinguish abilities from people's desire to exploit these abilities.

It is difficult to say exactly where styles come from. They seem to be largely a function of tasks and situations. Certain tasks are more optimally performed with certain styles. Rewarding students for using preferred styles on these tasks is likely to lead to greater display of the rewarded styles. More generally, a child's socialization into a value system will probably reward some styles more than others, leading to preferences for these styles. But the fact that some people retain less-rewarded styles despite environmental pressures suggests that socialization does not account fully for the origins of styles, and that there may be preprogrammed dispositions that are difficult to change.

According to this theory, the various styles of government we see in the world are not there by coincidence, but rather are external reflections or mirrors of the styles that we can find in the mind. Thus, in order to understand these styles of thought, we can look toward aspects of government for a sense of what is internally, as well as externally, possible. The theory deals with the functions, forms, levels, scope, and leanings of government as applied to the individual.

The functions of mental self-government

Just as governments carry out legislative, executive, and judicial functions, so does the mind. The *legislative* function of the mind is concerned with creating, formulating, imagining, and planning. The *executive* function is concerned with implementing and doing. And the *judicial* function is concerned with judging, evaluating, and comparing.

Mental self-government involves all three functions. However, in most people, one of the functions tends to be dominant. Thus the hallmark of a thinking style is that it is preferred over alternatives. In the case of Alex, Bob, and Charles, Alex is primarily executive in style, Bob, legislative, and Charles, judicial.

The legislative style characterizes people who enjoy creating, formulating, and planning for problem solution. Such individuals like to create their own rules and to do things in their own way. They prefer problems that are not prestructured or prefabricated. A student who has to come up with his own paper topic will benefit from a legislative style. For this student, most of the fun of doing a paper is in coming up with the topic and in organizing the paper, as opposed to actually writing it.

Individuals with an executive style are implementers. They like to follow rules, figure out which of already existing ways they should use to get things done, and prefer problems that are prefabricated or prestructured. Whereas the individual with the legislative style prefers to come up with the topic, the individual with the executive style prefers to be given the topic, and then to do the best possible job with it. She would probably prefer, however, a structured test to a paper, and is likely to eschew courses that require a lot of independent work.

The judicial style is seen in those people who like to evaluate rules and procedures, who like to judge things, and who prefer problems in which one analyzes and evaluates existing things and ideas. As students, they will prefer analytical essays, perhaps comparing and contrasting two points of view, or evaluating a position. They will also prefer analytical to straightforward memory-test questions (which are likely to be preferred by executive stylists).

The forms of mental self-government

Just as the functions of mental self-government resemble those of different branches of government, the *forms* of mental self-government resemble forms of government: monarchic, hierarchic, oligarchic, and anarchic.

In the *monarchic* form, a single goal or way of doing things predominates. People with a monarchic style tend to focus single-mindedly on one goal or need at a time. They are either oblivious to obstacles that stand in the way or are able to cast them aside. A student who is determined to turn in a paper by noon tomorrow, but who may face potential distractions, will benefit from a monarchic style. That student will not allow the distractions to get in the way of accomplishing his overriding priority.

The *hierarchic* form allows for multiple goals, each of which may have a different priority. People with a hierarchic style tend to enjoy dealing with many goals, to recognize that not all goals can be fulfilled equally well, to recognize that some goals are more important than others, to have a good sense of priorities, and to be systematic in their approach to solving problems. When a student needs to allocate time to several homework assignments of varying importance, that student will benefit from having a hierarchic style.

The *oligarchic* form allows for multiple goals, all of which are equally important.

A student who has an oligarchic style of thinking will do well in a course that includes several tests, weighted equally, or that requires a major paper that will count just as much as the final exam. Oligarchic individuals like dealing with multiple and often competing goals of equal perceived importance, but they experience conflict and tension when they have to assign priorities. Competing goals keep oligarchic individuals from completing tasks, because everything seems equally important to them.

For individuals with an *anarchic* thinking style, rules, procedures, and guidelines are anathema. Students who have an anarchic thinking style tend to perform best when tasks and situations are unstructured, when there are no clear procedures to be followed, or when the problems that they confront are most readily solved through insights that represent a departure from existing mindsets. People who have an anarchic style generally enjoy dealing with a potpourri of needs and goals that are often difficult to sort out. They tend to take a random approach to problem solving, often seem intolerant or unaware of the need for rules and regulations, and tend to resist authority.

Levels of mental self-government

Government functions at multiple levels: federal, state, county, city, and so on. In general, one can distinguish between global and local levels. Corresponding to these two levels are two more aspects of mental self-government.

A person with a *global* style prefers to deal with relatively large and abstract issues, and to ignore or at least to have someone else deal with details. The global person likes to conceptualize and work in the world of ideas. Metaphorically, he tends to see the forest, but not always the trees within it. A student with a global style will excel on assignments that require him to see a big picture in a novel, a historical event, or a scientific theory, but he will do much less well on assignments that require examining the specific details of the novel, historical event, or theory.

The *local* sort of person prefers more concrete problems requiring detail work, and tends to be pragmatically oriented. This person relishes the very small matters that the global person eschews, and likes to work on problems that require precision. A student with a local style may prefer a homework assignment with a lot of exercises on small problems to a conceptual essay that requires a global analysis of a phenomenon. This person, metaphorically, tends to see the trees, but not always the forest.

The scope of mental self-government

Governments need to deal both with internal, or domestic, affairs, and with external, or foreign, ones. Similarly, mental self-governments need to deal with both internal and external issues. People who are more *internal* in style tend to be introverted, task-oriented, and aloof, as well as socially less sensitive and interpersonally less aware than externalists. They also like to work alone. Essentially, their preference is to apply their intelligence to things or ideas in isolation from other people. An internalist will be happy working on his or her own in completing an assignment, but will probably be less than thrilled with cooperative learning activities, in which working with other people is a requirement.

People who are more *external* in their style tend to be extroverted, people-oriented, outgoing, and socially more sensitive than internalists. They like to work with others, and seek problems that involve working with other people or that are about other people. The group or cooperative learning experience so disagreeable to the internalist is exactly what the externalist will seek out and enjoy.

The leaning of mental self-government

Governments can have various political leanings. Optimally, these leanings are represented on a continuum, such as right-wing to left-wing, but, for present purposes, two major "regions" of leanings will be distinguished: conservative and progressive.

Individuals with a predominantly *conservative* style like to adhere to existing rules and procedures, minimize change, avoid ambiguous situations where possible, and prefer familiarity in life and work. A conservative style does not bar a simultaneously legislative one. A person may be both legislative and conservative if the person likes to come up with new ideas and ways of doing things that are essentially conservative in bent, drawing heavily upon what has been done in the past. Great conservative thinkers, such as Edmund Burke, would be examples of conservative legislative types.

A person with a *progressive* style likes to go beyond existing rules and procedures, maximize change, and find ambiguous and uncertain situations. This person becomes bored when things never seem to change. A person may be both executive and progressive, as would be the case of a person who is an underling to someone who advocates a very progressive point of view. This person likes the progressive stance, but follows rather than leads in it.

Having considered the various styles in the theory of mental self-government, consider next their implications for assessment.

The interface between thinking styles and assessment

Conventional assessment and thinking styles

Assessments are usually targeted at measuring abilities, whether general or particular, or at measuring achievements. In reality, of course, all assessments measure at least some of each. In assessments, there will always be unsystematic measurement error, which test-constructors seek to minimize but which they can never eliminate. More serious is the existence of consistent biases, that, unlike errors of measurement, always affect the same groups in the same ways, helping some and hurting others. The main thesis here is that type of test interacts with styles such as to create consistent biases. By always using tests of the same kind or kinds, we are always benefiting people with certain styles at the expense of people with other styles. In essence, we are confounding thinking styles, which are psychologically distinct from mental abilities and achievements, with these abilities and achievements. In other words, we are spuriously distorting the test scores in a consistent fashion.

Consider the various kinds of testing instruments we might have, the kinds of styles they would favor and disfavor, and how these effects might impact on what happens in our schools. I wish to state in advance what the conclusions of this analysis will be: Good testing does not use one format or another, but, rather, a combination of formats. Conventional multiple-choice tests have unfairly benefited children with certain styles but not others; but replacement of such tests with new, more "authentic" assessments will also benefit children with certain styles and not others. We will be replacing one mistake with another. Testing, like any other kind of scientific assessment, is best when it uses converging operations.

Multiple–choice/short-answer.   Far and away the most widely used form of assessment is the conventional multiple–choice/short-answer format found in almost all standardized tests (both group- and individually administered) and most teacher-made tests at the primary and secondary levels.

Various contemporary scholars have claimed that such tests cannot measure certain abilities in anything approaching an adequate way (e.g., Gardner, 1983). Regardless of the validity of this assertion, I believe that the main problem in measuring abilities via multiple-choice tests is not so much inadequacy in the measurement of abilities, but rather consistent biases in favor of certain styles.

Conventional tests strongly favor test-takers with an executive, local style, and favor somewhat those with internal and conservative styles as well. Why? First, the examinee is placed in a highly structured, usually very circumscribed kind of situation, where he is given the problem explicitly and told to solve it within the constraints presented. This is the kind of testing situation that is ideally crafted for the executive stylist. The problems are usually quite narrow in scope, at least relative to the larger problems of the discipline, favoring the local stylist. Students are not allowed to work with others; indeed, collaboration is usually considered to be cheating, and therefore, the internal stylist is favored. Finally, the scoring is according to a prefixed answer key that represents whatever the conventional wisdom may be for a certain kind of problem, favoring the conservative stylist.

Of course, there is nothing wrong with this particular profile of styles. Styles are not better or worse, just different. The problem is that if virtually all testing is of the conventional kind, then individuals with one profile of styles, or a profile close to it, will be systematically benefited, and will appear "smarter" than individuals with other profiles. Students will be given credit for attributes having nothing to do with ability or, really, even achievement.

What kind of effect could we expect this pattern of favoritism to have on our schools? We could expect to funnel through the system students who do what they are told, and usually do it well; who are best at working with problems in the small rather than in the large; who prefer to work individually rather than with others; and who are fairly conservative in their approach to problems. And this description fits quite well the description of the prototypical "good student" encountered by many professors who teach "better" students at both the undergraduate and graduate levels. But, especially at the graduate level, we need to ask ourselves whether these are the kinds of students we ideally want. They may have been very good at taking tests well and at getting good grades, but they are unlikely to be the students who are most creative when it comes to generating new ideas in their research, regardless of discipline (see Sternberg & Lubart, 1991a; 1991b). Creative students are more likely to show profiles of styles that are legislative and global, which are styles that are not favored by the conventional tests.

To the extent that more recent tests emphasize critical thinking and analysis, there will be a shift away from benefiting executive stylists toward benefiting judicial stylists. On the one hand, there is clearly value, in its own right, of measuring the ability to think with the material that is learned. After all, what good is it to know something if one is unable to use it? On the other hand, we are still benefiting certain styles at the expense of others so long as we do not use converging operations in our measurements.

Essay tests.   Who is benefited by essay tests will depend largely not upon the test itself but upon how it is scored. Consider three emphases a teacher (or testing company) might have in scoring.

One emphasis is on facts presented. When I took introductory psychology, we had what appeared to be an essay test. In fact, however, it was pretty much a straight recall test. The professor had in mind a list of 10 points he wanted students to make, and the essay was scored on a scale from 0 to 10, depending upon the number of these points that were made. Such a test really amounts to a recall rather than a recognition version of a conventional test. Its surface structure is that of an essay, but its deep structure is that of a conventional multiple-choice or short-answer test. The scorer is basically seeking recall of "facts" rather than understanding, use, or organization of these facts. The test benefits the executive, local, conservative stylist.

A second emphasis is on interpretation and analysis. Here, the scorer looks for the examinee's ability to criticize and otherwise analyze the material learned. Essay examinations in the form of "Compare and contrast . . . ," "Analyze . . . ," and "Eval-uate . . . ," are of this form. Here, the judicial style benefits over the legislative or executive. The global student may also benefit if the kinds of evaluations requested are on a larger as opposed to a smaller scale. To the extent that the scorer counts organization as well, which typically is considered important in evaluating essays of this type, students with a hierarchical style will also benefit: Such students tend to organize material in a way that emphasizes major points, downplays minor ones, and places the material in a logical sequence. Oligarchic students may do equally well if the various points to be made are of roughly equal importance, although such cases seem to be the exception rather than the rule.

A third emphasis is on creative synthesis. Here, the scorer is concerned less with the student's ability to repeat back what she has learned than with her ability to go beyond the information learned. Can she add something creative that shows she has achieved some kind of higher-order synthesis that extends beyond what was learned in class or in a book? Such an emphasis is likely to benefit legislative and possibly global students, if sufficient room is allowed for the student to express herself on larger issues. Again, to the extent that the scorer counts organization, the hierarchical student will tend to benefit, or the oligarchic student if the points to be made are of roughly equally importance. In rare cases, if the scorer can appreciate a more "stream-of-consciousness," "free-flowing" approach to creative production, a test-taker with an anarchic style may benefit. I suspect that the large majority of scorers, however, do not look fondly upon this style (unless its author is James Joyce or someone of similar repute!).

I have not discussed whether essay tests benefit students with a progressive style more than do multiple-choice or short-answer tests. I believe that the answer to this question lies entirely in the way the essays are evaluated. A teacher who values highly only students who agree with him, or with the conventional approach to the problems being studied, will tend to downgrade students with a progressive style and reward those with a conservative style that is simultaneously legislative and probably hier-archical. Clearly, very few people who evaluate essays, whether teachers or other-wise, will overtly state that they value only people who agree with them or some other standard source. What matters is not what they say, but what they do.

It is important to distinguish here between the progressive style and progressive politics. They are entirely different entities, and may or may not go hand-in-hand. Some of the most progressive thinkers are the most intolerant of dissent, a point that is being made, for better or worse, by the movement that is taking on so-called "political correctness." Intolerant people can come from anywhere on the political spectrum, not just the extreme right, or left, or whatever.

Projects. Projects are assessments that are done over a period of time and that involve some degree of independence and initiative on the part of the student. The more they require of each of these, the more they will benefit the legislative student. Not all projects are of this kind, however. If the teacher specifies what the project will be on, or gives the student only a fairly narrow range of topics, then the legislative student may not be left with much room for initiative. For example, I once went to a "project fair" involving my son, in which the projects were almost all on states of the union. Moreover, they all followed roughly the same format, obviously one preset by the teacher. Such projects were scarcely ones that would allow much room for student initiative.

Because there is so much possible information to handle in doing a project, such an activity will usually benefit a hierarchic student. But to the extent that there are many competing demands on the student and his time, so that it is difficult to allocate to the project the full set of resources it may ideally demand, the project format may benefit the monarchic student more than it benefits the other types of students. If such a student decides that the project is sufficiently important, then he or she will make sure that more than sufficient resources are allocated, regardless of competing demands on his time. The same principle holds true for other kinds of assessments that are resource-intensive but that compete for scarce resources, such as a take-home exam with a tight time limit.

Individual projects tend to benefit internal stylists, but projects that are assigned to groups will benefit external stylists. Most internalists are uncomfortable with group work, and if the group consists wholly or even mostly of internalists, they may have difficulty marshaling and integrating resources to make a collaborative venture a fully viable one.

Portfolio assessment. There is nothing approaching full consensus on how portfolio assessment should be done, or even regarding what should go into a student's portfolio. Some portfolios are little more than collections of test papers, whereas others may represent a collection of students' best projects. Moreover, sometimes the student decides what should go in the portfolio, other times the teacher, and still other times, both.

Who will be benefited from portfolio assessment therefore depends on exactly how the assessment is done. To the extent that a portfolio is simply a collection of conventional test papers, it will benefit the same student who is benefited by conventional tests. But to the extent that a student is actively involved in sorting out a variety of possible materials for inclusion in the portfolio, and especially project materials, this form of assessment will benefit the legislative and judicial, hierarchical student. The hierarchical style is best at setting priorities for what should and should not go in the portfolio. The oligarchic student will find this type of assessment particularly troublesome, in that his difficulties in setting priorities will render the task of deciding what to include in the portfolio a particularly daunting one.

Interview assessment. Interviews are routinely used for admissions purposes, and some examinations are given in an oral form that resembles an interview. In terms of abilities, interviews downplay written verbal skills while emphasizing oral verbal skills. But what changes, from the point of view of a theory of styles, when assessment is oral rather than written? What primarily changes is a shift from a more internal to a more external stylistic focus. When writing, one needs to take into account the point of view of a potential reader, but at a distance. One can do it in one's head. In an interview situation, one is managing a demonstration of knowledge or ability through a social vehicle, and one inevitably needs to attend to the social as well as the cognitive aspect of the interview. Having done a great deal of interviewing and at one time even analyzed college-admissions interview procedures (Sternberg,

1973), I am convinced that the social aspect of an interview is extremely important. Interviewers tend to prefer interviewees who are relaxed, who put the interviewers at ease, who are socially as well as verbally facile, and who have some degree of interpersonal sparkle. The person who sparkles in his writing may not in his speech, and vice versa. Thus, the interview tends to place the external stylist at an advantage, in contrast to most other testing media.

Assessment of thinking styles

We have discussed some general issues regarding the interface between thinking styles and assessment. The question now arises as to how thinking styles themselves can be assessed.

Elena Grigorenko and I have developed a number of converging operations for measuring styles, both in students and in teachers (Grigorenko & Sternberg, 1992). I will describe each in turn.

The *Thinking Styles Inventory* is a self-report measure in which students (or other examinees) rate themselves on a 1–9 scale, where 1 is low and 9 is high, for a number of behaviors. Consider examples of some of the items on the inventory:

I like tasks that allow me to do things my own way [legislative].
I like situations in which it is clear what role I must play or in what way I should participate [executive].
I like to evaluate and compare different points of view on issues that interest me [judicial].
I like to complete what I am doing before starting something else [monarchic].
When undertaking some task, I like first to come up with a list of things that the task will require me to do and to assign an order of priority to the items on the list [hierarchic].
I usually know what things need to be done, but I sometimes have trouble deciding in what order to do them [oligarchic].
When working on a written project, I usually let my mind wander and my pen follow up on whatever thoughts cross my mind [anarchic].
Usually when I make a decision, I don't pay much attention to details [global].
I like problems that require engagement with details [local].
I like to be alone when working on a problem [internal].
I like to work with others rather than by myself [external].
I like to do things in new ways, even if I am not sure they are the best ways [progressive].
In my work, I like to keep close to what has been done before [conservative].

We have also devised a *Thinking Styles Questionnaire for Teachers,* which measures teachers' preferences in styles for students for seven of the styles. Examples of items on this questionnaire are:

I want my students to develop their own ways of solving problems [legislative].

I agree with people who call for more, harsher discipline, and a return to the "good old ways" [conservative].

A third measure is the *Set of Thinking Styles Tasks for Students*. The idea here is to measure students' preferences for styles in actual tasks. Consider two examples:

When I am studying literature, I prefer to

  (a) follow the teacher's advice and interpretations of authors' positions, and to use the teacher's way of analyzing literature [executive]

  (b) to make up my own story with my own characters and my own plot [legislative]

  (c) to evaluate the author's style, to criticize the author's ideas, and to evaluate characters' actions [judicial]

  (d) to do something else (please indicate in the space below)

You are the mayor of a large northeastern city. You have a city budget this year of $100 million. Below is a list of problems currently facing your city. Your job is to decide how you will spend the $100 million available to improve your city. Next to each problem is the projected cost to eliminate a problem entirely. In the space on the next page list each problem on which you will spend city money and how much money you will budget for that problem. Whether you spend money on one, some, or all problems is up to you, but be sure your plan will not exceed the $100 million available. Whether you spend all the money to solve one or a few problems or divide the money partially to solve many problems is up to you . . .

  (1) Drug problem ($1 million)

  (2) Roads ($250 thousand)

  (3) Landfill ($250 thousand)

  (4) Shelters for the homeless ($500 thousand) . . .

The scoring of this problem is in terms of form of mental self-government. A monarchic person is likely to spend all or almost all the money on one problem. A hierarchic person will divide the money among problems, spending more money on problems of perceived importance. An oligarchic person will spend roughly equal amounts of money on each of the problems. An anarchic person will show no system at all, or will not conform to the constraints of the problem.

Finally, we have constructed a measure called *Students' Thinking Styles Evaluated by Teachers*. In these items, teachers evaluate the styles of their individual students. Sample items include:

S/he prefers to solve problems in her or his own way [legislative].

S/he likes to evaluate her or his own opinions and those of others [judicial].

Again, the idea of having a variety of measures is to use converging operations to assess the various styles. Not only do the kinds of measures differ, but who is doing the assessment (e.g., student or teacher) differs as well. But do these measures, and the theory underlying them, have construct validity? Consider some of the data we have collected to address this question.

Data testing the theory of mental self-government

Construct validation data

An initial study was done with Marie Martin in order to assess the construct validity of the theory and an early version of the *Thinking Styles Inventory*. Subjects were 75 college students. The results were promising for a "first pass."

Scale reliabilities ranged from .56 (executive) to .88 (global), with a median of .78. Most of the scale intercorrelations were low. The exceptions were ones that we anticipated. Correlations greater than .5 in absolute value were global with local (−.61), progressive with legislative (.66), conservative with legislative (−.50), conservative with executive (.59), and progressive with conservative (−.60). Thus, the legislative and progressive styles tend to be associated, as do the executive and conservative ones. Global and local styles tend to be negatively associated.

A factor analysis was generally although not totally supportive of the structure of the theory. Five factors accounted for 77% of the variance in the data. A first factor showed high loadings (greater than .7 in absolute value) for the conservative (.87), executive (.58), progressive (−.81), and legislative (−.78) styles. Thus, this factor combined the legislative–executive distinction with the progressive–conservative one. A second factor loaded separately for judicial (.70), with a high loading as well for oligarchic (.70). Whereas the legislative and executive styles are almost diametrically opposed, the judicial is not diametrically opposed conceptually to either, and so its loading on a separate factor makes sense. A third factor contrasted external (.72) with internal (−.80). The fourth factor contrasted the local style (.92) with the global one (−.82). And the fifth factor showed a high loading for the hierarchic style (.86).

Correlations were computed with the MBTI (Myers–Briggs Type Indicator) as well as the Gregorc measure of mind styles. For the MBTI, 30 of 128 correlations were statistically significant, whereas for the Gregorc, 22 of 52 were significant. These correlations are well above the levels that would be expected by chance, and suggest that the various style measures partition a similar space of the intelligence–personality interface, but in different ways. In contrast, the correlation of the measure of mental self-government with IQ was not significant, nor was the correlation with GPA. Three styles correlated significantly with SAT Math (judicial, global, and liberal; all positively), but none with SAT Verbal. Thus, styles do indeed appear to be largely distinct from intelligence or aptitudes.

Data on the relevance of styles to the schools

Elena Grigorenko and I (Grigorenko & Sternberg, 1992) have collected data assessing the relevance of styles to the schools. We did three studies in all.

In the first, we examined whether teachers' styles differ as a function of school.

Participants in the study were 85 teachers, 57 female and 28 male. They were in four schools of widely differing types. We found several interesting effects.

First, as we predicted, teachers at lower grade levels are more legislative and less executive than teachers at higher grade levels. In other words, the teachers at the lower levels are more encouraging of a style linked to creativity in their work with the students (Sternberg & Lubart, 1991a; 1991b).

Second, older teachers are more executive, local, and conservative than younger teachers. Of course, we do not know whether this result is a cohort effect or whether it represents an aging process. But the study indicates that on average, the younger teachers have a style more encouraging of creativity than the older ones.

Third, teachers show some differences in styles across subject-matter areas. Science teachers tend to be more local, humanities teachers more progressive. The latter finding was consistent with our expectation, but the former was a bit of a disappointment, suggesting as it does a more "molecular" view toward science than we would prefer among the science teachers.

Fourth, and perhaps most interestingly, we had an independent rater rate the ideology of each school for each of the style dimensions. The idea here was for the rater, who was blind to our hypotheses, to rate the ideology of the school, using catalogs, faculty and student handbooks, statements of goals and purposes, curricula, and related information. Some schools, for example, were rated as ideologically more legislative or more liberal than others. We found that six of seven planned contrasts were statistically significant when the actual styles of the teachers in the school were compared to the rated ideology. In other words, teachers' styles tend to match the ideology of their school.

In a second study, we looked at some of the demographics of styles. We found that father's, but not mother's education, was negatively related to the judicial, local, conservative, and oligarchic styles. Father's occupational level was also negatively related to the judicial, local, conservative, and oligarchic styles. Consistent with common beliefs, younger siblings were found to be more legislative than older ones. Perhaps most interestingly, we found that students tended to match their teachers in style. As students could not possibly have been placed in classes so as to achieve such a match, the results are consistent with our notion that styles are partially socialized – they develop by internalization of styles observed in role models.

In a third study, we queried whether students benefit if their styles match their teachers'. In other words, we know from the last study that there is a tendency to match. But do students who match actually do better than students who don't, independently of the students' abilities? We found that students were more positively evaluated by and received better grades from teachers who matched their styles than from those who did not. Moreover, teachers tended to overestimate the extent to which their students matched them in styles. In other words, people think others are more like them than they really are!

In conclusion, the set of studies suggest construct validity for the theory of mental self-government, and also suggest the usefulness of the theory in school settings.

Conclusions

Certain forms of testing benefit students with certain style profiles, whereas other forms of testing benefit students with other style profiles. Therefore, testing should be varied so as to avoid bias. Ability and achievement tests should measure what they are supposed to measure, and not measure these constructs confounded with styles. At the very least, these styles should be measured independently of abilities and achievements (Sternberg & Wagner, 1991; see Note).

Even converging operations in testing will not even out all inequities. There are certain styles that simply don't tend to be benefited by any (or, at least, hardly any) of the existing testing formats. Anarchic stylists, for example, will almost always be at a disadvantage, and hierarchic stylists will almost always do better than oligarchic ones. We can make testing more fair, but probably not completely fair.

Tests probably appear more statistically valid than they deserve to appear, in a certain sense, because the biases of the tests have also been those of the school, at least up to now. Ability tests, for example, tend to benefit executive, local, internal, conservative stylists, but so do most school environments. Thus, to some extent, we have been testing for what we value stylistically. The use of new, "authentic" assessment should prove interesting in one respect; they may lose validity not only because of the difficulty of scoring them objectively and because of their lower reliability over time, but because what is valued in such assessments may correspond less well to what the school values. Perhaps they will lead the way in changing what the schools value, although that remains to be seen. Testing has come more and more to rule instruction as our society increasingly emphasizes accountability. Thus, using new forms of tests may create new forms of valuing in the schools. In any case, considering the role of styles in all testing is of value to the extent it makes us question our educational practices and, particularly, whether we inadvertently reward some styles over others. If we do, we must ask ourselves why, and whether we wish to continue to do so.

Styles are not only important with regard to testing, but also with regard to teaching. We found that schools have different ideologies, and that teachers' styles tend to match those of their schools. Students then come to match their teachers, and those who do receive more positive evaluations and better grades from those teachers, regardless of abilities. Clearly, if we wish to fully understand the success of children in the school (and, we would speculate, adults on the job), we need not only to look at abilities and achievements, but at the interface between intelligence and personality – at thinking styles.

Note

The work reported herein was supported under the Javits Act program (Grant #R206R00001) as administered by the Office of Educational Research and Improvement, U.S. Department of Education. The findings and opinions expressed in this report do not reflect the positions or policies of the Office of Educational Research and Improvement or the U.S. Department of Education. Information regarding a Thinking Styles Inventory based on the theory of mental self-government (Sternberg & Wagner, 1991) can be obtained from Star Mountain Projects, Inc., 3237 Cranleigh Drive, Tallahassee, Florida, 32308. Requests for reprints of this article should be sent to Robert J. Sternberg, Department of Psychology, Yale University, Box 208205, New Haven, CT 06520-8205.

References

Gardner, H. (1983). *Frames of mind: The theory of multiple intelligences.* New York: Basic Books.

Garner, W. R., Hake, H. W., & Erikson, C. W. (1956). Operationism and the concept of perception. *Psychological Review, 63,* 149–159.

Gregorc, T. (1985). *Inside styles: Beyond the basics.* Maynard, MA: Gabriel Systems, Inc.

Grigorenko, E., & Sternberg, R. J. (1992). Thinking styles in school settings. Manuscript submitted for publication.

Holland, J. L. (1973). *Making vocational choices: A theory of careers.* Englewood Cliffs, NJ: Prentice-Hall.

Jung, C. G. (1923). *Psychological types.* New York: Harcourt Brace.

Kagan, J. (1976). Commentary on 'Reflective and impulsive children: Strategies of information processing underlying differences in problem solving.' *Monographs of the Society for Research in Child Development, 41* (5, Serial No. 168).

Kogan, N. (1983). Stylistic variation in childhood and adolescence: Creativity, metaphor, and cognitive styles. In P. H. Mussen (Ed.) (4th ed.), J. H. Flavell & E. M. Markman (Vol. Eds.), *Handbook of child psychology. Vol. 3: Cognitive development* (pp. 630–706). New York: Wiley.

Linn, R. L., Baker, E. L., & Dunbar, S. B. (1991). Complex, performance-based assessment: Expectations and validation criteria. *Educational Researcher, 20(8),* 15–21.

Malkiel, B. G. (1985). *A random walk down Wall Street* (4th ed.). New York: Norton.

Myers, I. B. (1980). *Gifts differing.* Palo Alto, CA: Consulting Psychologists Press.

Myers, I. B., & McCaulley, M. H. (1985). *Manual: A guide to the development and use of the Myers-Briggs type indicator.* Palo Alto, CA: Consulting Psychologists Press.

Renzulli, J. S., & Smith, L. H. (1978). *Learning styles inventory.* Mansfield Center, CT: Creative Learning Press.

Spearman, C. (1927). *The abilities of man.* New York: Macmillan.

Sternberg, R. J. (1973). Cost-benefit analysis of the Yale admissions office interview. *College and University, 48,* 154–164.

Sternberg, R. J. (1985). *Beyond IQ: A triarchic theory of human intelligence.* New York: Cambridge University Press.

Sternberg, R. J. (1988). Mental self-government: A theory of intellectual styles and their development. *Human Development, 31,* 197–224.

Sternberg, R. J. (1990). *Metaphors of mind: Conceptions of the nature of intelligence.* New York: Cambridge University Press.

Sternberg, R. J. & Lubart, T. I. (1991a). An investment theory of creativity and its development. *Human Development, 34,* 1–31.

Sternberg, R. J. & Lubart, T. I. (1991b). Creating creative minds. *Phi Delta Kappan,* 608–614.

Sternberg, R. J. & Wagner, R. (1991). *Thinking Styles Inventory.* Tallahassee, FL: Star Mountain Projects, Inc.

Stiggins, R. J. (1987). Design and development of performance assessments. *Educational Measurement: Issues and Practice, 6(3),* 33–42.

Strong, E. K., Jr., Campbell, D. P., & Hansen, J. C. (1985). *Strong-Campbell Interest Inventory.* Palo Alto, CA: Consulting Psychologists Press.

Thurstone, L. L. (1938). *Primary mental abilities.* Chicago: University of Chicago Press.

Wiggins, G. (1989). A true test: Toward more authentic and equitable assessment. *Phi Delta Kappan, 70,* 703–713.

Witkin, H. A. (1978). *Cognitive styles in personal and cultural adaptation: The 1977 Heinz Werner lectures.* Worcester, MA: Clark University Press.

7 A living systems approach to the integration of personality and intelligence

Martin E. Ford

Introduction

In the psychological study of humans, there are four basic questions that one can address:

1. The *process* question: What is happening when a person functions? What are the basic events that comprise human functioning?
2. The *content* question: What is the substance, meaning, or organization of a person's thoughts, feelings, perceptions, or actions?
3. The *effectiveness* question: How well is the person functioning with regard to some internally or externally defined criterion?
4. The *developmental* question: What kinds of enduring changes have occurred, are occurring, or are likely to occur in the processes, content, and/or effectiveness of a person's functioning, and how do such changes occur?

Most of the major concepts in psychology represent different kinds of component *processes* of human functioning – for example, cognition, emotion, motivation, behavior, attention, perception, memory, and so forth. Because these are the basic psychological phenomena that students, scholars, and practitioners must deal with, this is an important and legitimate focus. However, these processes are intimately interconnected in complexly organized ways to form a whole person who is continually interacting with the environment in goal-directed sequences of activity designed to create desired states and outcomes in the person or in the relationship between the person and environment (M. Ford, 1992). Consequently, the study of functional processes takes on deeper meaning and practical significance only when they are addressed in the context of the other three questions. As Bevan (1991) explains, "specialized knowledge derives its meaning . . . from the context of larger perspectives and questions. When it loses touch with that larger context, it loses its coherence and meaning" (p. 475).

Personality is the core psychological construct used to address the content question in psychological research and practice; *intelligence* is the most common concept used to address the effectiveness question; and *learning* and *development* are the primary concepts used to address the developmental question. It is therefore not surprising that these latter four concepts are among the most important and historically prominent concepts defining psychology as a unified discipline capable of generating

useful knowledge. However, even in fields organized largely around these concepts
(e.g., personality and cognitive and developmental psychology), there is a tendency
to focus narrowly on particular components of human functioning rather than to
frame problems in terms of broader issues that emphasize the meaning and
significance of these component processes in people's everyday lives. As a result,
there is a critical and growing need for broad, integrative theorizing in psychology.
Indeed, the continued coherence of psychology as a unified field of study may depend
on such theorizing.

> ... [P]sychology suffers from a crisis of disunity.... Psychology has so many unrelated
> elements of knowledge with so much mutual discreditation, inconsistency, redundancy, and
> controversy that abstracting general meaning is a great problem.... We need many unified
> theorists to save us from ever-increasing redundancy and artificial diversity.... Sheer produc-
> tion must be counterbalanced by an equally strong investment in weaving the unrelated
> knowledge elements together into the fabric of organized science.... Psychology has enor-
> mous potential power in its building materials, but that potential will only be realized by adding
> the architectural direction of unification efforts. (Staats, 1991, pp. 899, 905, 910)

In particular, theories are needed that link concepts focused on content, effectiveness, and developmental issues with each other and with detailed conceptualizations
of component processes. Although there are a few exceptions (e.g., Bandura, 1986;
Deci & Ryan, 1985, 1991; M. Ford, 1992; Gardner, 1983; Keating, 1984, 1990;
Sternberg, 1985a; Vygotsky, 1978), most theories address just one or two of the basic
questions described earlier (e.g., information-processing theories; causal-attribution
theories; expectancy–value theories; emotion theories; developmental theories of
component processes; psychometric theories of personality and intelligence). This is
generally true of most systems theories as well (e.g., control-system models that focus
narrowly on process components; general systems models that focus on the content
themes organizing a system's functioning without explicating the processes involved
in such functioning). A striking exception to this pattern, however, is D. Ford's (1987)
Living Systems Framework (LSF), a comprehensive theory of human functioning
and development that addresses in a direct and systematic way all four of the basic
questions guiding the science and application of psychology.

What follows is, in part, a necessarily brief summary of the LSF concepts and
principles pertaining to the problem of integrating the study of personality and
intelligence. To obtain a more complete understanding of the living systems approach
described in this chapter and its potential utility for scholars and professionals, the
reader should consult *Humans as Self-Constructing Living Systems: A Developmental
Theory of Behavior and Personality* (D. Ford, 1987), *Humans as Self-Constructing
Living Systems: Putting the Framework to Work* (M. Ford & D. Ford, 1987), and/or
Motivating Humans: Goals, Emotions, and Personal Agency Beliefs (M. Ford, 1992).
To avoid repetitive citations of these volumes, they are not referenced further in this
chapter except to highlight very specific contributions. However, the reader should
understand that they are the source of much of the information included in this
chapter.

Overview of the living systems framework

The roots of the Living Systems Framework (LSF) were firmly established three decades ago when D. Ford and Urban (1963), after devoting several years to the task of analyzing and comparing influential theories of psychotherapy, published their classic work, *Systems of Psychotherapy: A Comparative Study*. Based on this effort and his subsequent experiences in scholarly, professional, and administrative work, which convinced him of the need for multidisciplinary, multiprofessional approaches to understanding and improving the human condition, D. Ford formulated the core ideas of the LSF in the late seventies. After several years of elaborating, refining, and testing these ideas, a two-volume set of books was published describing the LSF and illustrating its utility for stimulating theoretical advances, guiding research, and facilitating the work of health and human service professionals (D. Ford, 1987; M. Ford & D. Ford, 1987).

Congruent with Staats' (1991, p. 910) emphasis on "adding the architectural direction of unification efforts" to the powerful "building materials" available in psychology's many areas of specialization, the LSF was constructed by wedding together the best that psychological science has to offer in terms of component minitheories and supporting evidence within a common framework representing human functioning and development in terms of a self-organizing, self-constructing adaptive control system (i.e., a living system). Thus, it is not an alternative to existing theories in fields such as cognition, motivation, behavior, personality, and development; rather, it is an integrative framework designed to help psychological scholars and professionals organize and build upon the useful theory and solid empirical work produced in many different specialized fields of study. Consistent with this goal, the LSF has recently produced two theoretical offspring – Motivational Systems Theory (MST; M. Ford, 1992) and Developmental Systems Theory (DST; D. Ford & Lerner, 1992) – each of which was created by integrating major components of the LSF with other recent theoretical advances.

Substantively, the LSF is composed of a variety of integrated conceptualizations which focus on:

1. *the unitary functioning of the whole person-in-context*, as manifested in complexly organized, goal-directed patterns of activity (including both content and process aspects of these patterns);
2. *the functioning of the component parts of the person*, including directive cognitions (personal goals), regulatory cognitions (evaluative thoughts), control cognitions (planning and problem-solving thoughts), information processing and memory functions, attention- and consciousness-arousal processes, emotional-arousal processes, transactional processes (e.g., motor and communicative actions), activity-arousal processes, and biological processes (environmental processes are also included in the framework since the basic unit of analysis is the person-in-context);
3. *processes of change and development* in the functioning of the component parts of the person and the person-as-a-whole, including concepts and principles representing stability maintaining, incremental change, and transformational change phenomena.

Thus, the LSF provides a way of thinking about not only the component processes of human functioning, but also the dynamic, integrated functioning of these processes in content-laden patterns designed to produce effective functioning (i.e., the attainment of relevant personal goals). It also describes how these patterns can "add up" over time and across contexts to produce a unique, self-constructed personality and developmental history. Moreover, it explains how behavior patterns can be strengthened or altered through a diversity of change processes.

Basic strategy of the living systems framework

Science and practice often advance by taking a model of demonstrated utility in one field and transforming it in a way that makes it applicable and useful for some other field. As has become increasingly popular in the social and behavioral sciences (Campion & Lord, 1982; Carver & Scheier, 1981, 1982, 1985, 1990; Hollenbeck, 1989; Hyland, 1988; Klein, 1989; Lord & Hanges, 1987; Lord & Kernan, 1989; Powers, 1973, 1989), the starting point for the construction of the LSF was the familiar model of a control system. In a simple control system (e.g., a thermostat), activity is generated whenever a discrepancy is perceived between current conditions and some desired state or consequence. In other words, the system is designed to "control" some variable that is being monitored by an information-collection function and evaluated by a comparator or regulatory function, based on the command of a directive function. This is a flexible arrangement, but limited in several important ways. For example, such systems are unable to invent new goals, to construct new action capabilities, or to alter or repair their "hardware" or "software" if they no longer are able to produce the desired consequence. They are designed to function in one way, and can never function in any other way.

By adding multiple options to one or more components of a simple control system (e.g., multiple goals, plans, regulatory rules, or action capabilities), one can construct an adaptive control system in which increasingly complex and flexible functional patterns are possible (e.g., chess playing by a computer or automatic piloting of an airplane). Such systems can not only react to current conditions (using "feedback" information from a variety of sources), they can also anticipate possible future consequences (using "feedforward" information) and adjust their behavior accordingly. Nevertheless, an adaptive control system, no matter how sophisticated, is still just a "fancy machine."

In contrast, human beings not only have the properties of an adaptive control system, they also have two additional capabilities that enable them to transcend the fundamental limitations of a mechanistic control system: biological self-constructing capabilities and behavioral self-constructing capabilities. In other words, unlike a "fancy machine," people can construct, elaborate, and repair their own "hardware" or biological structure (e.g., through biological growth and maturation and repair of damaged tissue), as well as construct, elaborate, and revise their own "software" or behavioral repertoire (e.g., through learning and skill development). That is how a young infant can develop into a mature adult, how a novice can become an expert, and how people can change major components of their basic "personality." Thus, a human being is a self-constructing adaptive control system, or in simpler terms, a living system.

Basic concepts representing the content and effectiveness of human functioning

The principle of unitary functioning

Perhaps the most fundamental guiding assumption of the LSF is the Principle of Unitary Functioning, that is, the assumption that a person always functions as a unit in coordination with the environments in which he is functioning. The key to maintaining unitary functioning among the diversity of biological systems, thought processes, emotional states, motor skills, communicative patterns, and other functions that a person is capable of displaying is *organization*. Indeed, organization is the essential defining property of a system. Organization exists when various components are combined in such a way that the whole is different from the sum of the parts. This "difference" involves both gains and losses. In one sense, the whole is greater than the sum of the parts because new qualities or capabilities emerge from the relationships among the parts that none of the parts could accomplish on their own (e.g., a tree house can emerge from a pile of wood; a stronger and more secure relationship can emerge from a marriage). However, in another sense the whole is less than the sum of the parts because the functioning of each of the parts has been restricted by virtue of being "locked in" to a particular organizational form (e.g., the pieces of wood can no longer be used in some other creation; the spouses will need to accept certain restrictions on their personal freedom). Relationships between system components that yield new properties and possibilities are called *facilitating conditionalities*. Relationships between system components that reduce the range of possibilities to some smaller subset are called *constraining conditionalities*.

The concept of behavior episode

Understanding the organization of complex behavior patterns is the key to understanding the overall content and effectiveness of a person's functioning. Thus, some practical way of representing the organized flow of a person's complex behavior patterns is needed. The LSF uses the concept of *behavior episode* to represent coherent sequences of unitary person-in-context functioning. A behavior episode is defined as a context-specific, goal-directed pattern of behavior that unfolds over time until one of three conditions is met: (1) the goal organizing the episode is accomplished, or accomplished "well enough" (sometimes called "satisficing"); (2) the person's attention is preempted by some internal or external event, and another goal takes precedence (at least temporarily); or (3) the goal is evaluated as unattainable, at least for the time being (cf. Pervin, 1983; Simon, 1967). For example, a weekend exam-grading episode initiated by a college professor may continue until (1) she has finished grading all of the exams; (2) she is distracted by hunger, a telephone call, a crying child, or some other compelling event; or (3) she decides she is unable to complete the task, at least for now (e.g., because she is too tired to concentrate on the task at hand).

The goal of the episode (i.e., the person's cognitive representation of the desired state or outcome he would like to achieve) provides direction for the episode, and triggers an organized pattern of cognitive, emotional, biological, and perceptual–motor activity that, in coordination with the opportunities and constraints in the environment, is designed to attain the goal. Thus, goals and contexts are the anchors that organize and provide coherence and meaning to the activities within a behavior episode. These activities (or *behavior patterns*) are often varied and complex, since many behavior episodes involve the simultaneous pursuit of multiple goals in some-what unpredictable environments. Indeed, it is impossible to understand the meaning or significance of most human activities without understanding the goals and contexts that organize them (D. Ford, 1987; Schutz, 1991).

Virtually all human activity – whether it involves work, play, social relationships, or solitary activity – is organized in behavior-episode form. Some episodes may be directed by goals that are vague, transient, or out of awareness (e.g., episodes in which people are daydreaming, watching TV, or "hanging out" with their friends), but even in these episodes there is usually some degree of coherence evident in the ongoing stream of activity (Csikszentmihalyi, 1990; Larsen, Ham, & Rafaelli, 1989; Pervin, 1983). Thus, behavior episodes are like stories on a television news show that is on 24 hours a day, every day. One episode follows another, each one coherent and meaningful in its own right. Many episodes are, like most news stories, rather mundane and repetitive; other episodes build upon one another to tell a larger story (like a news program's coverage of a war or a baseball pennant race); and still other episodes are isolated, one-of-a-kind events that have little to do with the rest of life's activities (like coverage of a freak accident or special human interest story).

It is useful to distinguish among three qualitatively different kinds of behavior episodes (D. Ford, 1987). In an *instrumental episode,* the person is actively engaged in some motor or communicative activity ("output") designed to influence the environment in some way, and is actively seeking feedback information ("input") from the environment about the results of that activity. In an *observational episode,* the person is seeking relevant informational "input" from the environment through sensori-perceptual processes such as looking, listening, or touching, but there is no "output" to speak of because the person is not trying to influence the environment. In a *thinking episode,* both the output and input processes are inhibited, and there is only "throughput" – that is, instead of trying to influence or obtain information from the environment, the goal is to try to improve the organization of some information that the person already has, or to construct or rehearse a plan for future action from such information.

Many complex activities involve all three kinds of episodes. This is a productive arrangement because different kinds of episodes tend to focus a person's attention on different component processes (e.g., knowledge acquisition in observational episodes versus planning and evaluation in thinking episodes versus acting and perceiving in instrumental episodes). For example, a father teaching his son how to hit a baseball might first demonstrate this skill, then explain the basic concepts involved in successful performance of the skill, and then help his son practice this skill. Similarly, a therapist trying to help someone overcome a phobia might use a combination of imagery, observation, and guided practice techniques to accomplish this objective.

The concept of behavior episode schema/schemata

Behavior episodes are temporary phenomena that come and go like stories on a news program, but with one notable exception: it is impossible to rerun a behavior episode. And yet, people do guide their behavior in new episodes by using experiences from past episodes. That is possible because, like a VCR with fancy editing capabilities, people can remember past episodes and combine them with memories of similar episodes. Thus, behavior episodes provide the raw materials from which people can construct a complex repertoire of enduring behavior patterns. The concept of *behavior episode schema/schemata* (BES; schemata is the plural of schema) is used in the LSF to represent the product of this behavioral self-construction process. A BES is an integrated internal representation of a particular kind of behavior episode experience or, more commonly, a set of similar behavior episode experiences (including episodes that have only been imagined or observed). "Similarity" is in the eye of the beholder, but it is primarily a function of the degree to which different behavior episodes involve the pursuit of similar goals in similar contexts (recall that goals and contexts are the anchors that organize behavior episodes).

A BES represents the functioning of the whole person-in-context, since that is what is involved in any given behavior episode. The BES concept is therefore similar to concepts such as motor schema (e.g., Schmidt, 1975), perceptual schema (e.g., Arbib, 1989), cognitive schema (e.g., Neisser, 1976), or self-schema (e.g., Markus, Cross, & Wurf, 1990), but broader in that it represents an integrated "package" of thoughts, feelings, perceptions, actions, biological processes, and relevant contexts. Some parts of a BES are accessible to consciousness and some are not. Moreover, the parts that are consciously accessible may vary across BES.

Functionally, a BES provides guidance about what one should pay attention to and how one should think, feel, and act in a specific behavior episode. In this sense, it is analogous to Neisser's (1976, 1985) concept of anticipatory schema. The quality of this guidance can vary tremendously, however (Arbib & Hesse, 1986). The guidance provided may be very concrete and detailed or quite general and vague. Key components may be fully automatized or require a great deal of attentional effort and conscious control to maintain effective functioning (Sternberg, 1985a). The organization of a BES is therefore a primary factor in determining the effectiveness of a behavior pattern. For example, a physician or psychologist specializing in a particular type of problem will be able to proceed with great efficiency and confidence when a patient or client presents a familiar symptom pattern. Conversely, if the best available BES for a given situation is weak or disorganized, the person's activity is likely to be erratic, tentative, or inappropriate for that situation. For example, a teenager who has recently learned to drive may display poor judgment or react slowly to a situation that a more experienced driver could handle easily and automatically.

Like the behavior episodes from which they are constructed, BES are anchored by goals and contexts. Consequently, only those BES that include goal and context characteristics similar to those of the current behavior episode will be potentiated and available for use in organizing that new episode. Arbib and Hesse (1986) also emphasize this point in discussing their related concept of schema:

We must specify the goal of the actor and the environmental situation . . . to be able to specify the action appropriate within a particular schema. The execution of the action brings with it certain expectations as to consequent changes in the environment; and the match or mismatch that results will determine the ensuing course of action. (p. 68)

Understanding the anchoring role of goals and contexts in behavior episodes and BES can help explain a diversity of behavior patterns that may seem ineffective or inappropriate to an observer, but that are actually quite sensible and productive given what the person is trying to accomplish. For example, a normally gentle parent may respond harshly and abruptly to a misbehaving child if the transgression is unusually severe (e.g., running out into the street), or if her primary concern at that time is the completion of some urgent task. A student who is perfectly capable of answering a teacher's questions may avoid doing so if he believes that his peers disapprove of academic effort or accomplishment, and he cares more about the approval of his peers than the approval of his teacher.

The principal that behavior patterns are organized around goals and contexts can also help account for the commonplace finding that people often do not use the capabilities they have learned in one situation in other seemingly relevant situations. For example, educators and psychotherapists have found that transfer of training (i.e., application of a learned skill to new situations) is unlikely to occur unless one explicitly attempts to promote such transfer (Goldstein & Kanfer, 1979). Child-development researchers have also been misled by the pervasive belief that behavior should be consistently controlled by highly generalized "mental structures." Because the initial BES that young children construct tend to be goal-, behavior-, and context-specific, researchers often mistakenly infer that a child lacks some capability on the basis of evidence that he or she failed to display that capability on a particular experimental task. Yet, in many cases it may simply be that the experimental task is sufficiently different from the kinds of episodes normally experienced by the child that it does not activate the child's relevant BES. Indeed, the decline of generalized stage theories of development can be attributed largely to repeated empirical demonstrations of "inconsistency" in performance across tasks viewed as similar by researchers, but not by children (e.g., Demetriou & Efklides, 1981; McDevitt & Ford,

1987), including demonstrations of "precocious" performance on tasks designed to be familiar and understandable to the child (e.g., Borke, 1971; Maratsos, 1973; Menig-Peterson, 1975).

As the preceding examples illustrate, the anchoring of BES to goals and contexts, while facilitating the process of constructing concrete and meaningful guides to behavior, can constrain the process of transferring useful BES to new episodes. To overcome this limitation, humans have developed the capability of constructing cognitive representations of BES components and component relationships, typically called concepts (or constructs) and propositions (or rules or theories), respectively. Concepts and propositions are powerful tools in learning and communication because they are much less constrained by the contexts, goals, and activities involved in the BES from which they were constructed. This allows them to be integrated into other BES and combined with other concepts and propositions with relative ease. This not only facilitates knowledge construction and skill development within the individual, it also plays a key role in the cultural transmission of knowledge. That is because it is much easier to construct shared meanings from abstracted BES components, which tend to be relatively simple and general, than from whole BES units, which tend to be complex and somewhat idiosyncratic.

On the other hand, it is important to understand that concepts and propositions, by themselves, lack meaningful content and personal significance precisely because they have been divorced from particular goals, contexts, and activities. It is only when concepts and propositions are embedded back into a personalized BES that they become infused with personal meaning and utility. This is the "missing link" in much of education – information is taught in the form of abstract concepts and propositions to facilitate communication and generalization, but is too often left unconnected to the real-world contexts and purposes for which it can be used. Having students use concepts and propositions in personally meaningful behavior episodes helps bring their meaning to life.

Once a BES has been constructed, it can be elaborated or combined with other BES and BES components. Over time, this can yield a very powerful BES encompassing a diverse repertoire of optional behavior patterns organized around a related set of goals and contexts. By combining a number of such BES together, a qualitatively superior kind of expertise called *generative flexibility* can emerge. This ability to quickly and flexibly generate effective options for achieving a particular set of goals is characteristic of exceptionally resourceful people such as clever lawyers, imaginative chefs, elusive NFL quarterbacks, expert video game players, and highly skilled auto mechanics.

BES can also be elaborated by linking them together in sequential fashion to produce a "script." A script serves as a template for a stereotyped sequence of events (Abelson, 1981), as illustrated by the performance of a musician in an orchestra, a politician giving a speech, or a gymnast executing a routine. Well-rehearsed scripts (sometimes also called "habits") can greatly facilitate the execution of precise, efficient behavior patterns; however, they tend to be lacking in generative flexibility.

In fact, the essential value of "automated" scripts or habits is to eliminate such variability! Scripts are therefore most effective in contexts that require close conformity to a set of rules or conventions (e.g., behaving properly in school or church), and in repetitive situations where efficiency is highly valued (e.g., driving to work, shopping for groceries, putting the kids to bed).

The concept of personality

The field of personality psychology seeks to distinguish itself from other specializations by its focus on the content and organization of enduring patterns of functioning, particularly those that transcend particular situations or particular component processes. Unfortunately, traditional methods of representing such patterns (e.g., traits, dispositions, and attitudes) have been of limited utility because they have failed to deal adequately with the functional variability characterizing most behavior patterns (Mischel, 1968). Some personality theorists (e.g., Bandura, 1986; Carver & Scheier, 1981, 1982; Dweck & Leggett, 1988; Mischel, 1973) have addressed this problem by trying to identify cognitive and social-cognitive processes that are variable in content but that nevertheless may play a major role in organizing an individual's functioning (e.g., goal orientations, beliefs about personal agency, self-regulatory processes, coping strategies, etc.). This has been a useful and productive approach; however, because most such theories lack a broader conception of unitary functioning in which to anchor their major constructs, it has left many wondering what happened to the "person" in personality. Indeed, this is currently the major barrier to progress in the field of personality psychology. Without some way of representing how the component processes of the person function as a unit, personality researchers cannot put their "person variables" together to make a person (D. Ford, 1987). For example, Mischel's cognitive social learning theory (Mischel, 1973) and Bandura's social cognitive theory (Bandura, 1986) offer a rich menu of person variables, but no clear set of propositions specifying how these variables operate in an organized fashion at the level of the whole person-in-context.

The LSF resolves these dilemmas by defining personality as the person's repertoire of stable, recurring behavior episode schemata. In particular, stable, recurring BES that are psychologically anchored by salient personal goals (i.e., BES that are particularly meaningful and significant to the person) are seen as the core defining features of an individual's personality. Because BES represent coherent, dynamic patterns of person-in-context organization, this definition provides a way of focusing on both process and content considerations in human functioning. Moreover, because BES may be anchored to very broad or very specific sets of goals and contexts, and because the number and range of optional components and ways of combining those components in any given BES may vary tremendously, the LSF conceptualization of personality enables one to resolve the longstanding debate regarding person versus situational determinants of behavior (i.e., both consistency and variability in functioning can be understood in BES terms). For example, people can be expected to manifest a high degree of temporal and situational consistency in their behavior patterns if their most prominent BES are anchored by unusually broad sets of goals and contexts, or if they have developed highly scripted or stereotyped patterns of goal seeking for a diversity of goals and contexts. Conversely, people may manifest a great deal of situational and temporal variability if they are involved in an unusually diverse range of activities or social roles involving very different kinds of goals and contexts, or if they are suffering from problems of "personality integration" in which they are unable to coordinate important subsets of their BES repertoire (as illustrated by identity crises, multiple-personality disorders, and the like).

Since BES representations include all aspects of an individual's functioning, personality attributes or "traits" may be defined in terms of thought patterns (e.g., an "optimistic," "paranoid," or "analytical" person), emotional patterns (e.g., an "anxious," "hostile," or "depressed" person), action patterns (e.g., a "shy," "aggressive," or "compulsive" person), or any other component process or combination of component processes that are particularly salient features of a stable, enduring set of BES (e.g., "hardiness," "Type A" behavior, or "dysfunctional" personality). However, because personal goals provide the psychological anchors for BES, a particularly informative way to describe the basic content of a person's functioning (i.e., their personality) is through assessments that yield information about the most significant and meaningful goals in a person's life. As Csikszentmihalyi (1990) explains, "more than anything else, the self represents the hierarchy of goals that we have built up, bit by bit, over the years" (p. 34). Indeed, one of the most promising recent developments in the field of personality psychology is an emerging emphasis on goal content, goal hierarchies, and the use of goal assessments to represent the core features of personality (e.g., Cantor & Kihlstrom, 1987; Csikszentmihalyi, 1990; Emmons, 1986, 1989; M. Ford, 1992; M. Ford & Nichols, 1991, 1994; Lazarus, 1991; Markus & Nurius, 1986; Markus & Ruvolo, 1989; Nichols, 1991; Pervin, 1989; Winell, 1987).

Recent efforts to study broad patterns of goal content have led to the development of several new procedures for representing goal hierarchies at the BES level of analysis. For example, M. Ford and Nichols (1987, 1991, 1994) have constructed the Assessment of Personal Goals (APG) to measure the general strength of each of the 24 goals in their Taxonomy of Human Goals (see Table 7.1). The APG is a self-administered paper-and-pencil instrument composed of 24 five-item scales. A diversity of item content is included in each scale in an effort to insure that, in each case, the overall estimate of goal strength is representative of the broadest possible range of contexts. Goal hierarchies can then be represented in terms of a profile of scores that highlights goals that are particularly likely or unlikely to be of concern to the individual in contexts that afford the attainment of that goal.

Because the personality profiles provided by the APG are described in terms of standardized categories (i.e., those included in the Taxonomy of Human Goals), they are particularly useful when groups of people are being assessed (i.e., when data must be aggregated across individuals) or when comparisons across individuals need to be made. For example, the APG can facilitate the efforts of marriage and relationship counselors who need some way of comparing the goal priorities of different clients. It can also provide useful information to an employer who wants to compare a particular goal profile with that of some normative or exemplary group. However, idiographic methods of assessing goal content are generally preferable in research designs and applied settings involving the individual case. Such procedures can utilize the self-constructed labels or mental images of the individual being assessed to describe the person's interests and concerns, thus yielding a more precise representation of the hierarchy of goals defining the basic content of a particular individual's personality.

For example, Nichols (1991) has developed a companion measure to the APG, called the Assessment of Core Goals (APG), in which an idiographic process is used to accomplish essentially the same purpose as the APG, namely, the identification and verbal labeling of broad, pervasive goals that may often function outside of awareness. the ACG is a carefully organized sequence of structured exercises through which an individual can move in incremental fashion toward a highly specific and personalized definition of their most central and powerful sources of motivation. This process involves four steps. In Step 1, participants recall and list past experiences that were exceptionally satisfying or enjoyable. Because strong positive affect signals the attainment of important personal goals (D. Ford, 1987; Nichols, 1990), it is assumed that core goals were probably involved in most of these experiences. The Ford and Nichols Taxonomy of Human Goals is used in this step as a prompt to help insure that a broad range of experiences is considered in generating the list. In Step 2, participants more carefully examine up to 15 of these experiences and try to identify for each one the moment of peak satisfaction and the specific event that triggered that feeling. This step is designed to help the person focus on the specific behavior episode in which the core goal was actually attained. In Step 3, participants search for common underlying themes with regard to the goals being satisfied by these 15 experiences and begin the process of trying to construct accurate verbal representations of these themes. This is accomplished by grouping together experiences that seem to have produced the same or a similar ultimate result. This convergence of different experiences that satisfy the same underlying goal is essential to the identification of fundamentally important goals that guide behavior across many different contexts. Finally, in Step 4, participants work to refine and test their initial goal representations until they have defined their unique set of core goals with the greatest clarity and precision possible. Clinical evidence collected thus far indicates that most people define between one and five core goals through this process (Nichols, 1990, 1991).

The ACG's selective focus on "core" goals is based on the clinical observation that people generally have a small set of personal goals that are so important to them that a large portion of their strong feelings of satisfaction and frustration can be traced to these central organizing concerns. Indeed, some ACG respondents have reported having trouble thinking of any highly satisfying experiences that did not satisfy at least one of their core goals. In other cases the connections between core goals and

Table 7.1. *The Ford and Nichols taxonomy of human goals*

	Desired within-person consequences
Affective goals	
Entertainment	Experiencing excitement or heightened arousal; Avoiding boredom or stressful inactivity
Tranquility	Feeling relaxed and at ease; Avoiding stressful overarousal
Happiness	Experiencing feelings of joy, satisfaction, or well-being; Avoiding feelings of emotional distress or dissatisfaction
Bodily sensations	Experiencing pleasure associated with physical sensations, physical movement, or bodily contact; Avoiding unpleasant or uncomfortable bodily sensations
Physical well-being	Feeling healthy, energetic, or physically robust; Avoiding feelings of lethargy, weakness, or ill health
Cognitive goals	
Exploration	Satisfying one's curiosity about personally meaningful events; Avoiding a sense of being uninformed or not knowing what's going on
Understanding	Gaining knowledge or making sense out of something; Avoiding misconceptions, erroneous beliefs, or feelings of confusion
Intellectual creativity	Engaging in activities involving original thinking or novel or interesting ideas; Avoiding mindless or familiar ways of thinking
Positive self-evaluations	Maintaining a sense of self-confidence, pride, or self-worth; Avoiding feelings of failure, guilt, or incompetence
Subjective organization goals	
Unity	Experiencing a profound or spiritual sense of connectedness, harmony, or oneness with people, nature, or a greater power; Avoiding feelings of psychological disunity or disorganization
Transcendence	Experiencing optimal or extraordinary states of functioning; Avoiding feeling trapped within the boundaries of ordinary experience
	Desired person–environment consequences
Self-assertive social relationship goals	
Individuality	Feeling unique, special, or different; Avoiding similarity or conformity with others
Self-determination	Experiencing a sense of freedom to act or make choices; Avoiding the feeling of being pressured, constrained, or coerced
Superiority	Comparing favorably to others in terms of winning, status, or success; Avoiding unfavorable comparisons with others
Resource acquisition	Obtaining approval, support, assistance, advice, or validation from others; Avoiding social disapproval or rejection
Integrative social relationship goals	
Belongingness	Building or maintaining attachments, friendships, intimacy, or a sense of community; Avoiding feelings of social isolation or separateness
Social responsibility	Keeping interpersonal commitments, meeting social role obligations, and conforming to social and moral rules; Avoiding social transgressions and unethical or illegal conduct
Equity	Promoting fairness, justice, reciprocity, or equality; Avoiding unfair or unjust actions
Resource provision	Giving approval, support, assistance, advice, or validation to others; Avoiding selfish or uncaring behavior

Task goals

Mastery	Meeting a standard of achievement or improvement; Avoiding incompetence, mediocrity, or decrements in performance
Task creativity	Engaging in activities involving artistic expression or creativity; Avoiding tasks that do not provide opportunities for creative action
Management	Maintaining order, organization, or productivity in daily life tasks; Avoiding sloppiness, inefficiency, or disorganization
Material gain	Increasing the amount of money or tangible goods one has; Avoiding the loss of money or material possessions
Safety	Being unharmed, physically secure, and free from risk; Avoiding threatening, depriving, or harmful circumstances

satisfying and dissatisfying life experiences are harder to establish, either because the person has difficulty with the process of identifying and labeling their core goals, or because their goal hierarchy has many context-specific goals that are not clearly linked to more fundamental terminal goals. In this respect it is useful to think of core goals as being analogous to factors in a factor analysis – usually a small number of them are responsible for a large proportion of the "variance" in an individual's personality, but in some instances a less interpretable "factor solution" will emerge.

Another measure designed to abstract broad patterns of goal content from idiographic descriptions of specific behavior-episode experiences is Winell's AIMS (Adult Intentional and Motivational Systems) Interview (Wadsworth [Winell] & Ford, 1983; Winell, 1987). This measure, which is also available in a self-administered paper-and-pencil format as part of the Personal Goals Inventory (PGI), yields a matrix representation of a person's short-, medium-, and long-term goals in six life domains: work and school, family, social life, leisure activities, personal growth and maintenance, and material/environmental concerns (i.e., the AIMS Chart). Attributes of these goals (e.g., importance, opportunity, difficulty, and clarity) are then assessed using the second part of the PGI, called the Goal Description Scales.

Emmons' (1986, 1989) "personal striving" approach to personality provides yet another way to represent goal hierarchies using idiographic descriptions of goal content. "Personal strivings refer to the typical types of goals that a person hopes to accomplish in different situations. . . . A personal striving . . . unites what may be phenotypically different goals or actions around a common quality or theme" (Emmons, 1989, p. 92). Personal strivings can be thought of as personalized and contextualized versions of the abstract goal categories represented in the Ford and Nichols Taxonomy of Human Goals, as illustrated by these examples of personal strivings provided by Emmons (1989): "set aside time for 'emotional rest' each day" (Tranquility), "make a good impression" (Resource Acquisition), "show that I am superior to others" (Superiority), "make life easier for my parents" (Resource Provision), and "have as much fun as possible" (Entertainment). The *Personal Striving Assessment Packet* (Emmons, 1986) provides the tools needed to represent the nature of and relationships among a diversity of goals represented in this form, which Emmons (1989) characterizes as "the level of analysis that conveys an optimal amount of information about an individual" (p. 121).

Strategies for assessing goal hierarchies at a somewhat more context-specific level of analysis – usually in terms of temporally extended, goal-directed patterns of activity (or potential activity) – have also been developed in recent years, as illustrated by Klinger's (1977, 1987) work on "current concerns," Little's (1983, 1989) research on "personal projects," Cantor's focus of "life tasks" (Cantor & Fleeson, 1991; Cantor & Kihlstrom, 1987; Cantor & Langston, 1989), and Markus' work on "possible selves" (Markus & Nurius, 1986; Markus & Ruvolo, 1989). These efforts further illustrate the importance and heuristic value of trying to represent personality in terms of broad patterns of goal content.

The concepts of achievement and competence

The LSF approach to conceptualizing the content and organization of behavior and personality leads very logically to an emphasis on *goal attainment* as the primary criterion for defining and assessing the effectiveness of human functioning. At the level of a particular behavior episode, this means successfully achieving the goal of the episode within the circumstances and criteria defined by the context anchoring the episode. Thus, *achievement* is the concept used to describe effective functioning at the behavior-episode level of analysis. Achievement is defined as the attainment of a personally or socially valued goal in a particular context.

At the BES (i.e., personality) level of analysis, *competence* is the concept used to describe effective functioning. Because evaluations of effectiveness at this level of analysis must take into account possible consequences for a diversity of behavior episodes beyond the immediate episode, competence is defined by adding ethical and developmental boundary conditions to the anchoring criteria of goals and contexts. Specifically, competence is defined as the attainment of relevant goals in specified environments, using appropriate means and resulting in positive developmental outcomes.

Although not a major focus of this chapter, it is useful to note that, with regard to component processes, there are four major prerequisites for effective functioning in any given behavior episode: (1) the person must have the motivation needed to initiate and maintain activity until the goal directing the episode is attained (this category includes the component processes of personal goals, emotional-arousal patterns, and personal-agency beliefs); (2) the person must have the skill needed to construct and execute a pattern of activity that will produce the desired consequences (this category includes transactional processes, information processing and memory functions, attention- and consciousness-arousal processes, activity-arousal processes, and control- and performance-evaluation cognitions); (3) the person's biological structure and functioning must be able to support the operation of the motivation and skill components; and (4) the person must have the cooperation of a responsive environment that will facilitate, or at least not excessively impede, progress toward the goal (i.e., the environment must be congruent with an individual's "agenda" of personal goals and the person's biological, transactional, or cognitive capabilities; it must have the material or informational resources needed to facilitate goal attainment; and it must provide an emotional climate that supports and facilitates effective functioning). Thus, at a broad level it is possible to describe the processes contributing to effective person-in-context functioning using the following heuristic formula (M. Ford, 1992):

$$\text{Achievement/Competence} = \frac{\text{Motivation} \times \text{Skill}}{\text{Biology}} \times \text{Responsive Environment}$$

In other words, effective functioning requires a motivated, skillful person whose biological and behavioral capabilities support relevant interactions with an environment that has the informational and material properties and resources needed to facilitate (or at least permit) goal attainment. If *any* of these components is missing or inadequate, achievements will be limited and competence development will be thwarted.

The concept of intelligence

Like the concept of competence, intelligence is a concept used to characterize effective functioning at the BES level of analysis – that is, intelligence represents a pattern of effective functioning, or the potential for effective functioning, across a variety of behavior episodes. Indeed, the concept of intelligence is sometimes defined essentially as a synonym for competence – that is, in terms of criteria representing the attainment of relevant goals in specified environments (as in definitions emphasizing performance accomplishments or adaptation to the values and demands of a particular social–cultural context) (e.g., M. Ford & Tisak, 1983; M. Ford, 1986a, 1986b; Kornhaber, Krechevsky, & Gardner, 1990; Sternberg & Wagner, 1986). Of course, many theories of intelligence do not take such an explicitly outcome-oriented approach. In fact, it is perhaps more common for definitions of intelligence to emphasize particular component processes (e.g., information-processing capabilities, reasoning and problem-solving skills, or neural processes) that contribute to effective functioning but that do not actually represent effective functioning (e.g., Eysenck, 1987). Nevertheless, virtually all conceptions of intelligence pertain, at least indirectly, to the bottom-line issue of functioning effectively with respect to a broad range of goals and contexts. Thus, intelligence can be defined, at least in very general terms, as a characteristic of a person's functioning associated with the attainment of relevant goals within some specified set of contexts and evaluative boundary conditions.

By specifying more precisely the different characteristics of a BES repertoire that may be associated with effective functioning in various kinds of behavior episodes, it should be possible to develop a taxonomy of the different prototypical meanings associated with the concept of intelligence. This strategy is somewhat analogous to the efforts of Sternberg and his colleagues to identify prototypes of competence and intelligence (Sternberg, 1985b, 1990; Sternberg, Conway, Ketron, & Bernstein, 1981). However, the present analysis uses the LSF as a starting point rather than beginning with people's judgments about effective functioning. This way of proceeding enables one to focus on effectiveness criteria that can be applied to *any* content rather than confounding effectiveness criteria with the specific content valued by a particular set of respondents.

Such an approach addresses one of the most persistent problems in efforts to conceptualize intelligence, namely, the failure to draw a careful distinction between those aspects of an intelligence assessment that involve value judgments (i.e., content judgments about the qualities or accomplishments that should be valued by a particular culture, context, or individual), and those that involve "factual" matters that are subject to some kind of empirical evaluation (M. Ford, 1992). Without such a distinction, it is almost inevitable that scientific debates about the nature of intelligence will become entangled with value-laden disagreements about what kinds of qualities or accomplishments should be considered in an assessment of intelligence. For example, the question of whether social or artistic competence is relevant to such an assessment is basically a value question, not a matter for scientific analysis. Only *after* such questions have been answered for some particular assessment purpose can one sensibly begin the process of seeking evidence of effective or ineffective functioning.

Seven different qualities associated with broad patterns of effective functioning are described in Table 7.2, along with the prototypical conceptions of intelligence that correspond with each of these qualities. Although these conceptions are potentially applicable to any given content domain, they are not really content-free, since any assessment of intelligence must be anchored to some content. Rather, they provide a framework for assessment by defining a set of general criteria that might be used to evaluate the effectiveness of a person's functioning with respect to the identified content of interest (i.e., depending on the relevance of each criterion to the content being assessed), and by specifying where content must be filled in (i.e., one must identify in some manner the BES and BES components of interest). This implies that intelligence tests should be regarded as evolving tools that can and should be changed whenever there is a significant change in either the content that is valued for some assessment purpose, or in the knowledge gained about the nature of effective functioning with regard to such content.

Integrating conceptions of personality and intelligence

As implied in the preceding sections of this chapter, the key to integrating the fields of personality and intelligence is linking evaluations of effectiveness to the content relevant for a particular individual or group of individuals. In other words, definitions and measures of characteristics associated with effective functioning (i.e., intelli-

Table 7.2. *A living systems conceptualization of the variety of meanings associated with the concept of intelligence*

Qualities associated with an effective BES repertoire	Prototypical meanings of intelligence
1. Quantity of accurate, useful information represented in the BES (and associated concepts and propositions) relevant to some general set of contexts (i.e., in some "domain" of human functioning).	Breadth of knowledge in a general domain of expertise.
2. Quantity of accurate, useful information represented in the BES (and associated concepts and propositions) relevant to a relatively circumscribed set of contexts.	Depth of knowledge in an area of specialization.
3. Degree to which BES enactments (i.e., actual performances) meet objective standards representing mastery, excellence, or high levels of achievement.	Performance accomplishments in a general domain or area of specialization.
4. Degree to which BES enactments meet subjective criteria representing smooth, polished functioning (e.g., effortlessness, grace, elegance, etc.).	Automaticity or ease of functioning in a general domain or area of specialization.
5. Probability of successfully enacting relevant BES under highly evaluative, arousing, difficult, or distracting conditions.	Skilled performance under highly challenging conditions.
6. Degree to which relevant BES are rich and varied with regard to potential combinations of optional components.	"Generative flexibility"—ability to alter behavior patterns in response to varying circumstances.
7. Degree to which existing BES can be incrementally improved in rapid fashion, or readily replaced in favor of more adaptive patterns.	Speed of learning and behavior change.

gence) must be anchored to content that is meaningful for a particular individual or group of individuals given their developmental history, cultural background, social and occupational roles, and personal circumstances (i.e., personality).

In some cases, content definitions may be broadly applicable to very large groups of people. This possibility is particularly well illustrated by assessments of infant intelligence, which focus largely on markers associated with biological maturation, and by the general dimensions identified in studies of people's conceptions of intelligence and competence – dimensions such as verbal ability, practical problem-solving competence, prosocial behavior, and the like (e.g., M. Ford & Miura, 1983; Sternberg, 1985b; Sternberg, Conway, Ketron, & Bernstein, 1981). However, even in these cases effectiveness criteria must still be operationalized in terms of behavior episodes representing personally or socially relevant content. For example, the kinds of practical problems relevant to an assessment of practical problem-solving ability may vary considerably across socioeconomic, cultural, ethnic, or occupational groups. Moreover, assessments of intelligence that are limited to a few general categories may not adequately or fully represent the range of content relevant for a particular individual or group of individuals (e.g., individuals who have a rich, varied, or unique hierarchy of personal goals). Thus, to be maximally useful and informative, assessments of intelligence and personality must be tied together at the level of the individual person or at the level of a relatively homogeneous group of people. This is an increasingly important principle to consider as the range of goals and contexts in which target individuals can invest themselves becomes more variable and complex (e.g., as a result of increased capabilities for self-direction, increased opportunities for autonomous decision making, or increased variability produced by social–economic–political circumstances).

In short, although some of the content relevant for evaluations of effective functioning might be defined by relatively fixed biological parameters or by widely shared cultural values, much of that content is defined by the individual's personal choices and local circumstances (i.e., by the goals and contexts that anchor their most important, recurring BES). Thus, intelligence must be defined, at least in part, on the person's own terms if it is to be a meaningful concept.

This way of conceptualizing intelligence is consistent with the move toward a "multiple intelligences" approach (Gardner, 1983), but expands the menu of possibilities to include virtually any domain or category of effective functioning that a person or social group might value, at levels of abstraction ranging from broad, general expertise across a diversity of contexts to highly focused accomplishments in a narrow range of contexts. Thus, the "fixed" part of the LSF approach to integrating personality and intelligence is not a set of content categories or dimensions such as verbal ability, visual–spatial ability, etc., but rather the set of seven generic criteria for describing an effectively functioning set of behavior episode schemata (see Table 7.2). In other words, this approach weds an idiographic conceptualization of personality with a nomothetic understanding of intelligence. It also suggests that descriptions of a person's functioning that do not incorporate both of these elements are likely to be somewhat impoverished.

Operationalizing the LSF approach to integrating personality and intelligence

The conceptual framework presented in this chapter suggests a basic strategy for integrating assessments of personality and intelligence. Specifically, to operationalize this approach one would need to cross an idiographically defined set of (one or more) content categories with a nomothetically defined set of (one or more) criteria representing some characteristic associated with an effectively functioning BES repertoire. The simplest version of such an assessment would involve the measurement of one aspect of effective functioning in one content domain (e.g., breadth of verbal knowledge as represented by a vocabulary test, mechanical aptitude as represented by proficiency in constructing or repairing machinery, or artistic creativity as represented by flexibility in combining elements into new or unique patterns). A somewhat broader application of this strategy might involve assessing multiple content dimensions on a particular criterion of effective functioning (e.g., depth of knowledge in various academic specialty areas as represented by an achievement-test battery; effectiveness in a professional job as represented by a portfolio of performance accomplishments).

The unique contributions of the LSF approach to the integrated assessment of personality and intelligence are more clearly revealed, however, by considering examples in which multiple criteria representing different aspects of effective functioning are simultaneously applied to a particular content domain. Four such examples are outlined in Table 7.3. In each example, a single content category of particular relevance to a group of people with similar BES is crossed with the seven characteristics associated with effective functioning described earlier in Table 7.2.

Although these examples of highly intelligent functioning with respect to a particular role or activity reveal some of the descriptive richness afforded by the LSF approach to integrating personality and intelligence, the ultimate application of this approach is designed to yield an even more informative result. In such an application, one would cross the seven evaluative dimensions representing the concept of intelligence with multiple content dimensions representing an idiographically defined set of personally or socially valued roles and activities. Table 7.4 displays an assessment format designed to serve this purpose, called the Assessment of Personal Intelligence (or API for short).

The API makes explicit the fact that it is impossible to conduct a meaningful assessment of intelligence without first specifying the precise content dimensions that are relevant for a particular individual (or set of similar individuals). Moreover, it highlights the fact that a variety of alternative criteria representing somewhat different meanings of intelligence can be used to define effective functioning. As a consequence of these two unique features, the API is capable of providing researchers and practitioners with an unusually relevant and revealing profile of an individual's functioning.

In an effort to further clarify this method of operationalizing the LSF approach to integrating the study of personality and intelligence, and to illustrate the potential advantages of this approach compared to traditional tests of personality and intelligence, two concrete examples of a completed Assessment of Personal Intelligence, each combining quantitative scoring with a verbal summary, are presented in Tables 7.5 and 7.6.

These examples illustrate several characteristics of a typical API. First, the focus on multiple content domains representing a diversity of valued goals and achievements affords the advantages of a "multiple intelligences" approach (Gardner, 1983), but with much greater flexibility than an approach that is limited to nomothetically defined categories of human functioning. From the perspective of the LSF, an infinite variety of content domains could, in principle, be defined, at whatever level of abstraction makes sense for the particular individual (or individuals) being assessed. In other words, by allowing content domains to be defined in terms of idiographically defined goals and achievements of particular concern to the individual and/or the contexts of the individual being assessed, it is possible to integrate the objectives of personality and intelligence assessments.

Table 7.3. *Profiles of highly intelligent individuals*

Criterion	Student	Counselor	Quarterback	Pianist
Breadth of knowledge in a general domain of expertise	The student knows a lot of relevant facts, concepts, or solution procedures in some academic domain or across several such domains.	The counselor has extensive knowledge about different kinds of counseling techniques and their utility for different kinds of clients and problems.	The quarterback has extensive knowledge of the game of football, the team's playbook, and when to call particular plays.	The pianist knows how to play many different songs (i.e., the pianist has a large repertoire).
Depth of knowledge in an area of specialization	The student has acquired a great deal of knowledge about a particular subject or special area of interest.	The counselor has the expertise and wisdom needed to understand a particular kind of client or problem in great detail.	The quarterback has an unusually clear and detailed understanding of how to attack a particular kind of defense (e.g., a zone defense, nickel defense, etc.).	The pianist has a repertoire that is particularly well suited for a particular audience or occasion (e.g., wedding music; children's songs).
Performance accomplishments	The student routinely performs well in classroom activities, on class assignments, and on exams.	The counselor successfully facilitates effective or improved cognitive, emotional, biological, and/or behavioral functioning in most clients.	The quarterback is able to execute plays successfully on virtually every down (within the constraints of the defense), and consistently makes key plays that help his team win games.	The pianist is able to perform songs from his or her repertoire in a technically proficient and stylistically appropriate manner.
Automaticity or ease of functioning	The student is able to complete academic tasks successfully with a minimum of effort.	The counselor is able to recognize and deal with clients' problems in a relaxed, efficient, and professional manner.	The quarterback can quickly size up a situation and decide what to do, and then implement that decision with machine-like precision or unusual grace.	The pianist is able to play with a natural, polished style that seems smooth, reliable, and relatively effortless.

Skilled performance under highly challenging conditions	The student is able to do his or her best even under difficult or highly evaluative conditions (e.g., hard or important exams; highly public performances).	The counselor is able to handle highly distressed, disorganized, or dangerous clients.	The quarterback is able to "come through in the clutch" and remain cool and in control in the face of adversity.	The pianist is able to perform at an optimal level despite the pressure of playing before a large or significant audience.
Generative flexibility	The student can generate alternative strategies or novel approaches to challenging tasks and problems.	The counselor displays ingenuity and versatility in dealing with clients' problems.	The quarterback is clever and resourceful in calling and/or executing plays.	The pianist can improvise on well-practiced routines or newly learned material in creative and interesting ways.
Speed of learning and developmental change	The student is able to learn new facts, concepts, and procedures in a rapid and enduring manner.	The counselor is readily able to incorporate new concepts, techniques, and approaches into his or her work.	The quarterback can quickly learn and master a new play, formation, or game plan.	The pianist can quickly learn a new song or new way to play an old song.

Table 7.4. *The basic measurement framework for the Assessment of Personal Intelligence*

Scoring instructions

Quantitative Assessment (optional). If this option is used, scores should represent levels of knowledge, mastery, performance, or success relative to domain-specific exemplary standards. (These standards should be defined in terms of developmentally appropriate, real-life human achievements rather than hypothetical ideals representing "perfection.")

1 -------------- 2 -------------- 3 -------------- 4 -------------- 5 -------------- 6 ---------------- 7

| Little or no expertise or competence | Modest level of expertise or competence relative to an exemplary standard | High level of expertise or competence but clearly less than an exemplary standard | Approaching or meeting an exemplary standard |

Verbal Assessment (required). In this option, levels of knowledge, mastery, performance, or success are summarized in words that are clearly anchored to particular achievements or to a developmentally appropriate exemplary standard.

Relevant Goals/Content Domains

Dimensions of intelligence	Domain one	Domain two	Domain three	Domain four	Domain five
Breadth of general knowledge base					
Depth of knowledge in specialized area					
Performance accomplishments					
Automaticity or ease of functioning	etc.				
Skilled performance under challenge					
Generative flexibility					
Speed of learning and behavior change					

(Table entries may be numbers or words, as explained above. However, if numbers are used, these must be supplemented by a verbal interpretive summary of each score or the overall profile of an individual's scores in each content domain. The selection of content domains may reflect goals that are of high personal relevance and/or those that are highly valued by the culture or contexts in which the person is functioning.)

Second, by restricting content domains to a relatively small number of goal pursuits representing a person's most important "core goals" (Nichols, 1990, 1991), "current concerns" (Klinger, 1977, 1987), "personal strivings" (Emmons, 1986, 1989), "personal projects" (Little, 1983, 1989), or "life tasks" (Cantor & Fleeson, 1991; Cantor & Kihlstrom, 1987; Cantor & Langston, 1989), it is possible to summarize that individual's personality and intelligence in a way that is broad in scope but reasonably concise. One might also try to increase the depth and precision of such an assessment by defining a set of relevant subgoals (i.e., areas of specialization) for some content domains. For example, the goal of "academic success" might be defined in terms of subdomains representing traditional subject matter categories. "Golfing

Table 7.5. *Completed Assessment of Personal Intelligence for "Jason," a 15-year-old male high school student*

Dimensions of intelligence	Relevant Goals/Content Domains				
	Academic Success	Social life/dating	Golfing mastery	Video game expertise	Artistic competence
Breadth of general knowledge base	6	3	5	7	3
Depth of knowledge in specialized area	6	2	6	7	3
Performance accomplishments	6	2	4	7	4
Automaticity or ease of functioning	7	1	4	7	4
Skilled performance under challenge	5	1	3	7	3
Generative flexibility	6	1	5	7	2
Speed of learning and behavior change	7	4	4	7	3

Verbal Summary

With regard to academics, Jason is an extremely bright youngster in the sense of breadth and depth of knowledge across academic subjects (compared to others at his level of development). He routinely earns high grades in all academic subjects with little effort because he learns so quickly and easily. His performance is less remarkable under conditions requiring extra effort or performance under pressure, but still above average compared to his peers.

Jason is very interested in dating and improving his social reputation, but is very shy around girls, especially those who are particularly popular or attractive. Consequently, he has learned a fair amount about this aspect of social competence but has almost no direct experience relevant to this domain.

Jason took up golf two years ago and has developed an intense passion for the game. He reads a lot about the game and is particularly knowledgeable about chipping and putting. His handicap has been gradually dropping, and is now at 15. He has a somewhat awkward swing, and performs erratically under pressure, but often exceeds observers' expectations due to his resourcefulness around the greens.

A major activity among Jason's male peers is playing video games. He has fully mastered many games, and is particularly skilled at games requiring intellectual skill and creativity along with excellent perceptual-motor skills. In fact, he is so experienced and clever in this domain that it is difficult to find games that provide him with a meaningful challenge.

From an early age, Jason has had a strong interest in art and continues to be interested in occupations that require artistic competence. Despite very little instruction or exposure to high quality artwork, he has produced impressive artwork on a number of occasions. However, the thematic and stylistic aspects of these products have been rather stereotyped and limited, and his skills have not progressed much in the last few years.

Table 7.6. *Completed Assessment of Personal Intelligence for "Sharon," a 29-year-old female stockbroker*

Dimensions of intelligence	Relevant goals/content domains				
	Financial market expertise	Close family relations	Maternal competence	Astute shopping	Piano playing skill
Breadth of general knowledge base	5	5	6	7	4
Depth of knowledge in specialized area	7	5	4	6	6
Performance accomplishments	6	3	4	6	5
Automaticity or ease of functioning	4	4	2	7	4
Skilled performance under challenge	6	3	3	7	5
Generative flexibility	4	5	3	7	3
Speed of learning and behavior change	4	4	3	6	3

Verbal summary

With regard to her chosen occupation, Sharon has performed very well for her clients by developing not only general expertise about the financial world, but also a very strong understanding of international markets. She is not particularly clever or insightful in this regard, but simply works very hard to obtain and analyze information that others choose to ignore.

Sharon comes from a very close-knit but troubled family, and invests a great deal of time and effort trying to maintain good relations among family members. As a Human Development major in college, she learned a fair amount about the dynamics of family relationships, and has learned to be persistent and resourceful in trying to manage family conflicts. However, she has had only limited success in helping her family alter their dysfunctional patterns of relating to one another.

Three months ago Sharon had her first child, a boy. She read everything she could find on the topic of how to be a good mother, but admits that she does not yet fully appreciate the meaning and significance of much of that information. Although things seem to be going reasonably well in terms of the baby's development, Sharon is clearly not yet comfortable in her role as a mother, and feels that she is just beginning to learn how to respond appropriately to her baby's needs.

In part because of her financial savvy, but largely due to years of experience in malls, department stores, and specialty stores, Sharon has become an expert shopper with detailed knowledge of formal and informal store policies and how to find the highest value merchandise for the least amount of money. Although she sometimes settles for a less than ideal price due to time and transportation constraints, she is also a remarkably efficient and creative shopper who can quickly locate and purchase desired goods and services from among hundreds of stores and catalogs to which she has access.

Sharon has studied classical piano for 17 years and has developed considerable technical proficiency, as evidenced by her successful participation in numerous recitals and concerts. However, her style is somewhat mechanical and it takes her many months to master each new piece of music. Nevertheless, she enjoys performing and is very concerned that she will be unable to continue investing time in this domain of expertise.

mastery" might be subdivided into the various kinds of shots required to play well (e.g., wood play, long iron play, short iron play, chipping and putting, sand play, etc.). Similarly, the goal of "piano proficiency" might be assessed with regard to different categories of music (e.g., classical, pop, religious music, etc.), or even with regard to specific pieces that are currently of primary interest or concern (e.g., a Beethoven sonata, Billy Joel's greatest hits, or piano accompaniments for an upcoming concert).

Third, the data in Tables 7.5 and 7.6 clearly convey both the interrelatedness and distinctiveness of different dimensions of intelligence. That is, because each dimension is intended to reflect different aspects of the same general phenomenon (i.e., the effectiveness of a person's functioning with regard to some set of stable, recurring BES and BES components), one would usually not expect a broad range of scores within a particular content category. On the other hand, even relatively small variations among these scores can convey meaningful information about the idiosyncratic character of the person's intelligence within a particular domain.

Finally, the verbal information provided for each domain in the person's API addresses the problem of how to translate numerical information of the kind yielded by most personality and intelligence tests into a meaningful understanding of the content and effectiveness of an individual's functioning. Although numbers anchored by clear content labels and specific effectiveness criteria can efficiently summarize a great deal of information, verbal interpretative material can provide additional detail about relevant goals and contexts and help bring these numbers "to life."

Limitations of the Assessment of Personal Intelligence

It is important to note that there are several potential obstacles and limitations inherent in the LSF approach to the integrated assessment of personality and intelligence that must be carefully considered before attempting to apply this approach. First, the API is simply a framework for assessment. It does not provide or even specify the kinds of measuring tools that one will ultimately need to use to fill in the cells of the API. That is intentional, of course, since it is impossible to specify in advance the precise measurement strategies (e.g., self-ratings, observer ratings, interviews, paper-and-pencil tests, performance assessments, etc.) needed to conduct a reliable and valid assessment of a particular content domain for an individual of a given development level.

Second, it is impossible to conduct an "assessment of personal intelligence" without first carefully defining the particular content domains that should be involved in such an assessment. This itself may be a complex measurement problem – certainly more complex than simply accepting the (usually implicit) definitions of valued content represented in most intelligence measures. At a minimum one must consciously consider whether an available assessment "makes sense" given the personal goals and circumstances of the person being assessed. Often, however, it may require a separate, initial assessment of personally, culturally, and/or developmentally salient goals and activities like those described earlier in this chapter.

Related to this limitation is the possible incongruity of the API approach with the goal of conducting a standardized assessment of intelligence. Although one might be able to rely on a standardized set of content categories up through the early school-aged years based on normative developmental criteria (e.g., Waters & Sroufe, 1983), it is difficult to justify a nomothetic approach beyond this age range given the increasingly diverse range of goals and contexts represented in the BES repertoire of older children, adolescents, and adults. On the other hand, because the criteria for defining different aspects of intelligence are fixed in the API, it may be possible to conduct standardized assessments *within* domains, assuming that a common "exemplary standard" can be defined against which to anchor the measurement process.

This assumption points out another potential limitation of the API, namely, the problem of identifying appropriate assessment standards. This problem is not unique to the API; all intelligence tests must define such standards (e.g., through item selection and/or norming procedures). However, because it will often be the case that different sets of standards will be needed for different individuals (i.e., because of the diversity of content domains represented in their assessments), this may be a particularly challenging problem in efforts to apply an idiographic approach such as that represented by the API to the assessment of intelligence.

Summary

In this chapter a conceptual and methodological approach to the integrated study and assessment of personality and intelligence was described. This approach is based on D. Ford's Living Systems Framework, a comprehensive theory of human functioning and development, and M. Ford's conceptualization of competence and intelligence (D. Ford, 1987; D. Ford & M. Ford, 1987; M. Ford, 1985, 1986a, 1986b, 1992; M. Ford & Tisak, 1983). The basic premise of this approach is that, by understanding human functioning in terms of individually constructed behavior patterns anchored by goals and contexts, it is possible to conceptualize personality and intelligence in a way that makes it possible to wed these concepts together in a productive way. Specifically, the LSF enables one to derive a set of criteria for evaluating the effectiveness of a person's functioning, and suggests a way of linking these criteria to content domains that have real-world significance for the individual (as exemplified by the Assessment of Personal Intelligence). Recent advances in the idiographic assessment of goal content (e.g., Cantor & Fleeson, 1991; Cantor & Langston, 1989; Emmons, 1986, 1989; Little, 1983, 1989; Markus & Nurius, 1986; Markus & Ruvolo, 1989; Nichols, 1990, 1991) provide further evidence of the feasibility and utility of this approach to integrating personality and intelligence.

References

Abelson, R. P. (1981). Psychological status of the script concept. *American Psychologist, 36,* 715–727.
Arbib, M. A. (1989). *The metaphorical brain 2: Neural networks and beyond.* New York: Wiley.
Arbib, M. A., & Hesse, M. B. (1986). *The construction of reality.* Cambridge: Cambridge University Press.

Bandura, A. (1986). *Social foundations of thought and action: A social cognitive theory.* Englewood Cliffs, NJ: Prentice-Hall.

Bevan, W. (1991). Contemporary psychology: A tour inside the onion. *American Psychologist, 46,* 475–483.

Borke, H. (1971). Interpersonal perception of young children: Egocentrism or empathy? *Developmental Psychology, 5,* 263–269.

Campion, M. A., & Lord, R. G. (1982). A control system conceptualization of the goal-setting and changing process. *Organizational and Human Performance, 30,* 265–287.

Cantor, N., & Fleeson, W. (1991). Life tasks and self-regulatory processes. In M. L. Maehr & P. R. Pintrich (Eds.), *Advances in motivation and achievement, Vol. 7* (pp. 327–369). Greenwich, CT: JAI Press.

Cantor, N., & Kihlstrom, J. F. (1987). *Personality and social intelligence.* Englewoods Cliffs, NJ: Prentice-Hall.

Cantor, N., & Langston, C. A. (1989). Ups and down of life tasks in a life transition. In L. A. Pervin (Ed.), *Goal concepts in personality and social psychology* (pp. 127–167). Hillsdale, NJ: Erlbaum.

Cantor, N., Markus, H., Niedenthal, P., & Nurius, P. (1986). On motivation and the self-concept. In R. M. Sorrentino & E. T. Higgins (Eds.), *Handbook of motivation and cognition: Foundations of social behavior* (pp. 96–121). New York: Guilford.

Carver, C. S., & Scheier, M. F. (1981). *Attention and self-regulation: A control-theory approach to human behavior.* New York: Springer-Verlag.

Carver, C. S., & Scheier, M. F. (1982). Control theory: A useful conceptual framework for personality–social, clinical, and health psychology. *Psychological Bulletin, 92,* 111–135.

Carver, C. S., & Scheier, M. F. (1985). A control-systems approach to the self-regulation of action. In J. Kuhl & J. Beckmann (Eds.), *Action control: From cognition to behavior* (pp. 237–265). Berlin: Springer-Verlag.

Carver, C. S., & Scheier, M. F. (1990). Origins and functions of positive and negative affect: A control-process view. *Psychological Review, 97,* 19–35.

Csikszentmihalyi, M. (1990). *Flow: The psychology of optimal experience.* New York: Harper & Row.

Deci, E. L., & Ryan, R. M. (1985). *Intrinsic motivation and self-determination in human behavior.* New York: Plenum.

Deci, E. L., & Ryan, R. M. (1991). A motivational approach to self: Integration in personality. In R. Dienstbier (Ed.), *Nebraska Symposium on motivation, Vol. 38: Perspectives on motivation* (pp. 237–288). Lincoln, NE: University of Nebraska Press.

Demetriou, A., & Efklides, A. (1981). The structure of formal operations: The ideal of the whole and the reality of the parts. In J. A. Meacham & N. R. Santilli (Eds.), *Social development in youth: Structure and content* (pp. 20–46). Basel, Switzerland: Karger.

Dweck, C. S., & Leggett, E. L. (1988). A social-cognitive approach to motivation and personality. *Psychological Review, 95,* 256–273.

Emmons, R. A. (1986). Personal strivings: An approach to personality and subjective well-being. *Journal of Personality and Social Psychology, 51,* 1058–1068.

Emmons, R. A. (1989). The personal striving approach to personality. In L. A. Pervin (Ed.), *Goal concepts in personality and social psychology* (pp. 87–126). Hillsdale, NJ: Erlbaum.

Eysenck, H. J. (1987). Speed of information processing, reaction time, and the theory of intelligence. In P. A. Vernon (Ed.), *Speed of information processing and intelligence* (pp. 21–67). Norwood, NJ: Ablex.

Ford, D. H. (1987). *Humans as self-constructing living systems: A developmental perspective on behavior and personality.* Hillsdale, NJ: Erlbaum.

Ford, D. H., & Lerner, R. M. (1992). *Developmental systems theory: A synthesis of developmental contextualism and the living systems framework.* Newbury Park, CA: Sage.

Ford, D. H., & Urban, H. B. (1963). *Systems of psychotherapy.* New York: Wiley.

Ford, M. E. (1985). The concept of competence: Themes and variations. In H. A. Marlowe & R. B. Weinberg (Eds.), *Competence development* (pp. 3–49). Springfield, IL: Charles C. Thomas.

Ford, M. E. (1986a). A living systems conceptualization of social intelligence: Outcomes, processes, and developmental change. In R. J. Sternberg (Ed.), *Advances in the psychology of human intelligence* (Vol. 3, pp. 119–171). Hillsdale, NJ: Erlbaum.

Ford, M. E. (1986b). For all practical purposes: Criteria for defining and evaluating practical intelligence. In R. J. Sternberg & R. K. Wagner (Eds.), *Practical intelligence: Nature and origins of competence in the everyday world* (pp. 182–200). Cambridge: Cambridge University Press.

Ford, M. E. (1992). *Motivating humans: Goals, emotions, and personal agency beliefs.* Newbury Park, CA: Sage.

Ford, M. E., & Ford, D. H. (Eds.). (1987). *Humans as self-constructing living systems: Putting the framework to work.* Hillsdale, NJ: Erlbaum.

Ford, M. E., & Miura, I. T. (1983). Children's and adult's conceptions of social competence. Paper presented at the annual meeting of the American Educational Research Association, New York.

Ford, M. E., & Nichols, C. W. (1987). A taxonomy of human goals and some possible applications. In M. E. Ford & D. H. Ford (Eds.), *Humans as self-constructing living systems: Putting the framework to work* (pp. 289–311). Hillsdale, NJ: Erlbaum.

Ford, M. E., & Nichols, C. W. (1991). Using goal assessments to identify motivational patterns and facilitate behavioral regulation and achievement. In M. L. Maehr & P. R. Pintrich (Eds.), *Advances in motivation and achievement, Vol. 7* (pp. 51–84). Greenwich, CT: JAI Press.

Ford, M. E., & Nichols, C. W. (1994). *Manual: Assessment of Personal Goals.* Palo Alto, CA: Consulting Psychologists Press.

Ford, M. E., & Tisak, M. S. (1983). A further search for social intelligence. *Journal of Educational Psychology, 75,* 196–206.

Gardner, H. (1983). *Frames of mind: The theory of multiple intelligences.* New York: Basic Books.

Goldstein, A. P., & Kanfer, F. H. (Eds.). (1979). *Maximizing treatment gains: Transfer enhancement in psychotherapy.* New York: Academic Press.

Hollenbeck, J. R. (1989). Control theory and the perception of work environment: The effects of focus of attention on affective and behavioral reactions to work. *Organizational Behavior and Human Decision Processes, 43,* 406–430.

Hyland, M. E. (1988). Motivational control theory: An integrative framework. *Journal of Personality and Social Psychology, 55,* 642–651.

Keating, D. P. (1984). The emperor's new clothes: The "new look" in intelligence research. In R. J. Sternberg (Ed.), *Advances in the psychology of human intelligence, Vol. 2* (pp. 1–35). Hillsdale, NJ: Erlbaum.

Keating, D. P. (1990). Charting pathways to the development of expertise. *Educational Psychologist, 25,* 243–267.

Klein, H. J. (1989). An integrated control theory model of work motivation. *Academy of Management Review, 14,* 150–172.

Klinger, E. (1977). *Meaning and void: Inner experience and the incentives in people's lives.* Minneapolis, MN: University of Minnesota Press.

Klinger, E. (1987). The interview questionnaire technique: Reliability and validity of a mixed idiographic-nomothetic measure of motivation. In J. N. Butcher & C. D. Spielberger (Eds.), *Advances in personality assessment, Vol. 6* (pp. 31–48). Hillsdale, NJ: Erlbaum.

Kornhaber, M., Krechevsky, M., & Gardner, H. (1990). Engaging intelligence. *Educational Psychologist, 25,* 177–199.

Larsen, R., Ham, M., & Rafaelli, M. (1989). The nurturance of motivation attention in the daily experience of children and adolescents. In M. L. Maehr & C. Ames (Eds.), *Advances in motivation and achievement, Vol. 6: Motivation enhancing environments* (pp. 45–80). Greenwich, CT: JAI Press.

Lazarus, R. S. (1991). *Emotion and adaptation.* New York: Oxford University Press.

Little, B. R. (1983). Personal projects: A rationale and method for investigation. *Environment and Behavior, 15,* 273–309.

Little, B. R. (1989). Personal projects analysis: Trivial pursuits, magnificent obsessions and the search for coherence. In D. M. Buss & N. Cantor (Eds.), *Personality psychology: Recent trends and emerging directions* (pp. 15–31). New York: Springer-Verlag.

Lord, R. G., & Hanges, P. J. (1987). A control system model of organizational motivation: Theoretical development and applied implications. *Behavioral Science, 32,* 161–178.

Lord, R. G., & Kernan, M. C. (1989). Application of control theory to work settings. In W. A. Herschberger (Ed.), *Volitional action* (pp. 493–514). Amsterdam: Elsevier.

McDevitt, T. M., & Ford, M. E. (1987). Understanding young children's communicative functioning and development. In M. E. Ford and D. H. Ford (Eds.), *Humans as self-constructing living systems: Putting the framework to work* (pp. 145–175). Hillsdale, NJ: Erlbaum.

Maratsos, M. P. (1973). Nonegocentric communication abilities in preschool children. *Child Development, 44,* 697–700.

Markus, H., Cross, S., & Wurf, E. (1990). The role of the self-system in competence. In R. J. Sternberg & J. Kolligian, Jr. (Eds.), *Competence considered* (pp. 205–225). New Haven, CT: Yale University Press.

Markus, H., & Nurius, P. (1986). Possible selves. *American Psychologist, 41,* 954–969.

Markus, H., & Ruvolo, A. (1989). Possible selves: Personalized representations of goals. In L. A. Pervin (Ed.), *Goal concepts in personality and social psychology* (pp. 211–241). Hillsdale, NJ: Erlbaum.

Menig-Peterson, C. L. (1975). The modification of communicative behavior in preschool-aged children as a function of the listener's perspective. *Child Development, 46,* 1015–1018.

Mischel, W. (1968). *Personality and assessment.* New York: Wiley.

Mischel, W. (1973). Toward a cognitive social learning reconceptualization of personality. *Psychological Review, 80,* 252–283.

Neisser, U. (1976). *Cognition and reality.* San Francisco: W. H. Freeman.

Neisser, U. (1985). The role of invariant structures in the control of movement. In M. Frese & J. Sabini (Eds.), *Goal directed behavior: The concept of action in psychology* (pp. 97–108). Hillsdale, NJ: Erlbaum.

Nichols, C. W. (1990). *An analysis of the sources of dissatisfaction at work.* Unpublished doctoral dissertation, School of Education, Stanford University, Stanford, CA.

Nichols, C. W. (1991). *Manual: Assessment of Core Goals.* Palo Alto, CA: Consulting Psychologists Press.

Pervin, L. A. (1983). The stasis and flow of behavior: Toward a theory of goals. In M. M. Page (Ed.), *Personality: Current theory and research* (pp. 1–53). Lincoln, NE: University of Nebraska Press.

Pervin, L. A. (1989). (Ed.). *Goal concepts in personality and social psychology.* Hillsdale, NJ: Erlbaum.

Powers, W. T. (1973). *Behavior: The control of perception.* Chicago: Aldine.

Powers, W. T. (1989). *Living control systems.* Gravel Switch, KY: Control Systems Group Press.

Schmidt, R. A. (1975). A schema theory of discrete motor skill learning. *Psychological Review, 82,* 225–260.

Schutz, P. A. (1991). Goals in self-directed behavior. *Educational Psychologist, 26,* 55–67.

Simon, H. A. (1967). Motivational and emotional control of cognition. *Psychological Review, 74,* 29–39.

Staats, A. W. (1991). Unified positivism and unification psychology: Fad or new field? *American Psychologist, 46,* 899–912.

Sternberg, R. J. (1985a). *Beyond IQ: A triarchic theory of human intelligence.* New York: Cambridge University Press.

Sternberg, R. J. (1985b). Implicit theories of intelligence, creativity, and wisdom. *Journal of Personality and Social Psychology, 49,* 607–627.

Sternberg, R. J. (1990). Prototypes of competence and incompetence. In R. J. Sternberg & J. Kolligian, Jr. (Eds.), *Competence considered* (pp. 117–145). New Haven, CT: Yale University Press.

Sternberg, R. J., Conway, B. E., Ketron, J. L., & Bernstein, M. (1981). People's conceptions of intelligence. *Journal of Personality and Social Psychology, 41,* 37–55.

Sternberg, R. J., & Wagner, R. K. (Eds.). (1986). *Practical intelligence: Nature and origins of competence in the everyday world.* Cambridge: Cambridge University Press.

Vygotsky, L. S. (1978). *Mind in society: The development of higher psychological processes.* Cambridge, MA: Harvard University Press.

Wadsworth (Winnell), & Ford, D. H. (1983). Assessment of personal goal hierarchies. *Journal of Counseling Psychology, 30,* 514–526.

Waters, E., & Sroufe, L. A. (1983). Social competence as a developmental construct. *Developmental Review, 3,* 79–97.

Winell, M. (1987). Personal goals: The key to self-direction in adulthood. In M. E. Ford & D. H. Ford (Eds.), *Humans as self-constructing living systems: Putting the framework to work* (pp. 261–287). Hillsdale, NJ: Erlbaum.

Part IV

Personality, intelligence, and culture

8   Intelligence and Personality in the Psychological Theory of Activity

*Sergei D. Smirnov**

The theory of activity is one of the most influential and extensive theories in Russian psychology. Theorists contributing to its development have included Davydov, Gal'perin, Leont'ev, Luria, Zaporozhets, and Zinchenko. The central construct of the theory is the concept of object-oriented activity, and it is impossible to discuss intelligence and personality within the framework of the theory without referring to that concept.

The reason activity holds such a central position is that, within the theory, activity is viewed not simply as a combination of various physical actions mediated by cognitive processes. Rather, object-oriented activity forms the connection between the individual and the world, and this connection is bidirectional. That is, the individual acts on and changes the environment through activity, but, as a result, the individual himself is also changed as he absorbs a wider and wider range of experiences from the environment. Hence, cognitive structures and personality are created via activity.

The purpose of this chapter is to discuss the relation of intelligence and personality within the framework of the theory of activity. Special attention will be paid to the concept of the image of the world – the mental image an individual holds of his environment and himself. The image of the world is formed in activity and the concept has its origin in Leont'ev's writings on the theory of activity. The concept of the image of the world originally appeared in one of the last articles written by Leont'ev (1979). The concept has since been further developed by Leont'ev's students, including Smirnov (1983) and Petukhov (1984). Some of the results of that effort are presented in this chapter. But, because a full description of the theory of activity is beyond the scope of this chapter, the discussion will be limited to those aspects of the theory that are related to the image of the world.

The chapter itself has a "circular" structure. The first sections describe the theory of activity in some detail, concentrating on the role of activity in the development of consciousness, personality, and cognitive processes. The middle section (the main body of the chapter) presents the concept of the image of the world as the interface of intelligence and personality. The final section is devoted to experimental studies

*Translated from the Russian by Elena Grigorenko and Patricia Ruzgis.

in Russian psychology, designed within the framework of the theory of activity, that have special significance for understanding the relation of intelligence and personality.

The main characteristics of activity

Activity, in the present context, is *object oriented.* An object is understood as not only a natural object but also as a cultural object. Whenever activity occurs, a culturally developed manner of interacting with the object takes place. The external object, therefore, dominates the process of activity. The development of the individual, and his activity, results from mastering an increasing range of new objects and incorporating a larger and larger part of the world into the structure of his activity.

The second characteristic of activity is its *social, historical–cultural* nature. An individual cannot develop new forms of activity independently. For development to take place other people must demonstrate new patterns of activity and involve the individual in shared activity. The transition from a shared (interpsychic) activity to an individual (intrapsychic) activity constitutes a major component of the process by which new psychological information is internalized.

An activity is always *mediated,* with objects, signs, symbols (such as language), and interaction with other people serving as mediators. In acting, we are always aware of others' attitudes toward our actions, even when they are not present at the moment of performing the activity.

Human activity is always *goal directed*; the goal is represented in consciousness as the planned result of activity. A goal coordinates activity and corrects its movement. That is, we have an expected result of activity or a goal in mind throughout the process of activity.

Activity is always initiated by the individual, not activated by outside stimuli. That is why activity is not merely a combination of reactions, but a system of actions linked together by motivation. A motive is what precipitates the activity – the meaning underlying the individual's actions.

Finally, an activity is always *productive.* If we view activity as a bipolar dimension, activity results in changes at the pole of the object (the outside world is changed by an attempt to reach a goal) and at the pole of the subject (the individual himself is changed – motivation, knowledge, abilities, etc.). By identifying which changes have greater weight, it is possible to distinguish different types of activities such as work activity, cognitive activity, and so on.

Psychological analysis requires the separation of activity into different levels of regulation, to determine their relationships. Leont'ev (1975) provides useful ideas regarding the structural components of activity:

1. An activity itself is a system of actions subordinated to a particular motive. A motive, according to Leont'ev, is a particular need that impels an activity. An individual is not always aware of the motive behind his activity, or may conceive of

it in a false way. An individual who has a need, but has been unable to find an object to satisfy it, is able to create only searching actions. But, whether conscious or unconscious, motive distinguishes activities; motive gives activity its specific quality. Some motives exist only in the imagination, but there is no activity without a motive.

2. An integrated activity can be viewed as series of separate actions; each action is performed to achieve an intermediate result. The motive tells us why the activity is being performed and what need impels the activity. A goal tells us what endpoint the individual is trying to reach through his actions. For example, if a person's motive for a travelling activity is to satisfy a need to see new places and meet new people, his goal would be to plan and embark on an appropriate vacation trip. But motives are not always conscious. A person may believe he is going to an art exhibition to satisfy an aesthetic motive, but his true motive may not be an aesthetic one. It may be a desire to meet someone at the exhibition or to appear knowledgeable when the exhibition is discussed at a future social gathering. But in each case, he will engage in similar actions, such as travelling to the exhibition, buying a ticket, and so on.

However, a motive is not necessarily singular. Usually an activity is poly-motivated, or, in the case of a hierarchical organization of motives, a single main motive, which can be divided into components, gives the whole activity its meaning. In addition, the same motive might be satisfied through a variety of actions. An aesthetic motive might be satisfied by going to an art exhibition, buying a work of art, or even commissioning an artist to produce a painting. The ticket to the exhibition could be bought, stolen, or even falsified. But the character of a motive places limitations on the choice of goals, restricting the choice to goals that do not contradict the true motive underlying activity. If our motive for giving money to charity is to help other people, we would rarely feel satisfied if we obtained the money by stealing it from a poor person. The process of creating goals from motive does not happen automatically. It is a very complex process that depends on the level of knowledge and the abilities of an individual, his peculiarities, the objective conditions of activity, and so on.

3. The structure of an action is defined by the conditions necessary for its performance. For example, satisfying a need for food requires the action of going to a restaurant or grocery store. There are a number of possible means of performing this action such as walking, taking a bus or a boat, driving a car, etc. The motive limits the choice of goals, and the goals and concrete conditions limit the choice of actions.

When actions are automatized and no longer consciously controlled, they are called operations. Operations provide means of completing already mastered actions. For example, when an adult is learning a foreign language, pronouncing a sound in the language becomes a separate action and serves a particular goal such as pronouncing an "n" in French. But immediately after mastering the sound, the action loses the aspect of conscious control and becomes an unconscious operation, serving the production of words and sentences in the foreign language. At this point, the grammatical content of speech is controlled at the conscious level and the sound content is controlled unconsciously. But such an operation could once again become an action that is under conscious control, especially if pronunciation is poor and needs correction.

Just as actions and operations can be transformed by the need for conscious control, the motive underlying an activity can be lost, turning the activity into an action. The reverse is also true – actions can acquire independent motives and become activities. For example, a person may perform the action of taking pictures to serve the motive of having photographic memories of a summer vacation. But should the person develop an interest in photography itself, the process of taking pictures acquires an independent motive and becomes an artistic activity. An example of losing an independent motive can occur during the activity of speaking in a foreign language. Initially, while we are learning, speaking French correctly is a motive in itself. Later, after we have gained some mastery of the language, we are no longer motivated by the goal of speaking correctly; the goal becomes one of using French, say, to communicate with foreign business associates, and the process of speaking the language becomes an action subordinated to a new motive. This phenomenon is called "displacement of a motive to a goal." These transformations are not exceptions. Rather, they create the life dynamics of activity and serve to enrich activity and its development. New motives, goals, tasks, and needs constantly appear inside activity as we learn and internalize new information.

One of the most important ideas in the psychological theory of activity is the common structure of external and internal activity. The notion of a common structure follows from the concept that internal, psychic activity originates from external, material activity. This notion of internalization of external forms of activity is presented in its most complete form in "the theory of directed formation of mental actions and concepts" (Gal'perin, 1965). The theory states that external action, in becoming mental action, goes through a number of stages, and at each of these stages gains new characteristics. As we noted earlier, external material action initially requires the participation of other people (parents and teachers) to provide examples of the action, be involved in its shared performance, and provide standards and ensure that it is performed correctly. But, in becoming mental action, the function of control is internalized and the individual begins to pay attention to and correct his own performance.

While most of the discussion up to this point has focused on external, material activity, it is important to note that there are no purely external or internal activities. Any external activity necessarily includes some internal involvement; for example, in formulating a plan of action. The reverse is also true; internal, mental activity (e.g., development of a scientific theory) at some point includes outside action. Furthermore, internal activity, like external activity, includes motives, goals, actions, and operations. The common structure of internal and external activities provides an opportunity for their interaction.

Furthermore, internal psychic activity has the same mediated, instrumental character as external activity. Here, too, systems of signs, primarily language, act as instruments that are not invented by the individual but which he must master. Signs have a historical–cultural nature and can be transmitted to another person only during shared, initially external, activity. We internalize language skills by listening to others talk and conversing with them. As a result of these interactions with others and our internalization of the knowledge gained during social interactions, a special form of psychic reflection, consciousness, evolves that cannot be reduced to a sequence of internal actions. It is interesting to note that in Russian *consciousness* also means shared knowledge. Consciousness is irreducible to a sequence of internal actions because in internal and external activities there is the simultaneous existence of two modes of observation: one that attends to the order, the sequence of actions, and another that simultaneously reflects on the "whole picture," including initial conditions, the movement of activity, and expected results. This latter aspect of consciousness is an image and it provides any activity with an integrated quality. In the next section we will discuss the concept of image of the world in more detail and describe its three components, each of which is related to a specific aspect of consciousness.

Activity and consciousness

Consciousness, as it arises in an individual, is an image of the world containing an image of the individual himself. This image is the point of origin of any activity because an activity is directed by a conscious image of an expected result. As the results of activity are incorporated into the image, the image changes. According to Leont'ev (see Smirnov, 1983), three strata or components of the image of the world are present in consciousness.

The first component of the image of the world, and its most basic level, is the sensory essence of consciousness, which includes the impressions experienced through each of the senses. Sensory essence is not usually received by an individual in pure form. Although it may appear to an individual that he is seeing or hearing "what is really there," through special efforts or special conditions (e.g., experimental conditions where visual perception is inverted through use of special lenses) it is possible to separate and distinguish the sensory information that is received by each of the senses from the object in which it is contained. In consciousness, sensory essence serves to supplement the sense of reality of reflected objects and the image of the world. The role of sensory essence in supplementing reality becomes particularly evident when one of the sense systems is destroyed.

The second component of the image of the world is meanings. Because meanings are not perceived by the senses but develop in social interaction, destruction of entire sensory systems does not destroy consciousness and does not stand in the way of its development. But consciousness and its development can be affected by circumstances that destroy the system of meanings through lack of social interaction, such as when a life is spent in isolation. This is because language is the primary conduit of culture and because the ways of dealing with reality are socially developed and reside in the system of meanings. While meanings exist in culture and in language, during the process of mastery by an individual meanings also become units of individual consciousness. Once meanings are internalized they do not require the reinstantiation of earlier, external forms of activity.

The third component of consciousness is personal sense. The interpretation of an event, a phenomenon, or a concept by an individual may not be identical to its objective content and/or the social meaning. Human beings do not simply learn uniform ways and means of activity. For the individual, activity is a means of achieving self-realization and satisfying the individual's particular needs. It follows that, because motives will vary from person to person, so will personal attitudes toward mastering operations and performing actions. Operations and actions are experienced in relation to interests, desires, and emotions. Therefore, personal sense of events may differ not only from individual to individual, but also from the objective meaning, although the individual may fully understand the objective meaning of the situation.

Leont'ev (1975, 1981) notes that, under certain circumstances, the lack of correspondence may make personal sense and objective meaning quite alien to each other. For example, the objective meaning of an event such as the destruction of many windows of a city as a result of a powerful explosion is clear to all the citizens of the city. But the subjective experience of this event may be different for the glass-cutters of the city, who stand to make a great deal of money from this event. Still a different meaning will be experienced by individuals who are forced to spend large sums of money replacing windows in the damaged buildings. Similarly, a biologist may be fully aware of the objective meaning of death, but death acquires a different personal sense and emotional coloring when the biologist learns about the death of a family member or of his own imminent death as a result of terminal illness.

Personal senses provide human consciousness with its emotional nature. The system of personal senses always changes and develops, as interests and desires change and as life experience adds to the content of the image of the world. However, a personal sense does not have an independent existence. It can be transmitted from one person to another only through symbol systems that are somewhat removed from an event as experienced by the individual. One purpose of the arts is the communication of personal sense, whereas the main purpose of science is to produce "pure" objective meanings. However, because the "objective meanings" produced by science live in individual consciousness, they inevitably include some expression of the personal sense of the scientist. Although the ideal in modern society requires the "cleansing" of personal senses from objective meanings, it is a task that is probably impossible (Polanyi, 1962), given the nature of consciousness.

Activity not only influences the content of individual consciousness; it has an equally profound influence on the expression of individual consciousness, that is, on personality. The following section describes the role of activity in personality.

Activity and personality

Personality is the most complete expression of subjective activity. Personality is born in activity and in the interpersonal sphere. It cannot be equated with individual traits. Rather, personality is a social quality. Hence, individual traits and genotype are not the basis of personality but its prerequisites. Simply knowing that an individual possesses certain traits does not predict the effect the trait will have on his personality. Leont'ev (1975) notes that "the same traits of a man may have different relations to his personality. In one case they are indifferent, in another the same traits may characterize his personality essentially" (p. 165). For example, a physically strong child may become used to solving problems by using his strength and will develop this physical quality to the detriment of his intellectual and emotional development. The emphasized trait, physical strength, will become essential in the structure of his personality and in his way of relating to other people. However, it is also possible that the same quality will remain in the background, exerting little influence on the development of personality. The same can be said of the range of possible qualities, including beauty or ugliness, traits of temperament, artistic talent, and even intelligence. External living conditions such as economic or education levels also do not directly determine the development of personality. All of these parameters can influence personality only indirectly, by limiting and narrowing the field of individual potential. In other words, to understand an individual's personality we need to know which traits are emphasized and how they are used in activity, particularly activity in the social domain.

Specifically, the activity-oriented approach argues against the notion that personality is the combined result of two factors, biological traits (genotype) and social traits. Rather, the influence of both of these factors is seen as mediated by the individual's choice of activity. Unlike the individual himself, personality does not exist prior to activity, it creates itself in activity. It is the resolution of contradictions and conflicts, encountered in activity, that creates personality. Furthermore, the development of personality does not take place in a uniform forward motion; there are critical periods and turning points when the experience of activity determines whether additional positive development and integrity will occur or whether personality will be degraded and disintegrate.

According to the theory of activity, three general parameters affecting integrity and change in personality can be identified: the breadth of the individual's connections with the world, the hierarchy of these connections, and their general structure.

The nucleus of personality is the totality of "activity attitudes" toward the world. As was noted earlier, the main characteristic of activity is its motive and the basis of personality is the individual's hierarchy of motives, particularly social motives. The first "kernels" of personality are formed in activity in the social domain because personality is socially constructed. Although all motives are initially individual, some individual motives become subordinated to social motives. The individual, to a greater or lesser degree, incorporates other people into his motive hierarchy. The incorporation of others into the motive hierarchy is the first turning point in the development of personality. The second turning point is the moment when self-consciousness appears and the individual begins "creating himself" consciously and purposefully. Here the individual develops selective attitudes toward past experiences, actively neglecting others, giving still others a higher value, and leaving some in a neutral position. This process allows a person to take control of his own development and "be born" as a personality of his own construction.

Activity, cognitive processes, and the image of the world

While the senses, from which the sensory essence of consciousness is derived, have a reflexive nature and react to stimuli, perception and thinking are active and characterized by the processes of activity, including motives, goals, actions, and operations. This means that for an image or concept to appear requires active processing or activity-like relationships between the person and the object of cognition. Therefore, as in any activity, cognitive processes have their own motivation and particularities of goal construction, and their own set of operations (for a more detailed discussion, see Tikhomirov, 1969). In thinking, for example, these operations are analysis and synthesis, generalization and abstraction, operations of logical conclusions, mathematical operations, and so on. All of these operations result from the internalization of external, practical, material actions such as learning language, and mastering actions with objects and cultural norms. Because this learning is accomplished under the guidance of others and according to standards set by others, the results of social–historical practice are incorporated into an individual's thinking. Thinking goes through developmental stages analogous to Piaget's stages of intellectual development: sensorimotor, image oriented, and conceptual (verbal).

The nature of knowledge in the theory of activity can be summarized as follows:

1. Knowledge is a product of activity, the result of the movement of activity from the objective, external to the subjective, internal realm. Through this movement, the mental image of an object incorporates knowledge gained from the external world.
2. Because there is a range of information that can be obtained from any object, the process of gaining knowledge is determined by the character of an activity with an object, not by the object itself. The parameters of an activity may be set in advance by providing the activity with a particular organization and means, and by creating adequate motivation (Gal'perin, 1965; Talyzina, 1975). This, of course, is the objective in school settings, where lessons are designed so children will learn particular skills from their activities.
3. In the process of activity, an image of the activity is created, and the general ability to reflect on reality and draw knowledge from it is developed. Sensory standards and socially developed normative actions, in particular, develop in activity and later mediate the process of cognition.
4. Because activity is a process and has a temporal organization and a successive structure, the image of the activity provides the activity with continuity, integrity, and unity as it unfolds in time. More simply, the image allows the individual to monitor what knowledge has been gained and what is still missing, what actions have been completed and what still remains to be done, what knowledge will be

necessary to complete the activity, and so on. Without an image, activity would be fragmented and successful completion would be impossible. Hence, action and image are two different aspects of cognitive functioning that are not qualitatively reducible to each other. Rather, they are connected and their connection develops in activity, with each altering and adjusting according to movement in the other as activity progresses.

5. It was noted earlier that personality reaches a turning point and is altered when the individual develops self-consciousness, that is, when the individual becomes aware of himself and his own activity. Similarly, when the psyche reaches a point of sufficient development, self-knowledge becomes an object in activity, leading to a reorganization of cognitive processes.

Because cognition, particularly thinking, is a special form of human activity and has all the attributes of any activity, cognitive activity, like activity in general, is regulated by an image of expected results. But here is an apparent paradox: The image we want to obtain through cognition must exist, in some form, at the outset of cognitive activity. But the paradox can be resolved by developing some of Leont'ev's ideas on the "image of the world."

By itself the concept of the "image of the world" is not new. Variations of this concept have been presented in earlier psychological theories, although usually referred to by different terms including "picture of the world," "model of the universe," and "representation of the self and the universe" (English & English, 1958; Neisser, 1967). In these alternative interpretations, the image of the world is a combination of separate images, representing separate objects and concepts, that take primacy over the total picture. However, there is substantial evidence that the cognitive sphere of personality develops as a unit, and it is the notion of unity that distinguishes the present conceptualizations of image of the world from alternative conceptions.

In the present approach, the image of the world is a unitary mental image an individual holds of his environment and the nature of that environment. It includes an image of the individual himself, his abilities, traits, behavior, and place in the world.

But the image of the world is not static, it is continually revised, modified, "fine-tuned," and corrected through a combination of two interrelated processes. One process is from "object to subject," that is, from external stimuli to the internal image of the world. As stimuli are encountered and perceived they are assimilated into the existing image of the world. But it is important to note that the new stimuli do not lead to new, single-element images that are separate from the existing image of the world or that simply became attached to it. Rather, the result of any cognitive process is the modification and enrichment of the existing image of the world. Any particular images of objects or situations are simply elements in the overall image of the world, not independent entities. For example, a person encountering a Venus's-flytrap plant for the first time would not simply develop a separate mental image of a unique carnivorous plant. Rather, his view of plants in general and probably his beliefs about what distinguishes plants from animals will likely be altered by this carnivorous plant.

Of course, the individual may begin to search for other varieties of plants that are carnivorous, view new plants he encounters as possibly carnivorous, or even try to recategorize the features of plants and animals according to criteria that can accommodate the Venus's-flytrap. This example leads us to the second process that contributes to modification of the image of the world, that of movement from subject to object, or from the individual's image of the world to the external environment.

This process is a form of hypothesis formation and testing. The individual constantly tests the adequacy and accuracy of his image of the world by formulating hypotheses and attempting to confirm or disconfirm them, although not always on a conscious level. The hypothesis-making process is a necessary condition for the integration of new information into the existing image of the world. Hypotheses turn "raw" sensory data into material from which the image of the world is constructed, modified, altered, and confirmed. The hypothesis-making process is also a precondition for experiencing outside stimuli. If a person is taking a walk through the woods and, out of the corner of his eye, catches sight of a long cylindrical object, he will feel calm or fearful depending on whether his hypothesis is that the object is a snake or a tree branch. The hypothesis-making process has a spontaneous character, providing the image of the world with constant confirmation or the possibility of adjustment depending on the adequacy of the initial image. The process ceases to operate only if the individual becomes unconscious.

As noted in the previous section, there are three levels or strata of consciousness, and the hypothesis-making and testing process varies in difficulty and complexity depending on what level of consciousness is involved. Hypotheses at the level of sensory essence are generally simple and relatively easy to confirm or disconfirm. Hypotheses at the sensory level are also easy for the image of the world to assimilate; for example, the expectation that a substance that looks like chocolate will taste sweet. But, at the level of meanings and/or personal senses, hypotheses tend to be more complex and their disconfirmation can have profound implications for the image of the world. If an individual's image of the world includes the belief that graduating from college will lead to a good job and a satisfying life, his image of the world will be seriously challenged should he find himself chronically unemployed and dissatisfied after graduating from college.

The most important characteristic of the image of the world, incorporating both processes, is its social and activity-born nature. But the relation of the image of the world to activity is a reciprocal one. In a functional sense, the image of the world is the beginning of activity. The formation of motives and goals, which is a necessary component of activity, is impossible without the orientation that comes from a plan that consists of images. But once initiated, activity continually exerts an influence back on the image of the world, enriching and modifying it.

This reciprocal influence also has implications for childhood development. The formation of the initial forms of the image of the world, in a child's development, is also connected with activity. While the image of the world is constructed throughout the lifespan, the beginning of its formation may be connected to the inhibition of the innate and automatic responses that are evident only in the first minutes, hours, and days of a child's life. The child's first actions are a synergistic union of motor, sensory, and affective components, and the image of the world, activity, and personality begin to develop in these initial actions.

The first form of the subject-to-object or hypothesis-making process is evident in motor activity. Later, impressions from external stimuli will be added to the child's initial image of the world, continually building and modifying it. More specifically, through a child's actions there is a meeting of the two processes discussed earlier, the subject-to-world process, consisting of imitation of actions and the world-to-subject process, consisting of sensory impressions from external stimuli. The combination of both of these processes is responsible for the child's first images. The initial images come not from external stimulation, as a mechanistic approach would maintain, nor are they innate. Rather, they result from the child's activity as a whole.

Generally, the initial activity is socially based; specifically, it is the shared activity of a child and mother, operating through the world-to-subject process. A child touches and senses objects with the aid of the mother's hands and masters space with the aid of the mother's legs. It is only when the child's ability to reflect on reality, developed in this shared activity, reaches a certain level that a child starts to identify and use the same reference points that originally directed the child's and mother's shared activity. But, independence develops only because the child begins actively to search for reference points through the hypothesis-making process with its role in confirming and disconfirming the adequacy of the child's image of the world.

Therefore, because of the social nature of human activity, other people (starting with the mother), have a special role in the formation of the individual's activity, his image of the world, and his personality. However, the social aspect of activity and the development of the image of the world are not limited to aiding the individual in his physical movements. Perhaps more importantly, the initial image of others influences the role they will play in the developing of the image of the world. For example, should an individual experience a great deal of rejection early in development and include an image of others as rejecting in his image of the world, he may go through life seeking to confirm his hypothesis that others will reject him.

As we have seen, the image of the world is conceived and developed in the process of mastering activity and social communication. But once developed, the image of the world allows an individual to discern and evaluate qualities of objects that would be impossible to separate through simple sensory interaction. These qualities form two distinct classes, utilizing two forms of subject–object interaction.

First are those qualities that are discernible by interacting with other objects, termed Subject–Object–Object interaction. For example, one can judge the relative weights of two objects and determine that one is heavy and the other light, by comparing those objects or by comparing one object to an image of a second object that is part of the image of the world. Such judgments of relative qualities would not be possible without stored images.

The second class includes the qualities and objects of consciousness that appear in interactions with other people, such as values, morals, intelligence, creativity, and other "nonphysical" qualities. These qualities become apparent only in shared activity. This type of interaction is called Subject–Object–Subject interaction. Knowledge and beliefs about this type of quality are more essential and more persistent once integrated into the image of the world than are qualities discovered in Subject–Object interaction.

These most essential and "deepest" of the world's characteristics form the nuclear structure of the image of the world. This level of symbolic sign representation of the world forms in individual subjectivity from socially developed meanings contained in languages, cultures, standards, and norms of human activity.

As part of the cognitive sphere of personality, the image of the world has a uniquely individual or idiosyncratic character and is closely connected with the emotional–motivational sphere. This is because emotional regulation is involved in the substance of any cognitive event. In addition, as a reflection of the future, a system of prognoses and hypotheses, the image of the world has a selective character. This selectivity appears primarily in the content of personally significant and important events that are connected to an individual's needs and activity. Activity is most intensely directed toward those objects that will satisfy needs, whether they are interpersonal needs, biological needs, or needs for knowledge, etc. However, in order to identify an object or event as significant and something toward which activity should be directed, some kind of "preknowledge" is necessary. One of the functions of this preknowledge is the selection of a direction for cognitive activity because, in order to learn something we have to imagine, in advance, that this knowledge will be useful to us, that it will aid us in satisfying some need. In other words, we don't simply act or learn; we choose where to act or what to learn, where to direct our mental energies. This mechanism is at work in practical activities and in activities that are not usually classified as practical. For example, when psychologists decide to address a particular question through research, they do so with some anticipation that they will successfully answer the question. Anticipation of success or failure constitutes emotional preknowledge and is one intersection of knowledge and emotion. As noted earlier, in order to experience an emotion we must already possess some knowledge, at least enough knowledge to construct a hypothesis. Piaget made a similar point, stating that the existence of any feeling is impossible without a certain level of understanding and distinction. But before attempting to gain knowledge of some subject, that subject must be identified as something that will serve our cognitions.

It follows that both our personal sense, including emotions, and the objective meaning of an object are part of the image of the world and direct our activity. In addition, because of their role in directing activity, personal sense and objective meaning are seen as preceding stimulation, not as simply extracted from external stimuli.

Furthermore, if the image of the world constantly generates hypotheses directed toward the world, then any cognitive activity, even the most elementary, begins with an initiative from the individual and ends in a subjective image. That is, the first step in cognitive activity has an internal source. Similarly, Leont'ev (1975) has stated that the inner acts through the outer and in the process the inner changes itself. Translated into symbolic language, cognitive activity would not be symbolized as Stimulus–Image–Reaction. Rather, the two types of cognitive activity follow two different patterns. When there is a discrepancy between predicted and actual stimuli that requires adjustment, cognitive activity follows a scheme symbolized as Image–Stimulus–Reaction–Image–Stimulus–Reaction, etc. But when cognitive activity is directed toward "trying things out in the world," to determine the results of action, it can be symbolized as Image–Action–Stimulation modified by Action–Image–Action–Stimulation modified by Action, etc.

In the next section we will discuss the role of activity, and particularly the image of the world, in interaction of intelligence and personality.

Theoretical analysis of intelligence and personality

A variety of definitions of intelligence have been proposed, including defining intelligence as the totality of all cognitive functioning, as an ability to adapt to new situations, and as thinking. In the present analysis intelligence will be defined as thinking, and it appears that all types of cognitive processes, including thinking, have some degree of personality inherent in them.

Therefore, when discussing intelligence, we must appeal to personality to explain its functioning. It is impossible to separate performance on intellectual tasks from personality. Under different circumstances varying degrees of separation are possible, but the connection between intellectual activity and personality is always there to some degree.

The connection between intelligence and personality is a "two-way street." It appears that intelligence depends on the need–motivational sphere of personality to an even greater degree than personality depends on intelligence. Specifically, personality determines the individual's choice of both an object of cognitive activity (e.g., artistic or scientific pursuits) and the type of cognition he will use (e.g., analytical or creative thinking). Intelligence also influences personality, by widening or narrowing the field of options available to an individual and by providing him with the means to move along his chosen path. Personality without intelligence is blind; intelligence without personality is a warehouse of unused instruments. Of course, intelligence and personality are never totally separate in real-world functioning, that is, there are no purely intellectual tasks and no individual needs that do not involve some cognitive activity. Any actual activity is always a function of some combination of both intelligence and personality.

In addition, different types of knowledge exert different influences on the formation of personality. Of particular significance is knowledge about other people and about the self, that is, the ability to understand others and to reflect on one's own feelings and behavior. These particular aspects of human understanding appear to require a different type of intelligence than that needed to understand the physical world. Also, as noted earlier in the discussion of activity and personality, the same individual traits may exert different influences on personality depending on an individual's attitudes towards the trait. The same point applies to intelligence. One person may devalue his intelligence and do little to develop or utilize it. But another person may place great importance on developing his intelligence and turn it into a central trait. He may engage in primarily intellectual pursuits, at the expense of physical and social skills, judge others mainly in terms of their intelligence, and so on. For the first individual, intelligence will play a relatively minor role in his personality structure and his image of the world, but for the latter individual, intelligence will be the primary component of both constructs.

Beyond this general approach, a framework for understanding the relation of personality and intelligence depends primarily on our understanding of the process of cognition itself. If cognition is viewed as a passive, reflective process, then personality becomes a simple mediating factor, a condition that is necessarily secondary to, and outside of, cognition itself. But, if cognition is viewed as it is in the theory of activity, with the image of the world acting as a primary cognitive structure, it becomes an active creator of an individual's view of reality. A main function of cognition in this latter approach is hypothesis-making or projecting the results of cognitive action. Viewed this way, personal characteristics, motives, values, attitudes, and even moral qualities, have a crucial influence on the process of cognition itself and on its results. In the following pages we will examine in more detail, some of the mechanisms and channels of this influence, using the main concepts of the activity approach as discussed earlier.

You will recall that the triad activity–action–operation represents the theoretical separation of the unified stream of activity into its major components. These components and their relations to activity are displayed in Figure 8.1. Motives, goals, and conditions of activity are the major determinants of the quality of activity as a whole, its separate actions, and its operational contents. Personal sense, objective meaning, and sensual essence are components of consciousness that regulate the direction and movement of activity, each on the basis of its own form of knowledge and approach to cognition (for details see Stetsenko, 1983).

The personal sense is an individual's system of values and personal attitudes toward objects of cognition and including the self, other people, and the world. This level is experienced as emotional stages and feelings. The innermost circle of Figure 8.1 is the personal-sense level of the image of the world, associated with the greatest degree of subjectivity and it is the most unique, individual, and inimitable in content. Hence, this level can also be considered the personality level of the image of the world.

In contrast, meanings provide more objective knowledge, which is comparatively free of subjective, immediate impressions. This kind of knowledge can be called "cold" knowledge to distinguish it from the emotional or "hot" knowledge that is contained in the personal sense. It includes cultural knowledge, knowledge of the physical world, knowledge of symbol systems such as language, and so on. The

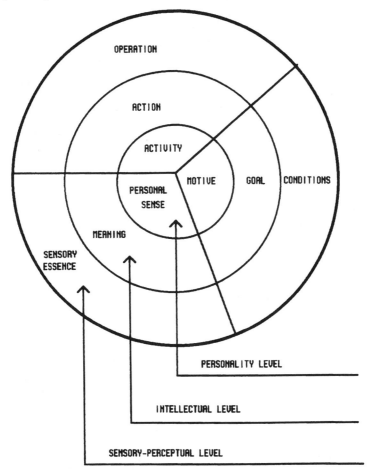

Figure 8.1. The relation of components of activity and structures of the image of the world.

second level of Figure 8.1 represents the level of cultural and objective meanings and knowledge. Here, goal-directed actions are the primary component of activity. This level is sometimes referred to as the intellectual level of the image of the world, because at this level we "think rather more than we feel." The subjective impressions that accompany meanings are sometimes called intellectual emotions, to separate them from emotions at the level of personal sense. In everyday terms we distinguish between the personality and intellectual levels when we say about a particular incident, "I can understand it intellectually, but emotionally it still upsets me."

Finally, sensory essence of consciousness is the totality of sensory information through all modalities and provides the subject with information from the physical environment. The outermost circle of Figure 8.1 represents the sensory–perceptual level of consciousness which is the site of sensory essence. Operations or automatized, unconsciously controlled actions are associated with this level of consciousness. The sensory essence of consciousness is accompanied by its own type of emotion. According to Wilhelm Wundt, any sensory experience is accompanied by a "simple feeling" that can be located as a point in three-dimensional space, the axes of which are pleasant–unpleasant, excitation–calm, and tension–relaxation. Therefore, it appears that each component of consciousness has its own relation to activity and to emotion, and emotion is one of the channels of communication and connection between the components. However, the degree of emotional expression and the role of emotion are different in personal senses, meanings, and sensory essence of consciousness.

You will recall that the image of the world is the initial point and the result of any cognitive action, and that the image of the world itself is a multilevel system that constantly generates hypotheses. These levels differ in the languages they use to formulate hypotheses. Specifically, hypotheses are formulated in the language of personal senses at the inner level, in the language of meanings or object hypotheses (Gregory, 1970) at the middle level, and in the language or sensory impressions at the outer level. Of course, dividing the image of the world into different levels is a tool for scientific analysis; it is experienced as a coherent unit by the individual. Furthermore, interlevel movement takes place constantly, but is experienced most acutely when there is a discrepancy between a predicted result and the actual stimuli received by the "sensory entrance" to the system. Such a discrepancy has to reach a threshold to be detected by the individual, and differences in the threshold is a point of individual variation. But generally, the more likely the hypothesis is, the higher is the threshold. Rarely would an individual test a hypothesis that has a probability close to 1, and rejecting this hypothesis requires a very strong perceived discrepancy. This is the reason for many of the mistakes that are made in perception and thinking.

Clearly there are differences and similarities at the personality, intellectual, and sensory levels of the image of the world. Next we will try to analyze, step-by-step, the specificity of personality and intelligence in the image of the world.

One difference in intelligence and personality, mentioned earlier, is that the levels of the image of the world differ in the "languages" in which hypotheses are formulated and tested. At the personality level all "conversations" are in terms of personal senses and individual feelings. The intellectual level uses a language of relatively objective knowledge and meanings, and at the sensory level the language is one of sensory essence or impressions.

The components of the image of the world, constructed from hypotheses, also differ in the following ways:

1. By degree of subjectivity, which is higher at deeper levels. That is, at the personality level the image of the world is more subjective than it is at the intellectual level, and the intellectual level is more subjective than the sensory level. At deeper levels, assimilation predominates accommodation, in Piaget's (1969) terms. Put in different terms, at the personality level, the overall image of the world determines the nature of specific images subsequently incorporated into it (Smirnov, 1983).
2. By the degree of rigidity/flexibility. Deeper structures are more conservative and change in them takes more time and requires more frequent and stronger dis-

crepancies between predicted and real results. Change is most difficult at the personality level of the image of the world. For example, if someone's closest friend dies, his connections with the friend are immediately changed at the intellectual level of the image of the world. But the process of altering connections at the personality level of the image of the world can take years. Although the person intellectually knows that his friend is gone, he doesn't feel it yet, and may find himself expecting to see the friend at places they both frequented, or thinking about a gift to buy for his friend's birthday. Even though at the intellectual level he knows there is no possibility of seeing his friend, hypotheses involving the friend continue to occur at the personal level for quite some time.

3. By the frequency of hypothesis-testing and the criteria for identifying discrepancies between hypotheses and reality. At the sensory level of the image of the world, the hypothesis-testing process is constant and virtually any discrepancy is sufficient to initiate change in the original hypothesis. For example, the hypothesis that a cloud of steam will feel hot is relatively easy to change if we touch it and find it is cold vapor. Hypotheses involving meanings and personal sense are tested much less frequently, and their modification has more serious implications for the image of the world as a whole. It is rare for a discrepancy at one of these levels to result in a change in only one hypothesis. More often a discrepancy requires rebuilding the whole system, or at least a subsystem, or hypotheses as well as their connections to the initial hypothesis. Hypotheses at deeper levels have more connections to other hypotheses, and more tests are necessary to prove or disprove them. The deepest hypotheses (e.g., a hypothesis about the meaning of life) may be tested and modified throughout the lifespan.

4. By the types of objects and events about which hypotheses are formulated. At the personal level hypotheses tend to be about a person himself and significant others; for example, "what I am feeling is love." Objects of material and ideal knowledge are the focus of hypotheses at the intellectual level; for example, a hypothesis that a particular formula can be used to solve a math problem. At the sensory level, hypotheses are about sensory impressions. Of course, some hypotheses involve an interaction of levels, like a teenage girl's hypothesis that a boy she has a "crush" on likes her too because he smiles at her often.

5. By the type of regulators. Personal senses are regulated by feelings, meanings are regulated by thoughts, and sensory essence is regulated by sensations or "simple feelings" (in Wundt's terms).

6. By their uniqueness and idiosyncrasy. The deeper levels of the image of the world, particularly the personality level, are more subjective in content and have a greater degree of individual variation than do surface levels. Sensory essence, the most surface level, regulates the individual's direct experience of the external environment, and here there is considerably less individual variation.

7. By the degree to which the component is dominated by axiomatic values. The personality level of the image of the world is connected to an individual's hierarchy of values and preferences. The intellectual level is associated primarily with means and tools, and at the sensory level the function is simply receiving and processing incoming stimuli. But it is interpreted by the personality level. For example, the sensory level perceives variations in skin color as just that: darker or lighter coloring. The intellectual level "knows" that each of these colors identifies a different racial group. But the personality level provides individual reactions and attitudes toward color and racial group whether they be tolerant, accepting, or prejudiced. The values attached to color by the personality level are far from the objective color information at the sensory level.

But the main characteristic of the personality level of the image of the world is that this level is the starting point of the hypothesis-making process. It is the emotional source of the hypothesis-making process, because the personality level gives rise to "gut feelings" and intuitions that serve as preknowledge.

The implications of these gut feelings or intuitions can be illustrated by a metaphor. Intelligence is like a flashlight that illuminates various parts of reality, clarifying those areas it shines on and allowing the individual to gain knowledge from them. But the choice of an area to illuminate is made by personality on the basis of gut feelings, from the personal sense component of the image of the world. (Possible sources of such preknowledge were described earlier in this chapter.) Put in its simplest terms, before we direct our intelligence to a particular place to look for knowledge or a solution, we must have some sense of where to direct the search. The role of anticipation in decision-making is played by emotions at the personality level of the image of the world.

The major conclusion that can be drawn from the foregoing discussion is that the quality of knowledge obtained by intelligence and the process of cognition itself depends on the initial hypothesis of expected results. Such hypotheses are the starting point of cognition, and are generated continuously at the personality level of the image of the world. Once generated, hypotheses are tested by determining if they match concrete results at the intellectual and sensory levels.

But the levels of consciousness do not necessarily develop in the same direction, producing discrepancies in functioning across the levels. For example, the intellectual level may be highly developed but the individual may be unmotivated at the personality level. Such an individual would be very intelligent but unable to choose a proper avenue for his intelligence. Therefore, the ability to use intelligence effectively depends on personality.

Similarly, personality depends on the level of development of intellectual and sensorimotor abilities. Some aspects of the individual's interpersonal relationships (e.g., interpersonal perception, ability to evaluate the behavior of others, causal attribution) and relationships mediated by objects (e.g., using tools in shared activity) are influenced by levels of cognitive and sensorimotor development.

But regardless of the quality of development, the relation of levels of image of the world and the dominance of each component do not remain stable throughout the lifespan. Vygotsky (1956) made this point in his theory of the development of higher mental functions. According to that theory, the early period of development is dominated by sensorimotor processes, the following period by intelligence, and for the remainder of a person's life personality is the dominant component. At each stage in child development, cognition is a function of all three components, but the relative weight of each and their contribution to cognition varies.

There are clear-cut cases that illustrate the interrelations and influences of personality and intelligence. Vygotsky's analysis of the causes of mental retardation in children suggested retardation is not simply a defect of intelligence. According to Vygotsky, retardation is a function of deficiencies in the motivational–emotional sphere, specifically the destruction of connections between intelligence and emotion.

Autism is an extreme example of mental retardation related to lack of emotionality. In addition, autism is an example of the dependence of intellectual development on the emotional content and frequency of child–adult and child–child interactions.

A second example of the connection between cognitive abilities and personal characteristics is found in studies of creative personality. Research in this area indicates that training exerts a direct influence on an individual's personal confidence in solving creative tasks and that this relation influences success in such tasks. This suggests that creativity is influenced by a combination of personality and intelligence. In addition, the evidence is consistent with the theory of different levels in the image of the world. The major characteristics of creativity are the flexibility, originality, and details of hypotheses. Remember that images grow from deeper to more surface levels. Specifically, the process of creativity starts at the personality level, which determines the focus and content of hypotheses. These hypotheses are then concretized at the intellectual and sensorimotor levels.

Similarly, the role of concrete combinations of personality and intelligence in directing cognitive abilities has been demonstrated in research on roles and division of labor in scientific collectives (see *Problemy Rukovodstva Nauchnym Kolletivom,* 1982). The results of this research suggest that personality and intellectual qualities are equally important in characterizing and differentiating "idea-producers," critics, executives, organizers, experts, and so on.

Studies on cognitive, intellectual, or thinking styles, often view personality as a regulatory factor in cognition (see, for example, Sternberg's chapter in this volume) and have contributed to the understanding of the influence of personality traits on cognitive activity. The influence of personality traits (e.g., motivation, anxiety, risk-taking, introversion–extraversion, conformism, etc.) on intellectual achievement has been studied from a wide range of psychological perspectives, including the theory of activity.

The next and final section of this chapter is designed to acquaint the reader with some of the experimental work on intelligence and personality within the framework of the theory of activity.

Personality and intelligence: a brief overview of experimental studies in the theory of activity

A little more than ten years ago, Tikhomirov and his colleagues Kornilova, Vasil'ev, Berezanskaya, and particularly Telegina outlined particularly important future directions for the study of the role of personality in the process of thinking using the framework of the theory of activity (*Psikhologicheskie Issledovaniya Intellectual'noi Deyatel'nosti,* 1979). They suggested the following issues as particularly deserving of attention:

1. The interaction of specific personality characteristics and particular aspects of thinking;

2. The role of personal attitudes in the process of thinking;
3. The emotional components of thinking;
4. Strength and type of motivation as factors in thinking.

Following the suggestion of Tikhomirov et al., the remainder of the chapter will focus on empirical studies addressing some of these issues.

Research on the interaction of personality characteristics, personal attitudes, and thinking

Petraitite (1981) studied the relation of social introversion–extraversion (using an adapted version of the MMPI), perceptual introversion–extraversion (using the Rorshach test), self-confidence, and indicators of creativity to ability to solve open-ended and spatial tasks. The results indicated that there is no simple connection between introversion–extraversion at the social level and at the perceptual level. This suggests that perceptual and social forms of interaction with reality have different bases. If perception is viewed as a substructure of intelligence, then the results also support the independence of different levels of the image of the world. In addition, creativity, extraversion at the social level, and introversion at the perceptual level were positively correlated, lending further support to the notion of separation of the three levels of the image of the world.

Grigorenko (1990) investigated the relation between cognitive style and level of IQ. The results suggest that level of IQ is higher for more reflective and more field-independent types, as measured by Kagan's MFFT (1965) and Witkins's EFT (1972). The degree of dogmatism, measured with a Russian version of Rokeach's questionnaire, was negatively related to subject's level of productivity in the hypothesis-making process. In contrast, sociability was positively related to ability to solve tasks under uncertain conditions. Similarly, the number of trials required to solve a task correlated positively with shyness, conformity, and diffidence. Finally, the originality of hypotheses formulated under uncertain task conditions positively correlated with level of psychoticism and general activity as measured by Yanpolsky's Personality Questionnaire. The author interprets the results as suggesting that personality traits determine the qualitative and quantitative characteristics of the hypothesis-making process, including the production and originality of hypotheses. This interpretation is consistent with the presentation of the hypothesis-making process in the theory of activity.

Ovchinnikova (1980) studied the relation of intelligence and aspects of thinking to values in children. The results indicated that children differ in their approach to cognitive tasks as a function of their value structures. Specifically, when a child's primary values are practical, the child tends to finish a task in the same way he started it. Such children tend to have lower levels of IQ than children who value cognition. They also perform poorly in the analysis of task conditions, primarily because they orient to concrete, practical features of a task, such as shape and color of objects, rather than to more abstract, figurative aspects.

Children who value cognition look for the most interesting ways to solve a task; these children preanalyze tasks before acting, show flexibility and variability in their choice of actions, understand abstract and figurative meanings, and move easily from one level of abstraction to another. They also had the highest IQs of the three groups tested.

Children whose dominant value is communication tend to be skilled at general-situation analysis, but less skilled at specific-task analysis. They easily adjust their strategies in response to the experimenter's feedback. Furthermore, all three types of "intellectual strategies" are evident in different types of activity and appear to be stable. Overall, the study supports the notion that the character of motivation in thinking activity is determined by the child's structure of values and influences the productivity and quality of thinking activity.

Similarly, Sunitova (1986) found a positive correlation between subjects' level of anticipation prior to participating in a task, and personality characteristics involved in activity regulation, specifically independence and flexibility. Again, the results suggest that differences in personal, individual motivation affect the process and results of thinking activity.

But while internal motivation appears to influence thinking activity, external pressure does not have the same effect. That is, personality characteristics and their role in motivation of thinking activity appear to be unaffected by suggestions from an external source. Berezanskaya (in *Iskusstvennyi Intellect i Psikhologiya*, 1976) asked children to construct different shapes from plastic pieces. A profile of each child's preferred shapes was then constructed through the frequency of each type of shape created by each child. Then the children were given a second set of plastic pieces in the same shapes but different colors. The experimenter indirectly suggested that if children constructed the same shapes they preferred earlier, the shapes would look bad because of the color of the pieces. Three groups of children were identified: Children who stopped constructing the bad looking shapes (26%) in response to the experimenter's suggestion, children who displayed a reverse reaction and constructed more of the bad looking shapes (20%), and children who did not alter their preferred pattern (54%). But no direct connection was found between the children's flexibility and their speed of cognitive activity.

Further support for the connection between personal disposition and intellectual regulation was investigated in a study using a computer task (Kornilova & Tikho-mirov, 1990). Two types of computer tasks were used, a computer game and a task in concept formation. The results suggest that state anxiety (measured by a Russian version of Spilberg's questionnaire) correlates with time per trial and time needed to reach a solution. That is, more anxious subjects performed each aspect of the task in a slower and more conscious manner. For such subjects, fewer aspects of the task were automatized operations and more were conscious actions. Trait anxiety (measured by the Russian version of Taylor's questionnaire) was also related to an increase in the time spent solving a problem, but only at the stage preceding the choice of a strategy.

In addition, the tendency to take risks, measured by Azarov's questionnaire, was related to the choice of a more risky strategy in solving the experimental tasks. But the same personality trait appears to make subjects more cautious in choosing a strategy when the subject is aware of his tendency to be impulsive and take risks and tries to control these tendencies. This indicates the necessity of distinguishing personality traits and the way those traits are used in performing intellectual tasks. The typologies commonly developed in personality psychology (e.g., caution–risk, intuition–logic), do not give any indication of how a personality trait will actually be manifested. For example, cognitive risk-taking and pragmatic risk-taking may both influence types of intellectual solutions, but with very different behavioral results. But the difference is not reflected in the general trait termed "risk-taking."

Research on the role of emotion in thinking activity

The theory of activity maintains that emotions influence and direct thinking activity. The studies discussed below support that idea, demonstrating that differences in emotional expression are related to variations in intelligence and thinking.

Kepalaite (1982) found that subjects who experience a greater frequency of negative emotions than positive emotions tend to have a high performance IQ and a relatively low verbal IQ, as measured by the Wechsler scales. In subjects with positive emotions dominant, verbal IQ was either high or low and related to moderate performance IQ. The study further indicated that there is a connection between emotions, IQ, and features of brain anatomy, specifically the location of the speech center. People with positive emotions dominant and high verbal IQ have speech centers located only in the left hemisphere, while people with negative emotions dominant and high performance IQ have speech centers either in the right hemisphere or both hemispheres.

Ol'shannikova and Pacyavichus (1981) obtained similar results in an investigation of the relation of emotions to self-regulation. Their results indicated that a tendency to experience negative emotions is related to high levels of self-regulation of activity, including thoroughness in planning, using information provided, and anticipation of important conditions. But a tendency to experience positive and neutral emotions appears to be unrelated to self-regulation.

Tikhomirov and his collaborators (1969) demonstrated that there is a relation between emotion and ability to solve intellectual tasks. More specifically, emotion, measured by galvanic skin response and simultaneous verbal reports, always follows moments of insight. But when subjects were given instructions that limited emotion, either to "remain composed" or to read instructions in an indifferent, monotone voice, they were unable to solve similar tasks. The results further support the idea that emotional expression is related to solving intellectual tasks. In addition, more complex tasks, requiring more creativity to solve, were related to greater levels of emotional tension.

The search for solutions appears to have two phases. First, there is an attempt to narrow the range for further search, that is, to identify the approximate zone where the solution is likely to be found. This phase is followed by an attempt to find the specific solution. Emotional activation appears to be connected to the first phase, giving the subject an indication of the relative value of each possible direction in further search for a solution. Therefore, emotions appear to act as heuristics by limiting the zone of search and functioning as regulators of thinking activity (Tikhomirov, 1969).

Particularly interesting for the study of emotion and thinking are cases involving extreme emotion and psychopathology. One such example is the tendency to produce empty and wordy statements based on surface analogies. A study conducted by Tepenicinoi (in *Psikhologicheskie Issledovaniya Intellektual'noi Deyatel'nosti,* 1979) showed that such disturbances are specific to a very narrow range of themes and situations that have special emotional significance to the individual. But in experimental situations, this tendency only becomes evident when the experimenter is able to evoke an acute reaction in an individual. This reaction is usually in response to a change in the relationship with the experimenter or another significant person. If the experimenter asks questions that are unrelated to persons or events that are important to the subject, the tendency to produce empty statements may not appear. Even more interesting is the observation that even in mentally healthy people situations that evoke a strong need for self-affirmation or self-defense may produce this phenomenon. The tendency is also common in teenagers because they are not yet intellectually mature and their critical thinking skills are not fully developed although they have strong needs for self-affirmation.

Research on strength and type of motivation in thinking activity

Another major direction of research into personality and intelligence in the framework of the theory of activity is the study of the motivation of intellectual activity. According to the theory, a motive provides activity with both meaning and stimulation. Hence, the quality of motivation is critical in determining both content and dynamics in the intellectual process.

Analysis of cases of psychopathology is useful because psychopathology often acts as a microscope, revealing principles of psychological functioning. The major studies were done under Zeigarnik's (1962) supervision.

Schizophrenics frequently exhibit "superflexibility," defined as a tendency to focus on secondary aspects of a topic and an inability to choose one aspect of a topic as most important for a particular situation. The basis of this disturbance appears to lie in the high level of lability and ambivalence of personality-motivational attitudes. As a result, the bonds between meanings and personal senses is diminished. Schizophrenics also show less regulatory function of motive than do nonschizophrenics, so thinking becomes uncontrolled and overly spontaneous. In addition, schizophrenics fail to notice their own mistakes or to respond when their mistakes are commented on or pointed out to them. Yet the operational aspect of thinking remains fully functional.

Additional examples come from the thinking disturbances of epileptics and alcoholics. The thinking of epileptics is characterized by stereotypicality, an inability to abstract, and a pedantic style of reasoning. The cause appears to be rigid attitudes toward personal motivation. This is basically the opposite of the labile attitude of schizophrenics. The thinking of alcoholics has a "partial" character, that is, they engage in reasoning but it is not related to either task goals or conditions and not directed toward task solution. All of these examples support the hypothesis that many disturbances of thinking are related to disturbances at the personality level.

Moreover, even for the normally functioning individual, motivation is crucial and influences the quality of thinking processes. In a series of studies, Telegina and Bogdanova (in *Psikhologicheskie Issledovaniya Intellektual'noi Deyatel'nosti*, 1979) altered subjects' motivation by embedding the intellectual acts in the context of different activities. Specifically, subjects completed tasks in either the context of the performance of an experimenter's instructions, participation in a competition, or an evaluation of mental abilities under the guise of a search for gifted individuals. The intellectual tasks were either verbal, mixed (verbal and performance), or creative and open-ended. Productivity of thinking, measured through the number of solutions offered, was higher in the "evaluation" condition than for the "instruction" condition for all types of tasks. Specifically, subjects offered twice as many solutions in the evaluation condition for verbal tasks, three times as many for mixed tasks, and five times as many for creative tasks. The authors concluded that the "structure, dynamics, and content of thinking are determined by motivation" and suggested that motivation affects a number of specific aspects of performance on intellectual tasks.

First, motivation influences an individual's understanding, evaluation, and acceptance of a thinking task. Regarding the latter, it is obvious that an individual must accept the need to perform well before he will be motivated to do so.

Motivation is also important in goal setting. That is, expectation of performance is based on the evaluation of abilities and anticipation of the results of activity. Simply put, motivation is most useful if it results from a realistic assessment of abilities and possibilities. Underestimating limits an individual's potential; overestimating sets the stage for frustration.

Finally, motivation influences the choice of meanings, actions, and operations and the way they are used in activity. A student who must take a difficult course in order to graduate could view the course as an obstacle, a threat, or a challenge. His choice of actions and operations (studying harder, cheating on exams, etc.) will depend on his motivation and the meaning he attaches to the situation.

By analyzing the motives of thinking activity we can describe the particular combinations of characteristics that are typical of different "types" of subjects' motivation and strategies in solving intellectual tasks. One type of strategy is full involvement in the search for a solution. This type of strategy is characterized by an intent to progress in solving a task. Typical of this strategy is a focus on solving the task by actions directed toward overcoming obstacles. In contrast, a second type of strategy involves a focus on "exiting" from the task, including circular behavior, negative self-appraisals (e.g., "I am too stupid to succeed in solving this"), references to physical and emotional conditions, and attempts to discredit the task. All of these "exits" are attempts to achieve some goal that is not connected to the object content of the task (Vasil'ev & Khusainova, 1989).

The same study investigated the influence of stable personality traits such as type of achievement motivation, heuristic competence, and action control (measured by questionnaires developed by Magomed-Eminov, Do'iner, and Kule, respectively) on the process of solving a variety of tasks. They found that a combination of heuristic competence and achievement motivation produced persistent and independent efforts directed toward reaching a goal along with a focus on the objective contents of a task. This "action orientation" produces an approach to activity that is consistent, goal-directed, and integrated. In contrast, low heuristic competence combined with avoidance motivation leads to attempts to "escape" from activity, reliance on external appraisals of failures and successes, and a focus on emotional condition instead of task requirements. This combination leads to loss of productivity and, as a result, to the destruction of the consistency and logic of activity.

Particularly interesting among studies of intelligence and personality is research on "the process and the result of interaction of two major subsystems – mental abilities and the motivational sphere of personality" (Bogoyavlenskaya & Susokolova, 1985, p. 156). Here the focus is on the ability to switch from outer, situational to inner, cognitive motivation. One study used a task with a number of levels of meaning, called the "method of creative field" (Bogoyavlenskaya, 1983). The task was designed to produce change in motivation. Subjects were instructed to solve a number of chess problems of the same type as quickly as possible; for example, producing checkmate on a cylindrical chess board. The subjects were given a relatively simple but superficial solution that could be used to solve all the tasks. The results indicated that there were distinct groups of subjects, distinguished by their use of the superficial solution and their response to instructions. "Reproductive" subjects used the superficial solution to solve all tasks and followed the instructions to solve the tasks as quickly as possible. A second group of subjects showed more "intellectual initiative." They searched for a common rule or principle to apply to all the tasks rather than using the superficial solution. Their search for such a principle was not stimulated by the experimenter and conflicted with the instruction to solve the problems as quickly as possible. These subjects were labeled "heuristicists" because of their focus on underlying principles and inner, cognitive motivation. A third group of subjects, labeled "creativists," not only searched for a common principle but looked for its theoretical explanation. For creativists, a heuristic is not only a rule of thumb but a theoretical problem. Because of their interest in solving the theoretical problem, creativists will ignore the experimenter's instructions and stop or interrupt their own activity when necessary. In random samples, the percentage of creativists is approximately 1–2%, and the percentage of heuristicists is roughly ten times that number. There is some evidence that the tendency toward "intellectual initiative" is controlled primarily by environmental rather than genetic factors (Bogoyavlenskaya & Susokolova, 1985).

This overview of experimental research within the framework of the theory of activity is not a complete one. However it does reflect the major directions of research in intelligence and personality within the context of that theory. A number of theoretical issues discussed in this paper await experimental validation, the results of which will necessarily alter aspects of the theory itself. But the studies clearly indicate that personality and intelligence, from the point of view of the theory of activity, are inseparable and interact in activity. Therefore, we believe that this and related theories raise issues that are deserving of further research.

References

Bogoyavlenskaya, D. B. (1983). *Intellectual'naya activnost' kak problema tvorchestva* (Intellectual initiative as a problem of creativity). Rostov-on-Don: Roston-on-Don State University.

Bogoyavlenskaya, D. B., & Susokolova, I. A. (1985). Opyt psykhologicheskogo issledovaniya intellectual'noi aktivnosti (An exerimental study of intellectual initiative). *Voprosy Psikhologii, 3*, 154–159.

English, H. B., & English, A. C. (1958). *A comprehensive dictionary of psychological and psychoanalytical terms: A guide of usage.* New York: Longmans, Green.

Gal'perin, P. Ya. (1965). *Osnovnyi resul'taty issledovanii po probleme "formirovaniya umstvennykh deistvii i ponyatii"* (Main results of studying the problem of "formation of mental acts and concepts"). Moscow: Moscow State University.

Gregory, R. L. (1970). *The intelligent eye.* New York: McGraw-Hill.

Grigorenko, E. L. (1990). *Experimental'noe issledovanie protsessa vydvigeniya i proverki gipotez v structure poznavatel'noi aktivnosti* (Experimental study of hypothesis-making in the structure of cognitive activity). Unpublished doctoral dissertation, Moscow State University.

Iskusstvennyi intellekt i psikhologiya (Artificial intelligence and psychology) (1976). Moscow: Moscow State University.

Kagan, J. (1965). Impulsive and reflective children: Significance of conceptual tempo. In J. D. Krumboltz (Ed.), *Learning and the educational process* (pp. 133–161). Chicago: Rand McNally.

Kepalaite, A. (1982). Znak emotsional'nosti i osobennosti intellekta (Emotions and characterics of intelligence). *Psikhologicheskii Gurnal, 2*, 120–126.

Kornilova, T. V., & Tikhomirov, O. K. (1990). *Prinyatie intellektual'nykh reshenii v dialoge s komp'uterom* (Intellectual decision-making in a dialogue with a computer). Moscow: Moscow State University.

Leont'ev, A. N. (1975). *Deyatel'nost', soznanie, lichnost'.* Leningrad: Izdatelstvo Politecheskoi Literatury. Published in English as *Activity, consciousness, personality* (Englewood Cliffs, N.J.: Prentice-Hall, 1978).

Leont'ev, A. N. (1979). Psikhologiya obraza (Psychology of image). *The Moscow University Herald, Series 14 – Psychology, 2*, pp. 3–13.

Leont'ev, A. N. (1981). *Problemy razvitiya psikhiki* (Problems of the development of mind). Moscow: Moscow State University.

Neisser, U. (1967). *Cognitive psychology.* New York: Appleton-Century-Crofts.

Ol'shannikova, A. E., & Pacyavichus, I. V. (1981). Rol' individual'no-tipichnych kharakteristic emotsional'nosti i samoregulyatsii deyatel'nosti (Individually-typical emotional characteristics and activity self-regulation). *Psikhologicheskii Gurnal, 1*, 70–81.

Ovchinnikova, T. N. (1980). Issledovanie lichnostnykh kharakteristik myslitel'noi deyatel'nosti (Study of personality characteristics of thinking activity). *Voprosy Psikhologii, 1*, 70–81.

Petraitite, A. M. (1981). Syvas' intellektual'nykh tvorcheskikh sposobnostei s ekstraversiei–introversiei (Correlations of intellectual and creative abilities with extraversion–introversion). *Voprosy Psikhologii,* 6, 111–115.

Petukhov, V. V. (1984). Obraz mira i psikhologicheskoe izuchenie myshleniya (Image of the world and psychological study of thinking). *The Moscow University Herald, Series 14 – Psychology,* 4, pp. 13–21.

Piaget, J. (1969). *Izbrannye psikhologicheskie trudy* (Selected psychological papers). Moscow: Pedagogika.

Polanyi, M. (1962). *Personal knowledge.* Chicago, Illinois: The University of Chicago Press.

Problemy rukovodstva nauchnym kollektivom (Problems of management of a scientific collective) (1982). Moscow: Moscow State University.

Psikhologicheskie issledovaniya intellektual'noi deyatel'nosti (Psychological studies of intellectual activity) (1979). Moscow.

Smirnov, S. D. (1983). *Psikhologiya obraza* (Psychology of image). Moscow: Moscow State University.

Stetsenko, A. P. (1983). K voprosu o psikhologicheskoi klassifikatsii znachenii (Towards a question of psychological classification of meanings). *The Moscow University Herald, Series 14 – Psychology,* 4, pp. 22–30.

Sunitova, R. I. (1986). *Vozrastnye i psikhologicheskie osobennosti prognozirovaniya v protsesse resheniya zadach uchaschimisya* (Developmental and individual characteristics of anticipation in pupils' task-solution). Unpublished doctoral dissertation, Moscow Pedagogical Institute.

Talyzina, N. F. (1975). *Upravlenie protsessom usvoeniya znanii* (Managing of learning). Moscow: Moscow State University.

Tikhomirov, O. K. (1969). *Structura myslitel'noi deyatel'nosti* (The structure of thinking activity). Moscow: Moscow State University.

Vasil'ev, I. A., & Khusainova, N. P. (1989). K voprosu o lichnostnykh determinantakh myslitel'noi deyatel'nosti (Towards the question of personality determination of thinking activity). *The Moscow University Herald, Series 14 – Psychology,* 3, pp. 33–41.

Vygotsky, L. S. (1956). *Izbrannye psikhologicheskie issledovaniya* (Selected psychological investigations). Moscow: Academy of Pedagogical Sciences.

Witkin, H. A., Oltman, P. K. (1972). *Manual for the Embedded Figures Test.* Palo Alto: Testing Service.

Zeigarnik, B. V. (1962). *Patologiya myshleniya* (Pathology of thinking). Moscow: Moscow State University.

9   Cultural meaning systems, intelligence, and personality

Patricia Ruzgis and Elena L. Grigorenko

An old Russian adage states, "We all view the world from our own belfry," and something of the same sentiment has been expressed by psychologists conducting cross-cultural research. Indeed, it is becoming clear that it is difficult to discuss psychological constructs without reference to the cultural environment in which behavior occurs, and nowhere is this more evident than in discussions of intelligence and personality. Consider the following descriptions:

John is an intelligent person. He describes himself as outgoing and outspoken. He has clear plans for his own future and goals he intends to pursue even though his family and friends do not agree with his preferences. They note that John is very self-reliant and independent. He speaks clearly and articulately and is very consistent about expressing his true opinions because he believes it is important to be frank and honest at all times. John plans to pursue a graduate degree in mathematics. He works hard to get top grades because he knows that he will need them if he wants to pursue his goals.

Eva is careful to keep her opinions to herself and is usually very quiet in public, although she is open and talkative with her friends. Eva lives with her parents and her two brothers. Her teachers describe her as obedient and polite in the classroom, preferring to maintain the harmony of the classroom by keeping her opinions to herself. Her friends think Eva's most noteworthy qualities are her witty conversational style and insightful observations. Eva is following her family's and teacher's advice and pursuing a degree in chemistry. She works hard to achieve top grades in school because she knows she will need them to get into a good college and college offers her the best opportunity to contribute to her family and her country.

Clearly each of these descriptions of intelligence is different, yet each represents conceptions of "intelligence" within a cultural context. It is likely that to each reader one of the descriptions will seem more intuitively accurate or a more reasonable description of intelligence than will the other. It is also likely that the preference of the reader will vary according to his or her cultural background. This recognition has been receiving considerable attention in recent years because as data accumulated from numerous cross-cultural studies involving both implicit and explicit theories, notions of intelligence held by various cultural groups were found to vary substantially from the "quick-analytical-abstract" conceptions held in Western societies

248

(Berry, 1984), raising questions about the way we define and measure intelligent behavior (Goodnow, 1984). Cross-cultural research has been of two general types, representing the two "types" of theories of intelligence.

Explicit theories are the most widely known "type" of theory within the scientific community. Sternberg, Conway, Ketron, and Bernstein (1981) define explicit theories of intelligence as "constructions of psychologists or other scientists that are based on, or at least tested on, data collected from people performing tasks presumed to measure intelligent functioning" (p. 37). When psychologists refer to theories it is generally explicit theories to which they are referring.

In general, the goal of cross-cultural explicit theories research has been to attempt to assess the patterns of intellectual abilities arising in different cultural contexts (Irvine & Berry, 1988). Here, group membership is often treated as an independent variable and scores on tests of cognitive abilities are treated as dependent variables. Most of this research follows the assumption of the law of cultural differentiation, which states that "cultural factors prescribe what shall be learned and at what age, consequently different cultural environments lead to the development of different patterns of ability" (p. 121).

A second area of research, and a less sizable body of studies, investigates implicit theories (Sternberg, 1987, 1990a; Sternberg, Conway, Ketron, & Bernstein, 1981), everyday models (Goodnow, 1980, 1984), or folk conceptions (Berry, 1984) of intelligence. Implicit theories are the informal theories that people hold regarding the nature of intelligence. The data in implicit theories research do not consist of scores on cognitive tests, but rather, people's notions of intelligence, often in the form of definitions, lists of characteristics typical of an intelligent person, synonyms for intelligence and so on. Implicit theories need to be discovered rather than invented because they already exist, and appear to form the basis of everyday assessments of intelligence (Sternberg, 1990a, 1987; Sternberg, Conway, Ketron, & Bernstein, 1981). While cross-cultural research directed toward testing and developing explicit theories attempts to discern who has how much of what type of intelligence, cross-cultural research using the implicit theories approach follows Irvine's suggestion that "psychologists should examine the layman's use of the word 'intelligence' as a key to the way societies designate acts as intelligent" (Irvine, 1970, p. 24).

The recognition of cultural variation in conceptions of intelligence has been, as Berry (1987) noted, both rewarding and threatening because, by conducting cross-cultural investigations, "one may discover a lot, but what one discovers may be challenging to one's established beliefs and practices" (p. 401). But Berry was also quick to note that calling attention to the linkages between the cultural prejudices and scientific practices and therefore reducing ethnocentrism was the initial goal of cross-cultural psychology. While cross-cultural investigations have been successful in raising questions about the nature of intelligence, the same investigations have produced a new dilemma. Because, although the majority of psychologists would probably agree with Ceci's (1990) observation that there is nothing new to the opinion that many traditional conceptions of intelligence are inadequate, there is considerably less agreement on how to conceptualize the relationship between intelligence and culture. At present there is a range of theoretical positions on the relationship between culture and intelligence that is almost as broad as the range of conceptions of intelligence that appears to be present in the data themselves.

At one extreme is a position that has been termed radical cultural relativism, which "requires that indigenous notions of cognitive competence be the sole basis for the generation of cross-culturally valid descriptions and assessments of intelligence" (Berry, 1974, p. 225). Hence, no comparison is really possible. At the other extreme are the views of theorists like Eysenck (1982) who view intelligence as the same in all cultures, and here there is no problem making cross-cultural comparisons in levels of ability. Falling between these two extremes are theoretical positions that vary largely according to the likelihood of finding universals of intelligence and the possibility of making cross-cultural comparisons. Cole and his colleagues of the Laboratory of Comparative Human Cognition (1982), for example, agree that there is no single conception of intelligence that is appropriate for members of all cultures. However, they maintain that the radical cultural relativist position does not take into account that cultures interact and suggest that a kind of conditional comparison is possible through investigation of how different cultures deal with equivalent types of tasks.

Possibly the most influential and widely held position at present is that of intelligence as adaptation. Ceci (1990) notes that "recently, cognitive psychologists like Sternberg, developmental psychologists like Charlesworth, and social psychologists like Berry and Dasen have sounded a similar theme of 'intelligence as adaptation' " (p. 30). Charlesworth (1976) views intelligence as adaptation to environmentally posed problems but notes that although adaptation is the universal goal of intelligence, what constitutes adaptive behavior is likely to vary for different cultural and subcultural groups. Specifically, Charlesworth defines intelligent behavior as "behavior under the control of cognitive processes and employed toward the solution of problems which challenge the well-being, needs, plans, and survival of the individual" (p. 150). Sternberg (1985, 1988) views intelligence as the mental activity underlying purposive adaptation to, shaping of, and selection of real-world environments relevant to one's life. Berry (1980) distinguishes four levels of context (ecological, experiential, performance, and experimental) and suggests that adaptive intelligence is exhibited in the experiential and ecological contexts. Ceci (1990) has stated that the role of context was long given "short shrift" in theories of intelligence and asserts that "one's way of thinking about things is determined in the course of interactions with others of the same culture; that is, the meaning of the cultural context is always negotiated between people of that culture. This in turn, modifies both culture and thought" (p. 97). A major theme running through the majority of contextual theories of intelligence is the observation that context influences the content of intelligent functioning, and that culture is a major force in determining the nature of the context. However, most theorists are not satisfied to leave theory at the cultural-relativist position where comparison is not possible and each culture must be considered entirely on its own. Instead, support is for Berry's (1984) goal of developing a universal theory of cognitive competence where universal is used in the anthropological sense of meaning a feature common to all mankind rather than limited to single populations.

But, the dilemma remains one of finding a useful and cross-culturally valid approach to conceptualizing culture that limits ethnocentrism, a problem that has apparently been exacerbated by the overall separation of the work of theorists investigating culture per se and those investigating intelligence. This is not unlike the separation of intelligence research and personality research that prompted this volume, a separation that appears, particularly in light of cross-cultural findings, to be quite artificial.

Our purpose in writing this chapter is to propose a broad framework for analyzing the relation of intelligence and personality to cultural context. Culture, in the present approach, will be defined in a way that is more typical of psychological anthropology than psychology, that is, as a system of meanings that produces a particular sense of reality and includes both values and variations in conceptions of personhood. Personality will be defined similarly, as an individual motivational system that is linked to and shares elements with the cultural meaning system. Intelligence will be viewed as adaptation, but adaptation to the cultural meaning system, incorporating and expressing cultural values. As a broad general framework we will adopt the individualism–collectivism dimension and the constructs of idiocentrism–allocentrism and independent–interdependent self-concepts as representative of cultural values and beliefs about the nature of persons. By examining current implicit-theories studies we will note that, like cultures, implicit theories are of two broad types, those that involve adaptation to a collectivistic culture with an interdependent view of the person and those that involve adaptation to an individualistic culture with an independent view of the person. This will be particularly evident in the social competence aspects of implicit theories. Therefore, our goal is not to define what intelligence *is,* but to discuss what intelligence means and how that meaning is related to other aspects of cultural meaning systems including values and prescribed personality attributes, across cultures.

Defining culture as meaning system

Reality, according to Goodman (1968), is not independent of our version of it and our version of reality is determined in large part by cultural context. This observation is reflected in current definitions that focus on culture as a system of meanings. Schneider (1976) views culture as "a body of definitions, premises, statements, postulates, presumptions, propositions, and perceptions about the nature of the universe and man's place in it" (p. 202), and further suggests that culture is intersubjectively shared, with the result that everyone assumes others see the same things they see. Similarly, Geertz (1973) describes culture as "an historically transmitted pattern of meanings embodied in symbols, a system of inherited conceptions expressed in symbolic form by means of which men communicate, perpetuate, and develop their knowledge about and attitudes toward life" (p. 89).

It is interesting and informative to note that the idea that culture shapes reality is not a specifically "Western notion," unlike many theories in the social sciences. In the Soviet Union, A. N. Leont'ev (1979) proposed that the pattern of meanings created and understood by the shared practices of groups of people constitute culture and express reality. Within this pattern of meanings, people from any particular culture have fixed and idealized their ideas about the world and embedded in these patterns culturally determined actions and types of behavior. According to Leont'ev, each individual experiences the cultural pattern as something existing "outside" of himself and as objective (even though it is invisible and untouchable), that is, as reality. Further, because they are socially constructed, cultural meaning patterns are learned when an individual is surrounded by people who demonstrate and share cultural patterns. Leont'ev notes that, through this process, cultural meanings and patterns originating outside the individual become a dimension of individual consciousness. In addition, because the pattern of meanings within individual consciousness includes a learned structure of connections between "things in the world" (objects, actions, and behaviors) it is no less a dimension in individual experience than are physical dimensions, such as time or space. Culture places the individual at a certain point in time and space, just as physical dimensions do, and therefore, is considered the fifth dimension by Leont'ev.

The point that is clearly made by each of these definitions of culture is that culture is not simply the "objectively" observable and measurable elements of society such as dietary practices, art, artifacts, farming methods, and so on. It is, most importantly, the set of conceptions of reality that are shared by members of the culture. Very simply, culture tells us how to think about things (Ceci, 1990).

Culture also tells us how to feel and what to do. D'Andrade (1984) notes that the shared meaning system of culture has not only representational functions, however, extensive they may be, but directive, constructive, and affective functions as well, that can create cultural entities and a particular sense of reality. More specifically, meaning systems "represent the world, create cultural entities, direct one to do certain things, and evoke certain feelings" (p. 96). D'Andrade uses the example of "success" as a class of culturally created entities to illustrate the point, and notes that unlike brute facts such as rocks or trees, culturally created entities like "success" exist because there is social agreement about "what is out there" and a set of constitutive rules that are adhered to and that define the entity. According to D'Andrade, "success" in American culture is an important personal quality on which people are agreed to vary, a source of prestige, self-satisfaction and differential rewards, a means of evaluating performance, and a goal toward which individual effort is directed. Sufficient ability combined with sufficient hard work (and intelligence!) are believed to lead to "success."

Yet, in spite of the American admiration for successful people, the books, seminars, and courses designed to teach people how to become more successful, and the pride parents feel for a child who is a success, "success" has no objective meaning outside the social agreement that defines it and creates its existence. That agreeing on the importance of success, or any other cultural entity, and striving for success are so accepted is not surprising given D'Andrade's observation that culture also has directive functions such that adhering to the cultural meaning system is intrinsically rewarding and includes both direct personal reward and the rewards attached to accepting and expressing cultural values. Culture provides members of a group with the shared definitions that make social living possible, and one of the purposes of the directive function of culture is to ensure that all members of a culture define situations similarly. Just consider the pressure and concern brought to bear on a student who is agreed to have high ability but who does not attempt to be successful and achieve more than average grades. He or she is usually labeled an underachiever (another cultural entity) and a great deal of effort is usually directed toward discovering the "problem" that is limiting his "success," perhaps a personality or psychological problem, difficulties at home, drug use, or even poor nutrition! Hence, because success is a culturally created entity, it appears that one cannot be a success without social consensus regarding what it means to be a success. Similarly, one cannot be regarded as an intelligent person without social consensus as to the meaning of intelligence, and this meaning varies with cultural context. Therefore, the notion of an "intelligent person" appears to represent one category of culturally created entities, as we will see.

Personality, like intelligence, is at least partially a function of culture. D'Andrade (1984) suggests that personality is a second kind of meaning system that is related to cultural meaning systems. This type of definition avoids a content-based formulation that artificially forces attributes into a "personality or culture framework," which, D'Andrade argues, is rather like chemists and biologists forced to divide the world into physical objects that are chemical and physical objects that are biological. Societies socialize children to internalize the personality characteristics that will allow them to function most effectively within the particular cultural system (Laboratory of Comparative Human Cognition, 1982). According to D'Andrade, whether specific aspects of human learning are categorized as part of culture or part of personality depends on how they are placed within a system of relationships and processes. Those aspects that are reasonably placed within the cultural meaning system are those that involve the adaptation of groups of people to their environment and to each other. But, "in the study of personality these relationships and processes involve the organization of behavior, impulse, affect, and thought around the drives of the individual. If one considers personality and culture to be open systems that are linked together, then there must be items belonging to both systems that form the links" (D'Andrade, 1984, p. 113). For example, the ideas that are involved in the cultural meaning system, like the importance of success and the competition related to it, then play a role in motivational systems. Essentially, the cultural meaning system is reflected, in these cases, in the personality systems of individuals. While this is a somewhat unusual notion in Western cultures, and therefore, difficult to discuss, both the connection and the distinction are reflected in the Russian language. In Russian the word *znachenie* means "culturally-fixed meaning" and *smysil* designates cultural meaning in the personal system of the individual. Furthermore, even in the cases where culture represents adaptation of groups of people to their environment, the form that adaptation takes develops within a system of cultural values (Miller, 1988). Therefore, both the adaptation of large groups of people and the personality systems of individuals can be viewed as linked to cultural meaning systems.

The goal of cultural analysis is to make the versions of reality held in other cultures accessible (Geertz, 1973) because often the versions of reality that appear irrational, delusional, ideological, etc., by outsiders, nonetheless seem entirely rational to the insider and are versions of reality that one can live by (Shweder, 1986). According to Shweder, these "divergent rationalities" can be explained by reference to processes legitimately classified as rational and are what allow members of a particular culture to have rational discussions within their respective versions of reality, but not across them. (Perhaps they explain the surprise and disbelief that often greet psychological studies conducted with subjects from other cultures that produce results very different from those obtained in our own culture).

Cultural interpretations are judged for validity by their ability to provide holistic accounts of diverse domains of behavior (Miller, 1988). Such interpretations, if they are to account for both intelligence and personality, obviously must include the cultural values and, perhaps less obviously, the culture's conception of personhood. It seems self-evident that if what it means to be a person varies with culture, then both desirable and actual personality attributes and beliefs about intelligence are also likely to vary. Research indicates that there is considerable variation in conceptions of personhood. The Western notion of the person as a "bounded, unique, more or less integrated motivational and cognitive universe, a dynamic center of awareness, emotion, judgment, and action organized into a distinctive whole and set contrastively both against other such wholes and against its social and natural background" (Geertz, 1975, p. 48) is far from universal. The majority of the world's cultures hold conceptions of the person that can be more accurately described as "self-in-relation-to-other" (Markus & Kitayama, 1991), or as human beings as occupants of social roles (Miller, 1984), and therefore less boundary-oriented.

Among the conceptions of the person that differ from the Western notion of the individual as a bounded set of personality traits are the highly stylized, role-oriented, and contextual conceptions of the Balinese (Geertz, 1975), the Cheyenne emphasis on relationships rather than personality traits (Strauss, 1973), and the Zapotec of Mexico references to a taxonomic realm of types of persons rather than to personality traits to explain behavior (Selby, 1975). Overall, the evidence suggests that the tendency to focus on individual abstract properties in isolation from social relations and context is related to Westernization in values but not to schooling, literacy, socioeconomic status, information, language, or cognitive facility in abstraction (Miller, 1988; Shweder & Bourne, 1982). But, although it is clear from the cross-cultural literature that values, conceptions of personhood, and conceptions of intelligence vary with culture, examining each individual cultural entity in each individual culture for its possible relation to personality and to intelligence is so daunting a task that it provides little that is useful, at least in the foreseeable future, and leaves us in much the same position as examining or measuring each attribute or ability associated with intelligence. There is still no useful conceptual framework for understanding cross-cultural variations in conceptions of intelligence as they relate to cultural meaning systems, no less one that includes their relations to personality. However, Triandis (1990a) notes that possibly "the most important dimension of cultural difference in social behavior, across the diverse cultures of the world, is the relative emphasis on individualism versus collectivism" (p. 42). The dimension has been compelling enough within the field of cross-cultural psychology that the 1980's have been called the decade of individualism–collectivism (Kim, submitted for publication). It is a dimension that may explain some of the variation in conceptions of intelligence across cultures. In addition, to individualism–collectivism for analysis at the cultural level, the psychological processes of idiocentrism–allocentrism provides a similar analysis of norms and values at the individual level (Triandis, 1990b), and the related dimension, independent and interdependent self-concepts, allows a cross-cultural comparison of conceptions of the person. Together they provide a coherent and consistent set of values and beliefs about the nature of persons that have clear implications for cultural variations in intelligence and personality. We will now discuss each of these constructs in turn, but it should be noted at the outset that idiocentrism and the independent self-concept are generally found in individualistic cultures and allocentrism and the interdependent self-concept are more typical of collectivistic cultures. The similarity in values and beliefs across the three constructs is unmistakable and striking.

The individualism–collectivism dimension

In recent years the individualism–collectivism dimension has proved a useful construct for advancing methodological and theoretical issues about culture and has generated considerable interest and commentary within the field of cross-cultural psychology. In particular, conceiving of cultures in terms of the individualism–collectivism dimension has allowed "the linkage of psychological phenomena to a cultural dimension" (Kim, submitted for publication, p. 2), particularly when the phenomena under consideration include motivation and cognition.

Individualism–collectivism is often conceived of as a bipolar dimension. However, it is important to note that cultures are more accurately described by the extent to which they are individualistic and collectivistic because all cultures contain elements of both types, but to different degrees. Triandis (1990b) notes that "the difference is that in some cultures the probability that individualistic selves, attitudes, norms, values, and behaviors will be used is higher than in others" (p. 2).

The United States is generally considered the most extremely individualistic of the world's cultures. Spindler and Spindler (1983) suggest that one of the forces contributing to immigration to the U.S. was the desire to escape restrictions associated with strict social stratification, and this type of social structure was never reconstructed. The countries of Western Europe and most English-speaking countries, including Canada and Australia, are also high in individualism. However, the majority of the world's cultures fall toward the collectivism side of the continuum, including Asian, African, and Latin American cultures as well as those in some parts of Europe such as Southern Italy and rural Greece (Kim, submitted for publication; Triandis, 1990a, 1990b).

At the most basic level the distinguishing factor of individualism and collectivism is in the relative emphasis on the individual versus the ingroup. Here an ingroup is defined as "a group whose norms, goals, and values shape the behavior of its members" (Triandis, 1990a, p. 53), e.g., an extended family, the community, the tribe, etc.; and an important aspect of collectivism is a sharp distinction between ingroups and outgroups. Much of the misunderstanding that occurs when relating individualism–collectivism to specific psychological findings is due to a misidentification of relevant ingroups in a particular culture. For example, to conclude that, for Chinese all other Chinese are part of the ingroup is to misidentify the ingroup. This would only be the case when other non-Chinese people are present, either in reality or in consciousness. In most instances, strangers in all collectivistic cultures represent outgroups.

Collectivism defines societies in which "people from birth onwards are integrated into strong cohesive ingroups, which throughout people's lives protect them in exchange for unquestioning loyalty" (Hofstede, 1980, p. 51). Collectivists respond as ingroup norms dictate, internalize group norms, show a great willingness to cooperate with ingroup members, and place ingroup goals ahead of personal goals (Triandis, 1990a). The emphasis in collectivistic cultures is on collective identity, emotional dependence, obligations to and the welfare of the group (Hofstede, 1980). Collectivists tend to have stable, enduring ingroup relations with many, often role-related, duties and obligations, and a primary concern is maintaining harmony within a stable ingroup. Ties to ingroup members tend to be strong and enduring. Hence, collectivists are concerned about the results of their actions on others (Hui & Triandis, 1986). Consistent with the emphasis on group welfare, the cardinal values of collectivists are reciprocity, obligation, duty, security, dependence, harmony, tradition, obedience to authority, proper action, and equilibrium. The major calamity for individuals in collectivistic societies is ostracism or exclusion (Triandis, 1990a, 1990b).

In contrast, in individualistic societies the focus is on the individual. The cardinal values of individualists are bravery, self-reliance, solitude, and frugality (Triandis, 1990a). Among additional values strongly associated with individualism are achievement, competition, expansion (Spindler & Spindler, 1983), autonomy, privacy, self-development (Lukes, 1973), emotional independence, and individual initiative (Hofstede, 1980). Hofstede notes that in individualistic cultures the ties between individuals are loose and each person is expected to take care of himself or herself and his or her immediate family. Individual goals are placed ahead of group goals (Doi, 1986) and Triandis (1990b) notes that "the more individuals rather than groups decide what norms are applicable, the more individualistic is the culture" (p. 4). For example, Bellah and his colleagues argue that in the extremely individualistic American culture individuals hold the belief that "anything that would violate our right to think for ourselves, judge for ourselves, make our own decisions, live our lives as we see fit, is not only morally wrong, it is sacrilegious" (Bellah, Madsen, Sullivan, Swidler, & Tipton, 1985).

Individualism is associated with affluence, cultural complexity, and social and geographic mobility (Triandis, 1990a). One corollary to cultural complexity is that nuclear families replace extended families; one is responsible for fewer people, but also has fewer people to rely on, with the result that individuals often feel and view themselves as isolated from others. Individualism tends to increase in all societies among members with greater levels of affluence and mobility. One result of cultural complexity and mobility and the related ease of moving among many potential ingroups is the tendency of individualists to have excellent, but often superficial, social skills and few intimate ties (Hsu, 1981). Social ties are often replaced or altered as interests, location, and personal needs change. Divorce and related social problems are higher in individualistic societies, one result of the looser social ties and fewer role-related obligations. Triandis (1990a) notes that the results of numerous factor analyses suggest that the factors most distinguishing individualism and collectivism are Family Integrity and Distance from Ingroups. Collectivists often live with their parents and extended family throughout adulthood, and find this desirable; individualists rarely do. One of the normative demands in individualistic cultures is to achieve separateness and independence.

In addition, the individualism–collectivism dimension appears to conform at least somewhat to the suggestion made by Berry and Irvine (1986) that what is necessary to develop a universal theory of intelligence is an ecological analysis. Here ecological analysis is defined as an attempt to find "explanations of cultural phenomena in terms of their interrelationship with natural phenomena within a particular ecosystem" (p. 278). Individualism and collectivism appear to develop partly in response to particular ecological demands. Ecology, according to Kim (submitted for publication), acted "like a filter that shaped and determined the types of cultures and individuals that survived" (p. 4) within any given ecosystem. Some thirty years ago, Kim notes, Barry, Child and Bacon (1959) found that migratory tribes emphasized autonomy, self-sufficiency, achievement, and assertiveness while agricultural, sedentary societies socialized tendencies to be obedient, compliant, and responsible. There is, it appears, a similarity between the qualities favored in migratory tribes and the cultural construct of individualism and a similar correspondence between the qualities emphasized in agricultural societies and collectivism. Individualists, Triandis noted (1990a), have frontiers, both real and ideological, to conquer.

Corresponding to individualism–collectivism at the cultural level, analysis at the individual level involves the psychological processes of idiocentrism and allocentrism (Triandis, 1990b) or independent and interdependent self-concepts (Markus & Kitayama, 1991). Here the analysis focuses on the study of individual norms, values, and conceptions of personhood. While it should be noted that all individuals, regardless of culture, possess both idiocentric and allocentric personality tendencies, Triandis (1990b) states that idiocentric elements are more likely to be sampled in individualistic cultures and allocentric elements in collectivistic cultures. Similarly, independent and interdependent self-concepts are more likely to be associated with individualistic and collectivistic cultures, respectively. As noted earlier, there are likely to be common or overlapping elements in the cultural meaning system and in the personalities of individuals, a probability that becomes clear when the analysis involves cultural individualism and individual idiocentrism and cultural collectivism and individual allocentrism. We will discuss these two forms of analysis at the individual level together because of the similarity in personality dimensions associated with each and the relation of both to cultural individualism and collectivism. Here the elements that predominate in the cultural meaning system appear to have an important role in the motivational, self-concept, and personality systems of individuals within that culture.

Idiocentrism–allocentrism and independent–interdependent self-concepts

In individualistic cultures, as described earlier, the focus is on the individual as the basic unit of society. Individuals are encouraged to strive for independence and self-actualization, and personal goals are given priority over group goals. Similarly, idiocentrics or people with independent self-concepts (primarily in individualistic cultures) are likely to see the individual as the basic unit and to explain behavior in terms of individual personality traits, attitudes, and abilities (Triandis, 1990a), and to believe those traits are context-free, enduring, stable attributes of the individual (Markus & Kitayama, 1991). The behavior of idiocentrics is regulated by personal values rather than ingroup values and high among those values are achievement, competition, freedom, autonomy, and the needs, rights, and capacities of the individual (Triandis, 1990b), reflecting the values of the individualistic culture.

The cultural emphasis on autonomy and self-reliance means that the primary task for idiocentrics is to separate and become independent from others and to develop and express his or her own abilities and potential (Markus & Kitayama, 1991). Achieving the cultural goal of independence requires "construing oneself as an individual whose behavior is organized or made meaningful primarily by reference to one's own internal repertoire of thoughts, feelings, and actions, rather than by reference to the thoughts, feelings, and actions of others" (p. 230). Understandably, with the cultural emphasis on independence and achievement of personal goals, the major calamity for the idiocentric is dependence (Triandis, 1990b).

In contrast to the focus on individuals typical of idiocentrics (and individualistic cultures), the allocentric or interdependent tends to reflect the values of the collectivistic culture of which he or she is more often a member. Just as collectivistic cultures place the ingroup's goals over the individual's and see the group as the basic unit of social perception, the allocentric tends to regulate his or her behavior primarily in terms of its implications for others. Recall that in collectivistic cultures there is a tendency to stress harmony, to share resources and good and bad results with ingroup members, and to be controlled by shame (Hui & Triandis, 1986). Similarly, allocentrics and those with an interdependent self-concept tend to have a "we consciousness," giving others more importance than they give to the self (Markus & Kitayama, 1991), and valuing qualities such as harmony and cooperation that promote the welfare of the group (Triandis, 1990b). Furthermore, where idiocentrics are likely to stress dispositional factors in causal explanations of behavior (e.g., "he is greedy"), allocentrics or people with interdependent self-concepts are likely to stress role relations or contextual factors (e.g., "it was his duty as the eldest brother," and "he speaks politely in class"), thereby taking a holistic, contextual view of the person (Miller, 1984; Markus & Kitayama, 1991; Triandis, 1990a).

In addition, Markus & Kitayama (1991) note that, because the motivation underlying goal-oriented behavior may be quite different for those with independent versus interdependent self-concepts, similar looking behavior may not be as similar in motivation as it appears to the cultural outsider. For example, studying hard to achieve good grades in school may have very different meanings in different cultural settings. For the independent self the behavior is likely to reflect personal goals ("I need to get good grades because I want to go to medical school"), whereas for the interdependent self the same behavior is performed to achieve the goals of the ingroup (good grades will bring honor to the family or fulfill elder relatives expectations and wishes). For example, Chinese children often strive to achieve the goals of others (Bond, 1986). This is an example of the type of overlap between culture systems and personality systems proposed by D'Andrade.

Furthermore, individual cognition appears to interact with cultural variation in the self-system; those with interdependent selves have relatively more knowledge of the other or self-in-relation-to-other than they do about the self while the reverse is true for those with independent selves (Greenwald & Pratkanis, 1984; Markus & Wurf, 1987). Furthermore, independent selves are more likely to refer to global, dispositional qualities in characterizing themselves and others, while interdependent selves more often refer to contextual, situational explanations (Miller, 1984; Shweder & Bourne, 1984). Therefore, the assumption that behavior is primarily motivated by individual knowledge and individual personality traits has little cross-cultural validity. Global characterizations in terms of individual personality traits is more accurately described as Western.

Achievement motivation clearly involves the self-system and interacts with cultural meaning systems. Yang (1982) distinguishes between individually oriented and socially oriented motivation. Bond (1986) suggests that the former is more typical of individualistic cultures and the latter more common in collectivistic cultures. Markus and Kitayama (1991) note that for those with independent selves, achievement motivation is generally directed toward reaching individual goals and expressing one's "unique" attributes and abilities. But actively seeking individual success is not universally valued or associated with self-esteem. Rather, interdependent selves express more socially oriented motives that have the other as referent and evaluator and with motivation directed toward achieving connectedness (Markus & Kitayama, 1991). Strong achievement motivation that is other-directed is associated with value placed on the ability to control personal desires and the goal of achieving connectedness and harmony. Even competitive reward situations do not necessarily produce competitive behavior among those with interdependent self-concepts. Bond (1986) reports that in Hong Kong and Taiwan school children tend to cooperate with opponents even in that type of situation and this tendency increases with age, whereas American children tend to display more competitiveness as they get older. For Chinese children, but not Americans, the goal of connecting appears to take precedence over the goal of winning a reward.

Implicit theories of intelligence and cultural meaning systems

As noted earlier, the majority of the world's cultures fall toward the collectivism end of the individualism–collectivism continuum, including Asian, African, and Latin American cultures. Cultures high in individualism include the countries of Western Europe, Canada, Australia, and the United States. One method of investigating the relation of culture to implicit theories of intelligence is to examine the conceptions previous research has suggested are representative of cultures known to be high in individualism or collectivism, beginning with studies conducted in Africa, an area generally agreed to be relatively high in collectivism.

Irvine (1969, 1970), working with African populations, conducted possibly the first empirical psychological investigation of folk conceptions of intelligence (Berry, 1984) by examining sayings, beliefs, and proverbs commonly used by the Mashona of Zimbabwe. According to Irvine, the Shona word for intelligence, *ngware,* means to be prudent and cautious, particularly in social relationships, because misfortunes are conceived of as part of a gestalt of human relationships. Irvine states that "intelligent acts are . . . of a conforming kind having primary reference to the affective climate of one's own relationships with the spiritual force of the living and ancestral spirits of the kin group" (Irvine, 1969, pp. 98–99). In addition, the Mashona consider knowledge of others more important for intelligence than knowledge of the self. Irvine (1970) noted that intelligence in Africa, if measured with conventional tests, would bear little relation to intelligence as conceived in the village unless tests were included to measure this socioaffective component so valued by the Mashona.

A similar emphasis on social aspects of intelligence was found among two other African groups, the Songhay of Mali and the Samia of Kenya (Putnam & Kilbride, 1980). In this study, subjects wrote essays describing an intelligent person. The content analyses of the essays suggest that for both the Songhay and the Samia individual qualities were less important than social and communal qualities in defining an intelligent person, a result that, like the Mashona inclusion of caution and prudence in social relationships, is consistent with both collectivism and an inter-dependent self-concept.

Serpell (1974, 1977) asked Chewa adults in Central Africa to rank village children on intelligence, to choose children to help with an important village task, and to give reasons for their choices. In choosing particular children, Chewa adults most often used native words meaning sensible or wise and clever, and additionally, referred to qualities such as obedience, cooperation, respectfulness, and willingness. Berry (1984) notes that there is a similarity to the results obtained by Irvine with the Mashona in the emphasis on "qualities of human relationships, particularly those which bind African communities together" (p. 348). Serpell noted that the cognitive skills measured by intelligence tests do not reflect the social component of coopera-tion and obedience that is an important part of the Chewa conception of intelligence. Furthermore, in the African populations investigated by Irvine, Putnam and Kilbride, and Serpell, the predominant features of conceptions of intelligence are those that facilitate and maintain harmonious and stable intergroup relations, as would be expected in collectivistic societies where the group, rather than the individual, is the primary unit of society.

Similar emphasis on social aspects of intelligence were evident in two additional African populations, the Baganda and the Baoule. Wober (1972, 1974) conducted a series of investigations with the Baganda of Uganda, including administration of semantic differential scales and an analysis of traditional children's literature. He concluded that the Bagandan conception of intelligence includes components usually referred to separately in English as intelligence and wisdom with an emphasis on correct behavior and social conformity. Ugandan Muslims, according to Wober (1974), conceive of an intelligent person as friendly, honorable, public, and happy.

Further evidence of the importance of social behavioral aspects in African con-ceptions of intelligence was provided by Dasen's (1984) work with the Baoule. Dasen states that what the Baoule value "are social skills: being helpful, obedient, respectful, but also being knowledgeable, taking responsibilities and showing initiative in tasks useful to the family and the community" (p. 430). Technological skills such as memory and manual dexterity are also valued, but only if they are used in the service of the social group. Theorists summarizing the African implicit theories of in-telligence have noted the overall inclusion, despite variation in emphasis on specific qualities, of a strong social component related a belief in the primacy of the family or collective over the individual (Berry, 1984; Mundy-Castle, 1983). Among the qualities most important to this social component are sensitivity to social atmosphere, interpersonal and social ease, acceptance of social values, and unselfconsciousness. Berry suggests that the results of African investigations seriously challenge the Western tendency to exclude all but cognitive components from tests of intelligence. It is clear, however, that African conceptions of intelligence stress those personality qualities and abilities that are consistent with the focus on the welfare of the ingroup in collectivistic cultures and have very little in common with the individualistic values typical of Western cultures and Western intelligence tests.

Of course, African cultures are not the only ones that have cultural meaning systems that are more collectivistic and interdependent than individualistic and independent. If these dimensions account only for African conceptions of intelligence they do not suggest a particularly useful framework. Fortunately, similar research has been conducted using Asian populations.

Azuma and Kashiwagi (1987) collected descriptors of intelligence and then asked Japanese subjects to rate whether or not the descriptors fit their notions of an intelligent person. Factor analysis of the ratings yielded five factors and two of the factors represented social competence. The first of these was labeled "positive social competence" comprising descriptors such as "sociable," "humorous," "effective speaker," and "good at getting along with others." The second social competence factor, labeled "receptive social competence," included descriptors like "can take another's point of view," "sympathetic," "modest," "admits mistakes in good grace," and "knows one's place." The authors note that this last descriptor is a typically Japanese value and represents the belief that "everyone has a role and should behave in accordance to that role and better not go beyond that" (p. 22). Note the similarity between this typically Japanese value and the concept of the person that stresses role-related obligations. A third factor "task efficiency" included such descriptors as "works efficiently," "good insight," "plans ahead," and "clear decisions." The final factors, accounting for a relatively small amount of the variance, were labeled "originality" (the descriptors included "original" and "sharp") and "reading and writing" (includes descriptors such as "good writer," "writes letters often," and "good reader").

The inclusion of a receptive social competence factor is interpreted by the authors as representative of the Japanese sample and the Japanese conception of intelligence. They further suggest that this factor sets the Japanese conception of intelligence apart from American conceptions (described below), and emphasizes the importance, in Japanese societies, of being adept at assessing expected social roles in Japanese societies. This factor also appears to reflect the values of collectivists in general and the collectivist emphasis on role-related obligations in particular. Most noteworthy for understanding conceptions of intelligence in the East are the investigations conducted by Keats and his associates (Gill & Keats, 1980; Keats, 1982) comparing Malayan and Chinese conceptions to those of Australians. Because Australia is generally agreed to be one of the world's most individualistic cultures and cultures in the Far East tend toward collectivism the studies allow a direct comparison of conceptions of intelligence in the two "types" of cultures.

In one study (Gill & Keats, 1980) questionnaires were administered to students from both cultures, and subjects were asked to list synonyms of "intelligent" and "not intelligent," rate behaviors, skills, and abilities of more and less intelligent individuals, and to describe "intelligence." Results were determined for both general competence areas and skills areas. In terms of the former, competence, subjects from both cultures gave the highest ratings to mental abilities and agreed that within the area of mental abilities, thinking and understanding were most important. Knowledge was given the second highest rating. However, important differences did result from ratings of importance in the skills area. Here Australians indicated that reading, speaking, and writing were the most important skills. Malays rated speaking and practical and social skills as the most important, again adding a social component that was not found among the Australians. Berry (1984) notes that the Malay conception of intelligence is similar to the results of African studies in the emphasis on social aspects of intelligence. In a second study, using diverse subject groups within each culture, Keats (1982) investigated Chinese and Australian beliefs regarding the characteristics of children and adults of higher intelligence. After classifying the responses into major themes, Keats reported that both Australian and Chinese subjects included problem solving, knowledge, and creativity as characteristics of intelligence. However, the Chinese, but not the Australians, included being careful, observing, imitation, and correct thinking, among characteristics of intelligence.

According to Keats (1982), the Chinese folk conception of intelligence can be summarized as a socially oriented person who gets things right, is pragmatic and responsible, observes and memorizes, but does not have a critical faculty or an inquiring mind. In contrast, the Australian folk conception involves a critical faculty and an inquiring mind, language and communication skills, and problem solving; an intelligent person reasons logically, has academic attainments, and is a success in society.

There is clearly a similarity in the Malay, Chinese, Japanese, and African conceptions of intelligence in that, in spite of differences in other attributes, all include an emphasis on qualities that are necessary for harmonious group functioning. These conceptions are also clearly different from the Australian model of intelligence where the emphasis is on individual cognitive abilities and related skills and individual attainments. But, as we will see, the individualistic Australians have similar conceptions of intelligence to individualistic Americans.

Bruner, Shapiro, & Tagiuri (1958) asked American college students to indicate personality traits displayed by intelligent people. They found that the traits associated with intelligence included clever, deliberate, efficient, and energetic.

Sternberg, Conway, Ketron, & Bernstein (1981) investigated conceptions of intelligence among adult American laypersons and experts (psychologists doing research on human intelligence in universities and research centers around the country). After collecting lists of behaviors associated with intelligence from both students and laypersons, Sternberg et al. asked the laypersons and experts to rate how characteristic each of the listed behaviors was of an intelligent person and then factor analyzed the ratings. The results suggest three interpretable factors in laypersons' conceptions of intelligence. The first was labeled "practical problem-solving ability" and comprised such behaviors as "reasons logically and well," "identifies connections among ideas," and "sees all aspects of a problem." The second factor, "verbal ability," included such behaviors as "speaks clearly and articulately," "is verbally fluent," and "is knowledgeable about a particular field of study." The third factor was labeled "social competence," including behaviors such as "displays interest in the world at large," "accepts others for what they are," and "is on time for appointments." But although there is a social component to Americans' conceptions of intelligence it is clearly of a different sort than the social component present in the conceptions of intelligence typical of the collectivistic cultures described. Nowhere is there the obedience, social responsibility, caution, and deference that would promote group welfare typical of all groups discussed so far with the exception of the Australians.

In the experts' conceptions of an ideally intelligent person even the social component included by American laypersons was absent. In experts' ratings the first factor was labeled "verbal intelligence" and included behaviors such as "reads with high comprehension," "displays a good vocabulary," and "displays curiosity." The second factor, "problem-solving ability," included behaviors such as "able to apply knowledge to the problem at hand," "makes good decisions," and "poses problems in an optimal way." The third factor, practical intelligence, comprises behaviors such as "sizes up situations well," "determines how to achieve goals," and "displays awareness of the world around him."

It is interesting to note here that, quite unlike the strong social component included in the folk models in relatively collectivistic societies, there appears to be little need for skills in interacting with other people in experts' conceptions. While it is true that experts' conceptions no doubt reflect a professional life spent studying individual intelligence, it is also true that individualism increases with social and geographic mobility and affluence in all societies, a more accurate description of a group made up exclusively of professionals than a group of randomly chosen laypersons in a Northeastern city.

In a third individualistic culture, Canada, Fry (1984) investigated conceptions of children's intelligence among primary school, secondary school, and college teachers. The results indicated that among primary school teachers, social competence and social aspects of intelligence were most important, including qualities such as friendliness, popularity, and interest in the environment. Secondary school teachers emphasized verbal abilities, including verbal fluency, and among college teachers, cognitive abilities were stressed, such as logical thinking, knowledge, reasoning ability, and the ability to solve problems in a mature way. Sternberg (1990b) notes that, taken together, the conceptions of intelligence among the Canadian teachers were similar to the three factors resulting from the study of implicit theories among American laypersons (Sternberg, Conway, Ketron, & Bernstein, 1981). However, because of the similarity to American conceptions of intelligence, the same point can be made regarding the lack similarity between Canadian and Japanese conceptions. Specifically, the Canadian subjects, like the Americans, do not include the receptive social-competence factor included in Japanese conceptions of intelligence.

Putting it all together

An intelligent person, Neisser (1979) states, is a prototype-organized Roschian concept with fuzzy boundaries, and intelligence is simply the degree of resemblance between two persons, one real and the other prototypical. Our confidence that another person deserves to be called intelligent is a function of his or her resemblance to the prototypically intelligent person. One need not possess all the characteristics of the prototype to be considered intelligent; it is the degree of similarity that matters, and at least one study has demonstrated that people do use prototypes in judging their own and others' intelligence (Sternberg, Conway, Ketron, & Bernstein, 1981). But Neisser also acknowledges that there is likely to be a covariance in many of the features of prototypes of intelligence because these attributes are sensitive to cultural factors.

Indeed, that observation seems to accurately reflect the implicit theories reviewed in this chapter. There are important differences in conceptions of intelligence across cultures that do appear to be sensitive to cultural factors. There appear to be two broad classes of conceptions of intelligence that are clearly sensitive to critical and fundamental aspects of cultural meaning systems. In particular, the culture's relative level of individualism–collectivism, which accounts for the relation of individuals to groups at the cultural level, and idiocentrism–allocentrism or interdependent–independent self-concepts, which account for differences in self-concept and personality motivational systems, appear to be related to differences in the content of prototypes of intelligence across cultures. This difference is particularly evident in the nature and importance of social-competence factors in implicit theories of intelligence. The universal aspect seems to be the overall inclusion of some social-competence component in all cultures studied, with the exception of the implicit theories of American intelligence experts! However, while that is an important observation, and suggests that it is the notions of experts that need "revision," to simply state that social competence is a universally important aspect of intelligence gives no indication of the evident differences in what it means to be socially competent nor does it allow an examination of the links between notions of intelligence and personality systems across cultures. To accomplish that goal requires examining notions of intelligence as part of the larger cultural meaning system.

In the individualistic cultures reviewed in this chapter, including Canada, the United States, and Australia, the social component of implicit theories of intelligence is of the type termed "positive social competence" by Azuma and Kashiwagi (1987). Among behaviors and qualities frequently mentioned as part of this positive social competence are speaking clearly and articulately, being a success in society, being frank and honest, displaying interest in the world at large, being on time for appointments, communicating well, and being friendly. That these are the behaviors considered both intelligent and socially competent is clearly consistent with individualistic values. Recall that individualists are described as having excellent but often superficial social skills of the type that allow easy movement among many ingroups but are less useful for developing and maintaining intimate ties (Hsu, 1981). We have

also noted that self-actualization and self-expression are more valued in individualistic cultures than are group harmony and the ability to respond to the needs of
others. Clearly the components of social competence regarded as intelligent among
individualists are of the type that are more useful in self-expression than in understanding and responding to others.

Cultural meaning systems share links with personality systems when cultural
values are implicated in individual motivation. For idiocentrics or those with independent self-concepts the self is conceived of as a bounded configuration of unique
abilities, attributes, and personality traits. Because the self is considered to be self-
contained and unique, and because those with independent self-concepts are more
likely to be members of individualistic cultures, motivation is likely to be directed
toward individual goals that will allow expression of the unique self. Furthermore,
because each individual is unique and separate it is each person's responsibility to
make his or her needs known (Markus and Kitayama, 1991). In individualistic
cultures, "the squeaky wheel gets the grease."

Given the emphasis on the individual in individualistic cultures it is not surprising
that social competence as an aspect of intelligence is of the type that will aid the
individual in making his or her needs, opinions, and abilities known rather than being
aware of the needs, opinions, and abilities of others. It appears that an intelligent
person in an individualistic society is someone who is able to express himself,
communicate clearly, and succeed in society in an optimal way, and do it in a manner
that will make a fast, positive impression among a variety of fluid ingroups.

A very different picture arises in the collectivistic cultures we have discussed,
including Asian and African cultures. Social competence was considerably more
important to collectivistic conceptions of intelligence, and it was of a different type
than social competence in individualistic cultures. Here the type of social competence
most frequently mentioned was that aptly termed "receptive social competence" by
Azuma and Kashiwagi (1987). Behaviors that were typical of this second "type" of
social competence were, in African populations, prudence and caution in social
relationships, obedience, respect for and deference toward elders, and social conformity. Japanese subjects included attributes such as knowing one's place, admitting
mistakes with good grace, being sympathetic, and modesty. Chinese subjects included carefulness, imitation, correctness in thinking, responsibility, and social responsibility in conceptions of intelligence. Again, although the specific behaviors
show some differences, in all cases social competence in collectivistic societies is
consistent with the primary collectivistic values of maintaining harmony and stability
within ingroups. Collectivists show great willingness to cooperate with ingroup
members, have many role-related obligations, and place ingroup goals ahead of
individual goals.

There is a strong similarity between the social-competence qualities included in
collectivist conceptions of intelligence and personality qualities valued across various
collectivistic societies. Hispanics value "simpatico," the ability to share and respect
the feelings of others (Triandis, Marin, Lisansky, & Betancourt, 1984). Traditional

Greeks place importance on having "philotimo," that is, being virtuous, polite, reliable, tactful, and self-sacrificing. A person with "philotimo" behaves toward the ingroup as the ingroup expects him to behave (Triandis, 1972). For Filipinos, it is important that people remain agreeable even under difficult circumstances, have sensitivity to others' feelings, and are willing to adjust their behavior in accordance with the feelings of others (Church, 1987). Self-expression for collectivists is secondary to group welfare as evidenced in both the values and desirable personality attributes in collectivistic cultures. It appears that in collectivistic societies an intelligent person has the skills that maximize harmonious and cooperative social interaction.

Furthermore, as in individualistic societies, collectivistic cultural meaning systems are linked to individual personality systems, creating a particular kind of motivation. But in this case it is not the individually goal-oriented motivation typical of individualistic societies. Those with interdependent self-concepts and allocentric personalities do not see themselves primarily as unique and separate individuals. Rather, the individual's boundaries "overlap" with those of ingroup members forming a "we consciousness" (Hui & Triandis, 1986; Markus & Kitayama, 1991). Motivation is social, that is, individuals strive to achieve group goals and a strong emphasis is placed on the ability to control personal desires in favor of group needs. Among the Japanese, for example, the outright assertion of the ego is considered immature; one is expected to be polite even under difficult circumstances (Hamaguchi, 1985). In Japanese society "the nail that stands out get pounded down" (Markus & Kitayama, 1991).

Clearly, the self-expression and assertive behaviors typical of individualistic conceptions of intelligence, if unmodified by receptive social competence, would be both disruptive and viewed unfavorably in collectivistic societies. Intelligence, in terms of differences in social competence, appears to conform to the emphasis on intelligence as adaptation in current theories of intelligence. But it is adaptation not only to the physical aspects of the environment, but to the cultural meaning system, suggesting that in order to understand intelligence as adaptation across cultures we must expand our definition of environment to include cultural meaning systems.

Because the social competence that appears, at first glance, to be a "universal" factor of intelligence varies sufficiently in individualistic cultures to constitute two separate abilities, receptive and positive social competence, it seems likely that other abilities that appear universal also vary with cultural meaning systems. Knowledge is widely valued across cultures, but the existing research is insufficient to tell us what kind of knowledge is valued and if that variation is as noteworthy as the variation in social competence. It is likely that in individualistic cultures the knowledge that is valued will be primarily self-knowledge and knowledge of subjects of individual interest or of those that are useful for individual gain. We noted earlier that people in individualistic cultures have relatively more knowledge of the self than of others. By contrast, individuals in collectivistic cultures possess relatively more knowledge of other people, as would be expected in cultures where the emphasis is on the ingroup and on the self-in-relation-to-other. Hence, it is likely that in collectivistic cultures the knowledge that is included in conceptions of intelligence will be similarly "other-focused." Another widely cited element of prototypes of intelligence, understanding, is likely to reflect the same difference in cultural values. Specifically, understanding is likely to mean primarily understanding of others and their needs for collectivists, and understanding of issues of importance to individuals in individualistic cultures. As with social competence, we cannot conclude that these seeming "universals" are indeed universal until we are able to correctly place them within the system of cultural meanings, and understand what each of these components means to members of diverse cultures and how they are a part of the particular senses of reality that are culture.

Acknowledgement

The authors would like to express their appreciation to Joan G. Miller for the many hours spent discussing culture. Without her time, attention, and expertise the ideas presented in this chapter could not have been developed.

References

Azuma, H., & Kashiwagi, K. (1987). Descriptors for an intelligent person: A Japanese study. *Japanese Psychological Research, 29,* 17–26.
Barry, H., Child, I., & Bacon, M. (1959). Relation of child training to subsistence economy. *American Anthropologist, 61,* 51–63.
Bellah, R. N., Madsen, R., Sullivan, W. M., Swidler, A., & Tipton, S. M. (1985). *Habits of the heart: Individualism and commitment in American life.* New York: Harper & Row.
Berry, J. W. (1974). Radical cultural relativism and the concept of intelligence. In J. W. Berry & P. R. Dasen (Eds.), *Culture and cognition: Readings in cross-cultural psychology.* London: Methuen.
Berry, J. W. (1980). Ecological analyses for cognitive psychology. In N. Warren (Ed.), *Studies in cross-cultural psychology.* London: Academic Press.
Berry, J. W. (1984). Towards a universal psychology of cognitive competence. *International Journal of Psychology, 19,* 335–361.
Berry, J. W. (1987). The comparative study of cognitive abilities. In S. H. Irvine & S. E. Neusteud (Eds.), *Intelligence and cognition: Contemporary frames of reference.* Dordrecht: Martinus Nijhoff.
Berry, J. W., & Irvine, S. H. (1986). Bricolage: Savages do it daily. In R. J. Sternberg & R. K. Wagner (Eds.), *Practical intelligence: Nature and origins of competence in the everyday world.* New York: Cambridge University Press.
Bond, M. H. (1986). *The psychology of Chinese people.* New York: Oxford University Press.
Bruner, J. S., Shapiro, D., & Tagiuri, R. (1958). The meaning of traits in isolation and in combination. In R. Tagiuri & L. Petrullo (Eds.), *Person perception and interpersonal behavior.* Stanford: Stanford University Press.
Ceci, S. J. (1990). *On intelligence – more or less: A biological treatise on intellectual development.* Englewood Cliffs, NJ: Prentice-Hall.
Charlesworth, W. (1976). Human intelligence as adaptation: An ecological approach. In L. Resnick (Ed.), *The nature of intelligence.* Hillsdale, NJ: Erlbaum.
Church, T. A. (1987). Personality research in a non-Western culture: The Phillipines. *Psychological Bulletin, 102,* 272–292.
D'Andrade, R. G. (1984). Cultural meaning systems. In R. A. Shweder & R. A. LeVine (Eds.), *Culture theory: Essays in mind, self, and emotion.* New York: Cambridge University Press.

Dasen, P. R. (1984). The cross-cultural study of intelligence: Piaget and the Baoule. *International Journal of Psychology, 19,* 407–434.

Doi, T. (1986). *The anatomy of conformity: The individual versus society.* Tokyo: Kodansha.

Eysenck, H. J. (1982). *A model for intelligence.* Berlin: Springer Verlag.

Fry, P. S. (1984). Changing conceptions of intelligence and intellectual functioning: Current theory and research. In P. S. Fry (Ed.), *Changing conceptions of intelligence and intellectual functioning: Current theory and research.* Amsterdam: North-Holland.

Geertz, C. (1973). *The interpretation of cultures.* New York: Basic Books.

Geertz, C. (1975). On the nature of anthropological understanding. *American Scientist, 63,* 47–53.

Gill, R., & Keats, D. (1980). Elements of intellectual competence: Judgments by Australian and Malay university students. *Journal of Cross-Cultural Psychology, 11,* 233–243.

Goodman, N. (1968). *Languages of art.* New York: Bobbs-Merrill.

Goodnow, J. J. (1980). Everyday concepts of intelligence and its development. In N. Warren (Ed.), *Studies in cross-cultural psychology.* London: Academic Press.

Goodnow, J. J. (1984). On being judged "intelligent." *International Journal of Psychology, 19,* 391–406.

Greenwald, A. G., & Pratkanis, A. R. (1984). The self. In R. S. Wyer & T. K. Srull (Eds.), *Handbook of social cognition, (Vol. 3),* Hillsdale, NJ: Erlbaum.

Hamaguchi, E. (1985). A conceptual model of the Japanese: Towards a methodological innovation in Japan studies. *Journal of Japanese Studies, 11,* 289–321.

Hofstede, G. (1980). *Culture's consequences.* Beverly Hills, CA: Sage.

Hsu, F. L. K. (1981). *American and Chinese: Passage to differences.* Honolulu: University of Hawaii Press.

Hui, C. H., & Triandis, H. C. (1986). Individualism–collectivism: A study of cross-cultural researchers. *Journal of Cross-cultural Psychology, 17,* 225–248.

Irvine, S. H. (1969). The factor analysis of African abilities and attainments: Constructs across cultures. *Psychological Bulletin, 71,* 20–32.

Irvine, S. H. (1970). Affect and construct—a cross-cultural check on theories of intelligence. *Journal of Social Psychology, 80,* 23–30.

Irvine, S. H., & Berry, J. W. (1988). The abilities of mankind: A re-evaluation . In S. H. Irvine & J. W. Berry (Eds.), *Human abilities in cultural context.* New York: Cambridge University Press.

Keats, D. (1982). Cultural bases of concepts of intelligence. A Chinese versus Australian comparison. In: *Proceedings second Asian workshop on child and adolescent development.* Bangkok: Behavioral Research Institute.

Kim, U. (submitted for publication). Introduction to individualism–collectivism. To appear in U. Kim, H. C. Triandis, & G. Yoon (Eds.), *Individualism and collectivism: Theoretical and methodological issues.* Newbury Park, CA: Sage.

Laboratory of Comparative Human Cognition. (1982). Culture and intelligence. In R. J. Sternberg (Ed.), *Handbook of human intelligence.* New York: Cambridge University Press.

Leont'ev, A. N. (1979). The image of the world. *The Moscow University Herald, Series 14–Psychology, Issue 2.* (In Russian.)

Lukes, S. (1973). *Individualism.* Oxford: Basil Blackwell.

Markus, H., & Kitayama, S. (1991). Culture and the self: Implications for cognition, emotion, and motivation. *Psychological Review, 98,* 224–252.

Markus, H., & Wurf, E. (1987). The dynamic self-concept: A social psychological perspective. *Annual Review of Psychology, 38,* 299–337.

Miller, J. G. (1984). Culture and the development of everyday social explanation. *Journal of Personality and Social Psychology, 46,* 961–978.

Miller, J. G. (1988). Bridging the content–structure dichotomy. In M. H. Bond (Ed.), *The cross-cultural challenge to social psychology.* Newbury Park, CA: Sage.

Mundy-Castle, A. (1983). Are Western psychological concepts valid in Africa? A Nigerian review. In S. H. Irvine & J. W. Berry (Eds.), *Human assessment and cultural factors.* New York: Plenum.

Neisser, U. (1979). The concept of intelligence. In R. J. Sternberg & D. K. Detterman (Eds.), *Human intelligence: Perspectives on its theory and measurement.* Norwood, NJ: Ablex.

Putnam, D. B., & Kilbride, P. L. (1980). A relativistic understanding of social intelligence among the

Songhay of Mali and the Samia of Kenya. *Paper presented at Society for Cross-Cultural Research,* Philadelphia.

Schneider, D. (1976). Notes toward a theory of culture. In K. Basso & H. Selby (Eds.), *Meaning in anthropology.* Albuquerque: University of New Mexico Press.

Selby, H. A. (1975). Semantics and causality in the study of deviance. In M. Sanches & B. G. Blount (Eds.), *Sociocultural dimensions of language use.* New York: Academic Press.

Serpell, R. (1977). Strategies for investigating intelligence in its cultural context. *Institute for Comparative Human Development, Quarterly Newsletter 1(3),* 11–15.

Serpell, R. (1974). Aspects of intelligence in a developing country. *African Social Research, 17,* 576–596.

Shweder, R. A. (1986). Divergent rationalities. In D. W. Fiske & R. A. Shweder (Eds.), *Metatheory in social science: Pluralism and subjectivities.* Chicago: University of Chicago Press.

Shweder, R. A., & Bourne, E. (1982). Does the concept of the person vary cross-culturally? In A. J. Marsella & G. White (Eds.), *Cultural conceptions of mental health and therapy.* Boston: Reidel.

Shweder, R. A., & Bourne, E. J. (1984). Does the concept of the person vary cross-culturally? In R. A. Shweder & R. A. LeVine (Eds.), *Culture theory: Essays in mind, self, and emotion.* New York: Cambridge University Press.

Spindler, G. D., & Spindler, L. (1983). Anthropologists view American culture. *Annual Review of Anthropology, 12,* 49–78.

Sternberg, R. J. (1985). *Beyond IQ: A triarchic theory of human intelligence.* New York: Cambridge University Press.

Sternberg, R. J. (1987). Implicit theories: An alternative to modeling cognition and its development. In J. Bisanz, C. J. Brainerd, & R. Kail (Eds.), *Formal methods in developmental psychology: Progress in cognitive development research.* New York: Springer-Verlag.

Sternberg, R. J. (1988). *The triarchic mind.* New York: Viking Press.

Sternberg, R. J. (1990a). Wisdom and its relation to intelligence and creativity. In R. J. Sternberg (Ed.), *Wisdom: Its nature, origins, and development.* New York: Cambridge University Press.

Sternberg, R. J. (1990b). *Metaphors of mind.* New York: Cambridge University Press.

Sternberg, R. J., Conway, B. E., Ketron, J. L., & Bernstein, M. (1981). People's conceptions of intelligence. *Journal of Personality and Social Psychology, 41,* 37–55.

Strauss, A. S. (1973). Northern Cheyenne ethnosociology. *Ethos, 1,* 326–357.

Triandis, H. C. (1972). *The analysis of subjective culture.* New York: Wiley.

Triandis, H. C. (1990a). Cross-cultural studies of individualism and collectivism. In J. Berman (Ed.), *Nebraska Symposium on Motivation, 1989.* Lincoln: University of Nebraska Press.

Triandis, H. C. (1990b). Theoretical and methodological approaches. *Paper prepared for the workshop on individualism–collectivism,* Seoul, Korea.

Triandis, H. C., Marin, G., Lisansky, J., & Betancourt, H. (1984). Simpatia as a cultural script of Hispanics. *Journal of Personality and Social Psychology, 47,* 1363–1375.

Wober, M. (1972). Culture and the concept of intelligence. *Journal of Cross-cultural Psychology, 3,* 327–328.

Wober, M. (1974). Towards an understanding of the Kiganda concept of intelligence. In J. W. Berry & P. R. Dasen (Eds.), *Culture and cognition: Readings in cross-cultural psychology.* London: Methuen.

Yang, K. S. (1982). Causal attributions of academic success and failure and their affective consequences. *Chinese Journal of Psychology, 24,* 65–83.

10 Morality, authoritarianism, and personal agency in cultural contexts

Elliot Turiel

In *The Authoritarian Personality* (Adorno, Frenkel-Brunswik, Levinson, & Sanford, 1950), a classic but currently somewhat neglected tome on prejudice and ideology, antisemitic individuals are portrayed as possessing an authoritarian personality syndrome that is antidemocratic and ethnocentric. Characteristic of this syndrome of authoritarianism is the stereotyping of Jews, as illustrated by the researchers' descriptions of Mack, one of their subjects (p. 41): "The Jews as a whole are conceived of as constituting a closely knit group, the members of which are blindly loyal and stick together for mutual comfort and help. They have their own organizations because they are unwilling to mix with Gentiles. By sticking together, they accumulate wealth and power which will be used to benefit no one but themselves." Moreover, Adorno, et al. (p. 43) assert that Mack "seems to think of the Jews as constituting a relatively homogeneous group that is categorically different from the group to which he feels he belongs [the Irish]. . . . Most striking is the *stereotyped* way in which he speaks of the Irish and of the groups with which they are contrasted. Each ethnic group is regarded as a homogeneous entity, and little mention is made of exceptions." They describe Mack's ideology concerning minorities to include "stereotypy," which is "the tendency to subsume things under rigid categories," and the idea that groups are "homogeneous units which more or less determine the nature of their numbers." Persons are not treated as individuals and all social interaction is viewed in hierarchical and authoritarian terms.

The authors of this volume on authoritarianism were critical of the personality syndrome of prejudiced individuals on two grounds: that minority groups are judged negatively, and that they are stereotyped in homogeneous ways. The authors implicitly assumed that social, ethnic, or national groups could not, and should not, be characterized in homogeneous ways, and that when individuals do so, it entails a stereotyping of people that often reflects prejudiced attitudes toward that group. Note, however, that the researchers themselves judged the personality of prejudiced individuals negatively and accepted that the personality syndrome of these individuals can be characterized in homogeneous terms. They proposed that prejudiced individuals possess a constellation of coherent and consistent traits, entailing an "authoritarian" personality, which contrasts with another constellation of traits reflective of the "democratic" personality.

271

Although these parallels exist between the researchers' characterizations of their subjects and their own orientation to the subjects themselves, it could be argued that the researchers' constructs are valid for two reasons. One is that prejudice is morally condemnable, and the other is that the homogeneous personality syndromes were derived by the researchers through intensive social scientific analyses. The latter consideration, of course, has been discussed and debated extensively in recent years – especially as stimulated by Mischel's (1968, 1969) well known assertions that the construct of coherent patterns of personality is invalid because behaviors are variable in accord with situational factors (also see Shweder, 1975). It is of interest to note that these types of disputes over the nature of personality traits are not new and were occurring at the time of the writing of *The Authoritarian Personality*. Indeed, Adorno, et al. (1950, p. 744) believed that, "Hardly any concept in contemporary American psychology has been so thoroughly criticized as that of typology. . . . From the viewpoint of general dynamic theory of personality, it is objected that typologies tend toward pigeonholing and transform highly flexible traits into static, quasi-biological characteristics while neglecting, above all, the impact of historical and social factors." They went on to argue that psychological types exist, not because of biological features, but because they are produced by the social world.

Whereas the debates over personality typing continue, there is a form of typing that has not been much critiqued nor debated. Over the years, there has been a strong tendency to contrast "cultures" in their social–moral orientations, thereby characterizing them in homogeneous terms. In recent years, it is commonplace to find cultures contrasted on the dimensions of individualism and collectivism or traditionalism (Hogan, 1975; Sampson, 1977; Shweder & Bourne, 1982; Triandis, 1989, 1990). The "cultural orientation," in turn, is supposedly reflected in the sociomoral reasoning and practices of its members.

This form of typing has far-reaching implications for the substantive domains that are the topics of this chapter – moral and social development. There are developmental implications, since it is proposed that an overriding cultural orientation is acquired by most individuals in forming their judgments and actions. There are also implications for what constitute realms of social practice and reasoning. One central feature supposedly distinguishing individualistic from collectivistic or traditional cultures is the conception of the person. It is said that individualistic cultures define the person as detached from relationships and the community, and thereby construct a morality focusing on personal rights, freedom, and the equality of individuals. By contrast, in collectivistic and traditional cultures the person is defined in relation to others and by roles and status within the social system. Accordingly, morality in those cultures is based on fulfilling prescribed duties and adhering to one's place in a hierarchically ordered system; concepts of personal jurisdiction, rights, or equality are said to be nonexistent.

In this chapter, the question of typing of cultures is examined, leading to an alternative view of cultural contexts and their relations to individuals' development of moral, social and personal concepts. We take a critical look at several versions of the proposition that cultures can be characterized by their respective homogeneous orientations, focusing especially on the dichotomy between individualistic and collectivistic or traditional cultures. An examination of the proposed features of individualistic cultures indicates that such typing involves stereotyping in a not dissimilar manner to the way Adorno, et al. (1950) described the stereotyping of those with the "authoritarian personality" syndrome. As detailed below, there are indeed several similarities between the Adorno, et al. subjects' characterization of social, ethnic, and religious groups and the ways cultural orientations have been typed with one-dimensional orientations. It is our contention that the evidence shows that people in so-called individualistic cultures have multiple social orientations, including concerns with social duties, the collective community, interdependence, as well as personal rights, freedoms, and equality. Research on "domain specific" forms of social reasoning or social intelligences is reviewed in order to show that individuals do not solely acquire one type of social orientation. We put forth the position that individuals construct their social judgments through reciprocal interactions with a multifaceted social environment. In the context of differently organized social systems (e.g., more or less hierarchy and role distinctions), it is necessary to understand participants' thinking about personal agency and jurisdiction, moral duties and rights, as well as roles within the constituted sociocultural context.

The (stereo) typing of peoples

Over the years, national, ethnic, and, especially, cultural groups often have been characterized in homogeneous terms by sociologists, psychologists, anthropologists, and social commentators. Prominent examples include portrayals of "national character," of connections between culture and personality, and the recently emphasized dichotomies between cultural orientations toward individualism and collectivism. Three or four decades ago, the notion of national character distinguishing the peoples of different countries was considered seriously in some circles. Illustrative examples can be found in Gorer's efforts to describe national character in *American People* (1948) and *The People of Great Russia* (1949). Gorer's anthropological studies of these peoples were premised on his central presuppositions that national character is the embodiment of culture, which is pervasive and acquired in early childhood. He maintained that each society has an ideal character for its members, serving to guide the child-rearing practices of parents and other authorities. Even though individuals may possess particular characteristics that deviate from that national character, according to Gorer anyone who has fully participated in the society through childhood and adolescence will represent the core of the group character.

Gorer's analyses of the American character are far-reaching but do not cohere into related elements. However, he maintained that two major themes, including features of individualism, characterized Americans. These were "emotional egalitarianism" (the equality of persons) and a strong rejection of authority (a rejection that goes so far as to regard authority as inherently bad, morally detestable, and dangerous). For instance, Americans presumably treat all relationships like ones of love and friendship because of their emphasis on egalitarianism. However, Americans are so insatiable for the signs of friendship that they regard persons as commodities to be marketed (Gorer, 1948, chapter V). As marketable and manipulable commodities, people are viewed as "working machines" to fit into the economic system. Given this objectification of people, Americans are actually not oriented toward relationships but to the world of objects and to monetary success and material possessions (chapters VI and VII). Gorer asserts, in fact, that materialism and monetary success dominate American life. Americans are overly concerned with: personal appearance ("It is only a slight exaggeration to say that a young woman who didn't paint her finger nails today would not be able to proclaim 'I am an American' with as much conviction and fervor as her properly made-up sisters," p. 195); the appearance of their material goods (e.g., the proper positioning of window shades, the style of furniture, etc.); and, of course, conspicuous consumption ("Few Americans . . . would dare have only one car in a house which has a two-car garage," p. 183).

Most of the evidence documenting the descriptions of the American character entailed examples of what is typically done, put in anecdotal form (including the type of material just quoted). Anecdotal evidence mainly stemming from experiences (his own and that of an English physician–psychoanalyst) in the Soviet Great Russian Republic (Gorer, 1949) also contributed to the portrayal of Russian national character (material from informal interviews, history, and literature were also included). In contrast with Americans' focus on the equality of persons, Russia is described as a caste society in which the group determines the rights, duties, and privileges of persons. Two themes regarding Russian national character emerge (though not as explicitly put as in the description of Americans). These are a fusion of persons into the group and reverence for authority. Russians are collectivists who accept a hierarchical system in which authority is idealized and a "natural" inequality among persons is assumed. The acquisition of these features of the national character is mainly due to experiences in very early childhood. Gorer maintained that the Russian character is formed by the practice of swaddling, entailing long periods during the first nine months in which infants are tightly wrapped. Swaddling inhibits the type of exploration of the environment that would stimulate self–other differentiations and shapes an orientation toward reliance on external control.

Four features of Gorer's work are important for our understanding of culture and social development. First, it was proposed that cultures form integrated systems that can be characterized in homogeneous terms. Some cultures are contrasted by opposite orientations (e.g., Americans detest authority, Russians revere it). Second, individuals within a culture are characterized as possessing coherent, global characteristics of a homogeneous kind that correspond to the unitary orientation of the culture. Third, the correspondence between individual and cultural characteristics is due to consistent experiences in early childhood that constitute the origins of the characteristics of adults. The fourth feature is that highly general and difficult to pinpoint practices of the society are given in the form of evidence.

The concept of national character is, therefore, essentially typological. It is proposed that there are consistent orientations within cultures that may differ from one culture to another. The term national character currently seems to be out of favor and has not always been used in theorizing about connections between culture and personality (or character). Nevertheless, at least the first three features of Gorer's analyses are evident, to one extent or another, in most formulations linking culture and personality. For example, concurrently with analyses of national character there were influential postulates regarding culture and personality prominent in the 1940s and 1950s (see Shweder, 1979a, 1979b, 1980 for critical, comprehensive reviews). To put it briefly and simply, the culture and personality school (e.g., Benedict, 1934, 1946; Kardiner, 1945; Whiting and Child, 1953) sought consistency or an underlying pattern across different situations, contexts, and realms (e.g., religion, politics, economics, aesthetics, and, of course, morality) within a culture. Cultures were seen to form consistent, integrated patterns represented in the personalities of individuals. Thus, cultures were characterized in homogeneous terms and individuals typed with global traits. Early childhood experiences were generally proposed to influence the person's acquisition of the integrated cultural patterns.

These propositions raise the same types of considerations and debates over typologies as noted by Adorno, et al. (1950). One critic of the culture and personality approach put the question in the following way (Shweder, 1979a, p. 258): "Any attempt to describe either personality or culture must address two basic questions: (1) How widely do the thoughts, emotions, and actions of a person or a people generalize across diverse stimuli, contexts, or domains? (2) To what extent can the thinking, feelings, and doings of a person or a people be sorted into a limited number of descriptive categories?" Shweder's conclusions regarding these questions, based on his review of the evidence, was consistent with Mischel's (1969) proposition that individuals do not possess general or global traits manifested in behavior across situations or contexts (also see Geertz, 1966). Moreover, Shweder read the evidence to disconfirm the propositions of both cultural integration and that early experiences strongly influence adult behavior.

Not surprisingly, debates over personality typing continue (details on personality theories and the evidence are beyond the scope of the present discussion). However, much less debate occurs regarding the typing of cultures or societies. As already noted, there have reemerged in recent years characterizations of cultures as integrated by orientations to individualism or collectivism (orientations deemed central to fundamental cultural differences in concepts of the person and of morality). Propositions regarding cultural variations in individualism and collectivism have taken several forms. Some have taken an evangelical form in that the emphasis has been on the deleterious quality of individualism in Western societies (e.g., Bellah, Madsen, Sullivan, Swidler, & Tipton, 1985; Delattre & Bennett, 1979; Hogan, 1975; Sampson, 1977; Sommers, 1984). It is argued by some that because this society is first and foremost oriented to "self-contained individualism" (Sampson, 1977), it is experiencing a moral decay or degeneration that would be ameliorated by a greater concern with the type of interdependence that is assumed to exist in collectivistic societies. It has also been argued that social scientists, with their Western biases, have contributed to society's degeneration by espousing individualistic theories (see especially Hogan, 1975 and Sampson, 1977; for a critical appraisal of these positions, see Turiel, 1989b).

More dispassionate positions are taken by those whose primary aim is to describe the proposed central or core cultural orientations (e.g., Shweder & Bourne, 1982; Triandis, 1989, 1990). Fairly comprehensive descriptions and reviews of evidence are provided by Triandis, who maintained that the most important dimension, with regard to social behavior, of differences between cultures may be the emphasis placed on individualism or collectivism. Like others, Triandis treats the United States as the quintessential individualistic society but also regards Australia, Canada, England, and New Zealand as among the most individualistic cultures of the world. China and India are said to be prototypical collectivist cultures.

A basic contrast is that whereas in individualistic cultures social behavior is largely determined by personal goals, in collectivistic cultures it is determined by shared goals. Insofar as there is an ethos of individualism, people are oriented to self-sufficiency, self-reliance, self-realization, detachment from others, personal goals, and an autonomy that resists social pressures for conformity. Those cultures do not manifest the characteristics of collectivistic cultures – which include concerns with tradition, duty, obedience to authority, interdependence, and social harmony. Hierarchy, status, and role distinctions predominate. A consequence of the focus on the group is a strict differentiation between the in-group and other groups, such that one's own group is given preference over other groups. People act towards the out-groups in noncooperative, unhelpful, and manipulative ways (Triandis, 1990).

The two types of cultures are said to define the social unit differently. For collectivists it is the group; for individualists it is the person. It has been maintained that in these two types of cultures, the very concept of the person varies. Shweder and Bourne (1982) distinguish between "sociocentric" and "egocentric" relations of the individual to the group, which are "creations of the collective imagination." In the former, there is no distinction between the individual and the status or role occupied nor a separation from the social context. Individual interests are subordinated to the good of the collectivity and the idea of individual autonomy is alien. Instead, persons are interdependent and strictly regulated by rules and duties. In the egocentric, individualistic cultures, by contrast, society is seen to "have been created to serve the interests of some idealized, autonomous, abstract individual existing free of society yet living in society" (Shweder & Bourne, 1982, p. 190). The individual is regarded as a value and end in and of itself. Freedom of personal expression in a variety of manifestations is salient and protected from societal intrusion. The dichotomy between individualism and collectivism is viewed as central to cultural variations in the realm of morality (Hogan, 1975; Sampson, 1977; Shweder, 1986, 1990; Shweder, Mahapatra, & Miller, 1987). Shweder and his colleagues, especially, have attempted to apply the general characterizations of cultural orientations to more specific formulations through a proposed distinction between "rights-based" and "duty-based" moralities. The moral reasoning and practices of Western societies are said to be structured by concerns with individual rights, equality, justice, personal liberties, and freedoms. The foundations of the moral code in such societies lie in personal prerogatives and entitlements. A rights-based morality is contrasted with the divergent and incomparable moral code of collectivistic or traditional–authoritarian societies. Those duty-based moral codes are organized around social hierarchies and prescribed roles, authority relations, particular duties, and maintenance of tradition. Rights, personal agency, and personal entitlements are not relevant because the individual is submerged within interdependence in the social order.

Accurate descriptions or stereotyping of cultures?

The characterizations of cultures and their moral codes as individualistic or collectivistic bring with them the assertion that persons in the culture share in the orientation, having acquired it in childhood. As opposed to the earlier work on national character and on culture and personality, in these recent treatments the features possessed by persons are not necessarily assumed to represent personality traits or syndromes. In some cases (e.g., Kessen, 1979; Sampson, 1977; Shweder & Bourne, 1982; Triandis, 1990), the psychological characteristics making up persons' orientations to individualism or collectivism are left unspecified. In other cases, it is proposed that culturally divergent moral codes are rationally based (Shweder, 1986, 1990). Duty-based and rights-based moral codes, for instance, are rational social constructions, at the cultural level, that are acquired by individual members of the culture. The moral codes constitute divergent, incommensurate systems structured by concepts of persons and social order. In these formulations the personality construct employing global, consistent traits is not present, but the idea of cultural integration is embraced. As general orientations, albeit in rational form, that constitute cultural differences (and, of course, differences between individuals from different cultures), there is the presumption that the thoughts, emotions, and actions of people do generalize across diverse stimuli, contexts, and domains.

Therefore, whether it be through the use of personality and character constructs or that of divergent forms of rationality, we see depictions of coherent, consistent orientations to the social world. In the work of Adorno, et al. (1950), individuals were typed by personality syndromes but there was an avoidance of typing of racial, religious, and national groups. Adorno, et al. characterized some of their subjects as typing such groups, which was itself a significant part of the proposed personality configuration defining the "authoritarian personality" syndrome. Whereas Adorno, et al. proposed consistent individual differences within groups and not group differences, in the analysis of national character and cultural dichotomies of individualism and collectivism the proposed consistent group differences imply coherent patterns of traits or thoughts and practices in individuals (since it is also proposed that individuals acquire the national and cultural patterns).

In other words, cultures and their individual members are characterized in homogeneous, unitary terms. Cultures and people are seen as one or the other; that is, individualistic or collectivistic. Their orientation is either egalitarian or hierarchical. They are either concerned with personal rights or societal roles and duties. They are either antiauthority (as in Gorer's notion that Americans view authority as detestable) or obedient to authority (e.g., that the people of Great Russia idealize authority). They are centered on the self or on the group. They are self-reliant or embedded in a system of interdependence among people. They are independent and unconcerned with group cohesiveness or they are meshed with the group such that rigid in-group/out-group distinctions are made.

Characterizing cultures in such homogeneous terms is a form of typing that may indeed constitute stereotyping (in the sense of seeing it as a fixed pattern), entailing the imposition of a unity that is not actually there. Although diversity is proposed to exist between cultures, within a given culture the overarching conception is one of unity, homogeneity, and insularity. It is stereotyping insofar as diversity and heterogeneity are features that not only apply to comparisons between cultures but also characterize the orientations within cultures and the thoughts and social practices of persons. A contrasting position is that within cultures and within individuals there is a coexistence of orientations encompassing the variety of features used to distinguish the supposed individualism and collectivism. For instance, it may be that there are coexisting concerns with egalitarianism *and* social hierarchy, with rights and duties, with independence and interdependence, with the person and with the group.

As is often the case with stereotypes, the characterizations of groups in homogeneous, one-dimensional terms can take on evaluative and moralistic qualities. This is especially so on the part of those whose assertion that Western society is individualistic has an evangelical tone. Accordingly, individualistic societies are spoken of in negative terms, with the at least implicit assumption that they suffer in comparison with collectivistic or traditional ones. For example, the American has been described as a "self-contained" individualist, "who does not require or desire others for his or her completion of life. . . . Self-contaminant is the extreme of independence . . . needing or wanting no one" (Sampson, 1977, p. 770). Individualism of this sort is considered to entail "great cost to human welfare," and its opposite, interdependence, "holds out the best hope for democratic processes of governance and natural problem solving" (p. 779). Others put it more bluntly: "our individualism may ultimately be in a very real sense, the ruin of us all" (Hogan, 1975, p. 536); "the ideology of individualism and the personal conscience orientation that characterize much of American psychology appear symptomatic of a sick society" (p. 539). It has also been asserted that the individualism of this society leads to an increased incidence of clinical depression (Seligman, 1988) and is a source of drug addiction, crime (Hogan, 1975), and child abuse (Triandis, 1990, p. 75). Even in the more descriptive, dispassionate analyses, evaluative commentary seems to creep in (Shweder & Bourne, 1982, p. 195–196):

It is also sobering to reflect on the psychic costs, the existential penalties of our egocentrism, our autonomous individualism. . . . Many in our culture lack a meaningful orientation to the past. We come from nowhere, the product of a random genetic accident. Many lack a meaningful orientation to the future. We are going nowhere – at best we view ourselves as "machines" that will one day run down. . . . In our view, society is dependent on us. And what are our gods? Personal success and wealth. . . . Cut adrift from any larger whole, the self has become the measure of all things, clutching to a faith that some "invisible hand" will by sleight of hand right things in the end.

Another indication that the one-dimensional characterization of individualism stereotypes what may be multifaceted and heterogeneous aspects of the social orientations is that the culture is not always described in this way. A brief look at the near-term historical context shows that American society and its members are not always described in individualistic terms by social scientists and social commentators (Turiel, Smetana, & Killen, 1991). One example comes from the work already discussed in *The Authoritarian Personality,* as well as other analyses of prejudice. By the account of Adorno, et al., a substantial minority of members of this society possess the traits grouped under the authoritarian personality syndrome – traits that for the most part are akin to the constellation usually attributed to collectivism and traditionalism. That is, the authoritarian personality syndrome includes an orientation to hierarchy rather than equality, to obedience rather than liberty, and to duties rather than civil rights. Moreover, it is a syndrome in which sharp in-group/out-group distinctions are made, with great favoritism given to one's own group.

Whether this kind of individual personality syndrome is an accurate representation is, of course, open to question. Furthermore, the extent to which it exists in the society is unclear. It does show, however, that nonindividualistic orientations have been described by psychologists studying social issues with American subjects. Additionally, American society, in general, has been characterized in terms opposite to individualism. As one example, some psychologists with a psychoanalytic bent, such as Erich Fromm (1941), argued that modern capitalist societies foster authoritarianism and conformity. According to Fromm, authoritarianism, closely paralleling the Adorno, et al. definition, is most prevalent in Fascist societies. Conformity, most prevalent in democracies, entails a loss of identity in which a sense of self is attained primarily by living up to the expectations of others. The individual subordinates the self to others in personal relations, and to the social and economic system.

Like Gorer, Fromm drew from public events (e.g., the media, entertainment, life styles, politics) to support his characterization of the society. Fromm's major thesis was that authoritarianism and conformity are the result of the functions and goals of capitalistic production. The individual is but a "cog in the vast economic machine." Fromm's way of articulating the issue is stark in its nonindividualism (1941, pp. 131–132): "the individual is confronted by uncontrollable dimensions in comparison with which he is a small particle. All he can do is to fall in step like a marching soldier or a worker on the endless belt. He can act; but the sense of independence, significance, has gone."

The metaphor of people as cogs in machines, social and economic, was also evoked by several popularly received books written by sociologists and social commentators in the 1950s, including *The Lonely Crowd* (Reisman, Glazer, & Denney, 1950), *The Organization Man* (Whyte, 1956), and *White Collar* (Mills, 1956). Without invoking psychoanalytic concepts, these writers also viewed society to be oriented to conformity to and dependence upon the group. The theme of economic forces overwhelming individual initiative and self-reliance is evident here too. Especially for Mills and Whyte, it is the organizations of the society that stifle freedoms, personal control, and individual creativity. Society was viewed as consisting of bureaucratic and hierarchical social institutions that, to use the words of Mills, usurp freedom and rationality from individuals. The consequences are that persons in the society are primarily conformist, lacking initiative, and dependent on others for sources of direction. In this view, people are impersonal, interchangeable links in the system of social organization.

Additional examples of nonindividualistic perspectives on behavior and social orientations at levels more specific than the general society come from two sources. One source is in the variety of ways the morality of this society is portrayed (e.g., Gilligan, 1982; Kohlberg, 1969; Miller & Luthar, 1989). Most pertinent to our present purposes is that some have presented a view of the dominant morality as centered on traditions, duties, hierarchical relations, and authority (e.g., Bennett & Delattre, 1978; Ryan, 1989; Sommers, 1984; Wynne, 1986). The working assumption in that perspective is that individualism, in the sense of disconnectedness, freedom, and antipathy to traditions and authority, is unrepresentative of the society. That type of individualism represents a minority orientation that, insofar as it exists, has a deleterious effect on the moral fabric of the culture (i.e., drug addiction, crime, sexual promiscuity, etc.). The antidote to the influences of individualism is a reaffirmation of the fundamental cultural moral codes: traditional values, duties, obedience to authority, respect for cultural symbols. In essence, proponents of this position construe the dominant morality of this culture in terms similar to the way supposedly "duty-based" (collectivistic and traditional) cultures are construed by those who construe Western morality as individualistic and "rights-based" (Turiel, 1989a).

A second source is a body of social psychological experiments conducted in the United States, yielding findings of widespread obedience to the commands of authorities (Milgram, 1963, 1974) and conformity to the behaviors of a small group giving incorrect perceptual judgments (Asch, 1956). Furthermore, it has been found (Frager, 1970) that in the supposedly collectivistic society of Japan less conformity was obtained in the Asch experiment than had been obtained with subjects in the United States. Japanese subjects, unlike American subjects, also showed a tendency to go against the group even when its members gave correct judgments (labeled by the researchers as anticonformity). The findings of Frager's study were contrary to his expectation that, because of the great pressure to conform in the Japanese collectivistic culture (also see Benedict, 1946), there would be high levels of conformity. Indeed, it is still claimed (Triandis, 1990, p. 81) that in "Japan hierarchy is the essence of social order" and that Japanese "dislike stating personal opinions and prefer opinions that emerge from social consensus." Nevertheless, the findings of nonconforming behavior in Japan have been interpreted, in a posthoc fashion, as consistent with collectivism (Triandis, 1990, p. 88). The argument is that Japanese subjects did not conform in the experimental situation because the majority was composed of strangers who were not part of the in-group. Given the distinction held by collectivists between the in-group and the out-group, they would not be expected to conform to the behaviors of strangers.

That post-hoc explanation ignores that the "strangers" were themselves Japanese and, therefore, actually part of the supposed in-group. It also fails to account for the conformity with strangers of American subjects. From the perspective of the individualism–collectivism dichotomy, it should be said that if Americans go so far as to conform with perfect strangers (and even obey authorities previously unknown to them, as in the Milgram experiments) then they have a rather strong sense of collectivism – or conversely their individualism does not run very deep.

The interpretation of Japanese nonconformity as consistent with collectivism highlights a general problem in analyses of these cultural orientations, which is that there is sometimes a failure to distinguish clearly between characterizations of the cultural orientations and observed or measured outcomes expected to follow from those characterizations. Once a society is classified as of one kind or another, then observed practices in that society are interpreted from the viewpoint of the cultural orientation (as in the use of findings of nonconformity among the Japanese) or simply listed among the characteristics of the designated orientation (that is, the independent and dependent variables are not clearly distinguished). As a consequence, it is not likely that observed practices or judgments in a particular society would lead to reformulation of the proposed cultural orientations.

Another example illustrative of this problem can be seen in discussions of findings presumably showing that moral judgments in collectivistic societies are more absolute and more contextual than in individualistic ones (Shweder & Bourne, 1982; Triandis, 1990). Although there is a seeming inconsistency between absolute and context-dependent judgments, both are simply listed as part of collectivism. An alternative approach would be to question the original classification of a homogeneous orientation on the grounds that judgments are not of one kind.

Domains of social reasoning

It is apparent that different and sometimes opposing characterizations have been given of the social orientation of Americans. Some see a predominance of individualism in the society, while others see a predominance of conformity to faceless institutions in which the self is absorbed. In each of these polar interpretations it is assumed that members of the society are under the sway of social forces that buffet them into a condition that is maladaptive and contrary to their well-being. Both those viewing the society as individualistic or conformist lament a disintegration and destructiveness caused by that predominant orientation.

That there are opposing interpretations of presumed homogeneous cultural orientations or core moral codes suggests that each side of the polarities presents an overstated, stereotyped case. These views are one-sided in their assumption that individuals are buffeted by social forces. They fail to account for reciprocal interactions between the individual and social/cultural contexts. They also fail to account for heterogeneous interpretations made by individuals of a multifaceted social world and corresponding variety in their behaviors.

It is important to be clear that the kind of heterogeneity or multiplicity of orientations to which we are referring is not accounted for by the notion that there is variability among subgroups or subcultures within a larger group or cultural context. Variability exists within groups and within individuals. When we say that characterizations of individualism or collectivism are stereotypical, we mean that at all levels of units of analysis (groups, subgroups, or individuals) there is a failure to account for diversity.

Documenting that alternative and even opposing descriptions of Western society's orientation have been put forth serves to question the validity of these characterizations, suggesting they are stereotypical. It is likely that each is based on observed phenomena that only partially reflect the social practices of the society. Nevertheless, this is by no means conclusive since one characterization (say that of individualism) conceivably could be accurate while the other is not. Of more direct bearing on our proposition is evidence on attitudes and judgments of persons in this society. One such body of evidence comes from a series of large-scale public-opinion survey studies conducted by political scientists and sociologists of Americans' attitudes toward personal freedoms and rights (McClosky & Brill, 1983; Stouffer, 1955). Over the decades, the surveys have consistently shown that Americans do not simply uphold freedoms and rights. Whereas they endorse such rights under some circumstances, they also believe that under other circumstances, rights and freedoms should be restricted. It has been found that majorities of large samples (some studies sampled over 3000 persons) do state that they believe in freedom of speech, press, assembly, and religion as well as in rights to privacy, dissent, and divergent lifestyles. However, these same persons do not endorse most of these freedoms and rights when they are in conflict with traditions, community standards, and the maintenance of social order. Similarly, rights and freedoms are not endorsed when they conflict with other moral considerations; such as in cases where the assertion of a right or a freedom could result in physical or psychological harm to others and if it conflicts with the furtherance of the general welfare.

These survey data could be interpreted in a number of ways. For instance, from the perspective of critics of personality typing (Mischel, 1968, 1969; Shweder, 1975) the findings could be taken to support their basic proposition that individual behavior is highly dependent on external situational contingencies and varies by features of experienced contexts. As put by Mischel (1969, pp. 1014 and 1016): "A great deal of environmental specificity has been found regularly on character traits such as rigidity, *social conformity,* aggression, on *attitudes to authority,* and on virtually any other non-intellective personality dimension. . . . What people do in any situation may be altered radically even by seemingly minor variations in prior experiences or slight modifications in stimulus attributes or characteristics of the evoking situation" (italics added).

However, this way of explaining the response variations to stimulus items regarding freedoms and rights omits a necessary component – namely, the ways respondents interpret the stimulus situations. The systematic nature of variations in responses to the survey items indicates that respondents were not solely shifting with the wind, so to speak. There was general endorsement of the items which presented freedoms and rights in the abstract or in relatively weak conflict with other considerations. This suggests that individuals do have an understanding of freedoms and rights; that is, they actively think about and apply their intelligences to such matters. It was primarily when freedoms and rights were placed in conflict with competing moral and social considerations that respondents were less likely to endorse them. This suggests that individuals in this society also apply their intellectual functions to different realms of social life, that freedoms and rights are not the only kinds of social concepts held, and that in many circumstances the strongest commitments are not to freedoms and rights (for discussion of the shortcomings of the interpretation that the survey findings show individuals only give lip service to freedoms and rights, see Helwig, 1991, and Turiel, Killen, & Helwig, 1987).

Our proposal, which differs from the familiar contrast between consistency in personality syndromes or homogeneity in cultural orientations, on the one hand, and behavioral variability due to situational features, on the other hand, is that persons form coherent but distinct types of understandings of the social world. Broadly defined, intelligence or intellectual functioning is part of the social realms. However, by the term intelligence we do not mean a capacity measurable in quantitative terms. Rather, we use the term to refer to ways of thinking that persons construct as part of their reflections upon and adaptation to the environment (Piaget, 1966). We also propose that such ways of thinking constitute domains of social reasoning (Turiel, 1983; Turiel, et al., 1987; Turiel, Hildebrandt, & Wainryb, 1991). These distinct domains constitute a multiplicity of social orientations or intelligences evident in the reasoning of individuals. The multiple orientations include the sorts of matters usually classified under "individualism": self-interest, personal entitlements, and personal agency. However, other factors are also included. There are concerns with roles and status in social systems, with rules, authority, duties, and traditions. And there are concerns with morality in interdependent relationships bearing on justice, fairness, welfare, and the rights of groups and persons (civil and individual rights).

These domains, labeled as personal or psychological, societal, and moral, reflect major aspects of social life about which children learn as they grow. With regard to those aspects of social life, children's social interactions include features that may not be solely encompassed by the broad level of cultural context. Children interact with other people and, thereby form psychological concepts (see Heider, 1958 for an early exposition of the parameters of psychological concepts). During the past decade a voluminous literature has emerged, usually put in terms of "theories of mind," regarding young children's psychological understandings (e.g., Astington, Harris, & Olson, 1988; Harris, 1989). Studies examining understandings of persons' beliefs, desires, intentions, and mental perspectives document that by 4 or 5 years of age children have formed concepts of internal mental states (disputes regarding the age of these acquisitions are over whether they occur at age 4 or 5 or earlier; see Sodian, Taylor, Harris, & Perner, 1991). It has also been found in recent studies that concepts of internal mental states are acquired at about the same age in non-Western literate and in preliterate societies (Avis & Harris, 1991).

Children's social experiences also include persons in organized social interactions. Social institutions and systems of social organization include rules, commands, authorities with attributes different from those possessed by children (e.g., rights, power, position, and knowledge), and hierarchically ordered relations (Nucci & Nucci, 1982a, 1982b; Nucci & Turiel, 1978; Nucci, Turiel, & Encarcion-Garwych, 1983; Smetana, 1989). Additionally, there are social expectations and requirements of a moral kind that are entailed in social relationships and embedded in institutions.

Although children are exposed to all these aspects of social life, it is possible that because of particular social arrangements (cultural or otherwise) one type dominates over the others. If such were the case, personal agency could be subsumed under the system of social organization or social order, resulting in a lack of concepts of personal jurisdiction, entitlements, or rights (as has been claimed for so-called collectivistic societies). Alternatively, social order and most aspects of morality, except personal rights, could be subsumed under an emphasis on the freedoms and entitlements of persons (as has been claimed for so-called individualistic societies). There is a large body of evidence, however, strongly indicating that neither of these alternatives hold for this society. Children, adolescents, and adults make domain-specific judgments within the moral, societal, and personal realms (see Turiel, et al., 1987 and Helwig, Tisak, & Turiel, 1990 for reviews).

We can illustrate how individuals maintain a mixture of social orientations through a brief look at the research and its findings. The research showing that moral, societal, and personal concepts are not all of one piece, we should note, has been guided by philosophical propositions regarding differences between the standards, conventions, or practices of social organizations and institutions (Dworkin, 1978; Gewirth, 1978; Rawls, 1971). Morality refers to concepts of welfare, justice, and rights. Although morality applies to social systems, it is not defined by existing social arrangements. Central features of moral prescriptions are that they are obligatory, generalizable, and impersonal since they are grounded in concepts of welfare, justice, and rights. Conventions, by contrast, are shared behaviors whose meanings are defined by the social system in which they are embedded; conventions vary by socially constructed meanings. In turn, there are actions within the jurisdiction of personal choice (part of personal agency) which are considered outside moral or social regulation.

A focus of a number of studies has been on the characteristics used to define and identify different social actions and prohibitions (characteristics referred to as "criterion judgments"), as well as forms of reasoning in evaluating social actions (referred to as "justifications"). Analyses of children's criterion judgments have included whether acts are considered to be *contingent* on rules or authority status (i.e., whether the evaluation is dependent on a rule, law, or promulgation by persons in positions of authority), if they are generalizable (i.e., whether the evaluation applies across settings and situations), if they are based on consensus or personal choice. With regard to issues within the moral domain (e.g., inflicting physical harm on others, theft, unequal distribution, discrimination), it has been found that children and adolescents judge them to be obligatory, nonchangeable on an arbitrary basis, not contingent on existing rules or laws, not dependent on authority dictates, and applicable across situations and societal contexts. In their justifications individuals show concerns with the welfare of others, just or fair resolutions of competing claims among people, and the maintenance of rights. Moral judgments, therefore, bear upon interpersonal relations, the collectivity (since there is a concern with welfare and fairness in relations of interdependence), and the individual (since there are concerns with the rights of persons).

It is in judgments about social conventions (examples are forms of address, modes of dress, and forms of greeting) that we see understandings of institutional ties and a perceived need for conformity. Conventions are judged to be contingent on rules, authority, and existing social practice; they also are judged to be nongeneralizable and relative to social systems. In their justifications regarding conventions, individuals show concerns with maintaining social order and upholding traditions. Judgments about conventions, therefore, bear mainly on collectivities and the concern is with maintaining a system, with rules, uniformity, and authority, for the coordination of interrelationships.

These studies also show that the ways children and adolescents judge the legitimacy of authority commands reflects neither the idea that authority is abhorrent nor that there is an idealization of it. A consistent finding (Damon, 1977; Laupa, 1990; Laupa & Turiel, 1986, 1993; Tisak, 1986; Weston & Turiel, 1980) is that by a relatively young age (5 or 6 years) distinctions are made between legitimate commands, which are accepted, and those considered illegitimate, which are rejected. Boundaries are also drawn between contexts in which a person in authority has or has not jurisdiction (e.g., school vs. home). To illustrate. Individuals do not judge acts in the moral domain to be contingent on authority dictates. Acts like harming others or violating rights are considered wrong even if they are condoned by authorities; furthermore, it is considered legitimate to disobey an authority's command to engage in such acts. At the same time, acts in the conventional domain are contingent on authority; authorities can legitimately dictate behaviors that are part of conventional regulation in social contexts.

This type of coexistence of orientations to authority is also evident in behavioral analyses. Milgram's (1963, 1974) well known findings of obedience to authority are dramatic in their demonstration that American adults will obey authorities in unexpected ways. In direct contrast with the thesis of individualism, and certainly with

Gorer's assertion that Americans regard authority as detestable and dangerous, Milgram found that under certain circumstances large percentages of subjects in his experiments will inflict physical harm when commanded to by authority. He also found, however, that under other circumstances large percentages of subjects reject those commands.

Therefore, the research shows that individuals make moral judgments pertaining to interdependence among people, that they have understandings of and commitments to the social order and authority, and that they are willing to reject authority dictates. Not surprisingly, persons in this society are also concerned with many of the features grouped under the individualistic orientation – personal agency, self-determination, and personal choice. There is a recognition that people have interests, personal goals, and entitlements that are legitimate in their own right insofar as they do not conflict with others, do not cause harm, and do not constitute part of the conventional social order. In studies conducted in the United States, children and adolescents classified certain issues as out of the realm of legal regulation, moral generalization, and essentially up to individual choice (Miller & Bersoff, 1988; Nucci, 1981; Smetana, 1988; Stoddart & Turiel, 1985; Tisak, 1991; Tisak & Tisak, 1990). Examples of issues that subjects classified in this way include control over one's correspondence or creative works, friendship choices, prudential matters, aspects of the state of one's own body, and adherence to sex roles.

The nature of these issues and the contexts in which they are placed appear to play a role in whether they are consistently judged to be under personal jurisdiction. Many issues are considered personal except when a group agrees to their conventional regulation. For example, Miller and Bersoff (1988) found that children generally judge acts that are not highly instrumental in attaining common public goals (e.g., using silverware to eat, and formal dressing) to be under personal jurisdiction. However, the children considered it legitimate to conventionally regulate such acts when there is agreement to do so within a limited group operating in a nonpublic context. Other issues (e.g., sexual practices, use of recreational drugs, lifestyle choices, and occupational choices) hold a deeper sense of personal jurisdiction in that they are considered to be out of the boundaries of societal regulation. Here, too, the situational context has a bearing on the types of judgments applied. Institutional or even individual attempts to place restrictions on such personal choices are often regarded as violations of personal rights, and thus are judged from a moral standpoint.

In any event, the findings on concepts of personal agency indicate that children develop a sense of self with desires, goals, and interests that can be legitimately distinguished from social requirements. This sense of person is not restricted to oneself, but is also acknowledged to apply to others. When subjects assert that certain actions are legitimately part of personal choice (one's own business), they do so for self and others. The central feature of this realm, as we view it, is not selfishness (as opposed to, say, altruism) – though selfishness may indeed exist – but a conception of personal agency. The personal coexists with the social. Children develop concepts about the person (the self included) with short and long term private ends and personal goals (Nucci & Lee, 1993). As elucidated a long time ago by James Mark Baldwin (1896; especially chapter VII), the child develops more than one type of goal or end, including "egoistic" and "altruistic" ones. According to Baldwin, each of these goals can be a product of reason: "it is sometimes reasonable or intelligent for the child to act for himself, in a selfish way, and then on another occasion it is equally reasonable for him to act for another, in a generous way" (Baldwin, 1896, p. 278).

Baldwin's claim is reminiscent of Mischel's (1969) statements, quoted above, regarding behavioral shifts in accordance with situational contexts. In Baldwin's view, however, the individual applies different aspects of psychological and social understandings to varying contexts. Personal agency and awareness of others in social contexts are necessary for individual development and for social cooperation in community life. Personal agency is also an aspect of those moral judgments that account for reciprocity in relations between persons (Nucci & Lee, 1993).

The heterogeneity of social orientations represented in different but coexisting domains of social reasoning brings with it some important commonalities among members of the society. The domain differentiations themselves constitute common ground. Additionally, there is a great deal of consistency between individuals in evaluations and judgments about moral issues like inflicting harm, theft (Turiel, et al., 1991), injustice (Wainryb, 1991), and rights (Helwig, 1991). In the context of these commonalities and consistencies there is also intragroup variability in that disagreements and even heated disputes occur over social matters. Public disputes occur over social-policy issues, such as affirmative action, public subsidies of social programs, and the death penalty.

Intense public debates also occur over issues like abortion, homosexuality, and pornography. Studies of judgments about these issues (Turiel, et al., 1991) have documented that there are disagreements in the ways individuals evaluate them and that many reason about these issues differently from the ways they reason about "prototypical" moral, conventional, or personal issues. Many in this society consider abortion, or homosexuality, or pornography acceptable, while others evaluate them negatively. For the most part, those who view these issues as acceptable treat them as matters of personal choice in the deep sense. They are matters under personal jurisdiction that should not be legally regulated. We also ascertained that people evaluating those issues negatively were inconsistent and conflicted over imposing restrictions on behavior and permitting personal choice. For instance, subjects judged that abortion is wrong, but that it should be legal or even that it was a matter of individual discretion. This kind of juxtaposition never occurred for moral issues like inflicting harm, where the negative evaluations were coupled with the judgments that the acts should be illegal and not left to individual choice. Much of the variation between subjects was due not to differences in moral concepts, but to differences in assumptions regarding other central components of the issue. Abortion provides a clear-cut example. Those who considered abortion to be wrong generally made the assumption that the fetus is a life (thus abortion is killing), while those judging abortion acceptable assumed that the fetus is not yet to be defined as a life (for these reasons we have classified these types of issues as ambiguous or nonprototypical relative to the domains; see Turiel, et al., 1991 for details).

Personal agency elsewhere

Our interpretation of the data considered thus far is that cultures are heterogeneous, with their members holding diverse social orientations based on a variety of social experiences. Social thought is not of one kind. It could be argued, however, that findings from Western cultures merely show that those cultures are not homogeneous because they are comprised of several groups providing most people with a diversity of cultural experiences that results in the kinds of variations evident in the surveys of civil liberties and in the research on domain-specific judgments. Perhaps characterizing this culture as mainly individualistic is mistaken because of a failure to account for multiple cultural influences. Nevertheless, it would be argued, the underlying proposition holds: cultural orientations shape the social judgments and practices of individuals, and groups without various subcultures could be characterized in homogeneous terms. There may exist traditional, hierarchical, collectivistic cultures that define persons through their embeddedness in the group.

Before considering the issue of personal agency in specific, it should be pointed out that research on domains of social reasoning has been conducted among religious persons and in non-Western cultures. One set of studies included Amish–Mennonite and Orthodox Jewish subjects (Nucci, 1986; Nucci & Turiel, 1993). Although conducted in the United States (Amish residing in rural areas of Indiana and Orthodox Jews in Chicago, Illinois), these studies investigated judgments about rules that constitute binding duties within religious systems which are traditional and hierarchically organized. In addition to eliciting judgments about moral issues (e.g., hitting, stealing, slander), judgments were made about nonmoral religious rules (e.g., day of worship, avoiding work on the Sabbath, head coverings, Baptism, circumcision). Among these groups, too, rules pertaining to moral issues were judged as nonalterable by religious authorities [consensus among the congregation and ministers (for the Amish) and Rabbis (for Jews)], applicable to members of other religions, and noncontingent on God's word (i.e., violations of the moral rules would be wrong even if they were not prohibited in the bible and even if commanded by God). Moreover, these types of judgments were justified by reasons of avoiding harm and promoting justice and fairness. By contrast, the nonmoral religious rules were judged to be contingent on God's word and relative to particular religions. In these cases, it was not clearly judged that nonmoral rules could or should be changed by religious authorities; the locus of authority for their establishment and possible alterability was in the authority of God.

Similar results were obtained in studies conducted in Nigeria (Hollos, Leis, & Turiel, 1986), Korea (Song, Smetana, & Kim, 1987), Indonesia (Carey & Ford, 1983), and Zambia (Zimba, 1987). In those cultural contexts, children, adolescents, and adults do make judgments about moral and conventional issues that are char-

acterized by the same criteria used by individuals in Western settings. M
were judged to be obligatory, noncontingent on rules or laws, and ge
across societal contexts. Conventional issues, in turn, were judged as contingent on
rules or authority and as relative to their particular social contexts.[1]

These studies, then, show that the development of differentiated domains of social
reasoning is not restricted to secular or Western settings; there is a mixture of social
orientations among devoutly religious persons and in some non-Western societies.
However, whether concepts of personal agency and jurisdiction are part of the
heterogeneity of social orientations in those and other non-Western settings is still an
open question – such concepts were not directly investigated in those studies. The
role of personal agency and concerns with personal jurisdiction and entitlements in
social thought and practices need to be carefully considered before they can be ruled
out of the psychological makeup or cultural orientations of any peoples, given that
the personal realm, in one form or another, has been regarded as important in most
major psychological explanations. Most notably, the various manifestations of the
noncognitive socialization approach have considered self-interest and personal needs,
as well as their countervailing forces, central to social development. These theories
range from radical behaviorism (e.g., Skinner, 1971), to less radical behavioristic
(e.g., Aronfreed, 1968) and social-learning perspectives (e.g., Bandura & Walters,
1963; Mischel & Mischel, 1976), to psychoanalytic theories (e.g., Erikson, 1950;
Freud, 1930).

Common to these approaches is the general proposition that early life is characterized by a predominance of biologically based behaviors aimed at satisfying needs,
desires, wants and the like (from the straightforward drives postulated in behavioris-
tically inclined approaches to complex instincts in psychoanalytic ones). Social
developmental changes of these types of initial states are due to countervailing forces
in the social environment, such as alternative behaviors that are rewarded and promoted, the frustration of needs and desires, and the imposition of social norms and
values. In spite of the shifts engendered by those countervailing forces, the force of
self-interest is seen to remain as a relevant factor in the psychology of social behavior
beyond early childhood. In the first place, self-interest and the motivation to satisfy
needs are not said to be entirely suppressed or eliminated. Rather, they occur in
socially appropriate circumstances (e.g., when they are not in conflict with socially
mandated norms). Moreover, it is thought that self-interest manifests itself even when
alternative social values have been acquired. In behavioristic perspectives, for instance, it is seen in the proposition that there are commonly found discrepancies
between espoused moral values or judgments and behavior (Aronfreed, 1968).

In psychoanalytic accounts it is proposed that tensions between instinctual forces
and developmental–social outcomes are enduring and profound. Fundamental to
Freud's view was the idea that the requirements of civilization, which serve the
well-being of humanity, also result in serious discontents for individuals because of
the repression of instinctual needs. As put by Freud (1930, p. 43): "A good part of
the struggles of mankind center around the single task of finding an expedient

accommodation – one, that is, that will bring happiness – between this claim of the individual and the cultural claims of the group; and one of the problems that touches the fate of humanity is whether such an accommodation can be reached by means of some particular form of civilization or whether this conflict is irreconcilable." Freud's position, as is well known, was that the problem is never entirely reconcilable, such that the individual in civilization gives up "a portion of his possibilities of happiness for a portion of security" (p. 62). In a similar vein, Adorno, et al. (1950, p. 239) attribute much of the dysfunctional quality of prejudiced persons to inadequacies in a sense of self and to compensations for overly frustrated needs:

the antidemocratic individual, because he has had to accept numerous externally imposed restrictions upon the satisfactions of his needs, harbors strong underlying aggressive impulses. . . . One outlet for this aggression is through displacement onto outgroups leading to moral indignation and authoritarian aggression.

In these views, therefore, the self with needs, desires, and personal goals becomes modified or transformed to one extent or another by social forces, but does not become totally absorbed by the group. It has been thought that in some situations the individual does become absorbed into groups (LeBon, 1895/1960). Especially in temporary, or transient groups, such as in mob-action, the individual becomes extremely suggestible and loses all sense of autonomy. However, immersion in a mob also was seen to allow the emergence of repressed or suppressed instinctual drives (Freud, 1922). Furthermore, in some cases of extreme contagion, there can be a lasting total submergence of personal interest to the group that resembles a hypnotic state of an automaton kind (LeBon, 1895/1960).

The characterizations of collectivistic, hierarchically organized societies we have been considering neither regard the absorption of an autonomous self into the group as temporary nor include tensions between personal goals and group goals. Matters of self-interest, personal needs, or self-preservation are not part of the formulation of how individuals' social functioning is guided by cultural orientations. In a sense, initial psychological states are presumed to be neutral; they are shaped by the dominant ethos or worldview in the society. In some formulations (e.g., Shweder, et al., 1987; Shweder, 1990) the child's acquisition of concepts of morality and persons is rationalistic. However, rationality is presumed to be of one piece (again, collectivistic or individualistic) with a particular way of construing persons, morality, and the social order. Individuals form a way of thinking about the social world that reflects a rationality that can be located at the cultural level.

Whereas our position is also that the individual's orientation to the social world is rational, we do not assume that solely one form of thinking develops nor that there are overarching cultural orientations to be acquired. In our view, positing a unitary cultural orientation is insufficient to explain social functioning because it does not account for the ways individuals interpret different elements of social interactions. Individuals do not solely accommodate to prepackaged cultural systems. As stated earlier, our position is that children form concepts of the different elements in their social world, including persons (self and others) with needs, interests, and goals.

Alongside concepts of self and persons (the psychological domain), there is concern with the welfare of persons and the organization of systems of social interaction. As has often been stressed (Baldwin, 1896; Durkheim, 1925/1961; Freud, 1930; Piaget, 1932), there coexist tendencies – egoistic and altruistic, selfish and generous, self-directed and empathic of others – which form the basis for the development of coordinated and cooperative social relationships.

As a start, this can be approached as a question of whether or not concerns with personal agency, jurisdiction, and entitlements exist in traditional hierarchical cultures, where it has been said they do not exist because the person is defined by duties and role relationships. Our alternative hypothesis is that individual entitlements and prerogatives, and concepts of rights, are embedded in hierarchical social systems. This hypothesis is predicated on the idea that social relationships in hierarchical systems are not static and that individuals have mutual expectations. Furthermore, the dynamics of equalities, inequalities, and authoritarianism in such relationships may include perceptions of unfairness and ignored rights. This can be put more concretely. The other side of the coin of fixed duties and roles in a social hierarchy is that those with privileged status conceive of themselves and others in like positions as having personal entitlements due to them because of their roles in the system and, especially by those in subordinate positions.

A sense of personal entitlements in hierarchical social systems can be manifested in a number of ways. Two obvious instances where such entitlements may hold are for those in higher castes or social classes relative to those in lower castes or classes and in gender relationships. On the one hand, a person's position may dictate particular duties and prescribed behaviors seen to stem from roles held in the system. On the other hand, holding a position of dominance (social class or gender-related) may bring with it a strong sense of personal prerogatives and entitlements expected from those in subordinate positions. In such a case, concepts of duties and social obligations would coexist with concepts of personal agency, personal jurisdiction, and entitlements. Furthermore, it may be that while persons in subordinate positions, in part, accept their status, they also, in some respects, view their roles as entailing ignored rights and unfair expectations.

Dramatic examples illustrating that social hierarchies entail more complex concepts of persons than what is defined by particular roles in the system come from recent public reports of events occurring in traditional, hierarchical societies. The first pertains to caste or social-class relations in India, as vividly reported in a *Los Angeles Times* article (May 14, 1990) titled, "Untouchables: Murder Sparks Outcry for Outcasts' Rights." The person murdered, named Dhanraj, was a 26-year-old Hindu of the untouchable caste (herijans) who had recently married within his caste. Husband and wife lived in a tiny mud hut in the small village of Sato Dharmapur in the state Uttar Pradesh, working in the fields of a feudal lord (of the Thakur caste). One day, the feudal lord demanded that Dhanraj give him his wife to become part of what amounts to his "modern-day harem." When Dhanraj would not acquiesce, the following interchange was reported to have occurred. The feudal lord laughed and said, "Don't you worry. I am a rich man. I will purchase two bullocks, and they will do your work in the field. You give me your wife, and I will keep her like a rani (princess). Now do as I say." Dhanraj responded, "She is my wife. Not yours. I will not stay here any longer. I will never work for you again." The husband and wife then ran away to their hut, as the feudal lord shouted, "I will get what I want. I will take you by force, and after that nobody will help you."

That very afternoon the feudal lord obtained the help of two nephews to pour kerosene on Dhanraj and set him afire. Dhanraj managed to jump in a well to douse the fire, but was very badly burned. The local police refused to take a statement from him. Only after several hours were relatives able to get the police to drive him to a place where he could receive medical care. He died the next morning.

The feudal lord told the local police a story they accepted, namely, that Dhanraj had stolen a little money, got drunk and burned himself to death. However, Dhanraj's family, along with a number of other untouchables, took some action. They carried his body to where an autopsy was performed; it showed no alcohol in his blood. They then held a sit-in at the office of the district collector, who eventually arranged for the feudal lord to pay the family $500 in compensation.

This incident dramatically illustrates how an authoritarian, hierarchical structure can include presumptions of personal prerogatives and entitlements ensuing from one's higher status or position. This particular higher caste person was willing to take drastic measures to get what he wanted. The incident also illustrates that persons in subordinate positions do respond to such events as entailing unfairness and violations of rights. Although this incident is extreme, according to the newspaper report its most unusual feature is not that it occurred but that it received further public attention. It was reported that in modern India "the raping and killing of harijans is a daily event" and that 10,000 atrocities are recorded every year against untouchables.

The event received attention because two political activists who are proponents for the rights of untouchables and women happened to see a local newspaper account of the settlement. One of them, a woman named Kristina Rawet, is in the opposition party to that of then Prime Minister V. P. Singh. She convinced Dhanraj's reluctant widow to talk to her by telling her that "if we can get justice for you, others like you will not have to suffer." The other political activist, Kanchi Ram, is the head of a new political party fighting for untouchables. His comments are informative: "There are two identical countries in the world where a minority rules over the majority. One is South Africa, and the other is India. The difference is that in India it is not color. It is caste. This case of Dhanraj and the poor widow is a usual thing here, a routine case involving only one death."

Life and death issues also bring to the fore the relevance of personal agency in gender relations. As reported in *The New York Times* ("Toll of AIDS on Uganda's Women Puts Their Roles and Rights in Question," October 28, 1990), in Uganda the inequalities that typically result in greater privileges for men has particularly dele- terious effects on women because of the AIDS epidemic: "While AIDS is affecting men and women in Africa about equally, social workers say that the disease in many ways has a disproportionate effect on African women. They are obviously over-burdened as the main agricultural producers, the ones who bear and care for children, and the lowest-paid members of society who often have little say over their destiny." It was also reported that African social workers contend that "the African male maintains unrestrained and unchallenged dominance over the African woman," and "it is the economic impoverishment of women in African society combined with the sexual demands of men that leave many women so vulnerable to AIDS."

African women who engage in difficult physical labor that men consider beneath them ("Uganda's Women: Children, Drudgery and Pain," *The New York Times,* February 24, 1991) are also dominated by men sexually. In that economic context, many infected men demand that their wives engage in sex; men claim that they have a right to sex with their wives. When women refuse, there are other consequences. For example, a woman who refused to take care of a husband dying of AIDS because he had three other wives and expected her to have sex with him, had her possessions taken by his angry relatives. After the husband died she was left penniless, since the relatives emptied a shop she ran with him and kicked her out of her house. This problem came to the attention of a legal-aid society composed of women lawyers. Members of that society claim that cases involving AIDS and women's rights outstrip any other new referrals they receive.

Other recent journalistic reports have appeared pertaining to similar phenomena in India and other parts of the world, such as South America and the Middle East. In India, for instance, a serious problem for women stems from abuses of a still commonly practiced, though illegal, dowry system ("The High Price of Marriage in India: Burning Brides," *San Francisco Chronicle,* July 2, 1989). In these cases, when demands (even after marriage) for larger and larger dowries are unmet, the husbands and their families either murder the wives or through physical and mental torture provoke them to commit suicide: "The strong patriarchical tradition of India . . . and growing lust for material possessions account for exorbitant dowry demands." Again, these are not isolated incidents since 72,00 brides in the 15-to-20-year old age group have died in India in the last 41 years. More generally, the patriarchal tradition is blamed for the exploitation and physical abuse of women when husbands feel their needs are not adequately met. Even working wives are exploited, as claimed by a female editor of *The Hindu,* South India's largest circulation newspaper (*San Francisco Chronicle,* July 2, 1989): "They are often farmed out to work and their earnings are seized by husbands and in-laws who unhesitatingly take charge of the household finances. These women remain hopeless prisoners of an overbearing social tradition that views women as less than human."

In another part of the world where patriarchal traditions exist, Brazilians have been confronting the widespread problems of family violence and the killings of wives who commit adultery. In rejecting the claim that a man was justified in killing his wife and her lover on the grounds that he was defending his honor, the Brazilian Supreme Court wrote that embedded in the notion of honor is self-interest and personal concerns (as reported in " 'Honor' Killing of Wives is Outlawed in Brazil," *The New*

York Times, March 29, 1991): "Homicide cannot be seen as a normal and legitimate way of reacting to adultery. Because in this kind of crime what is defended is not honor, but vanity, exaggerated self-importance and the pride of the lord who sees a woman as his personal property." Also, in Egypt complaints have been voiced about the violation of women's rights by Nawal El Saadow, a doctor who has been the country's director of public health ("Fighting Against the Veil," *The Monthly,* Berkeley, California, February 1991). She argues that the patriarchal system is based on economic expediency and inequality that favors the interests of men.

These few examples are not meant to be conclusive evidence for the proposition that personal agency is part of the structure of traditional, hierarchical societies. These examples serve several other purposes. First, they demonstrate how interpersonal relations within a hierarchical organization can present conditions for the assertion of personal entitlements and produce conflicts around issues of justice, welfare, and rights. Note that the incident in India included a strong assertion of personal entitlements on the part of the feudal lord (he asserted: Do what I say, I will get what I want, etc.), an assertion of personal jurisdiction and implied rights by persons in subordinate positions (Dhanraj stated: she is my wife, not yours), and reactions reflecting concerns with issues of justice and welfare (Dhanraj's relatives engaged in protest and the political activists spoke of achieving justice and ensuring the welfare of untouchables). Second, they show that interpersonal relationships, as well as moral–political goals, are not simply preestablished by social codes and prescribed roles. Interpersonal relations include demands, counter-demands, and conflicts with their own dynamics (as seen in both examples). Third, these public reports should be sufficient to take seriously the hypothesis that personal agency and rights are part of so-called collectivistic cultures.

Further evidence for the proposition that concepts of personal autonomy exist in traditional, hierarchically organized cultures comes from research conducted in the Middle East (Wainryb & Turiel, in press). Studies with males and females were done with members of a Druze Arab community living in villages in Northern Israel (for a description of the Druze community, see Turiel & Wainryb, in press). The research did not examine judgments about life and death issues or atrocities committed by one group upon another. Instead, it focused on judgments about everyday activities in relationships between men and women in family settings. The concerns of the research were how males (in positions of dominance) conceive of personal agency and jurisdiction and how females (in subordinate positions) think about their roles and the demands placed on them. Subjects were presented with conflicts between persons in dominant (i.e., husbands and fathers) and subordinate (wives, daughters, and sons) positions in the social hierarchy and posed with questions regarding decision-making power and authority. The findings showed that there is a strong sense of personal entitlements on the part of males, and that women recognize that men assert personal entitlements. Women attribute validity to those entitlements (reflecting an acceptance of their roles), and yet have a sense of rights ignored and legitimate entitlements denied (reflecting conflict over their roles). The findings, therefore, are consistent with the picture conveyed by the events in India and Uganda as reported in the newspaper articles, indicating that personal agency, justice, and welfare are all concerns in those cultures.

Conclusion

In citing the examples of events reported in the public media we are suggesting neither that the supposedly collectivistic societies are primarily characterized by relations of exploitation that can result in atrocities nor that such relations are restricted to those societies. No doubt, an ample number of examples of exploitation and atrocities could be cited for Western societies as well. These examples illustrate that personal and moral concerns are part of the hierarchies, status distinctions, and power relations in traditional, collectivistic societies. Also, this should not be taken to mean that power relations or status distinctions are the unique realm of non-Western cultures. Taking different forms, they are part of so-called individualistic cultures, too (Okin, 1989). Conflicts and struggles over personal entitlements and moral demands occur in Western and non-Western settings.

Nor is it the intent here to maintain that there are no differences between cultures. To understand similarities and differences, it is necessary to recognize the heterogeneity of social judgments and practices in individuals, as well as the multiplicity of social contexts within cultures. Drawing global distinctions between cultures, as in the individualism–collectivism dichotomy, fails to account for the different domains of social judgments formed by persons and the variety of ways those judgments are applied in concrete social situations. Curiously, many of those who accentuate the influence of a homogeneously conceived cultural orientation do maintain that thought varies by domains and that particular stimuli, situations, and social contexts affect behaviors and judgments. These components are used to argue against propositions of global, unitary psychological processes, such as a constellation of personality traits, or a general structure of the mind, or a central mechanism of learning and development. Yet, a central organizing feature is proposed for the environment, in the form of the general cultural orientations or schemes, that is not consistent with the heterogeneity of domains of judgment and the variability of stimulus situations and social contexts. Ultimately, those positions return to postulating general internal psychological constructs, since the proposed cultural orientation is said to become the central aspect of the individual's social functioning.

It is necessary, instead, to account for the heterogeneity of thought, as represented by distinct conceptual domains, and for comparable distinctions in social experiences and the social environment. From that perspective, individuals are in reciprocal interaction with their social environments. Social relationships, institutional arrangements, social hierarchies, and personal jurisdiction all constitute part of the individual's multiple relations to culture. Social experiences influence and alter social thinking, but reciprocally, thought entails interpreting and conceptually altering social contexts.

Note

1 Research has also been conducted in India. On the basis of their research in the temple town of Bhubraneswar (the state capitol of Orissa), Shweder, et al. (1987) maintained that moral and conventional issues are not distinguished in that hierarchically organized society. However, in that research many of the actions classified as conventions were practices tied to assumptions held by Hindus regarding an afterlife, souls of the deceased, and ancestral spirits. As reinterpreted by Turiel, et al. (1987), many of those practices are assumed to have harmful consequences to souls in an afterlife and therefore entail moral considerations. As consequences in the afterlife, these types of events are not directly observable to those on earth (e.g., the effects on a deceased man of his widow's ways of dressing). A recent follow-up study by Madden (1992) in the same temple town examined judgments and justifications (Shweder, et al. did not report findings of justifications) made by priests and college students regarding actions classified as moral and conventional, and ones associated with assumptions pertaining to souls in an afterlife (labeled belief-mediated issues). Madden found that the Indian students distinguished moral from conventional and the belief-mediated issued on criterion judgments and justifications. The findings with the priests were less straightforward. The priests judged the moral issues as noncontingent and generalized them across contexts. Priests judged conventional and belief-mediated issues as noncontingent and generalizable to a lesser extent than the moral issues but to a greater extent than did the students. However, the justifications given by the priests for moral issues clearly differed from those given for conventional or belief-mediated issues. Whereas judgments for moral issues were justified with reasons of welfare and fairness, judgments for conventional and belief-mediated issues were mainly justified with reasons pertaining to social organization and the dictates of the natural, religious, or supernatural.

References

Adorno, T. W., Frenkel-Brunswik, E., Levinson, D. J., & Sanford, R. N. (1950). *The authoritarian personality*. New York: Harper & Row.

Aronfreed, J. (1968). *Conduct and conscience: The socialization of internalized control over behavior*. New York: Academic Press.

Asch, S. E. (1956). Studies of independence and conformity: A minority of one against a unanimous majority. *Psychological Monographs, 70*, (no. 9).

Astington, J. W., Harris, P. L., & Olson, D. R. (1988). *Developing theories of mind*. New York: Cambridge University Press.

Avis, J. & Harris, P. L. (1991). Belief–desire reasoning among Baka children: Evidence for a universal conception of mind. *Child Development, 62*, 460–467.

Baldwin, J. M. (1896). *Social and ethical interpretations in mental development*. New York: Macmillan.

Bandura, A. & Walters, R. (1963). *Social learning and personality development*. New York: Holt, Rinehart, & Winston.

Bellah, R. N., Madsen, R., Sullivan, W. M., Swidler, A., & Tipton, S. M. (1985). *Habits of the heart: Individualism and commitment in American life*. New York: Harper & Row.

Benedict, R. (1934). *Patterns of culture*. Boston: Houghton Mifflin.

Benedict, R. (1946). *The chrysanthemum and the sword. Patterns of Japanese culture*. Boston: Houghton Mifflin.

Bennett, W. J. & Delatree, E. J. (1978). Moral education in the schools. *The Public Interest, 50*, 81–98.

Carey, N. & Ford, M. (1983). Domains of social and self-regulation: An Indonesian study. Paper presented at the meeting of the American Psychological Association, Los Angeles.

Damon, W. (1977). *The social world of the child*. San Francisco: Jossey-Bass.

Delattre, E. J. & Bennett, W. J. (1979). Where the values movement goes wrong. *Change, 11*, 38–43.

Durkheim, E. (1961). *Moral education*. Glencoe, IL: The Free Press. (Originally published 1925)

Dworkin, R. (1978). *Taking rights seriously*. Cambridge, MA: Harvard University Press.

Erikson, E. H. (1950). *Childhood and society*. New York: W. W. Norton & Co.

Frager, C. (1970). Conformity and anti-conformity in Japan. *Journal of Personality and Social Psychology, 15,* 203–210.

Fromm, E. (1941). *Escape from freedom.* New York: Holt, Rinehart, & Winston.

Freud. S. (1922). *Group psychology and analysis of the ego.* New York: W. W. Norton & Co.

Freud, S. (1930). *Civilization and its discontents.* New York: W. W. Norton & Co.

Geertz, C. (1966). Person, time and conduct in Bali: An essay in cultural analysis. Yale Southeast Asia Program, Cultural Report Series, #14.

Gerwirth, A. (1978). *Reason and morality.* Chicago: University of Chicago Press.

Gilligan, C. (1982). *In a different voice: Psychological theory and women's development.* Cambridge, MA: Harvard University Press.

Gorer, G. (1948). *The American people: A study in national character.* New York: W. W. Norton & Co.

Gorer, G. (1949). *The people of great Russia: A psychological study.* London: The Cresset Press.

Harris, P. L. (1989). *Children and emotion: The development of psychological understanding.* Oxford: Basil Blackwell.

Heider, F. (1958). *The psychology of interpersonal relations.* New York: Wiley.

Helwig, C. C. (1991). Adolescents' and young adults' conceptions of civil liberties: Freedom of speech and religion. Unpublished doctoral dissertation, University of California, Berkeley.

Helwig, C. C., Tisak, M., & Turiel, E. (1990). Children's social reasoning in context. *Child Development, 61,* 2068–2078.

Hogan, R. (1975). Theoretical egocentrism and the problem of compliance. *American Psychologist, 30,* 533–539.

Hollos, M., Leis, P. E., & Turiel, E. (1986). Social reasoning in Ijo children and adolescents in Nigerian communities. *Journal of Cross-cultural Psychology, 17,* 352–374.

Kardiner, A. (1945). *Psychological fronteers of society.* New York: Columbia University Press.

Kessen, W. (1979). The American child and other cultural inventions. *American Psychologist, 34,* 815–820.

Kohlberg, L. (1969). Stage and sequence. The cognitive-developmental approach to socialization. In D. Goslin (Ed.), *Handbook of socialization theory and research* (pp. 347–480). Chicago: Rand McNally.

Laupa, M. (1990). Children's reasoning about three authority attributes: Adult status, knowledge, and social position. *Developmental Psychology, 27,* 321–329.

Laupa, M. & Turiel, E. (1986). Children's conceptions of adult and peer authority. *Child Development, 57,* 405–412.

Laupa, M. & Turiel, E. (1993). Children's concepts of authority and social contexts. *Journal of Educational Psychology, 85,* 191–197.

LeBon, G. (1960). *The crowd: A study of the popular mind.* New York: The Viking Press. (Originally published 1895)

Madden, T. (1992). Cultural factors and assumptions in social reasoning in India. Unpublished doctoral dissertation, University of California, Berkeley.

McClosky, H. & Brill, A. (1983). *Dimensions of tolerance: What Americans believe about civil liberties.* New York: Russell Sage Foundation.

Milgram, S. (1963). Behavioral study of obedience. *Journal of Abnormal Social Psychology, 67,* 371–378.

Milgram, S. (1974). *Obedience to authority.* New York: Harper & Row.

Miller, J. G. & Bersoff, D. M. (1988). When do American children and adults reason in social conventional terms? *Developmental Psychology, 24,* 366–375.

Miller, J. G. & Luthar, S. (1989). Issues of interpersonal responsibility and accountability: A comparison of Indians' and Americans' moral judgments. *Social Cognition, 7,* 237–261.

Mills, C. W. (1956). *White Collar: The American middle class.* New York: Oxford University Press.

Mischel, W. (1968). *Personality and assessment.* Stanford: Stanford University Press.

Mischel, W. (1969). Continuity and change in personality. *American Psychologist, 24,* 1012–1018.

Mischel, W. & Mischel, H. N. (1976). A cognitive social-learning approach to morality and self-regulation. In T. Lickona (Ed.), *Moral development: Theory, research and social issues* (pp. 104–107). New York: Holt, Rinehart, & Winston.

Nucci, L. P. (1981). The development of personal concepts: A domain distinct from moral or social concepts. *Child Development, 52,* 114–121.

Nucci, L. P. (1986). Children's conceptions of morality, societal convention, and religious prescription. In C. Harding (Ed.), *Moral dilemmas: Philosophical and psychological reconsiderations of the development of moral reasoning* (pp. 138–174). Chicago: Precedent Press.

Nucci, L. & Lee, J. (1993). Morality and personal autonomy. In G. G. Noam & T. Wren (Eds.), *The moral sefl: Building a better paradigm* (pp. 123–148). Cambridge, MA: MIT Press.

Nucci, L. P. & Nucci, M. S. (1982a). Children's social interactions in the context of moral and conventional transgressions. *Child Development, 53,* 403–412.

Nucci, L. P. & Nucci, M. S. (1982b). Children's responses to moral and social conventional transgressions in free-play settings. *Child Development, 53,* 1337–1342.

Nucci, L. P. & Turiel, E. (1978). Social interactions and the development of social concepts in preschool children. *Child Development, 49,* 400–407.

Nucci, L. & Turiel, E. (1993). God's word, religious rules and their relation to Christian and Jewish children's concepts of morality. *Child Development, 64,* 1475–1491.

Nucci, L. P., Turiel, E., & Encarnacion-Gawrych, G. E. (1983). Children's social interactions and social concepts: Analysis of morality and convention in the Virgin Islands. *Journal of Cross-cultural Psychology, 14,* 469–487.

Okin, S. M. (1989). *Justice, gender, and the family.* New York: Basic Books.

Piaget, J. (1932). *The moral judgment of the child.* London: Routledge and Kegan Paul.

Piaget, J. (1966). *The psychology of intelligence.* Totowa, NJ: Littlefield, Adams & Co. (Originally published 1947)

Rawls, J. (1971). *A theory of justice.* Cambridge, MA: Harvard University Press.

Riesman, D., with N. Glazer and R. Denney. (1953). *The lonely crowd: A study of the changing American character.* New York: Doubleday & Co.

Ryan, K. (1989). In defense of character education. In L. Nucci (Ed.), *Moral development and character education: A dialogue* (pp. 3–17). Berkeley: McCutchan.

Sampson, E. E. (1977). Psychology and the American ideal. *Journal of Personality and Social Psychology, 35,* 767–782.

Seligman, M. (1988). G. Stanley Hall Lecture. Meeting of the American Psychological Association, Atlanta.

Shweder, R. A. (1975). How relevant is an individual difference theory of personality? *Journal of Personality, 43,* 455–484.

Shweder, R. A. (1979a). Rethinking culture and personality theory. Part I: A critical examination of two classical postulates. *Ethos, 7,* 255–278.

Shweder, R. A. (1979b). Rethinking culture and personality theory. Part II: A critical examination of two more classical postulates. *Ethos, 7,* 279–311.

Shweder, R. A. (1980). Rethinking culture and personality theory: Part III: From genesis and typology to hermeneutics and dynamics. *Ethos, 8,* 60–94.

Shweder, R. A. (1986). Divergent rationalities. In D. W. Fiske & R. A. Shweder (Eds.), *Metatheory in social science: pluralisms and subjectivities* (pp. 163–196). Chicago: University of Chicago Press.

Shweder, R. A. (1990). In defense of moral realism. *Child Development, 61,* 2060–2067.

Shweder, R. A. & Bourne, E. J. (1982). Does the concept of person vary cross-culturally? In A. J. Marsella and G. M. White (Eds.), *Cultural conceptions of mental health and therapy* (pp. 97–137). Boston: Reidel.

Shweder, R. A., Mahapatra, M., & Miller, J. G. (1987). Culture and moral development. In J. Kagan and S. Lamb (Eds.), *The emergence of morality in young children* (pp. 1–83). Chicago: University of Chicago Press.

Skinner, B. F. (1971). *Beyond freedom and dignity.* New York: Knopf.

Smetana, J. G. (1988). Adolescents' and parents' conceptions of parental authority. *Child Development, 59,* 321–335.

Smetana, J. G. (1989). Toddlers' social interactions in the context of moral and conventional transgressions in the home. *Developmental Psychology, 25,* 499–508.

Sodian, B., Taylor, C., Harris, P. L., & Perner, J. (1991). Early deception and the child's theory of mind. *Child Development, 62,* 468–483.

Sommers, C. H. (1984). Ethics without virtue: Moral education in America. *American Scholar, 53,* 381–389.

Song, M. J., Smetana, J. G., & Kim, S. Y. (1987). Korean children's conceptions of moral and conventional transgressions. *Developmental Psychology, 23,* 577–582.

Stoddart, T., & Turiel, E. (1985). Children's concepts of cross-gender activities. *Child Development, 56,* 1241–1252.

Stouffer, S. (1955). *Communism, conformity and civil liberties.* New York: Doubleday.

Tisak, M. S. (1986). Children's conceptions of parental authority. *Child Development, 57,* 166–176.

Tisak, M. S. (1991). Preschool children's conceptions of moral and personal events involving physical harm and property damage. Unpublished manuscript, Bowling Green State University.

Tisak, M. S. & Tisak, J. (1991). Children's conceptions of parental authority, friendship, and sibling relations. *Merrill-Palmer Quarterly, 36,* 347–367.

Triandis, H. C. (1989). The self and social behavior in differing cultural contexts. *Psychological Review, 96,* 506–520.

Triandis, H. C. (1990). Cross-cultural studies of individualism and collectivism. In J. J. Berman (Ed.), *Cross-cultural perspectives. Nebraska Symposium on Motivation: 1989 Vol. 37* (pp. 41–133). Lincoln: University of Nebraska Press.

Turiel, E. (1983). *The development of social knowledge: Morality and convention.* Cambridge, England: Cambridge University Press.

Turiel, E. (1989a). The social construction of social construction. In W. Damon (Ed.), *Child development today and tomorrow* (pp. 86–106). San Francisco: Jossey-Bass.

Turiel, E. (1989b). Multifaceted social reasoning and educating for character, culture and development. In L. Nucci (Ed.), *Moral development and character education: A dialogue* (pp. 161–182). Berkeley: McCutchen.

Turiel, E., Hildebrandt, C., & Wainryb, C. (1991). Judging social issues: Difficulties, inconsistencies, and consistencies. *Monographs of the Society for Research in Child Development, 56* (2).

Turiel, E., Killen, M., & Helwig, C. C. (1987). Morality: Its structure, functions and vagaries. In J. Kagan and S. Lamb (Eds.), *The emergence of moral concepts in young children* (pp. 155–244). Chicago: University of Chicago Press.

Turiel, E., Smetana, J. G., & Killen, M. (1991). Social contexts in social cognitive development. In W. M. Kurtines and J. L. Gewirtz (Eds.), *Handbook of moral behavior and development. Vol. 2: Research* (pp. 307–332). Hillsdale, NJ: Erlbaum.

Turiel, E., & Wainryb, C. (in press). Social reasoning and the varieties of social experience in cultural contexts. In H. W. Reese (Ed.), *Advances in child development and behavior* (Vol. 25). San Diego: Academic Press.

Wainryb, C. (1991). Understanding differences in moral judgments: The role of informational assumptions. *Child Development, 62,* 840–851.

Wainryb, C. & Turiel, E. (in press). Dominance, subordination, and concepts of personal entitlements in cultural contexts. *Child Development.*

Weston, D., & Turiel, E. (1980). Act-rule relations: Children's concepts of social rules. *Developmental Psychology, 16,* 417–424.

Whiting, J. M. W. & Child, I. L. (1953). *Child training and personality: A cross-cultural study.* New Haven: Yale University Press.

Whyte, W. H. (1956). *The organization man.* New York: Simon and Schuster.

Wynne, E. A. (1986). The great tradition in education: Transmitting moral values. *Educational Leadership, 43,* 4–9.

Zimba, R. F. (1987). *A study on forms of social knowledge in Zambia.* Unpublished doctoral dissertation, Purdue University.

Part V

Integration

11 Some final thoughts about personality and intelligence

Peter Salovey and John D. Mayer

The area of inquiry concerned with the recursive influences of personality and intelligence represents fertile ground for collaborative efforts between cognitive–developmental and personality–social psychologists. Volumes such as the present one provide an enormous service to the field of psychology by facilitating interaction among members of subfields who may increasingly find themselves isolated from like-minded colleagues located either physically or psychologically at great distance. As Martin Ford notes in his chapter, "There is a tendency to focus narrowly on particular components of human functioning rather than to frame problems in terms of broader issues that emphasize the meanings and significance of these component processes in people's everyday lives. As a result, there is a critical and growing need for broad, integrative theorizing in psychology." We could not agree more. The systematic study of personality and intelligence fosters intersubdisciplinary collaboration despite such boundaries to the benefit of the collaborators themselves and to the larger field of psychology.

The present volume is concerned with a number of important contributions to the study of intelligence. In this commentary, we shall review the ten chapters of the volume, organizing them around four levels of analysis in the study of personality and intelligence: (a) personality traits and intelligence; (b) personality development and intelligence; (c) theoretically broader inquiries concerning personality and the manifestations of intelligence; and (d) personality and intelligence in their cultural context.

The second half of this concluding chapter describes an area of inquiry honored primarily by its absence in the first ten chapters: emotion and intelligence. Although the emotional system constitutes one of the two primary divisions of personality, investigators of intelligence have remained largely uninterested in emotion, with a few exceptions that we shall point out. In this context, we discuss our recent thinking about a framework that we call *emotional intelligence.*

Levels of analysis in the study of personality and intelligence

Let us first, however, turn to the chapters that constitute the present volume and discuss them at the level of personality traits, personality development, and personality theories, respectively.

Personality traits and intelligence

For decades, investigators of personality trait–intelligence relationships have conducted correlational studies attempting to identify purportedly stable aspects of
personality – self-consciousness, field independence, need for cognition, and the like
– thought to be associated with intelligence. In many cases, relationships that seemed
intuitively plausible could not be confirmed empirically. Eysenck presents a compelling case that in the instance of examining personality–intelligence relations, we must
discard simple, atheoretical investigations of trait–IQ associations. (For those readers
unfamiliar with this literature, Eysenck's comprehensive review will be worth a
look.) Eysenck painstakingly summarizes the considerable work on intercorrelations
among personality traits and intelligence. Like others who have examined these
studies, he concludes that the most striking thing about these efforts is the lack of
significant correlations. For instance, it would seem reasonable to predict an inverse
relationship between trait anxiety and intelligence; overly anxious individuals should
perform more poorly on measures of intelligence. In fact, there is no reliable difference in intelligence between highly anxious and calmer individuals when anxiety is
measured as a trait, although inductions of state anxiety do inhibit performance in
predictable ways. There are, of course, a few simple empirical exceptions to the
pattern of low correlations between traits and intelligence (e.g., between sociopathy
and patterns of verbal versus performance IQ). But independence is the rule.

Can the question be asked in a more complex way? Might there be differences in
the factorial structure of intelligence for groups differing on a personality trait, say,
neuroticism? The evidence is mixed. Eysenck encourages these kinds of inquiries,
noting that the more theoretically generated the prediction, the more likely it is
confirmed.

The power of the theory-based approach can be seen in relations between introversion–extroversion and intelligence. The simple bivariate correlation between this trait
and intelligence is not significant. However, one might predict differences in style of
intellectual performance between introverts and extroverts, and, in fact, such a prediction is supported by the data. Extroverts work faster but less accurately on tasks than
introverts, for example. Certainly, such findings provide interesting evidence supporting the construct validity of the underlying measures of introversion and extroversion.
If the overall intellectual achievement of introverts and extroverts is about the same,
some obvious next steps include uncovering the conditions under which differences
between them in intellectual style might be of practical importance. A finding of
potential relevance is that as children grow older, introversion becomes increasingly
related to intelligence, perhaps because brighter children are encouraged more to
study on their own.

Moreover, fascinating relations between personality and divergent thinking styles
have been uncovered. Eysenck's review provides some tantalizing evidence that
psychoticism might be related to the kinds of creativity represented by "divergent"
cognition. Successful painters, for example, record higher psychoticism scores than

less successful painters or control groups. Similar relationships have been reported with scales of schizotypal behavior. Of course, such relationships between creativity and psychological disturbance require further exploration, lest we reinforce stereotypes about madness and artistic genius. It is certainly possible that beautiful works are created in spite of psychological disturbance rather than because of it.

Another theory-based examination of personality traits and intelligence that has produced promising findings emanates from factor-analytic studies of traits very closely related to intellectual function (Mayer, Caruso, Zigler, & Dreyden, 1989). These investigators first factor-analyzed personality measures closely related to intelligence (e.g., curiosity, interest) and concluded that there are three basic dimensions of intellectually related personality traits: intellectual absorption (similar to hypnotic absorption and Csikszentmihalyi's (1990) concept of *flow*), intellectual pleasure, and intellectual apathy. Gifted children score higher on intellectual absorption and intellectual pleasure than mental- and chronological-age matched control children.

A clever personality–intelligence connection is represented in the present volume by Haslam and Baron's construct of *prudence*. They introduce prudence as an intelligent way for the individual to behave rather than as a trait related to intelligence as measured by intelligence tests. Haslam and Baron believe that the prudent individual essentially behaves altruistically toward one's future self. As the authors admit at the outset, prudence is a matter of intelligent character rather than intelligence per se. The authors take a normative approach to intelligent behavior rather than intellectual performance, and their well-written chapter is fascinating and stimulating. Of course, it does raise more questions that it answers. We wonder why so many of the intelligent (in the sense of *g*) individuals that we know behave so imprudently?

Ruzgis and Grigorenko write that according to Irvine, the Mashona (of Zimbabwe) word for intelligence "means to be *prudent* and cautious, particularly in social relationships . . . ." Must we accept this as a definition of intelligence at all? It certainly doesn't bear any relationship to the intelligence that psychologists have traditionally studied (i.e., *g*); rather, it sounds like cautiousness. If one wants to call it intelligence, fine. But in such an instance, perhaps we should reserve some other term for what researchers in the intelligence tradition have formerly considered intelligence (e.g., some variation of problem-solving or abstract reasoning).

Personality development and intelligence

In considering personality and intelligence, we can move to a different level of analysis by considering personality development more holistically and its relationship to intelligence. Such an approach characterizes the chapter by Maciel, Heckhausen, and Baltes. One of the most significant contributions of Maciel, Heckhausen, and Baltes's work is their application of Cattell (1971) and Horn's (1968) distinction between fluid and crystallized intelligence to the problem of maturation. These authors argue that as a people mature, they focus their intellectual energy on increasingly narrow domains of thought. Research by Baltes and his colleagues indicates that frequently challenged domain-specific mental activities remain intact and perhaps even grow with age.

For example, if a person entered a legal career, he or she would remain adept, and perhaps improve in legal problem-solving abilities. Such intellectual pursuits require extensive commitments of time and concentration, with resulting tradeoffs in other areas. Thus, a person selectively optimizes those tasks required by the individual's goals while losing ability to problem-solve in other domains in which the individual is increasingly less involved. As such, fields of mastery become narrowed, and the person may compensate in other areas using a variety of strategies.

We wrote this chapter at the time of the presidential debates prior to the 1992 election. One presidential candidate remarked that the average American will change jobs eight times during his or her adult life-span. With such rapidity of occupational change, it is not clear whether the advantages of the crystallization of intelligence within particular areas will be lost to individuals who are forced late in life to switch careers.

Perhaps one of the major challenges facing the university today is the termination of mandatory retirement for faculty members. Although this issue poses problems for provosts worrying about the financial costs of maintaining professors on the payroll well into their 80s or beyond, the Maciel et al. chapter suggests that we also concern ourselves with the selective optimization of the skills of such senior colleagues. Although most of the positive attributes encompassed in the Big Five personality structure are thought to decline with age, we nevertheless expect such individuals to be wise – as defined here to have special insights and to be empathic, introspective listeners. Why not create roles that optimize these particular attributes? Rather than ask the most junior members of the faculty to serve as residence-hall advisors, freshman counselors, career consultants, ombudsmen and mediators, instead turn to those wise colleagues thought to be especially well qualified for these jobs. We expect Maciel et al.'s provocative research on the relationship between wisdom and intelligence, creativity, and personality to be directly applicable to utilizing the particular intellectual talents of the elderly with the most benefit to society.

A major finding reported in Maciel et al.'s chapter is that there is life-span growth on selected intellectual capacities in a general context of decline. This pattern of intellectual performance over the life-span is also represented in lay theories of intelligence and aging. Toward the conclusion of their chapter, Maciel et al. discuss the possibly complex interactions between goal pursuit and intellectual development. For example, while repeated functioning in an area may preserve performance, greater *life satisfaction* may increase for those people who have flexible life goals.

A focus on lay theories of intelligence is also characteristic of the chapter by Chiu, Hong, and Dweck, who present interesting evidence about how one's conception of one's own intelligence may influence intellectual performance. They distinguish between a belief that intelligence is malleable and under instrumental control – an *incremental* theory of intelligence – versus a belief that intelligence is a fixed or unpredictable attribute – an *entity theory*. This new framework nicely incorporates Diener and Dweck's (1978, 1980) earlier work on mastery-oriented versus helpless response patterns in problem solving. In that earlier research, children were administered attributional measures associated with helplessness versus persistence in the face of failure. Mastery-oriented children use failure as an opportunity to teach themselves, whereas helpless children report a number of task-irrelevant thoughts.

More recently, Dweck and her colleagues have shown that people who believe intelligence is malleable (incremental theorists) choose more demanding problems to work on (thereby presumably taking more opportunity to learn) as well. Chiu, Hong, and Dweck present evidence that entity theorists, identified in grade school, show pronounced declines in their relative standing in the seventh grade, compared to the sixth grade. These differences between entity and incremental theorists may have more to do with coping with success versus failure than with actual success or failure. It may be that over the long term, better copers increase their intellectual performance to a greater degree, but to date, there is little convincing evidence for this idea.

Personality and the manifestations of intelligence

A very promising avenue toward understanding relationships between personality and intelligence concerns work on fundamental theories of personality that are rooted in individual differences in intellectual and problem-solving abilities, styles, and goals. Prototypic of this exciting style of inquiry is work on a cognitive theory of personality by Cantor and Kihlstrom (1987). Cantor and her colleagues' theory of social intelligence is both a theory of personality *and* a theory of intelligence. It is not surprising, then, that the chapter by Cantor and Harlow is one of the most integrative vis-à-vis the theme of this volume. Social intelligence theory suggests that individual uniqueness – personality – is rooted in the characteristic ways in which people go about solving representative problems of daily living. Often these problems are organized around a dominant life-task at a particular juncture – adjusting to college, finding a romantic partner, raising a family, planning retirement, and the like.

We wonder what kind of intelligence is it that is so domain specific? With no reference to a general ability or even a "social IQ," it may be at times difficult to distinguish such intelligence from luck, a societal rising tide of prosperity, or other such "confounds." For example, can theories of social intelligence distinguish between a genuinely high-ability (let's say, to be provocative about it, high IQ) person who writes a superb book and makes a modest amount of money from it versus a drunken professor who at the end of every week buys a lottery ticket and one week wins big? Each person has behaved adaptively at his or her given life task and come out a winner. Cantor and Harlow raise the issue of expertise, which may be used to answer some of these questions. Flexibility, attunement to, and discrimination among opportunities may distinguish between the drunken lottery winner and the book author. But expertise across such areas *is* intelligence (i.e., is highly related to traditional measures of IQ).

Cantor and Harlow raise an interesting point in light of the theme of Maciel et al.'s chapter discussed earlier. They worry that the skills displayed and tasks pursued by individuals are constrained by what is considered normative for someone of a particular age. As Cantor and Harlow note, "The contingencies for social feedback and social comparison are set against . . . standards of what a person *should* be doing at each point in their lifecourse." Cantor and Harlow thankfully view deviations from these social expectations as a core component of social intelligence, allowing them to take a constructive approach (rather than a deficit-based one) to the talents that an individual contributes to society. It is no accident that flexibility is the hallmark of intelligent behavior in this view.

A very different but equally grand model is suggested by Sternberg, who proposes a government metaphor to understand different thinking styles and the most advantageous ways to assess them. For instance, monarchs stick to a single way of accomplishing a task while oligarchic thinkers juggle multiple goals. Similarly, legislative thinkers develop rule systems, executives carry them out with fidelity, and judicial thinkers judge the adequacy of such systems. This metaphor is provocative in its application here and builds on other government metaphors in psychology such as Freud's (1917/1966, p. 139) discussion of the ego as a government censor, Greenwald's (1980) totalitarian ego, Murray and Kluckhohn's (1956) idea that personality is a superordinate government institution, as well as government metaphors found in contemporary philosophical discussions of cognitive organization, such as Minsky's (1986) *Society of Mind* and Dennett's (1978) comparison of cognitive functions to the various heads of executive-branch agencies. Fox (1992) even proposes that introductory social psychology courses can be organized around the government metaphor provided by an anarchist political framework – a decentralized stateless society in which communal individuality is promoted.

Ford also proposes a metatheoretical framework for understanding the interrelations of personality and intelligence based primarily on Living Systems Theory that he calls Motivational Systems Theory. Like Cantor and Harlow's chapter (and several of the others), Ford, too, sees goals as the linking construct between personality and intelligence (an idea with which we are also sympathetic; cf. Singer & Salovey, 1993). The *behavior episode,* a goal-directed pattern of behavior in a particular context, is the unit of analysis. In many ways, then, intelligence is the accuracy with which required behavior episodes are mentally represented, something like *behavior episode schemas* (defined here as including thoughts, feelings, perceptions, actions, biological processes, and contexts – one wonders what would not be included in such a representation) and the resulting pattern of effective functioning that should follow. And personality is part-and-parcel the individual's repertoire of characteristic behavior episode schemas. (We prefer *schemas* as the plural of *schema*; Ford prefers *schemata.* We are reminded of a particularly vitriolic reviewer of one of our journal submissions who opened his comments to us with "You say schemas; I say schemata. Let's call the whole thing off."). We have always found models of personality based on systems and control theories elegant and useful. At the same time, they must be stated carefully so that they are falsifiable and testable as wholes.

Personality and intelligence in their cultural context

Rather than using metaphors like social intelligence, governmental structure and functioning, or systems theory to understand personality and intelligence, Smirnov chooses instead to say simply that intelligence *is* thinking, no more, no less, and then assumes that personality is an inherent component of all thought processes. Personality, however, need not be necessarily incorporated into the popular models of thinking of late, which are rooted in neural networks and parallel processing at a neuronal level of analysis modeled in computational terms. Smirnov, however, notes that thinking – both in process and content – is motivated by individual personality differences.

Smirnov is in agreement with many of the other authors of this volume that the precise way that intelligence is expressed is determined by an individual's personality, in particular, his or her goals. The fact that personality is viewed as a moderator of the expression of intelligence shows that Russian and American psychologists are conceiving of the relation between personality and intelligence quite similarly. The chapter concludes with a nice summary of trait relations to IQ that is consistent with the American data on the subject.

Whereas to date there is little evidence in American research on the relation between mood and intelligence, there appear to be some provocative findings in the Russian literature. For example, Smirnov reports that sad people have higher performance than verbal IQs. In addition, the Russian literature points to some possible relationships between positive emotions and verbal intelligence, because both may be lateralized in the left hemisphere. When we discuss emotional intelligence later in this chapter, we shall return to these findings.

In their nicely written chapter, Ruzgis and Grigorenko argue that no matter what our favorite metaphor for intelligence (and personality) may be, both intelligence and personality are bound by culture. In particular, what is thought to be intelligent behavior is often behavior that allows the individual to adapt successfully in a cultural context. Ruzgis and Grigorenko adopt a view of intelligence as adaptation. Although provocative, there is always a concern when departing from the traditional, information-processing definitions of intelligence. So long as intelligence is defined as the ability to learn, remember, manipulate symbols, and reason abstractly, then it seems that most of the traditional research in intelligence (i.e., Galton, Spearman, Cattell, Eysenck, etc.) can be applied cross-culturally. By defining intelligence as adaptation, we require that its measurement be culture-bound, which is fine, so long as there is broad agreement about what is adaptive in a particular cultural context. For example, does protesting against an authoritarian government in China represent high or low intelligence from the adaptation point of view? An adaptation view of intelligence is not sufficiently worked out to answer such a question. Further, many plants and animals adapt to their situation. Sunflowers move their petals so as to face the sun. Is this intelligence? Well, no, because it doesn't require conceptual abstraction. The sunflower neither knows what the sun is nor could it change from sun to moon. The problem is, the sunflower is quite adaptive, as is the porcupine, squirrel, and urban rat. None of these creatures are especially intelligent, however.

Ruzgis and Grigorenko state "For example, studying hard to achieve good grades in school may have very different meanings in different cultural settings. For the independent self, the behavior is likely to reflect personal goals . . . whereas for the interdependent self the same behavior is performed to achieve the goals of the ingroup . . . ." Granted, but it is precisely the information-processing definition of intelligence that avoids this problem. Intelligence, as defined by Western psychology, is the property of the individual, and that individual, idiocentric or allocentric, can have his or her intelligence gauged by abilities at manipulating symbols. Certainly intelligence can exist at a group level. Ants are often said to be very intelligent, as, presumably, certain cultures are more intelligent than others (or, at least differently intelligent). But this collective intelligence is disparate in its meaning from individual intelligence, and the loose slippage between the two ideas points up some of the advantages of rigorous (and not necessarily culturally relativistic) definitions.

These debates, in the end, come down to one's definition of intelligence. And controversy about such definitions is not new. In fact, the broader definition proposed by Wechsler (1958) that intelligence is the aggregate capacity of the individual to act purposefully, think rationally, and deal effectively with the environment would probably be acceptable to those individuals working in social intelligence or culturally based frameworks. Investigators of relationships between personality traits and intellectual skills would probably be happier with the more restrictive definition of intelligence proposed by Terman (1916), focusing primarily on the ability to think abstractly.

Perhaps a useful solution to these issues is a more precise demarcation between the constructs of *intelligence*, on the one hand, and *social competence*, on the other. There are many situations in which cultural expectations dictate appropriate behavior. In Japan one bows upon greeting another person, especially a social superior. If one were not to bow, we might assume that such a person lacked social competence. At the same time, we would probably not devise an intelligence test that scored someone as highly intelligent if he or she regularly bowed in appropriate social circumstances. Culture surely influences the situations in which intelligent behavior can be manifested, and so we cannot assume that it can be accurately measured the same way across all cultural contexts. Social competence, however, *is* knowledge of the reinforcement structure of one's culture and the ability to adapt behavior to it. Separating intelligence and social competence may provide greater conceptual clarity in this context.

A final note on the issue of culture. We find ourselves in strong agreement with Elliot Turiel's worry that although many psychologists heeded Mischel's (1968) warnings about the validity of personality typing, they feel free to engage in "culture typing." The danger here is that the increasing emphasis on culture in 1990s psychology has motivated a tendency to characterize cultures as monolithic along some fundamental dimensions and then to assume vast homogeneity within the culture on this dimension. Although we welcome the reintroduction of culture into mainstream psychology, at the same time we suggest that every investigator interested in cultural constraints on thinking and behavior read Turiel's chapter.

What is missing?

As should be obvious by this point, the present volume represents a broad sweeping look at relations between intelligence and personality, with levels of analysis ranging from traits and intellectual-test performance (e.g., Eysenck's chapter) to whole cultures (e.g., Turiel's chapter). We are primarily investigators of emotion, and what seems to be missing, from our perspective, in nearly all of these accounts is a role for emotion in the intelligence–personality interface.

Emotion is not entirely excluded from this volume. In fairness, Chiu, Hong, and Dweck discuss the importance of affect, but use the language of needs, motives, and psychoanalysis, almost as if emotions do not play a role in more modern, cognitive conceptualizations of intelligence and/or personality. Certainly, Cantor and Harlow's discussion of optimism and pessimism is relevant to the self-regulation of emotion – a set of skills that probably would be included in an adaptation-oriented definition of intelligence. But it is only the chapter by Smirnov in which actual research on the impact of moods and emotional states on intellectual performance is discussed directly.

In the remainder of this chapter, we shall argue that emotion plays an important role in linking personality (i.e., individual differences in the ways in which people confront the challenges of the world) with intelligence (i.e., the accuracy, efficiency, and success with which they do so). We should be clear: we certainly do not fault the authors of the chapters of this volume for ignoring the emotional system. Indeed, emotions often have been viewed in psychology as antithetical to clear thinking. Young (1936, pp. 457–458) described them as causing a "complete loss of cerebral control" and containing no "trace of conscious purpose." And Woodworth (1940) suggested that a scale to measure intelligence should contain items demonstrating *not* being afraid, angry, grieved, or inquisitive about things that arouse the emotions of younger children. Instead, we view emotions as organized responses, crossing the boundaries of many psychological subsystems, and thus propose that the adaptive processing of emotionally relevant information is part of intelligence and, at the same time, individual differences in the skills with which such processing occurs constitute core aspects of personality (Salovey & Mayer, 1990).

Emotional intelligence

We have proposed a framework called *emotional intelligence* as a way of identifying and organizing the specific skills needed to understand and experience emotions most adaptively (Mayer & Salovey, 1993; Salovey & Mayer, 1990; Salovey, Hsee, & Mayer, 1993). More formally, we define emotional intelligence as the ability to monitor one's own and others' feelings and emotions, to discriminate among them, and to use this information to guide one's thinking and actions (Salovey & Mayer, 1990, p. 189).

A case study

Before presenting a more thorough description of our emotional-intelligence framework, however, we shall try to persuade you of the utility of such a construct by discussing a political candidate from the presidential campaign of five years ago. Recall that in the 1988 election, in contrast to 1992, George Bush rather soundly defeated Michael Dukakis, the rather lackluster Democratic nominee. But earlier in the campaign for the Democratic nomination, it looked as though the Democratic standard bearer was more likely to be Gary Hart, the former Colorado senator. Although the front-runner for the nomination at the time, Hart's candidacy collapsed when, in the face of rumors concerning adulterous relationships, he dared the press corps to produce evidence of illicit affairs. And so they did – by staking out his Washington, DC condominium and monitoring its nighttime visitors. We ask – recall the discussion of *prudence* earlier – how could a seemingly intelligent individual so efficiently orchestrate his own self-destruction?

We would argue that just as decrements in visual–spatial tasks on the WAIS may indicate lateralized brain injury (Lezak, 1983, pp. 251–252), so can decrements in particular aspects of emotional intelligence be indicative of characterological impairment. Gary Hart's ability to build a successful 1988 presidential campaign by inspiring staffers and voters probably indicated high overall emotional intelligence. However, one or more decrements in emotional-information processing probably destroyed his presidential campaign. Hart was often depicted in the press as an emotionally constricted technocrat, so much so that when his voice broke during a campaign stop in his home town, his staff was thrilled with this brief expression of emotion (Dowd, 1987). (Recall, also, the disappointment of Dukakis supporters when months later at a debate with Bush, Dukakis reacted with little emotion to a question concerning the hypothetical rape of his wife.)

Hart's campaign as the Democratic front-runner collapsed amidst newspaper accounts of sexual indiscretion and lapses in judgment. In the ensuing analyses of how this occurred, David Spiegel, a psychiatrist at Stanford University Medical School was quoted as saying:

Such people come to feel that they can do no wrong and that they should be allowed to do whatever they want . . . it is only an educated inference on my part, but Gary Hart seemed to be so taken with himself and his accomplishments that he could not empathize, and he was so divorced from a sense of being involved that he could not consider the cost to his wife and to his supporters of not controlling his own impulses (Goleman, 1987, p. C-5).

Hart seemed unable to perceive or calculate the emotional reactions of his wife, family, and the public. He may also have been impaired in introspections about his own guilt and shame as evidenced in his speech that ended his campaign. According to William Schneider, a political analyst at the American Enterprise Institute:

Gary Hart had a blind spot . . . he thought his passions and foibles were irrelevant; he did not sense how important the character of the president is. The word around Washington was that Hart felt special and invulnerable (Goleman, 1987, p. C-5).

Further, as Louis Jolyon West, chairman of the Department of Psychiatry at UCLA, indicated:

[Hart] had a self-deceptive sense of invulnerability; he seemed to believe he would not be found out no matter the risks he took. In that way he seems similar to Ivan Boesky [the Wall Street broker who confessed to insider trading] (Goleman, 1987, p. C-5).

Thus, individuals may be high in emotional intelligence, others uniformly low, but a third, more interesting group show great abilities on some aspects of emotional intelligence but profound deficits in others.

The emotional-intelligence framework

In the next section of this chapter, we shall discuss the various aspects of emotional intelligence and the personalities of people skilled or unskilled on each of these dimensions. Although, historically, scientists of human intelligence often contrasted rational thought with emotional experience (Schaffer, Gilmer, & Schoen, 1940; Woodworth, 1940; Young, 1936), modern investigators recognize that emotions can serve as a source of information to individuals (Schwarz, 1990), and individuals are more or less skilled at processing this information.

Gardner (1983) has described what he calls personal intelligence in part as "access to one's own feeling life – one's range of affects or emotions: the capacity instantly to effect discriminations among these feelings and, eventually, to label them, to enmesh them in symbolic codes, to draw upon them as a means of understanding and guiding one's behavior" (p. 239). Our view of emotional intelligence encompasses these clearly adaptive skills, and more. Briefly, emotional intelligence can be de-scribed in three primary domains: the accurate appraisal and expression of emotion in self and in other people, the adaptive regulation of emotions in self and in other people, and the utilization of emotions to plan, create, and motivate action.

Accurate appraisal and expression of emotion. The ability to recognize, identify, and label what one is feeling is clearly the precursor to the adaptive use of the information that emotions convey. Work with young children suggests that the ability to recognize accurately the facial expressions of emotions increases linearly with age.

Children as young as three years are able to pose facial expressions suggested to them by an adult (Lewis, Sullivan, & Vasen, 1987). At about four years of age, children can identify correctly the emotion suggested by about half of the faces that they see. By six years of age, they are correct 75% of the time. For some emotions, such as happiness and disgust, correct identification on nearly every presentation is seen in children as young as four years (Profyt & Whissell, 1991).

At the same time, we are all familiar with adults who seem oblivious to their own feelings and insensitive to those of others (Salovey & Mayer, 1991). Some individuals have great difficulty identifying the feelings communicated to them through the facial expressions of other people (Buck, 1984; Campbell, Kagan, & Krathwohl, 1971; Kagan, 1978; Rosenthal, Hall, DiMatteo, Rogers, & Archer, 1979). People also vary in their ability to use their own facial expressions (and other nonverbal behaviors) in order to communicate what they are feeling (Buck, 1979; Friedman, Prince, Riggio, & DiMatteo, 1980). Moreover, there are vast differences in the ability to articulate feelings into words. Children begin to learn emotion words at quite a young age (Bretherton, Fritz, Zahn-Waxler, & Ridgeway, 1986; Whissell & Nicholson, 1991). Despite such fluency with emotional language demonstrated by children, some adults grope wildly with the affective lexicon when trying to report on their feelings. Others, of course, are much more facile, and perhaps gravitate toward professions that reward these skills such as psychotherapy, authoring novels, advertising, and the like.

Although the construct has yet to be measured in ways that would make psychometrists happy, there seems to be a group of individuals who are simply unable to use words to describe feelings at all. Labeled *alexithymics* (literally, "no words for feelings"), these individuals are thought to be at risk for a variety of psychological disorders, especially psychosomatic illnesses (Apfel & Sifneos, 1979; Krystal, Giller, & Cicchetti, 1986; Sifneos, 1972, 1973; Taylor, 1984). In some of our studies, we have examined people who replace emotional with nonemotional words. Such individuals seem to have reduced empathy for the feelings of others (Mayer, Salovey, Gomberg-Kaufman, & Blainey, 1991). We also have been able to identify individuals who vary with respect to how much attention they pay to and the clarity with which they perceive their moods (Mayer & Gaschke, 1988; Salovey, Mayer, Goldman, Turvey, & Palfai, 1992). Such perceptions may be related to the tendency to ruminate after distressing experiences and the frequency with which physical symptoms are reported in stressful situations (Goldman, Kraemer, Salovey, & Mayer, 1992).

Adaptive regulation of emotion.   Although not studied systematically until recently, people engage in all kinds of activities to regulate their moods. They may try to control their thoughts, drink alcohol, seek the company of others, or jog (see Morris & Reilly, 1987, or Parrott, 1993, for reviews). Children as young as four years recognize their ability to regulate their feelings. Brown, Covell, and Abramovitch (1991) asked children to listen to stories in which they might experience happy, sad, or angry emotions. They then indicated various cognitive (e.g., "try to think to yourself, 'it wasn't as bad as all that' ") and behavioral (e.g., "go and do something that you would really like to do") strategies they would use in order to regulate that emotional experience. Four-to-six-year-old children in this study were as likely to recognize effective emotion control strategies as teenagers.

Emotional intelligence, however, includes more than just an ability to regulate feelings in oneself. It also pertains to the ability to regulate adaptively the feelings of other people. We have all had the experience of being moved by a stirring orator, finding ourselves impressed by the professional demeanor of a job candidate, or becoming attracted to someone we hardly know. Some people seem to know how to create emotions in others that serve them in adaptive ways.

In the extreme, manipulating the feelings of another person for one's own gain may seen sociopathic or Machiavellian. But in less extreme situations, we may simply label such individuals as "charismatic" or, merely, charming (Wasielewski, 1985). A most advantageous strategy is to focus on the feelings of other people and inhibit a display of one's true emotional reactions to some situation. For example, Hochschild (1983) has studied the ways in which certain professionals, such as airline flight attendants, strongly regulate their displays of feelings and focus on and attempt to regulate the feelings of others. Emotional regulation may be accentuated among helping professionals, which may account for their high incidence of burnout.

Utilization of emotion-based knowledge. Individuals also differ in their ability to harness their own emotions in order to solve problems. Moods, generally, influence problem-solving outcomes. For instance, changes in feelings may facilitate the generation of multiple options (Mayer, 1986). And certain emotions may facilitate different kinds of problem-solving tasks (reviewed by Isen, 1987). For instance, creative and inductive reasoning may be improved by happy moods (Isen, Daubman, & Nowicki, 1987; Isen, Johnson, Mertz, & Robinson, 1985), while tasks requiring deductive reasoning and the careful consideration of multiple options may be facilitated by sad moods. In a recent set of studies, Palfai and Salovey (1993) found that happy moods interfered with performance on a deductive-reasoning task (such as those found on the LSAT exam), whereas sad moods led to slower performance on inductive reasoning problems, such as analogies.

It may be that happy and sad moods are associated with distinct information-processing styles that can affect performance on different kinds of problem-solving tasks. Emotions that signal danger, such as sadness, fear, shame, and guilt may switch individuals into a focused, sequential analytic mode of processing that leads to enhanced attention and reduced error on some kinds of problems (Kuhl, 1983). Anger and joy, on the other hand, may create a state of mind that allows for the diffuse, multiple processing characteristic of more intuitive and holistic tasks. An intuitive awareness of the kinds of cognitive tasks facilitated by different affective states may characterize the emotionally intelligent individual.

Mood also may facilitate problem solving by virtue of its impact on the organization and utilization of information in memory. Individuals find it easier to categorize aspects of problems as related or unrelated when happy (Isen & Daubman, 1984), which may facilitate creative thinking. It seems that when feeling good, individuals are better able to discover category-organizing principles and then use these principles to integrate and remember new information (Isen, Daubman, & Gorgoglione, 1987). This may account for their greater connectedness to and altruism toward other people (Salovey, Mayer, & Rosenhan, 1991). Finally, the positive impact that pleasant moods have on creative problem-solving tasks may be mediated by changes in persistence. Happy individuals feel more confident about their abilities (Kavanagh & Bower, 1985; Salovey & Birnbaum, 1989) and so may be more likely to continue to work even in the face of obstacles.

Conclusion

The contributors to this volume have made important advances to our understanding of personality and intelligence. Throughout the volume, as they trace the relations between discrete traits and IQ, intelligence in personality development, and theoretical discussions of the place of intelligence in models of personality, they have drawn together much of the diverse and widespread treatment of these topics that can be found in the literature today. To this enlightening discussion, we have tried to add one additional contribution concerning emotion. *Emotional intelligence* is an organizing framework for cataloguing abilities related to understanding, managing, and using feelings. Included in this array are abilities to recognize emotions in oneself and others and express emotion-laden concepts in words. Moreover, the individual functioning in an emotionally intelligent manner is able to regulate feelings in him or herself and in other people and to utilize emotions to aid in problem solving and decision making. It is our belief that the adaptive use of emotion-laden information is a significant aspect of what is meant by anyone's definition of intelligence, yet it is not studied systematically by investigators of intelligence. Moreover, individual differences in understanding, regulating, and using feelings constitute major aspects of personality. Emotions, we believe, provide an important keystone to understanding the personality–intelligence connection.

References

Apfel, R. J., & Sifneos, P. E. (1979). Alexithymia: Concept and measurement. *Psychotherapy and Psychosomatics, 32,* 180–190.

Bretherton, I., Fritz, J., Zahn-Waxler, G., & Ridgeway, D. (1986). Learning to talk about emotions: A functionalist perspective. *Child Development, 57,* 529–548.

Brown, K., Covell, K., & Abramovitch, R. (1991). Time course and control of emotion: Age differences in understanding and recognition. *Merrill-Palmer Quarterly, 37,* 273–287.

Buck, R. (1979). Individual differences in nonverbal sending accuracy and electrodermal responding: The externalizing–internalizing dimension. In R. Rosenthal (Ed.), *Skill in nonverbal communication: Individual differences.* Cambridge, MA: Olegeshlager, Gunn, & Hain.

Buck, R. (1984). *The communication of emotion.* New York: The Guilford Press.

Campbell, R. J., Kagan, N. I., & Krathwohl, D. R. (1971). The development and validation of a scale to measure affective sensitivity (empathy). *Journal of Counseling Psychology, 18,* 407–412.

Cantor, N., & Kihlstrom, J. F. (1987). *Personality and social intelligence.* Englewood Cliffs, NJ: Prentice Hall.

Cattell, R. B. (1971). *Abilities: Their structure, growth, and action.* Boston: Houghton-Mifflin.

Csikszentmihalyi, M. (1990). *Flow: The psychology of optimal experience.* New York: Harper and Row.

Dennett, D. C. (1978). Toward a cognitive theory of consciousness. In D. C. Dennett (Ed.), *Brainstorms: Philosophical essays on mind and psychology* (pp. 149–173). Cambridge, MA: Bradford Books.

Diener, C. I., & Dweck, C. S. (1978). An analysis of learned helplessness: Continuous changes in performance, strategy, and achievement cognitions following failure. *Journal of Personality and Social Psychology, 36,* 451–462.

Diener, C. I., & Dweck, C. S. (1980). An analysis of learned helplessness: 2. The processing of success. *Journal of Personality and Social Psychology, 39,* 940–952.

Dowd, M. (1987). With tears and revelation, '88 contenders soften images. *New York Times,* April 26, 1987, p. 1, 28.

Fox, D. R. (1992). A political framework for the introductory social psychology course. *Contemporary Social Psychology, 16,* 37–39.

Freud, S. (1917/1966). *Introductory lectures on psychoanalysis.* (trans. J. Strachey). New York: Norton.

Friedman, H. S., Prince, L. M., Riggio, R. E., & DiMatteo, M. R. (1980). Understanding and assessing nonverbal expressiveness: The Affective Communication Test. *Journal of Personality and Social Psychology, 39,* 333–351.

Gardner, H. (1983). *Frames of mind.* New York: Basic Books.

Goleman, D. (1987). Sex, power, failure: Patterns emerge. *New York Times,* May 19, 1987, p. C-1, 5.

Goldman, S., Kraemer, D., Salovey, P., & Mayer, J. D. (1992). *Emotional intelligence and the reporting of physical symptoms in stressful situations.* Submitted for publication.

Greenwald, A. (1980). The totalitarian ego: Fabrication and revision of personal history. *American Psychologist, 35,* 603–618.

Horn, J. L. (1968). Organization of abilities and the development of intelligence. *Psychological Review, 75,* 242–259.

Hochschild, A. R. (1983). *The managed heart: Commercialization of human feeling.* Berkeley, CA: University of California Press.

Isen, A. M. (1987). Positive affect, cognitive processes, and social behavior. In L. Berkowitz (Ed.), *Advances in experimental social psychology* (Vol. 20, pp. 203–253). San Diego: Academic Press.

Isen, A. M., & Daubman, K. A. (1984). The influence of affect on categorization. *Journal of Personality and Social Psychology, 47,* 1206–1217.

Isen, A. M., Daubman, K. A., & Gorgoglione, J. M. (1987). The influence of positive affect on cognitive organization: Implications for education. In R. Snow and M. Farr (Eds.), *Aptitude, learning, and instruction: Affective and cognitive factors.* Hillsdale, NJ: Erlbaum.

Isen, A. M., Daubman, K. A., & Nowicki, G. (1987). Positive affect facilitates creative problem solving. *Journal of Personality and Social Psychology, 52,* 1122–1131.

Isen, A. M., Johnson, M. S., Mertz, E., & Robinson, G. F. (1985). The effects of positive affect on the unusualness of word associations. *Journal of Personality and Social Psychology, 48,* 1413–1414.

Kagan, N. (1978, September). *Affective sensitivity test: Validity and reliability.* Paper presented at the meeting of the American Psychological Association, San Francisco.

Kavanagh, D. J., & Bower, G. H. (1985). Mood and self-efficacy: Impact of joy and sadness on perceived capabilities. *Cognitive Therapy and Research, 9,* 507–525.

Krystal, J. H., Giller, E. L., & Cicchetti, D. V. (1986). Assessment of alexithymia in post-traumatic stress disorder and somatic illness: Introduction of a reliable measure. *Psychosomatic Medicine, 48,* 84–91.

Kuhl, J. (1983). Emotion, cognition, and motivation, II. *Sprache und Kognition, 4,* 228–253.

Lewis, M., Sullivan, M. W., & Vasen, A. (1987). Making faces: Age and emotion differences in the posing of emotional expressions. *Developmental Psychology, 23,* 690–697.

Lezak, M. D. (1983). *Neuropsychological assessment.* New York: Oxford University Press.

Mayer, J. D. (1986). How mood influences cognition. In N. E. Sharkey (Ed.), *Advances in cognitive science* (Vol. 1, pp. 290–314). Chichester: Ellis Horwood.

Mayer, J. D., Caruso, D., Zigler, E., & Dreyden, J. (1989). Intelligence and intelligence-related personality traits. *Intelligence, 13,* 119–133.

Mayer, J. D., & Gaschke, Y. N. (1988). The experience and meta-experience of mood. *Journal of Personality and Social Psychology, 55,* 102–111.

Mayer, J. D., & Salovey, P. (1993). The intelligence of emotional intelligence. *Intelligence, 17,* 433–442.

Mayer, J. D., Salovey, P., Gomberg-Kaufman, S., & Blainey, K. (1991). A broader conception of mood experience. *Journal of Personality and Social Psychology, 60,* 100–111.

Minsky, M. (1986). *Society of mind.* New York: Simon Schuster.

Mischel, W. (1968). *Personality and assessment.* New York: Wiley.

Morris, W. N., & Reilly, N. P. (1987). Toward the self-regulation of mood: Theory and research. *Motivation and Emotion, 11,* 215–249.

Murray, H. A., & Kluckhohn, C. (1956). A conception of personality. In H. A. Murray & C. Kluckhohn (Eds.), *Personality in nature, society, and culture* (2nd ed., pp. 3–49). New York: Knopf.

Palfai, T. P., & Salovey, P. (1993). The influence of depressed and elated moods on deductive and inductive reasoning. *Imagination, Cognition, and Personality, 13,* 57–71.

Parrott, W. G. (1993). Beyond hedonism: Motives for inhibiting or maintaining good and bad moods. In D. M. Wegner & J. W. Pennebaker (Eds.), *Handbook of mental control.* Englewood Cliffs, NJ: Prentice-Hall.

Profyt, L., & Whissell, C. (1991). Children's understanding of facial expression of emotion: I. Voluntary creation of emotion-faces. *Perceptual and Motor Skills, 73,* 199–202.

Rosenthal, R., Hall, J. A., DiMatteo, M. R., Rogers, P. L., & Archer, D. (1979). *Sensitivity to nonverbal communication: The PONS Test.* Baltimore, MD: Johns Hopkins University Press.

Salovey, P., & Birnbaum, D. (1989). Influence of mood on health-relevant cognitions. *Journal of Personality and Social Psychology, 57,* 539–551.

Salovey, P., Hsee, C. K., & Mayer, J. D. (1993). Emotional Intelligence and the Self-Regulation of Affect. In D. M. Wegner & J. W. Pennebaker (Eds.), *Handbook of mental control.* Englewood Cliffs, NJ: Prentice-Hall.

Salovey, P., & Mayer, J. D. (1990). Emotional intelligence. *Imagination, Cognition, and Personality, 9,* 185–211.

Salovey, P., & Mayer, J. D. (1991). On emotional intelligence. *Dialogue,* Spring 1991, 9–10.

Salovey, P., Mayer, J. D., Goldman, S., Turvey, C., & Palfai, T. P. (1992). *The trait meta-mood scale and emotional intelligence: Measuring attention to, clarity, and repair of mood.* Submitted for publication.

Salovey, P., Mayer, J. D., & Rosenhan, D. L. (1991). Mood and helping: Mood as a motivator of helping and helping as a regulator of mood. In M. S. Clark (Ed.), *Prosocial behavior: Review of personality and social psychology* (Vol. 12, pp. 215–237). Newbury Park, CA: Sage.

Schaffer, L. F., Gilmer, B., & Schoen, M. (1940). *Psychology.* New York: Harper & Brothers.

Schwarz, N. (1990). Feelings as information: Informational and motivational functions of affective states. In E. T. Higgins and R. M. Sorrentino (Eds.), *Handbook of motivation and cognition: Foundations of social behavior* (Vol. 2, pp. 527–561). New York: Guilford.

Sifneos, P. E. (1972). *Short-term psychotherapy and emotional crisis.* Cambridge: Harvard University Press.

Sifneos, P. E. (1973). The presence of "alexithymic" characteristics in psychosomatic patients. *Psychotherapy and Psychosomatics, 22,* 225–262.

Singer, J. A., & Salovey, P. (1993). *The remembered self.* New York: Free Press.

Taylor, G. J. (1984). Alexithymia: Concept, measurement, and implications for treatment. *American Journal of Psychiatry, 141,* 725–732.

Terman, L. M. (1916). *The measure of intelligence.* Boston: Houghton-Mifflin.

Wasielewski, P. L. (1985). The emotional basis of charisma. *Symbolic Interaction, 8,* 207–222.

Wechsler, D. (1958). *The measurement and appraisal of adult intelligence.* Baltimore, MD: Williams & Wilkins.

Whissell, C. M., & Nicholson, H. (1991). Children's freely produced synonyms for seven key emotions. *Perceptual and Motor Skills, 72,* 1107–1111.

Woodworth, R. S. (1940). *Psychology, 4th Edition.* New York: Henry Holt.

Young, P. T. (1936). *Motivation of behavior.* New York: Wiley.

Name index

319

Subject index

abilities, as intelligence measure, 41–2
ability testing, *see* cognitive-ability testing
abortion, 287–8
absorption, intellectual, 305
ACE test, 14
achievement motivation, individually-oriented versus socially-oriented, 259–60
achievement-related goals, of Type A individuals, 153–4
achievement strategies, 145
achievement tasks, 149, 150
   optimistic vs. pessimistic approach to, 156, 157
acquired immune deficiency syndrome (AIDS), 292–3
action identification, 53
activity, 221–47
   cognitive processes as, 228–33
   consciounsess and, 225–6
   experimental studies of, 239–46
   external/internal nature of, 224–5
   goal-directed nature of, 222, 224, 230, 232, 234, 235
   image of the world concept of, 229–33, 234, 235
   knowledge and, 228–9
   main characteristics of, 222–5
   motivation of, 222–223, 224, 226, 227–8, 230, 234
   object-orientation of, 222
   as operations, 223–4, 226
   personality and, 226, 227–8
   social interactions and, 231
   theoretical analysis of, 233–9
adaptation
   cultural meaning systems and, 254
   as intelligence, 104, 105, 107, 137, 250–1, 309–10
   in personality functioning, 114–5
adaptive functioning, 126–30
adaptive responses, versus maladaptive responses
   to morality, 124–6, 127
   in problem-solving, 118–121
   in social interactions, 121–4
adultery, 293–4
Adult Intentional and Motivational Systems Interview, 201

affect, goal-directed behavior and, 145
affective processes, of personality, 108–12
affiliative tasks, 149, 150
Africans, intelligence concepts of, 256, 260–2, 263, 266
aging
   cognitive, 76–80, 93
   compensatory processes of, 64–5, 66, 79; *see also* life-span development
alcoholics, thinking styles of, 244
alexithymics, 314
allocentrism, 255, 257–60
altruism, of goals, 36–8, 287, 291
American People (Gorer), 273
Americans
   conformity of, 279–80, 281, 282–3
   cultural stereotyping of, 281
Amish, 288
anarchic style, 176
antisemitism, 271
anxiety, 3–4
   intelligence and, 14–17, 304
   independence-related, 148–9
   problem-solving and, 241
apathy, intellectual, 305
Aristotle, 41, 44, 45, 47
artists, psychoticism of, 18–19
aspiration level, during old age, 86–7
Assessment of Core Goals, 199, 201
Assessment of Personal Intelligence, 207, 211–4
Assessment of Personality Goals, 198–9
assessments, thinking styles and, 177–82
attitudes, as intelligence component, 106–7
attunement
   discriminative facility and, 153–5, 159
   in life-task pursuit, 151–2, 158, 159, 160–1
   in problem-solving, 146, 147, 148–50, 151–2
   in social intelligence, 307–8
Australia, as individualist culture, 276
Australians, intelligence concepts of, 262–3, 265
authoritarian personality, 271–272, 273, 277, 279, 290
Authoritarian Personality, The (Adorno et al.), 271–2, 279